The Big

Type 2

Diabetes Cookbook

Simple and Fast Diabetic Friendly Recipes for the Newly Diagnosed

Lisa Sadler

Table of Contents

Type 2 diabetes is a metabolic disorder in which the body's capacity to regulate and use sugar (glucose) as a fuel is hampered. As a result of this long-term (chronic) condition, too much sugar circulates in the bloodstream. In the long run, high blood sugar levels can cause problems with the circulatory, neurological, and immune systems.

There are essentially two interrelated illnesses at work in type 2 diabetes. Your pancreas does not create enough insulin, a hormone that regulates sugar transport into cells, and your cells do not respond to insulin adequately, causing you to eat less sugar. Type 2 diabetes is traditionally known as adult-onset diabetes, however both type-1 diabetes and type-2 diabetes can begin in childhood or later in life. Despite the fact that type 2 diabetes is more common in older people, an increase in the number of obese children has resulted in an increase in the incidence of type 2 diabetes in children.

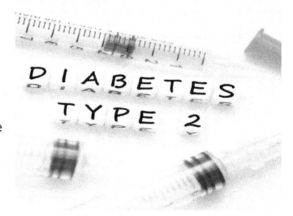

Type 2 diabetes has no treatment, but it can be managed by losing weight, eating a healthy diet, and exercising. If food and exercise aren't enough to keep your blood sugar under control, diabetes medications or insulin therapy may be necessary.

Differences Between Type-1 and Type-2 Diabetes

We understand that some people are confused by the differences between type 1 and type 2 diabetes. And we're frequently asked about the distinctions.

Type 1 and type 2 diabetes share many similarities, but they also have many differences. It's important to think about what causes them, who they affect, and how you should handle them. Gestational diabetes and MODY diabetes are two further types of diabetes. The distinctions between categories 1 and 2 are the topic of this website.

To begin with, type 1 diabetes affects 8% of all diabetics. Around 90% of people suffer from type 2 diabetes.

The distinctions between type 1 and type 2 diabetes are often misunderstood. This may necessitate you explaining why what works for one type of person does not work for another, as well as the many considerations.

The most crucial thing to keep in mind is that they are both really serious. Having high blood glucose (or sugar) levels, whether you have type 1 or type 2 diabetes, can have serious health consequences. You must take the required procedures to manage one of these conditions if you have one.

	Type 1	**Type 2**
What's going on?	Type 1 diabetes is thought to be caused by an autoimmune reaction that hamper the cells to create insulin because it is attacking the cells in your pancreas.	Type 2 diabetes is caused unable to produce enough insulin, or the insulin it does produce is ineffective.
Factors that are at risk	Some people with certain genes are more likely to develop type 1 diabetes; while many won't go on to have even if they have the genes. Diet and lifestyle habits don't cause type 1 diabetes.	Some factors, such as weight and ethnicity, can increase your chance of developing type 2 diabetes.
Symptoms	Type 1 symptoms develop more quickly.	Type 2 symptoms are more likely to go missed since they take longer to show.
Management	Insulin is used to control blood sugar in people with type 1 diabetes.	In comparison to type 1 diabetes, type 2 diabetes can be controlled in a variety of ways. Some of the solutions include medication, exercise, and diet. People with type 2 diabetes can also be given insulin.
Prevention and Cure	There is currently no cure for type 1 diabetes, however research is ongoing.	Type 2 diabetes cannot be cured, although there is evidence that it can be prevented and put into remission in many cases.

When the pancreas produces less insulin than the body requires, the body's cells stop responding to it, resulting in type 2 diabetes. They do not consume as much sugar as they should. In your blood, sugar builds up. Insulin resistance is the inability of cells to respond to insulin.

Obesity

Obesity is no longer solely a condition that affects the old, despite the fact that the risk increases with age, and an increasing number of young people are being diagnosed with the disease.

Nearly a third (31.2 percent) of children aged 2 to 15 are obese, according to Public Health England Data.

While the exact causes of diabetes are unknown, certain factors are known to raise the risk of developing various types of diabetes mellitus.

Being overweight or obese (having a BMI of 30 or higher) increases your chance of developing type 2 diabetes. There is a clear correlation between obesity and type 2 diabetes. The risk and severity of type 2 diabetes are connected to BMI (BMI).

Obese people have a seven-fold increased risk of diabetes compared to those of normal weight, while overweight people have a three-fold increased risk.

While it is well understood that body fat distribution is a significant determinant of diabetes risk, the exact mechanism of relationship is unknown. It's also unclear why not everyone who is obese develops type 2 diabetes, or why not everyone who has type 2 diabetes is obese.

According to studies, abdominal obesity causes fat cells to emit 'pro-inflammatory' substances, which can make the body less sensitive to the insulin it produces by affecting insulin responsive cells' activity and capacity to respond to insulin.

Insulin resistance is one of the most common symptoms of type 2 diabetes.

Obesity that is defined by excess abdominal fat is known as central or abdominal obesity (i.e. a large waistline).

Gestation Period

Gestational diabetes is a type of diabetes that develops in a pregnant woman who previously had never had diabetes. In some women, gestational diabetes can affect many pregnancies. In most cases, gestational diabetes appears during the third trimester of pregnancy. Doctors are more likely to screen for it between 24 and 28 weeks of pregnancy.

Managing gestational diabetes is often as simple as eating a well-balanced diet and exercising on a regular basis. In some cases, a woman with gestational diabetes may need to take insulin.

Although there is no established reason for GDM, there are some speculations as to why it happens.

The placenta not only provides nourishment and water to a growing fetus, but it also creates a range of hormones to keep the pregnancy going. Hormones like estrogen, cortisol, and human placental lactogen are all known to block insulin. This is referred to as the contra-insulin effect, and it usually occurs between 20 and 24 weeks of pregnancy.

As the placenta develops, more of these hormones are generated, raising the risk of insulin resistance. The pancreas can normally manufacture more insulin to overcome insulin resistance, but if the amount of insulin produced is insufficient to counteract the effect of placental hormones, gestational diabetes develops.

Hypertension

High blood pressure (hypertension) can cause or exacerbate a variety of diabetes problems, including diabetic eye disease and kidney disease. Most diabetics will develop high blood pressure, as well as other cardiac and circulation issues, over time.

Diabetes wreaks havoc on arteries, exposing them to atherosclerosis (hardening of the arteries). This can lead to high blood pressure, which can lead to complications like blood vessel damage, heart attacks, and renal failure if left untreated.

People with hypertension are more likely than individuals with normal blood pressure readings to have:

• Coronary artery disease, sometimes known as heart disease, is a type of cardiovascular illness.
• Strokes
• Hardening of the arteries in the legs and feet is known as peripheral vascular disease.
• Insufficiency of the heart
• Even blood pressure that is slightly above normal (120/80 to 129/80) has an effect on your health.

Over the course of ten years, studies reveal that you have a two to three times greater chance of developing heart disease.

Other Causes

Type 2 diabetes is caused by genes, but lifestyle decisions are also essential. You may have a genetic mutation that makes you vulnerable to type 2 diabetes, but if you take care of your body, you may avoid developing diabetes.

Let's say two persons share a genetic mutation. One eats well, keeps their cholesterol under control, and stays physically fit, whereas the other is overweight (BMI over 25) and inactive. Because certain lifestyle choices have a significant impact on how well your body uses insulin, a person who is overweight and inactive is significantly more likely to acquire type 2 diabetes.

Type 2 diabetes can be influenced by a variety of lifestyle decisions, including:

Lack of physical activity: Physical activity has numerous advantages, one of which is that it can help you avoid type 2 diabetes if you're at risk.

Unhealthy meal-planning options include: Type 2 diabetes is more likely if you eat a diet heavy in fat and low in fiber (which you can get from grains, veggies, and fruits).

Obesity/Overweight: A lack of exercise and poor diet planning can contribute to obesity or exacerbate it. Being overweight makes you more prone to develop insulin resistance, which can lead to a variety of other health problems.

How to Prevent and Control Diabetes

Diabetes is a life-threatening condition. Sticking to your diabetes treatment plan requires a 24-hour commitment. However, your efforts are commendable. Diabetes management can help you avoid serious — even life-threatening — consequences.

Develop Good Habits

When adopting dietary modifications to help prevent diabetes, the quantity and quality of your carb intake are both crucial elements to consider.

Carbs are broken down into little sugar molecules by your body and taken into your bloodstream. Your pancreas is stimulated to generate insulin, a hormone that helps sugar travel from your bloodstream into your cells, as a result of the rise in blood sugar.

Because the cells in patients with prediabetes are resistant to insulin, blood sugar levels remain high. As a result, the pancreas produces more insulin in an attempt to lower blood sugar levels.

This can result in gradually increased blood sugar and insulin levels over time, eventually leading to type 2 diabetes.

All carbohydrate sources, not just sugar and processed carbohydrates, boost insulin release. Although refined carbohydrates are absorbed more quickly than complex carbohydrates, there is conflicting evidence suggesting the increase in blood sugar caused by a diet is linked to diabetes risk.

As a result, reducing highly processed carbs is unlikely to be a better option for preventing diabetes than regulating overall carb intake and choosing high-fiber carbs.

Soda, candy, dessert, white bread, spaghetti, and sweetened breakfast cereal are all examples of meals and drinks high in added sugars or refined carbs.

Healthy substitutions include non-starchy veggies like broccoli and mushrooms, whole fruit, oats, and whole grain bread and pasta. Fiber is higher in these selections, which helps to prevent blood sugar increases.

Sticking to water as your primary beverage will help you avoid high-sugar beverages.

Adults with type 2 diabetes and latent autoimmune diabetes have been related to sugary beverages like soda and sweetened fruit juice.

A large observational research of 2,800 adults found that drinking more than two servings of sugary beverages per day raised the risk of LADA and type 2 diabetes by 99 percent and 20 percent, respectively.

Furthermore, one study found that drinking one serving of sugar-sweetened beverages per day may increase the risk of type 2 diabetes by 18%.

Increased water consumption, on the other hand, may result in improved blood sugar control and insulin responsiveness.

Getting enough fiber in your diet is good for gut health and weight loss. It may also aid in the prevention of diabetes.

This nutrient helps maintain blood sugar and insulin levels low in patients with prediabetes and older women with obesity, according to studies.

Fiber is split into two types: soluble fiber that absorbs water and insoluble fiber that does not.

In your digestive tract, soluble fiber and water produce a gel that inhibits food absorption, resulting in a more gradual rise in blood sugar. As a result, increasing soluble fiber consumption may lower fasting blood sugar and insulin levels.

Insoluble fiber has also been associated to blood sugar decreases.

While many research on fiber and diabetes employ fiber supplements rather than high fiber diets, obtaining more fiber from fruits and vegetables is a good idea.

Regular Exercises

Diabetes can be avoided by getting enough exercise on a regular basis.

Insulin sensitivity, also known as insulin resistance, is commonly lowered in people with prediabetes. To move sugar out of your blood and into your cells, your pancreas must produce more insulin in this state.

Exercise improves your cells' insulin sensitivity, which means you require less insulin to control your blood sugar levels.

In adults with prediabetes or type 2 diabetes, many types of physical activity have been demonstrated to lower insulin resistance and blood sugar levels. Aerobic exercise, high-intensity interval training (HIIT), and strength training are examples.

In a study of 29 persons with type 2 diabetes, HIIT, which involves bursts of intense activity followed by brief rest periods, was linked to better blood sugar control and longer endurance training sessions.

You don't have to exercise HIIT to gain the benefits, though. Exercises that last less than 10 minutes, such as brisk walking, are excellent choices. Start with short workouts and work your way up to 150 minutes per week if you're new to exercising.

Regular physical activity has numerous advantages. You can benefit from exercise in the following ways:

• Reduce your weight
• Reduce your blood sugar levels.
• Boost your insulin sensitivity, which helps you maintain a healthy blood sugar level.

Most adults have the following weight-loss and weight-maintenance goals:

Exercise that is aerobic in nature. For a total of at least 150 minutes per week, aim for 30 minutes or more of moderate to intense cardiovascular exercise on most days, such as brisk walking, swimming, biking, or running.

Exercising with resistance. Resistance training, done at least two to three times per week, improves your strength, balance, and capacity to stay active. Weightlifting, yoga, and calisthenics are all examples of resistance training.

Inactivity is kept to a minimum. Long periods of inactivity, such as sitting at a computer, can be broken up to help control blood sugar levels. Every 30 minutes, take a few minutes to stand, move around, or do some mild activity.

Diabetes is less likely if you lose weight. People in one large study reduced their risk of developing diabetes by nearly 60% after losing around 7% of their body weight with exercise and dietary changes.

To avoid disease progression, the American Diabetes Association recommends that persons with prediabetes lose at least 7% to 10% of their body weight. Greater weight loss will provide even more benefits.

Establish a weight-loss target that is proportional to your current body weight. Consult your doctor about establishing reasonable short-term objectives, such as losing 1 to 2 pounds each week.

You may be concerned that having diabetes may force you to give up things you enjoy. The good news is that you can still consume your favorite foods, albeit you may have to eat them in smaller portions or less frequently. Your health-care team will work with you to develop a diabetes meal plan that suits your specific needs and preferences.

The key to eating well with diabetes is to consume a wide variety of healthful foods from all food categories in the amounts recommended by your meal plan.

What to Eat

Carbohydrates

Carbohydrates (carbs) are the primary source of blood sugar elevation. Glycemic index and glycemic load are scientific terminology that describe how a carbohydrate affects blood sugar levels.

Foods having a low glycemic load (index) elevate blood sugar just slightly, making them healthier alternatives for diabetics.

The amount of fiber, fat, and protein in a dish (or meal) are the most important components in determining its glycemic load.

The difference between glycemic index and glycemic load is that the former is a standardized assessment, while the latter takes into consideration a real-life portion size. A bowl of peas, for example, has a glycemic index of 68 (per 100 gram), but only a 16 glycemic load (lower the better). You'd think peas were a horrible choice if you only looked at the glycemic index, but you wouldn't consume 100 gram of peas. Peas have a low glycemic index and are a good source of protein when eaten in a moderate portion size.

Carbohydrates are divided into two types: simple carbohydrates and complex carbohydrates.

Simple sugars or complex carbs

Whole-food complex carbs (low glycemic load foods, or foods that are part of a type 2 diabetes low-carb diet plan) contain additional nutrients such as:

Fibers \Vitamins

Protein and fat intake are reduced.

These extra nutrients help to reduce glucose absorption and maintain blood sugar levels more steady.

Complex carbs, sometimes known as low glycemic index foods, include:

Whole wheat and brown rice

Quinoa, steel-cut oatmeal, fruits, beans, and lentils

Vegetables

Non-starchy—includes broccoli, carrots, greens, peppers, and tomatoes

Starchy—includes potatoes, corn, and green peas

Fruits—includes oranges, melon, berries, apples, bananas, and grapes

Grains—at least half of your grains for the day should be whole grains, includes wheat, rice, oats, cornmeal, barley, and quinoa

examples: bread, pasta, cereal, and tortillas

What Kinds of Fats Are Suggested?

Fats have minimal direct influence on blood sugar, although they can help decrease the absorption of carbohydrates when eaten as part of a meal. Fats have health consequences that are unrelated to blood sugar.

Consider the following scenario:

The lipids included in animal meat raise the risk of cardiovascular disease. Dairy, particularly fermented dairy products like yoghurt, appears to reduce this risk.

Olive oil, nuts, seeds, and avocado are all plant-based fats that have been linked to a lower risk of cardiovascular disease.

Fat can also help manage overeating and carbohydrate cravings by contributing to feelings of satiety. A serving of good fats (such as avocado on whole grain toast) is far more filling and nutritious than jam on white bread.

What Kinds of Protein Are Suggested?

Protein delivers gradual, consistent energy with no impact on blood sugar levels. A meal or snack should always include protein, particularly plant-based protein. Protein helps with sugar cravings and feeling full after eating, as well as keeping blood sugar constant (satiety). Protein can be obtained from both animal and plant sources; however, animal sources sometimes contain undesirable saturated fats.

Proteins to consider include:

• Beans
• Legumes
• Eggs
• Fish and seafood
• Organic dairy products
• Peas
• Tofu and soy foods
• Lean meats such as chicken and turkey

To maintain stable blood sugar levels, pay attention to the macronutrient balance (fat, protein, and carbohydrates) in a meal. Fat, protein, and fiber, in particular, all inhibit carbohydrate absorption, allowing for a slower, lower insulin release and a consistent transit of glucose out of the blood and into the target tissues - all of which is beneficial.

What to Avoid

Reduce your intake of the foods and beverages listed below:

Liquids with added sugars, such as juice, regular soda, and regular sports or energy drinks foods high in saturated fat and trans fat, also known as sodium sweets, such as liquids with added sugars, such as juice, ordinary soda, and typical sports or energy drinks baked goods, candy, and ice cream

Instead of sugary drinks, drink water. In your coffee or tea, try using a sugar substitute.

If you do drink alcohol, keep it to one or two drinks per day for women and two drinks per day for men. If you use insulin or diabetes therapies that increase the amount of insulin your body generates, alcohol can cause your blood glucose level to drop too low. This is particularly true if you haven't eaten for a long period.

Some diabetics must eat at a same time each day. Others may find it easier to change their eating habits. Depending on your diabetes meds or insulin type, you must have the same amount of carbohydrates at the same time. You can be more flexible with your eating schedule if you use "mealtime" insulin.

Your blood glucose level may drop dangerously low if you use diabetes drugs or insulin and miss or delay a meal. Consult your doctor to determine when you should eat. You should also consider if you should eat before or after an exercise.

Spinach Egg Scramble on Bread

Prep time: 10 minutes. | Cooking time: 5 minutes. | Servings: 1

1 teaspoon canola oil
1½ cups baby spinach
2 eggs, lightly beaten
1 pinch kosher salt
1 pinch black pepper
1 slice whole-grain bread
½ cup raspberries

Inside the small nonstick skillet, add the oil over moderate-high heat. minutes Place the spinach on a serving platter. Clean your pan, set over moderate heat, and crack the eggs into it. Cook, stirring once or twice to ensure equal cooking, for 1-2 minutes, or till just set. Add spinach, salt, and Black pepper, to taste. With toast and strawberries, serve your scramble.

Nutritional information: Calories 298; Total Carbs 20.8; Net Carbs 2g; Protein 17.9g; Fat 15.9g; fibers: 3g; Sugars: 6g

Pineapple-Grapefruit Smoothie

Prep time: 10 minutes. | Cooking time: 5 minutes. | Servings: 2

1 cup part-skim coconut water
1 cup baby spinach
1 cup diced pineapple
1 grapefruit, peeled and segmented small
½ teaspoon ginger, grated
1 cup ice

Inside the blender, mix the coconut water, ginger, spinach, grapefruit and any juices, pineapple, and ice. Puree till the mixture is smooth and foamy.

Nutritional information: Calories 102; Total Carbs 25.8; Net Carbs 2g; Protein 2g; Fat 0.9g; fibers: 3g; Sugars: 6g

Oatmeal with Sausage

Prep time: 10 minutes. | Cooking time: 15 minutes. | Servings: 1

2 teaspoon canola oil
1 ½ ounce chicken sausage
1 cup vegetable broth
½ cup rolled oats
⅛ teaspoon salt
½ cup grape tomatoes halved
⅓ cup herbs packed
½ cup baby arugula
1 tablespoon pine nuts
1 large lemon wedge

Inside the small nonstick and cast-iron pan, heat 1 teaspoon oil on moderate heat. Cook the sausage and stir occasionally, until the sausage is uniformly browned, almost 10 minutes. Meanwhile, inside the small saucepan on high heat, bring the broth to a boil. Turn off the heat and cook, stirring periodically,

for 5 minutes, or till the oats become soft. Cut your sausage in coins by thinly slicing it. In a suitable mixing bowl, combine the cooked oats, sausage, tomatoes, and herbs. Place in a suitable mixing basin. Drizzle the leftover with 1 teaspoon oil over arugula and pine nuts. If desired, garnish with a lemon slice.

Nutritional information: Calories 391; Total Carbs 36.2; Net Carbs 0.5g; Protein 15.7.5g; Fat 22.4g; fibers: 3g; Sugars: 6g

Sausage Scrambled Eggs

Prep time: 10 minutes. | Cooking time: 10 minutes. | Servings: 2

nonstick cooking spray
2 eggs
2 tablespoons low-sodium chicken broth
black pepper
1 ounce turkey sausage
¼ cup cherry tomatoes
2 tablespoons part-skim cheddar cheese
1 English muffin, halved and toasted

Using the cooking spray, coat the large nonstick skillet. Preheat the skillet on medium-high heat. Whisk up eggs, broth, and black pepper inside the moderate bowl into sliced sausage. Fill a heated pan halfway with the egg mix. Cook, constantly stirring, over moderate heat until the mix solidifies just on the bottom and around the sides. Lift and fold the partly cooked egg mix with the spatula or even a big spoon so that the uncooked piece flows beneath. Cook on moderate heat till nearly done, then add the tomatoes and cheese. Cook for another min or till the egg mix is cooked properly but glossy and juicy. Serve with muffin halves together with the side.

Nutritional information: Calories 198; Total Carbs 15.2; Net Carbs 2g; Protein 13.4g; Fat 9.7g; fibers: 3g; Sugars: 6g

Breakfast Bark with Berries

Prep Time: 10minutes. | Cook Time: 0 minutes. | Servings: 8

3-4 strawberries, sliced
1 ½ cup plain Greek yogurt
½ cup blueberries
What you'll need from the store cupboard:
½ cup low-fat granola
3 tbsp. sugar-free maple syrup

Using parchment paper, line a baking sheet. Combine yoghurt and syrup in a medium mixing basin. Spread in a thin even layer on the prepared pan. Add the remaining Ingredients on top. Wrap in foil and place in the freezer for two hours or overnight. To serve, cut the cake into squares and serve right away. When bark thaws out too much, it loses its shape. Any leftover bark should be frozen in an airtight container.

Nutritional information: Calories 69; Total Carbs 18g; Net Carbs 16g; Protein 7g; Fat 6g; Sugar 7g; Fiber 2g

Waffle with Nut Butter Spread

Prep time: 5 minutes. | Cooking time: 10 minutes. | Servings: 1

1 cinnamon waffle
1 tablespoon almond butter
¼ sliced banana
1 teaspoon chocolate chips

Waffles should be toasted according to the guidelines. Put almond butter over the bread, then top with the banana slices and chocolate chips. Warm the dish before serving.

Nutritional information: Calories 222; Net Carbs 3g; Protein 5.7.5g; Total Carbs 25.2; Fat 12.4g; fibers: 3g; Sugars: 6g

Breakfast Salad with Egg

Prep time: 5 minutes. | Cooking time: 10 minutes. | Servings: 1

3 tablespoon salsa Verde
1 tablespoon olive oil
2 tablespoon chopped cilantro
2 cups mesclun
8 tortilla chips, blue corn
½ cup kidney beans red
¼ sliced avocado
1 large egg

Inside the suitable bowl, combine the salsa, 1 tablespoon oil, and cilantro. Inside the shallow dinner dish, toss half of the mix over mesclun (or other greens). Toss the salad with chips, beans, and avocado. Inside the small nonstick pan, heat the leftover 1 teaspoon oil on moderate-high heat. Add eggs, then cook for almost 2 minutes, or till the white is fully cooked; however, the yolk is somewhat runny. Serve your salad with the egg over the top. If preferred, drizzle with leftover salsa vinaigrette and top with more cilantro.

Nutritional information: Calories 527; Total Carbs 37.2; Net Carbs 4g; Protein 16g; Fat 34.4g; fibers: 3g; Sugars: 6g

Sweet Potato Frittata

Prep time: 30 minutes. | Cooking time: 30 minutes. | Servings: 4

6 large eggs
1 cup half-and-half
1 teaspoon kosher salt
½ teaspoon ground pepper
2 cups sweet potatoes
2 tablespoons olive oil
2 cups chopped kale
½ red onion
2 garlic cloves
3 ounces goat cheese, low-fat

At 350 degrees F, preheat your oven. Combine the eggs as well as the following 3 ingredients inside the mixing bowl. In a 10-inches of ovenproof nonstick pan, sauté potatoes using 1 tablespoon heated oil for 8 - 10 minutes, or until soft and golden; remove, then keep warm. In residual 1 tablespoon oil, sauté

kale and next 2 ingredients 3-4 minutes, or till kale becomes wilted and tender; mix in potatoes. Cook for another 3 minutes after pouring the egg mix equally over the veggies. Goat cheese should be sprinkled over the egg mix. Bake for almost 10-14 minutes, or till set, at 350 degrees F.

Nutritional information: Calories 199; Total Carbs 23.2; Net Carbs 2g; Protein 9g; Fat 9g; fibers: 3g; Sugars: 6g

Breakfast Quesadilla

Prep time: 10 minutes. | Cooking time: 2 minutes. | Servings: 1

Nonstick cooking spray
¼ cup refrigerated egg
1 flour tortilla
2 tablespoons shredded part-skim mozzarella cheese
2 tablespoons black beans
2 tablespoons chopped tomato

Using nonstick frying spray, coat a large nonstick skillet. Preheat the skillet on medium-high heat. Add the egg to the heated skillet and season with the spice mix. Cook, without mixing, over moderate heat till the egg starts to set here on the bottom and around the edges. Using a paper towel, wipe off the same skillet. Spray the skillet with nonstick cooking spray. Preheat the skillet to medium-high heat. Cook, rotating once, for almost 2 minutes in a hot pan or till tortilla becomes browned and filling gets cooked through. Add more (Pico de Gallo) over the top if preferred.

Nutritional information: Calories 175; Total Carbs 24.2; Net Carbs 5g; Protein 19.6g; Fat 5.1g; fibers: 3g; Sugars: 6g

Breakfast Pizza

Prep time: 10 minutes. | Cooking time: 5 minutes. | Servings: 1

nonstick cooking spray
4 slices turkey pepperoni
2 tablespoons green pepper
2 tablespoons pre-sliced mushrooms
2 egg whites
1 tablespoon low-fat milk
1 thin roll deli flat
2 teaspoons pizza sauce
1 slice part-skim mozzarella cheese
4 slices Roma tomato

Cook on moderate heat inside the small saucepan coated with the cooking spray. Cook for almost 2 minutes with pepperoni, mushrooms, and sweet pepper inside the saucepan. Mix the egg whites with milk inside the small dish, then pour the pepperoni mix inside the saucepan. Cook until the egg white mix starts to firm up. Fold the partly egg yolk white mix over with a spatula; heat for another 2 minutes or till well done. Half of the egg mix should be poured over every 1 of the deli flat pieces made. Toss in a tomato, if preferred.

Nutritional information: Calories 218; Total Carbs 23.2; Net Carbs 2g; Protein 21g; Fat 6g; fibers: 3g; Sugars: 6g

Oats Granola

Prep time: 1 hour 15 minutes. | Cooking time: 10 minutes. | Servings: 7

½ cup olive oil
¾ cup maple syrup (unsweetened)
2 tablespoons turbinado sugar
1 teaspoon kosher salt
3 cups rolled oats
1 cup coconut flakes
¾ cup sunflower seeds raw
¾ cup pumpkin seeds raw

At 300 degrees F, preheat your oven. Use parchment paper, paper-lined covered the baking sheet. Combine the oil, salt, sugar, and maple syrup inside the suitable mixing bowl. Stir in the oats, pumpkin seeds, sunflower, and coconut until uniformly mixed. Spread the prepared granola mixture onto the prepared baking sheet and bake for almost 45-55 minutes, mixing every 15 minutes, until the granola becomes light, nicely browned and dry. Allow cooling fully before serving. Granola with ginger and pecans: leave out the pumpkin seeds, then cut the sunflower seeds down almost ½ cup. 1 ½ cup pecans.

Nutritional information: Calories 142; Total Carbs 12.2; Net Carbs 5g; Protein 4.7g; Fat 15.7g; fibers: 3g; Sugars: 6g

Turmeric Tofu Scramble

Prep time: 5 minutes. | Cooking time: 10 minutes. | Servings: 4

⅓ cup low-fat almond milk
2 tablespoons nutritional yeast
2 garlic cloves
½ teaspoon Dijon mustard
¼ teaspoon ground turmeric
¼ teaspoon ground cumin
1 tablespoon olive oil
½ cup yellow onion, chopped
14 ounces tofu
Sea salt and black pepper, to taste

Mix turmeric, cumin, almond milk, mustard, ½ teaspoon salt, garlic, and nutritional yeast inside the suitable mixing bowl. Inside the suitable skillet, heat oil on moderate heat. Cook, occasionally stirring till the onion is tender, almost 5 minutes. Cook almost 3-5 minutes, and then bring to a simmer, till the tofu has been well cooked. Reduce heat to low and add almond milk mixture, stirring constantly. Cook about 3 minutes, stirring periodically. Season with some more salt than black pepper (freshly ground) Serve with vegetables, salsa, and tortillas.

Nutritional information: Calories 282; Total Carbs 33.2; Net Carbs 1.2g; Protein 14.7g; Fat 18.7g; fibers: 3g; Sugars: 6g

French Toast with Blueberries

Prep Time: 15 minutes. | Cook Time: 20 minutes. | Servings:8

4 eggs
1 ½ cup blueberries
½ cup orange juice
1 tsp. orange zest
What you'll need from store cupboard:
16 slices bread, (chapter 14)
3 tbsp. Splenda, divided
⅛ tsp. salt
Blueberry Orange Dessert Sauce, (chapter 16)
Nonstick cooking spray

Preheat the oven to 400 degrees Fahrenheit. Coat a large baking sheet in cooking spray., coat a large baking sheet. Combine the berries and 2 tablespoons of Splenda in a small bowl. On a work surface, arrange 8 slices of bread. Place the second slice of bread on top and top with about 3 tablespoons of berries. Slightly flatten. In a small mixing dish, combine the remaining Ingredients. Dip both sides of the bread into the egg mixture and place on the preheated pan. Cook for 7-12 minutes per side in the oven, or until gently browned. Warm the dessert sauce until it is warm. Top the French toast with 1-2 teaspoons of the sauce. Serve.

Nutritional information: Calories 208; Total Carbs 20g; Net Carbs 18g; Protein 7g; Fat 10g; Sugar 14g; Fiber 2g

Cottage Cheese with Walnuts

Prep time: 5 minutes. | Cooking time: 10 minutes. | Servings: 2

1 cup part-skim cottage cheese
1 handful walnut

Fill a suitable bowl halfway with the cottage cheese and walnuts. Top with 1 pinch of cinnamon and 1 pinch of salt.

Nutritional information: Calories 269; Total Carbs 22.2; Net Carbs 1.2g; Protein 9g; Fat 10g; fibers: 3g; Sugars: 6g

Avocado Pesto Zucchini Noodles

Prep Time: 10 minutes. | Cook Time: 05 minutes. | Servings:2

6 cups of spiralized zucchini
1 tablespoon olive oil
6 oz. of avocado
1 basil leaf
3 garlic cloves
⅓ oz. pine nuts
2 tablespoons lemon juice
½ teaspoon salt
¼ teaspoon black pepper

Spiralize the zucchini and place them on paper towels to absorb any excess liquid. Put avocados, basil leaves, garlic, pine nuts, and sea salt in a food processor and pulse until finely chopped. Then slowly drizzle in the vegetable oil until it is emulsified and creamy. In a skillet over medium-high heat, drizzle vegetable oil and add zucchini noodles, cooking for about 2 minutes or until cooked. Toss zucchini noodles with avocado pesto in a large mixing bowl. Serve with cracked pepper.

Nutritional information: Calories 110; Total Carbs 7.1g Net Carbs 12.6g Protein 2.3g Fat 9.2g Sugar 2.3g Fiber 3.3g

Sausage Pepper Skillet

Prep time: 20 minutes. | Cooking time: 10 minutes. | Servings: 2

½ tablespoon coconut oil
1 link kielbasa sausage, low-sodium
½ cup red peppers
½ cup yellow peppers
½ cup red onion
¼ teaspoon pepper flakes crushed
1 minced garlic clove
salt and black pepper, to taste
1 tablespoon parsley

Over moderate-high heat, heat the skillet. Add oil after the skillet gets heated. The sausage should then be added and browned on every side, turning periodically. Add your peppers and onions after the sausage has browned, then keep mixing. Add powder of garlic, pepper flakes (crushed), and just 1 pinch of pepper and salt after that. Cook for another five minutes, or till onions are transparent and peppers are cooked and have a small sharpness. Serve garnished with parsley.

Nutritional information: Calories 189; Total Carbs 11.2; Net Carbs 2g; Protein 8g; Fat 4g; fibers: 3g; Sugars: 6g

Pumpkin Pancakes

Prep time: 20 minutes. | Cooking time: 10 minutes. | Servings: 3

1 ½ cups rolled oats
½ cup pumpkin puree
½ cup cottage cheese
2 large eggs
2 tablespoons maple syrup (unsweetened)
2 teaspoons baking powder
1 teaspoon pie spice pumpkin
¼ teaspoon salt

Inside the high-powered blender, add all the recipe ingredients and mix until largely smooth. Preheat a pan on moderate heat, whereas the batter sits in a blender. Oil or even butter should be used to oil the pan. When the pan becomes heated, pour ⅓ of the batter into every pancake. To make a spherical pancake, smooth out batter using the back side of the spoon. Cook about 2-4 minutes, or till bubbles develop all around edges and the pancakes gently puff up. Cook for yet another 1-2 minutes on the opposite side, or till golden brown.

Nutritional information: Calories 295; Total Carbs 41.2; Net Carbs 1.2g; Protein 16g; Fat 7g; fibers: 3g; Sugars: 6g

Avocado Raspberry Smoothie

Prep time: 5 minutes. | Cooking time: 0 minutes. | Servings: 1

½ cup water
¼ medium avocado
1 tablespoon lemon juice
¾ cup frozen mango
¼ cup frozen raspberries
1 tablespoon agave

Inside the blender, combine the water, avocado, mango, raspberries, and lemon juice. Blend till completely smooth. Serve.

Nutritional information: Calories 188; Total Carbs 32.2; Net Carbs 2g; Protein 1.5g; Fat 7.4g; fibers: 3g; Sugars: 6g

Egg Banana Pancakes

Prep time: 15 minutes. | Cooking time: 5 minutes. | Servings: 2

2 large eggs
1 banana

Heat a wide nonstick skillet on moderate heat, lightly oiled. Drop four mounds of the batter into the pan, all using 2 tbsp. each batter. Cook for 2 to 4 minutes, or till bubbles emerge on the top and the edges seem dry. Flip your pancakes carefully with the thin spatula and cook for 1 - 2 minutes longer, or till browned mostly on the bottom. Place the pancakes on a platter and set them aside. Repeat with the remaining batter, carefully oiling the pan each time.

Nutritional information: Calories 124; Total Carbs 13.8; Net Carbs 0.5g; Protein 6.9g; Fat 4.9g; fibers: 3g; Sugars: 6g

Bean Breakfast Tacos

Prep time: 10 minutes. | Cooking time: 5 minutes. | Servings: 1

1 teaspoon olive oil
1 cup chopped kale
½ cup cannellini beans, rinsed
2 (5 inches) corn tortillas
1 tablespoon part-skim cheddar cheese
1-piece cooked bacon

Inside the suitable skillet, heat the oil on moderate heat. Cook and stir, until the greens and beans are heated, almost 2 minutes. Serve with the cheese and bacon on the corn tortillas.

Nutritional information: Calories 283; Total Carbs 33.2; Net Carbs 2g; Protein 12.7.5g; Fat 11.4g; fibers: 3g; Sugars: 6g

Rainbow Yogurt Meal

Prep time: 10 minutes. | Cooking time: 10 minutes. | Servings: 1

½ cup plain yogurt
1 teaspoon maple syrup, unsweetened
9 raspberries
3 clementine segments
3 green grapes
6 blueberries

Inside the broad, shallow dish, combine yogurt and syrup. Using raspberries, blueberries, grapes, and clementine, make a rainbow on top of the yogurt.

Nutritional information: Calories 128; Total Carbs 21.2; Net Carbs 5g; Protein 7g; Fat 2.7g; fibers: 3g; Sugars: 6g

Walnut Berry Oatmeal

Prep time: 10 minutes. | Cooking time: 0 minutes. | Servings: 1

1½ tablespoons Walnuts
½ cup quick and easy oatmeal
½ cup citrus and mint berries

Quick and easy oatmeal may well be reheated. Citrus and mint berries, as well as walnuts, go on top.

Nutritional information: Calories 212; Total Carbs 21.2; Net Carbs 1.2g; Protein 3.7g; Fat 5.7g; fibers: 3g; Sugars: 6g

Mint Berry Yogurt Bowl

Prep time: 15 minutes. | Cooking time: 10 minutes. | Servings: 1

¾ cup plain Greek yogurt
1 tablespoon chopped mint
2½ tablespoons chopped walnuts
½ cup citrus and mint berries

Fill a suitable bowl halfway with yogurt. Citrus and mint berries, mint, plus walnuts go on top. Keep refrigerated or eat fresh.

Nutritional information: Calories 172; Total Carbs 16.2; Net Carbs 2g; Protein 6.7g; Fat 8.7g; fibers: 3g; Sugars: 6g

Avocado Toast with Pickled Onions

Prep time: 20 minutes. | Cooking time: 10 minutes. | Servings: 2

2 slices bread
½ medium avocado
⅛ teaspoon sea salt
⅛ teaspoon black pepper
½ lime juice
few slices of pickled onions
1 sprinkle pepper flakes (red)

Toast the bread until it becomes golden brown. While the bread starts toasting, remove the peel off your avocado and set it inside the bowl. Squeeze with in lime, then season with black pepper and sea salt. Mash it with a fork till it reaches the desired texture. Evenly spread your avocado just on toasts. Sprinkle/apply the remaining subjects and have fun!

Nutritional information: Calories 195; Total Carbs 25.2; Net Carbs 2g; Protein 5g; Fat 8g; fibers: 3g; Sugars: 6g

Gruyère and Bacon Scrambled Eggs

Prep time: 10 minutes. | Cooking time: 10 minutes. | Servings: 4

8 large eggs
1 teaspoon Dijon mustard
salt and black pepper, to taste
1 tablespoon olive oil
2 slices low-sodium bacon thick-cut
2 cups spinach
2 ounces low-fat Gruyère cheese

Mix eggs, mustard, 1 tablespoon of water, and ½ teaspoon of salt and pepper inside the suitable mixing bowl. Inside the 10-inches of nonstick skillet, heat oil and butter over moderate flame. Cook, tossing with the rubber spatula every several seconds until eggs are done to your liking, about 2-3 minutes for moderate eggs. Combine the bacon, spinach, and cheese (Gruyère) inside the mixing bowl.

Nutritional information: Calories 189; Total Carbs 21.2; Net Carbs 1.2g; Protein 11g; Fat 7g; fibers: 3g; Sugars: 6g

Coconut Porridge

Prep Time: 02 minutes. | Cook Time:10 minutes. | Servings:4

4 cup vanilla almond milk, unsweetened
What you'll need from store cupboard
1 cup unsweetened coconut, grated
8 tsp. coconut flour

In a saucepan, roast the coconut over medium-high heat until it is lightly toasted. Make sure it doesn't burn. Bring the milk to a boil. Slowly add the flour, stirring constantly, and simmer and stir until the mixture thickens, about 5 minutes. Remove the pan from the heat; the mixture will thicken as it cools. Pour into bowls, top with blueberries. Serve and enjoy.

Nutritional information: Calories 231; Total Carbs 21g; Net Carbs 8g; Protein 6g; Fat 14g; Sugar 4g; Fiber 13g

Huevos Rancheros

Prep Time: 12 minutes. | Cook Time: 33 minutes. | Servings: 2

4 corn tortillas
1 can tomato(es) (14.5-ounce, no-salt-added, diced, drained)
1 teaspoon ground cumin
⅛ teaspoon cayenne pepper (optional)
½ teaspoon salt
4 large eggs
1 ounce part-skim mozzarella cheese or reduced-fat feta (shredded)
¼ cup cilantro (chopped)

Preheat oven to 425 degrees F. Put the tortillas in a pan and fry them on each side for 3 minutes. Meanwhile, place tomatoes, cumin, cayenne pepper, and salt in a medium non-stick pan and cook over medium-high heat. Reduce heat to medium-low and cook covered until soft or 3 minutes. Divide one egg into a beaker for the calculation. Carefully move the eggs over the tomato mixture. Repeat with the remaining eggs. Slowly simmer, covered, over medium, 2½ to 3 minutes or until the whites completely solidify and the yolks begin to thicken slightly. Place a tortilla to eat on each of the four plates. Cover with eggs and tomato mixture. Use cheese and coriander to spread and enjoy!

Nutritional information: Calories 162; Total Carbs 14.6g; Net Carbs 9g; Protein 10g; Fat 8g; Sugar 2g; Fiber 5g

Swedish Pancake with Apple Filling

Prep Time: 25 minutes. | Cook Time: 20 minutes. |
Servings:6

2 apples, cored and sliced thin
¾ cup egg substitute
½ cup fat-free milk
½ cup sugar-free caramel sauce
1 tbsp. reduced calorie butter
What you'll need from the store cupboard
½ cup flour
1½ tbsp. brown sugar substitute
2 tsp. water
¼ tsp. cinnamon
⅛ tsp. cloves
⅛ tsp. salt
Nonstick cooking spray

Preheat the oven to 400 degrees Fahrenheit. Place
the low-fat butter in a cast iron skillet or an
ovenproof skillet and bake until melted. Whisk together flour, milk, egg substitute, cinnamon, cloves,
and salt in a medium mixing bowl until smooth. Pour
batter into a heated skillet and bake for 20–25
minutes, or until golden brown and puffy. Using cooking spray, coat a medium saucepan. Heat over a medium heat setting. Combine the apples, brown sugar,
and water in a mixing bowl. Cook, stirring periodically, for 4–6 minutes, or until apples are soft and
golden brown. In a microwave-safe measuring glass,
pour the caramel sauce and heat for 30–45 seconds,
or until warmed through. To serve, put apples into
the pancakes and top with caramel sauce. Cut the
wedges in half.

Nutritional information: Calories 193 Total Carbs
25g Net Carbs 23g Protein 6g Fat 2g Sugar 12g Fiber
2g

Salad with Avocado and Chicken Dice

Prep Time: 05 minutes. | Cook Time: 10 minutes. |
Servings:2

10 oz. diced cooked chicken
½ cup 2% Plain Greek yogurt
3 oz. chopped avocado
12 teaspoon garlic powder
¼ teaspoon salt
⅛ teaspoon pepper
1 tablespoon lime juice
¼ cup fresh cilantro, chopped

Combine all of the Ingredients in a medium mixing
basin. Keep refrigerated until ready to eat. Cut the
salad in half and combine it with your favorite greens
to serve.

Nutritional information: Calories 403; Total Carbs
13.1g Net Carbs 20.6g Protein 50.6g Fat 13.2g Sugar
6.3g Fiber 4.3g

Pancakes with Coconut

Prep Time: 05 minutes. | Cook Time:15 minutes. |
Servings:4

1 cup coconut flour
2 tablespoons of arrowroot powder
1 teaspoon. baking powder

1 cup of coconut milk
3 tablespoons coconut oil

Combine all of the dry Ingredients in a medium container. Mix in the coconut milk and a couple of tablespoons of copra oil until thoroughly combined. 1 teaspoon copra oil, melted in a skillet Pour a ladle of batter onto the skillet and swirl it around to properly distribute the batter into a smooth pancake. Cook for
about 3 minutes over medium heat, or until firm.
Turn the pancake over and cook for another 2
minutes, or until golden brown on the other side.
Cook the remaining pancakes in the same manner as
before. Serve.

Nutritional information: Calories 258; Total Carbs
9.3g Net Carbs 4.3g Protein 1.9g Fat 25g Sugar 2.3g
Fiber 2.3g

Quinoa Porridge with Blueberries

Prep Time: 05 minutes. | Cook Time:25 minutes. |
Servings:2

2 cups of coconut milk
1 cup rinsed quinoa
⅛ teaspoon ground cinnamon
1 cup fresh blueberries

Boil the coconut milk in a pot over high heat. Allow
the quinoa to soak in the milk before bringing it to a
boil. Then, on medium heat, let it simmer for a quar-
ter-hour until the milk is reduced. The cinnamon
should be added last, and the mixture should be thoroughly mixed in the saucepan. Cook, covered, for at
least 8 minutes, or until the milk has been absorbed.
Cook for another 30 seconds after adding the blueberries. Serve.

Nutritional information: Calories 480; Total Carbs
68g Net Carbs 53g Protein 14g Fat 17.4g Sugar 7.2g
Fiber 7.9g

Chickpea Flour Omelet

Prep Time: 10 minutes. | Cook Time: 20 minutes. |
Servings: 1

1 cup chickpea flour
⅓ cup nutritional yeast
3 finely chopped green onions
4 ounces sautéed mushrooms
½ teaspoon onion powder
¼ teaspoon black pepper
½ teaspoon garlic powder
½ teaspoon baking soda
¼ teaspoon white pepper

In a bowl, combine the onion powder, white pepper,
chickpea flour, garlic powder, black and white pepper,
baking soda, and yeast. Add 1 cup water and mix
well until smooth batter formd. Heat the frying pan
over medium heat and add the batter like pancakes.
Sprinkle some green onion and mushrooms on top of
batter. Flip the omelet and cook evenly on both sides.
Serve the omelet with spinach, tomatoes, hot sauce,
and salsa.

Nutritional information: Calories 150; Total Carbs
2.4g; Net Carbs 1.5g; Protein 10.2g; Fat 1.9g; Sugar
0g; Fiber 2.2g

Paleo Hash

Prep Time: 7 minutes. | Cook Time: 33 minutes. | Servings: 5

8 ounces white mushroom, quartered
1 pound brussels sprout, quartered
Everything bagel seasoning
1 tablespoon olive oil or avocado oil
3 cloves of garlic, minced
1 small onion, diced
Crushed red pepper, optional
8 slices of nitrate free bacon sugar free, for Whole30, cut into pieces
Sea salt and pepper to taste
6 large eggs

Preheat the oven to 425 ° F for 5 minutes. On a baking tray, arrange the mushrooms and Brussels sprouts in a single layer. Drizzle with the olive oil and seasoned salt and pepper. Sprinkle the onions on top and place the strips of bacon equally over all the vegetables. Roast the veggies for 15 mins in the preheated oven, then sprinkle with the garlic and stir gently. Roast the veggies with garlic for another 10 minutes or until the bacon and vegetables are crisp and fluffy, then extract from the oven. Make tiny gaps in the veggies and place the egg gently on it, careful not to 'split' the yolk. Sprinkle the bagel seasoning and crushed red pepper over the top of hash. Bake the hash with eggs for another 5-10 minutes or until the eggs are fried. Remove from the oven and quickly serve. Enjoy!

Nutritional information: Calories 250; Total Carbs 14g; Net Carbs 10g; Protein 14g; Fat 18g; Sugar 4g; Fiber 5g

Avocado Toast

Prep Time: 5 minutes. | Cook Time: 13 minutes. | Servings: 4

1 avocado peeled and seeded
2 tablespoons chopped cilantro
Juice of ½ lime
½ tablespoon red pepper flakes optional
Salt & pepper to taste
2 slices of whole grain bread or bread of your choice
2 eggs fried, scrambled, optional

Toast 2 whole grain slices until they are crispy and golden. In a bowl, add the avocado, lime, cilantro and salt and pepper and crushed them until well incorporated. Spread the avocado sauce on all the toasted slices with ½ of the combination. Top with fried poached or scrambled egg, as desired and serve.

Nutritional information: Calories 501; Total Carbs 11g; Net Carbs 6g; Protein 16g; Fat 28g; Sugar 2g; Fiber g

Sprouted Toast with Avocado

Prep Time: 10 minutes. | Cook Time: 15 minutes. | Servings: 3

2 small sized bread sprouts
1 cup finely cut tomatoes
2 moderate size avocados

1 small cup alfalfa
Pure sea salt and bell pepper

In a bowl, add the avocado, alfalfa, and tomatoes and mix. Place the sauce to the bread and season to taste with pure sea salt and pepper. Have a delicious breakfast with any freshly extracted juice of your choice.

Nutritional information: Calories 82; Total Carbs 25g; Net Carbs 23g; Protein 30g; Fat 15g; Sugar 8g; Fiber 15g

Traditional Omelet with Turmeric

Prep Time: 8 minutes. | Cook Time: 15 minutes. | Servings: 2

4 large eggs
Kosher salt
1 tablespoon olive oil
¼ teaspoon brown mustard seeds Turmeric powder
2 green onions, finely chopped
¼ cup diced plum tomato
Dash of black pepper

Whisk the eggs and salt together. Heat oil in a large cast-iron skillet over medium heat. Use mustard and turmeric seeds. Stir constantly for 30 seconds or until the seeds crackled. Add the onions and cook for 30 seconds or until tender, stirring constantly. Add the tomatoes. Cook for 1 minute, stirring constantly, or until very tender. Pour the bowl with the egg mixture. Spread evenly. Cook until edges are set (about 2 minutes). Slide the edges of the spatula between the edges of the omelet and the plate. Carefully lift the edges of the omelet by tilting the pan so that it comes in contact with the egg mixture. Duplicate procedure from the opposite edge. Continue cooking until the setting is ready. Loosen the omelet and fold it in half with a spatula. Carefully slide the omelet onto the plate. Cut the omelet in half and sprinkle with pepper.

Nutritional information: Calories 216; Total Carbs 14g; Net Carbs 9g; Protein 13.3g; Fat 16.9g; Sugar 0.6g; Fiber 4g

Curried Apple Chicken Salad

Prep Time: 12 minutes. | Cook Time: 13 minutes. | Servings: 3

1 pound of cooked, diced chicken breast.
1 Granny Smith diced apple.
2 celery stalks, (diced)
2 green onions, (diced)
½ cup sliced cashew.
1 cup plain Greek yogurt
1 tablespoon tahini
4 teaspoons curry powder
1 teaspoon ground cinnamon

In a big mixing bowl, add the milk, tahini, curry powder, and cinnamon. Add the chicken, apple, celery, cashews and green onions. Stir to mix well. Serve with papya chunks if desire.

Nutritional information: Calories 139; Total Carbs 19g; Net Carbs 11g; Protein 14g; Fat 8g; Sugar 1g; Fiber 5g

Quinoa Burrito

Prep Time: 15 minutes. | Cook Time: 10 minutes. | Servings: 1

1 cup quinoa
2 cups black beans
4 finely chopped onions, green
4 finely chopped garlic
2 freshly cut limes
1 big tablespoon cumin
2 beautifully diced avocado
1 small cup beautifully diced cilantro

Boil quinoa as per instructions. Heat up beans over low heat. Add other Ingredients to the beans pot and let it mix well for about 15 minutes. Serve quinoa and add the prepared beans on top.

Nutritional information: Calories 117; Total Carbs 22g; Net Carbs 18g; Protein 27g; Fat 8g; Sugar 2g; Fiber 10g

Bulgur Porridge

Prep Time: 5 minutes. | Cook Time: 15 minutes. | Servings: 4

4 cups 1% low-fat milk
1 cup bulgur
⅓ cup dried cherries
¼ tablespoon salt
⅓ cup dried apricots, coarsely chopped
½ cup sliced almonds

In a large saucepan, put the milk, bulgur, dried cherries, and salt. Bring to a boil. Reduce heat to low and simmer, stirring constantly, until tender and oatmeal are tender for 10-15 minutes. Divide among 4 bowls. Garnish with apricots and almonds and serve.

Nutritional information: Calories 340; Total Carbs 21g; Net Carbs 18g; Protein 15g; Fat 6.7g; Sugar 2g; Fiber 5g

Savory Egg Muffins

Prep Time: 12 minutes. | Cook Time: 33 minutes. | Servings: 6

1 and ½ cups water
2 tablespoons unsalted butter
1 (6-ounce) package Stove, top lower-sodium stuffing mix for chicken
3 ounces bulk pork sausage
Cooking spray
6 eggs, beaten
½ cup nonfat (1.5 ounces) Monterey Jack cheese, shredded -
½ cup finely chopped red bell pepper –
¼ cup sliced green onions

Preheat oven to 400°F. Boil 1½ cups of water and butter. Mix the Ingredients. Cover, remove from heat, and let stand 5 minutes. Use a pork to fluff the filling. Leave it for 10 minutes. Cook the sausages in a small skillet over medium heat until they are brown while the stuffing is cooling. Stir to break. Press about ¼ cup into the bottom and sides of 12 oil-coated muffin cups. Pour in eggs equal to cups of filling. If desired, top the eggs evenly with cheese, ham, bell peppers, and green onions. Bake at 400°F for 18-20 minutes. Let stand 5 minutes before eating. Loosen the glass muffin with a thin, sharp knife along the edge. Remove from the casserole dish. Serve immediately.

Nutritional information: Calories 292; Total Carbs 18g; Net Carbs 12g; Protein 14.6g; Fat 16.7g; Sugar 3g; Fiber 9g

Cajun-Style Shrimp and Grits

Prep Time: 12 minutes. | Cook Time: 20 minutes. | Servings: 6

1 tablespoon olive oil
½ cup (2 ounces) of non-nitrite ham, minced
1 cup chopped onion
1 garlic clove, minced
36 medium shrimp, peeled (about 1 ¼ pounds)
1 teaspoon Cajun seasoning
2 and ½ cups water, divided
1 tablespoon unsalted butter
1 cup fat-free milk
1 quarter teaspoon salt
1 cup uncooked quick-cooking grits
1 cup (4 ounces) of sharp cheddar cheese, shredded
½ cup sliced green onions

Heat olive oil in a large skillet over medium heat. Add Tasso; Fry for 2 minutes or until edges are golden. Add onions. Fry for 2 minutes. Stir in the garlic. Fry for 1 minute. Sprinkle with Cajun seasoning, add the shrimp on the grill and cook in the oven for 3 minutes in turn. Use ¼ glass of water to loosen the brown flakes and scrape the pan. Remove from fire. Stir and mix with the butter until melted. Wrap up and stay warm. Add milk, salt, and 2 cups of water to a boil over medium heat. remove heat. Continue to add the oatmeal and cook until thick and crisp, stirring constantly with a whisk. Place the grain at room temperature. Add the cheese and stir with a whisk until the cheese is melted. Place an equal spoon on the plate. Mix together the eafood, mixed ham, and green onions for serving.

Nutritional information: Calories 346; Total Carbs 14g; Net Carbs 9g; Protein 24g; Fat 14g; Sugar 3g; Fiber 4g

Summer Fruits Smoothie

Prep Time: 12 minutes. | Cook Time: 0 minutes. | Servings: 4

1 cup fresh blueberries
1 cup fresh strawberries (chopped)
2 peaches (peeled, seeded and chopped)
Peach flavored Greek style yogurt (non-fat)
1 cup unsweetened almond milk
2 tablespoons ground flax seed
½ cup ice

Put all Ingredients in a blender and puree until creamy. Serve chilled.

Nutritional information: Calories 130; Total Carbs 23g; Net Carbs 20g; Protein 15g; Fat 4g; Sugar 1g; Fiber 4g

Scrambled Eggs and Onion for Lox

Prep Time: 12 minutes. | Cook Time: 15 minutes. | Servings: 4

6 eggs
4 egg whites
1 teaspoon canola oil
⅓ cup sliced green onions
4 ounces smoked salmon, cut into ½-inch pieces
¼ cup reduced-fat cream
nonfat cheese, cut into 12 pieces
¼ teaspoon freshly ground black pepper
4 slices pumpernickel bread, toasted

Place the eggs and egg whites in a bowl. Stir with a whisk until combined. Preheat a medium nonstick skillet to medium. Use oil in the shower. Swirl to coat Put the green onions in the pan. Fry for 2 minutes or until tender. Connect a bowl of the egg mixture. Cook without stirring until the mixture is on the edges. Draw a spatula to create a curd at the bottom of the pan. Add sour cream and salmon. Continue to draw a spatula on the bottom of the pan until the egg mixture is slightly thick but still moist. Do not stir. Removed directly from the pan. Sprinkle Pepper on egg mixture and serve.

Nutritional information: Calories 297; Total Carbs 11g; Net Carbs 6g; Protein 22g; Fat 14g; Sugar 2g; Fiber 7g

Chicken Nuggets

Prep Time: 15 minutes. | Cook Time: 23 minutes. | Servings: 2

½ cup almond flour
1 tablespoon Italian seasoning
2 tablespoons extra virgin olive oil
½ teaspoon salt
½ teaspoon pepper

Preheat the oven to 400° F. Using parchment paper to arrange a large baking dish. In a bowl, combine the Italian seasoning, almond flour, pepper, and salt together. Start cutting, remove the fat from the chicken breast, then cut it into 1 inch thick slices. Drizzle the chicken with extra virgin olive oil. Place each piece of chicken in a bowl of flour and toss until well covered in the mix, then transfer the chicken to a lined baking sheet. Bake chicken chunks for 20 minutes. To make the outside crispy, turn on the oven and place the chicken nuggets under the oven for 3-4 minutes.

Nutritional information: Calories 149; Total Carbs 29g; Net Carbs 22g; Protein 23g; Fat 9g; Sugar 3g; Fiber 8g

Baked Sweet Potatoes with egg

Prep Time: 30 minutes. | Cook Time: 60 minutes. | Servings: 4

For The Potatoes:
4 medium Sweet Potatoes
2 heads of garlic
2 teaspoons Extra Virgin Olive Oil
½ tablespoon Taco Seasoning
¼ cup fresh cilantro, plus additional for garnish
salt and pepper
4 eggs
For The Sauce:
½ cup avocado, about 1 medium avocado
1 tablespoon fresh lime juice
1 teaspoon lime zest
salt and pepper
2 tablespoons water

Preheat the oven to 395°F. Line the baking pan with foil. Place the potatoes in the baking pan. Make garlic pocket by placing garlic in the olive oil and little salt and roll in the foil. Then fold to make pocket. Place garlic pocket on the baking pan with potatoes. Bake the garlic and potatoes for about 40 minutes, until it is tender. Remove the garlic pocket from the pan and proceed to cook the potatoes for additional 25-35 minutes, until fork tender and soft. When the potatoes are tender, set them aside for about 10 minutes until they're cool. Lower the temperature of the oven to 375°. Break the potatoes into half and peel the skin back, leaving the skin intact on the sides. Carefully scoop out the pulp, leaving a little amount on the sides of the potato to help maintain its form. Mash the flesh of the sweet potato and then cut ½ of it from the bowl. Add in the taco seasoning, cilantro, salt, and pepper to taste into the mashed flesh. Squeeze all the fluffy garlic in the mash and blend well. Divide the flesh between the 4 sweet potatoes, spreading it softly to fill the mash, leaving a large hole in the middle of each potato. Place the potatoes boats on the baking sheet and crack an egg into each hole and season it with pepper and salt. Bake until the egg is well fried for about 10-15 minutes and blend until smooth. For the avocado sauce, add all Ingredients in a food blender along with little water and blend until well mixed. Sprinkle the sauce with salt and pepper to taste. Spread the avocado sauce between the potatoes until cooked, spreading it out on top. Garnish the potatoes with sliced tomatoes and cilantro in addition. And enjoy!

Nutritional information: Calories 399; Total Carbs 21g; Net Carbs 14g; Protein 18g; Fat 32g; Sugar 8g; Fiber 5g

Keto Salad

Prep Time: 11 minutes. | Cook Time: 0 minutes. | Servings: 2

4 cherry tomatoes
½ avocado
1 hardboiled egg
2 cups mixed green salad
2 ounce of chicken breast, shredded
1 ounce of low-fat feta cheese, crumbled
¼ cup cooked nitrate-free bacon, sugar-free, crumbled

Cut the avocado and tomatoes. Cut the hard-boiled eggs. Place the mixed vegetables on a large plate. Add the chicken breast, mashed bacon, and feta cheese. Arrange tomatoes, eggs, chicken, avocado, feta, and bacon in a horizontal line over the vegetables. Serve and enjoy.

Nutritional information: Calories 152; Total Carbs 24g; Net Carbs 19g; Protein 17g; Fat 9g; Sugar 1.1g; Fiber 6.2g

Pancakes with Blueberry and Peaches

Prep Time: 12 minutes. | Cook Time: 16 minutes. | Servings: 6

One and ½ cups all-purpose flour
2 tablespoons splenda
2 tablespoons flaxseed (optional) One tablespoon baking powder
½ teaspoon kosher salt
1 and ½ cups nonfat buttermilk
1 teaspoon grated lemon rind
2 eggs
1 cup fresh or frozen blueberries, thawed
1 cup chopped fresh or frozen peaches, thawed
2 tablespoons unsalted butter
Fresh blueberries (optional)

Whisk or gently pour the flour into a measuring cup. Level with a knife. In a large bowl, combine flour, splenda, flax seeds, baking powder, and salt as needed and stir with a fork. In a small cup, put the buttermilk, lemon zest, and eggs and stir with a fork. Use the buttermilk mixture to mix and stir until it is just moist. Thinly fold the blueberries and peaches. Heat a nonstick skillet or nonstick skillet over medium heat. Pour ⅓ cup of flour into a pancake in the pan. Cook over medium heat for 2-3 minutes or until the foam covers the top and fry the edges. Slowly turn the pancake over. Cook 2-3 minutes or until the underside is golden brown.

Nutritional information: Calories 238; Total Carbs 14g; Net Carbs 10g; Protein 8.1g; Fat 2.8g; Sugar 3g; Fiber 2.5g

Instant Pot Chicken Chili

Prep Time: 6 minutes. | Cook Time: 21 minutes. | Servings: 2

1 tablespoon vegetable oil
1 yellow diced onion
4 minced garlic cloves
1 teaspoon ground cumin
1 teaspoon oregano
2 and halls' chicken breasts, boneless & skinless
16 ounce of salsa Verde
For Toppings
2 packages of queso fresco(crumbled) or sour cream
2 diced avocados
Finely chopped radishes
8 springs cilantro (optional)

Set the Instant Pot to a medium sauté setting. Add oil and vegetables to the pot. Add the onion and simmer for 3 minutes, stirring constantly, until the onion begins to melt. Add the garlic and stir for 1 minute. Add oregano and cumin and simmer for 1 minute. Add ½ of the salsa verde to the pan. Top with the chicken breast and pour the chicken with most of the leftover salsa verde. Place the cover on the instant pot, change the nozzle to "Seal" and select "Manual". Set the timer for 10 minutes. Then let the pressure release naturally after done. Remove the lid and transfer the chicken to a small bowl and chop it with a fork. Transfer the meat to a pot and stir to combine most of the remaining Ingredients. Serve hot and enjoy.

Nutritional information: Calories 144; Total Carbs 20g; Net Carbs 18g; Protein 15g; Fat 7g; Sugar 3g; Fiber 8g

Black Beans and Egg Tacos

Prep Time: 9 minutes. | Cook Time: 13 minutes. | Servings: 4

½ cup red onion, diced
86-inch white soft corn tortillas, warmed
1 clove of garlic, minced
1 teaspoon avocado oil
¼ cup chopped fresh cilantro
4 eggs
1 15-ounce can black beans, rinsed and drained
1 small avocado, diced
¼ teaspoon ground chipotle powder
½ cup fresh or your favorite jarred salsa

Make scrambled egg as you always do. Take a pan and heat the avocado oil in it. Add onions and sauté for 3 minutes until tender. Add garlic and beans and cook for 2-5 minutes until heated through and shinny. Toast the tortillas until little tender . Put aside, wrapped to keep them warm, in a cloth napkin. Take a tortilla and layer the beans, ¼ cup per taco, then add the eggs. Top up the taco with salsa, avocado and cilantro.

Nutritional information: Calories 349; Total Carbs 12g; Net Carbs 9g; Protein 11g; Fat 15g; Sugar 5g; Fiber 6g

Beef Fajitas

Prep Time: 6 minutes. | Cook Time: 19 minutes. | Servings: 4

1 lbs. beef stir-fry strips
1 medium red onion
1 red bell pepper
1 yellow bell pepper
½ teaspoon cumin
½ teaspoon chili powder
Splash of oil
Salt
Pepper
½ juice of lime
Freshly chopped cilantro (also called coriander)
1 avocado

Steam a cast-iron saucepan over medium heat. Wash and clean the peppers, cut them into slices 0.5 cm thick, and leave them separately. Wash the red onions and cut them into strips. Separate. When the pan is heated, add a little oil. Add 2-3 packets of stir-fry strips while the oil is hot. In a skillet, lightly brown a loaf of beef with salt and pepper. Bake for 1 minute on each side and place on a plate to warm. When the beef is cooked, add the chopped onion and red pepper to the rest of the broth and set aside. Spice with chili powder and cumin, then simmer until desired consistency. Transfer the roasted vegetables and beef to a plate and serve with chopped avocado, a drop of lemon juice, and a drop of fresh cilantro.

Nutritional information: Calories 151; Total Carbs 27g; Net Carbs 20g; Protein 37g; Fat 6g; Sugar 0.4g; Fiber 11g

Berry Parfaits

Prep Time: 7 minutes. | Cook Time: 23 minutes. | Servings: 4

For The Nut Granola
2 cups mixed nuts
1 tablespoon flax seed
1 tablespoon sesame seeds
1 tablespoon chia seeds
2 tablespoons pumpkin seeds
2 tablespoons coconut oil, melted
Pinch of salt
For The Blueberry Sauce
2 cups frozen blueberries
3 tablespoons Xylitol or (sugar alternative)
1 tablespoon water
For The Parfait
Plain Greek yoghurt
Fresh raspberries or other fruit of your choice

Preheat the oven to about 175°C and line a baking tray with parchment paper. In a bowl, mix all the granola Ingredients and place them in a baking tray evenly. Place the granola in the oven and bake. Bake the granla until golden brown for 5-10 minutes. For blueberry sauce, mix all Ingredients in a saucepan and cook for 5 to 10 minutes to bring a boil on low flame until the juice is released. Cool the sauce. For serving, place the yoghurt with the granola, fresh fruit and blueberry sauce in a bowl to make the parfaits. Cool the parfait for at least 30 minutes or overnight in refrigerator.

Nutritional information: Calories 217; Total Carbs 12g; Net Carbs 8g; Protein 65g; Fat 16g; Sugar 3g; Fiber 1g

Salad with Pomegranate and Brussels Sprouts

Prep Time: 10minutes. | Cook Time:00 minutes. | Servings:6

3 cup Brussels sprouts, shredded
3 cup kale, shredded
1 ½ cup pomegranate seeds
What you'll need from store cupboard:
½ cup almonds, toasted & chopped
¼ cup reduced fat parmesan cheese, grated
Citrus Vinaigrette, (chapter 16)

In a large mixing basin, add all of the Ingredients. Mix the salad in the vinaigrette to thoroughly coat it. Serve.

Nutritional information: Calories 256 Total Carbs 15g Net Carbs 10g Protein 9g Fat 18g Sugar 5g Fiber 5g

Turkey Meatballs

Prep Time: 16 minutes. | Cook Time: 25 minutes. | Servings: 5

20 ounces ground turkey
4 ounces fresh or frozen spinach
¼ cup oats
2 egg whites
2 celery sticks
3 cloves' garlic
½ green bell peppers
½ red onion
½ cup parsley
½ teaspoon cumin
1 teaspoon mustard powder
1 teaspoon thyme
½ tablespoon turmeric
½ teaspoon chipotle pepper
1 teaspoon salt
Pinch of pepper

Preheat the oven to 350° F. Chop very finely the onion, garlic, and celery, and add to a large mixing bowl. In the dish, add the ham, egg whites, oats, and spices and combine well. Make sure the blend has no pockets of spices or oats. Spinach, green peppers and parsley are chopped. To the bowl, add the vegetables and mix it until well-combined. Line the parchment paper with a baking sheet. Roll the turkey mixture into 15 balls and put them on the baking sheet. Bake for 25 minutes, until fully baked.

Nutritional information: Calories 349; Total Carbs 7g; Net Carbs 4g; Protein 19g; Fat 7g; Sugar 0g; Fiber 1.2g

Berry Avocado Smoothie

Prep Time: 7 minutes. | Cook Time: 0 minutes. | Servings: 2

½ avocado
1 cup strawberries
¼ cup blueberries
½ cup low-fat milk
½ cup 2% Greek yogurt

Place the avocado, strawberries, blueberries and milk in a blender. Blend the fruits until perfectly smooth. Serve or put in a refrigerator for up to 2 days.

Nutritional information: Calories 350; Total Carbs 25g; Net Carbs 15g; Protein 24g; Fat 17g; Sugar 9g; Fiber 5g

Scrambled Tofu with Spinach

Prep Time: 5 minutes. | Cook Time: 15 minutes. | Servings: 4

1 crumbled serve of tofu
1 small cup finely chopped onions
1 teaspoon the fresh parsley
1 teaspoon coconut oil
1 cup soft spinach
1 small teaspoon Turmeric
2 avocado serves
75g of tomatoes
1 small spoon of roasted paprika

In a bowl, make tofu crumbs with your hands and keep it aside. In a pan, sauté diced onions in oil till it softens. Put your tofu, tomatoes, and other seasonings in a pan and mix well until combine till tofu is well prepared. Add veggies in it and stir. Serve in a bowl alongside some avocado and fresh salad.

Nutritional information: Calories 91; Total Carbs 5g; Net Carbs 3g; Protein 30g; Fat 3g; Sugar 4g; Fiber 8g

Asparagus Bacon Salad

Prep time: 5 minutes. | Cooking time: 5 minutes. | Servings: 1

1 hard-boiled egg, peeled and sliced
1- ⅔ cups asparagus, chopped
2 slices bacon, cooked crisp and crumbled
1 teaspoon olive oil
1 teaspoon red wine vinegar
½ teaspoon Dijon mustard
Pinch salt and pepper to taste

Boil the water in the pot, then add the asparagus and cook for almost 2-3 minutes. Drain and add cold water to stop the cooking process. In a suitable bowl, whisk together the mustard, oil, vinegar, salt and Black pepper to taste. Place the asparagus on a plate, top with egg and bacon. Drizzle with vinaigrette and serve.

Nutritional information: Calories 356; Total Carbs 10g; Net Carbs 5g; Protein 25g; Fat 25g; Sugar 5g; Fiber 5g

Turkey and Egg Casserole

Prep Time: 13 minutes. | Cook Time: 13 minutes. | Servings: 5

½ cup green chopped onions
2 cups nonfat milk
nonstick cooking spray
½ teaspoon mustard powder
¼ teaspoon salt
¼ teaspoon black pepper
egg substitute
4 slices of whole wheat bread, cut into ½ –inch cubes
3 precooked diced turkey breakfast sausage patties
¼ cup cheddar cheese, reduced-fat, shredded

Preheat oven to 350 degrees F. Grease a 9x13 baking tin with cooking spray. In a medium pot, mix skim milk, green onions, dried mustard, salt (optional), pepper, and egg substitute. Place the bread cubes and sausage under the pan and pour the egg mixture over the bread and sausage. Put cheddar cheese on top. Cover the baking pan with foil and bake for 20 minutes. Remove the foil and cook for another 40 minutes. Serve hot and enjoy.

Nutritional information: Calories 120; Total Carbs 9g; Net Carbs 5g; Protein 10g; Fat 3g; Sugar 0.5g; Fiber 1g

Goddess Bowl with Spiced Avocado Dressing

Prep Time: 10 minutes. | Cook Time: 20 minutes. | Servings: 4

3 heaping cups finely sliced kale
1 small cup diced broccoli florets
½ cup zucchini spiralized noodles
½ cup soaked Kelp noodles
3 cups tomatoes
2 tablespoons hemp seeds
Tahini dressing
1 small cup sesame butter
1 cup alkaline water
1 cup freshly extracted lemon
1 garlic, finely chopped clove

¾ tablespoon pure sea salt
1 spoon of olive oil
bell pepper
Avocado dressing
1 big avocado
2 freshly extracted lime
1 cup alkaline water
1 tablespoon olive oil
bell pepper
1 tablespoon powdered cumin

In a pan, simmer veggies, kale, and broccoli for about 4 minutes until tender. In a bowl, add all dressing Ingredients and noodles and mix well. Add cooked noodles and add prepared avocado cumin dressing in the veggies and toss well. Add tomatoes in it and combine well. In a blender add all tahini Ingredients and pulse until smooth. Put the cooked kale and broccoli in a plate, add Tahini dressing, add noodles and tomatoes. Add hemp seeds to the whole dish and enjoy it.

Nutritional information: Calories 109; Total Carbs 14g; Net Carbs 10g; Protein 25g; Fat 6g; Sugar 2g; Fiber 6g

Simple Amaranth Porridge

Prep Time: 05 minutes. | Cook Time:30 minutes. | Servings:2

2 cups of coconut milk
2 cups alkaline water
1 cup amaranth
2 tablespoons coconut oil
1 tablespoon ground cinnamon

In a pot, combine the milk and water and bring to a boil. Reduce the heat to medium after stirring in the amaranth. Cook, stirring occasionally, over medium heat for at least half an hour. Turn down the heat. Stir in the cinnamon and copra oil. Serve.

Nutritional information: Calories 520; Total Carbs 40.3g Net Carbs 27.3g Protein 9.9g Fat 38.2g Sugar 4.9g Fiber 8.1g

Low-Fat Cheddar Apple Muffins

Prep Time: 10 minutes. | Cook Time: 20 minutes. | Servings:12

1 egg
¾ cup tart apple, peel & chop
⅔ cup reduced fat cheddar cheese, grated
⅔ cup skim milk
What you'll need from store cupboard:
2 cup low carb baking mix
2 tbsp. vegetable oil
1 tsp. cinnamon.

Preheat the oven to 400 degrees Fahrenheit. A 12-cup muffin pan should be lined with paper liners. Lightly beat the egg in a medium basin. Stir in the remaining Ingredients until they are barely moistened. Divide evenly between the muffin cups. Bake for 17-20 minutes, or until golden brown. Serve warm.

Nutritional information: Calories 162; Total Carbs 17g; Net Carbs 13g; Protein 10g; Fat 5g; Sugar 8g; Fiber 4g

Omelet with Greens

Prep time: 35 minutes. | Cooking time: 10 minutes. | Servings: 4

3 tablespoons olive oil
1 yellow onion
8 large eggs
2 tablespoons unsalted butter
1-ounce low-fat parmesan grated
2 tablespoons lemon juice
3 ounces baby spinach

Inside the nonstick skillet, heat 1 tablespoon of oil on moderate heat. Add the onion and cook for almost 6 minutes, till it is soft. Place inside the suitable bowl. Mix egg, 1 tablespoon of water, plus ½ teaspoon of salt inside the large mixing dish. Return the skillet to medium-high heat, then add the butter. Cook, frequently whisking with such a rubber spatula, till the eggs are halfway set. Reduce heat, then simmer for 4-5 minutes, or till eggs are just set. Cut it in half, then top over the parmesan and fried onion. Mix your lemon juice and leftover 2 tablespoons of olive oil inside the suitable mixing bowl. Toss the spinach with the vinaigrette before serving with the omelet.

Nutritional information: Calories 152; Total Carbs 11.2; Net Carbs 1.2g; Protein 3.7g; Fat 2.7g; fibers: 3g; Sugars: 6g

Spinach Shakshuka

Prep time: 35 minutes. | Cooking time: 10 minutes. | Servings: 4

2 tablespoon olive oil
1 yellow onion
1 garlic clove
1 teaspoon ground cumin
salt and black pepper, to taste
1 lb. tomatoes
8 large eggs
¼ cup baby spinach

At 400 degrees F, preheat your oven. Inside the large oven-safe pan, heat the oil over medium. Add the onion and sauté for 8 minutes, or till golden brown and soft. Cook for 1 minute after adding the garlic, cumin, and ½ teaspoons salt and pepper. Stir in the tomatoes, and then bake for almost 10 minutes in the oven. Remove your pan from the oven, mix, and then form 8 tiny wells in the vegetable mix, gently cracking 1 egg into another. Bake eggs until done to your liking, around 7-8 minutes with crunchy exterior yolks. Serve with bread, if preferred, and a sprinkle of spinach.

Nutritional information: Calories 182; Total Carbs 21.2; Net Carbs 2g; Protein 8.7g; Fat 4.7g; fibers: 3g; Sugars: 6g

Cantaloupe Smoothie

Prep time: 5 minutes. | Cooking time: 0 minutes. | Servings: 2

4 cups cubed cantaloupe, frozen
¾ cup carrot juice
1 pinch of salt
melon balls, berries, nuts

Inside the food processor or even high-powered blender, mix the cantaloupe, juice, and salt. Pulse and combine alternately till thick and smooth, 1-2 minutes, pausing for stir, then scrape down both sides as required. If preferred, top your smoothie by adding extra melon, berries, almonds, or basil.

Nutritional information: Calories 135; Total Carbs 31.2; Net Carbs 4g; Protein 3.4g; Fat .7g; fibers: 3g; Sugars: 6g

Veggie Wrap

Prep Time: 12 minutes. | Cook Time: 13 minutes. | Servings: 2

2 teaspoons olive oil or other
1 cup sliced mushrooms
2 eggs
½ cup egg white or egg replacement
1 cup firmly packed spinach or other greens
2 tablespoons of sliced scallions.
nonstick cooking spray
2 whole wheat and low-carb flour tortillas
2 tablespoons salsa

Add the oil to the pan over a medium flame. Add the mushrooms and sauté until the edges turn golden (about 33 minutes). Beat the eggs with the whites or egg substitute in a medium sized bowl using a blender or by hand until they are emulsified. Mix sliced spinach and green onion. Add fresh or dried vegetables such as basil or parsley to taste like Moe. Start heating the medium/large pan to a medium-low temperature. Put on the pan with a change of spray. Go to the egg mixture and stir the mixture while cooking with a spatula. Once the eggs in the area unit are grilled as you feel, turn off the heat and stir in the mushrooms. Spread ½ egg mixture into 36 halves of each dough. High each with a spoonful of fresh herbs or alternate sauce in your alternative. Garnish with extra toppings such as avocado, bell, or tomato slices if desired, and then roll them up and create a wrapper.

Nutritional information: Calories 220; Total Carbs 14g; Net Carbs 10g; Protein 19g; Fat 11g; Sugar 2g; Fiber 2g

Avocado Toast

Prep time: 5 minutes. | Cooking time: 0 minutes. | Servings: 1

¼ avocado
¼ teaspoon ground pepper
⅛ teaspoon garlic powder
1 slice toasted bread
1 large fried egg
1 teaspoon sriracha
1 tablespoon scallion

Inside the suitable bowl, lightly mash the avocado with pepper and garlic powder. Toast is topped with a blend of avocado and fried egg. If desired, top with the sriracha and scallion.

Nutritional information: Calories 271; Total Carbs 18.2; Net Carbs 2g; Protein 11g; Fat 17.7g; fibers: 3g; Sugars: 6g

Tex-mex Migas

Prep Time: 9 minutes. | Cook Time: 15 minutes. | Servings: 4

3 large eggs - 3 egg whites
1 tablespoon canola oil
4 corn tortillas, cut into ½ -inch-wide strips
½ cup chopped onion
2 large seeded jalapeño peppers
⅔ cup lower-sodium salsa
½ cup non-fat Monterey Jack cheese, shredded
½ cup sliced green onions
Hot sauce (optional)
Lower-sodium red salsa (optional)
Lower-sodium green salsa (optional)

Place the eggs and egg whites in a bowl. Stir with a whisk until combined. Set to medium and heat in a medium nonstick skillet. Use oil in the shower. Swirl on the shirt. Spread tortilla strips on the pan and cook for 3 minutes or until golden brown, stirring constantly. Add the onions and jalapeño peppers to the sauce. Fry for 2 minutes or until tender. Add ⅔ cup of salsa and simmer for 1 minute, stirring constantly. Add the egg mixture. Cook for 2 minutes or until eggs is tender, stirring frequently. Sprinkle the cheese with the egg mixture. Bake 3 minutes or until cheese is melted. Cover with green onions and serve immediately. Serve with hot sauce, red salsa, or green salsa of your choice.

Nutritional information: Calories 193; Total Carbs 12g; Net Carbs 9g; Protein 10.2g; Fat 10.4g; Sugar 1.4g; Fiber 6.2g

Pumpkin Topped Waffles

Prep time: 10 minutes. | Cooking time: 10 minutes. | Servings: 1

1 frozen waffle
1 tablespoon canned pumpkin
½ ounce part-skim cream cheese
1 teaspoon toasted walnuts

Waffles should be toasted according to the guidelines. Combine the pumpkin and cream cheese inside the suitable mixing bowl. Top with the chopped walnuts and spread over the waffle.

Nutritional information: Calories 132; Total Carbs 15.2; Net Carbs 5g; Protein 4g; Fat 7g; fibers: 3g; Sugars: 6g

Cheese Coated Egg Muffins

Prep time: 08 minutes . | Cook Time: 18 minutes | Serves 4

4 egg whites
½ teaspoon fresh parsley, diced fine
3 tablespoons reduced fat Parmesan cheese, divided
2 teaspoons water
½ teaspoon salt
truffle oil to taste
nonstick cooking spray

Preheat at 400 degrees Fahrenheit (205 degrees Celsius). Using nonstick cooking spray, coat two muffin pans. Whisk together egg whites, water, and salt in a small bowl until well blended. Fill each muffin cup with just enough egg white mixture to just cover the bottom. On each egg white, a small amount of Parmesan cheese should be sprinkled. Bake for 10 to 15 minutes, or until dark brown around the edges, being careful not to burn them. Allow to cool for 3 to 4 minutes in the pans before transferred to a small bowl and lightly drizzling with truffle oil. Toss in the parsley and ½ tablespoon Parmesan. Serve.

Nutritional information: Calories 47; Total Carbs 0g; Net Carbs 0g; Protein 18.1g; Fat 3.0g; Sugar 0g; Fiber 0 g

Niçoise Salad Tuna

Prep Time: 12 minutes. | Cook Time: 5 minutes. | Servings: 1

4 ounces ahi tuna steak
1 whole egg
2 cups baby spinach (3 ounces)
2 ounces green beans
1 and ½ ounces broccoli
½ red bell peppers
3 and ½ ounces cucumber
1 radish
3 large black olives
Handful of parsley
1 teaspoon olive oil
1 teaspoon balsamic vinegar
½ teaspoon Dijon mustard
½ teaspoon pepper

Cook the eggs and let them cool. Steam the beans and broccoli and drain 2-3 minutes in the microwave or 3 minutes in boiling water. Heat oil at a high temperature in a pan. Pepper the seafood on each side and put them on the heat, stirring both sides for about 2 minutes. Place the spinach in a bowl. Cut the red peppers, oranges, and eggs into small pieces. Put the spinach on it. Cut the radish and toss the broccoli, beans, and olives together. Add the spinach salad on top. Cut the tuna into pieces and add to the salad. In a bowl, add olive oil, balsamic vinegar, mustard, salt, and pepper. Finely chop the parsley and add it to the vinaigrette. Use a spoon to spread the dressing over the salad.

Nutritional information: Calories 149; Total Carbs 21g; Net Carbs 15g; Protein 19g; Fat 6g; Sugar 1.5g; Fiber 2.5g

Salad with Pickled Cucumbers and Onions

Prep Time: 10minutes. | Cook Time:00 minutes. | Servings:2

½ cucumber, peeled and sliced
¼ cup red onion, sliced thin
What you'll need from store cupboard:
1 tbsp. olive oil
1 tbsp. white vinegar
1 tsp. dill

Mix all of the Ingredients together in a medium mixing basin. Serve.

Nutritional information: Calories 79 Total Carbs 4g Net Carbs 3g Protein 1g Fat 7g Sugar 2g Fiber 1g

Balanced Turkey Meatballs

Prep Time: 12 minutes. | Cook Time: 26 minutes. | Servings: 2

20 ounces ground of turkey
3 and ½ ounce of fresh or frozen spinach
¼ cup oats
2 egg whites
Celery sticks
3 cloves' garlic
½ green bell peppers
½ red onion
½ cup parsley
½ teaspoon cumin
1 teaspoon mustard powder
1 teaspoon thyme
½ teaspoon turmeric
½ teaspoon chipotle pepper
1 teaspoon salt
A pinch of pepper

Preheat the oven to 350 °F . Finely chop the onion, garlic, and celery (or use a food processor) and place them in a large mixing bowl. In a bowl, put the ham, egg whites, oatmeal, and spices and mix well. Make sure the mixture does not contain spices or oats. Finely chop the spinach, pepper, and parsley. Add the vegetables to the mix and mix until well combined. Place the parchment paper on the baking sheet. Roll the turkey mixture into 15 balls and place them on a baking sheet. Bake for 25 minutes, until fully baked and serve with salad.

Nutritional information: Calories 129; Total Carbs 22g; Net Carbs 17g; Protein 25g; Fat 9g; Sugar 2g; Fiber 3g

Pear Oatmeal

Prep time: 15 minutes. | Cooking time: 10 minutes. | Servings: 1

¼ cup rolled oats
⅛ teaspoon ground ginger
¼ cup pear
⅛ teaspoon ground cinnamon

Cook the oats as directed on the packet. Add the ginger and mix well. Serve with such a pear on top. Cinnamon should be sprinkled on top.

Nutritional information: Calories 108; Total Carbs 21; Net Carbs 0.5g; Protein 3g; Fat 2g; fibers: 3g; Sugars: 6g

Fig on Crispbread

Prep time: 5 minutes. | Cooking time: 0 minutes. | Servings: 1

2 rye crispbreads
2 tablespoon peanut butter
dried figs 4
2 teaspoon pepitas
1 teaspoon coconut flakes

Add 1 tablespoon of peanut butter, half of the fig pieces, 1 teaspoon of pepitas, and ½ teaspoon of coconut flakes upon every crispbread

Nutritional information: Calories 407; Total Carbs 45.2; Net Carbs 2g; Protein 11g; Fat 20g; fibers: 3g; Sugars: 6g

Cucumber Toast

Prep time: 5 minutes. | Cooking time: 0 minutes. | Servings: 1

1 slice whole-grain bread
2 tablespoons quark
2 tablespoons diced cucumber
1 tablespoon cilantro leaves
1 pinch sea salt

Add quark, sea salt, cilantro, and cucumber on top of the bread.

Nutritional information: Calories 141; Total Carbs 13.2; Net Carbs 0.5g; Protein 7.6g; Fat 5.1g; fibers: 3g; Sugars: 6g

Peanut Butter and Jelly Oats

Prep time: 10 minutes. | Cooking time: 10 minutes. | Servings: 2

1⅓ cups water
⅔ cup rolled cereal
¼ teaspoon salt
1 tablespoon peanut butter
1 tablespoon strawberry preserves
2 strawberries, sliced

Mix water, oats, and salt inside the large microwave-safe dish. Microwave the mixture over high heat about 3-5 minutes. Remove from the oven and let aside almost 1-2 minutes. For almost 20 seconds, vigorously whisk your peanut butter into oats, or till fully incorporated and creamy. Microwave your strawberry jams inside the microwave-safe dish on high for almost 10 seconds, or till thinned and warmed completely. Drizzle strawberry preserves over the oats in 2 separate bowls. Add the few strawberries slices to each dish as a finishing touch.

Nutritional information: Calories 179; Total Carbs 28.2; Net Carbs 2g; Protein 6.6g; Fat 5.5g; fibers: 3g; Sugars: 6g

Hummus Toast

Prep Time: 30 minutes. | Cook Time: 4 hours. | Servings: 2

1 soft boiled egg, halved
6 tablespoons plain hummus
2 pieces gluten-free bread, toasted
1 pinch of paprika
2 teaspoons everything bagel Spice
drizzle of olive oil

Spread hummus on each bread slice approximately 3 tablespoons each. Place the halved egg on it top with 1 teaspoon 'Bagel' spice each. Sprinkle small amount of paprika, muzzle with olive oil and make sandwich and serve at once.

Nutritional information: Calories 213; Total Carbs 15g; Net Carbs 8g; Protein 6.5g; Fat 11g; Sugar 4g; Fiber 9g

Strawberry Coconut Breakfast Cake

Prep Time: 11 minutes. | Cook Time: 23 minutes. | Servings: 2

½ cup chopped walnuts
2 cups unsweetened coconut flakes
1 teaspoon cinnamon
¼ cup chia seeds
2 cups diced strawberries
1 ripe banana, mashed
1 teaspoon baking soda
4 large eggs
¼ teaspoon of salt
1 cup unsweetened nut milk
2 tablespoons coconut oil, melted

Preheat the oven to 375 °F for 10 minutes. Grease a square 8-inch baking pan and set aside. In a bowl, combine the dried Ingredients walnuts, chia seeds, cinnamon, salt and baking soda. In another bowl, whisk the eggs and milk together. Add mashed banana and coconut oil to the egg mixture. Add the wet Ingredients to the dry Ingredients and mix properly. Fold the strawberries in. Pour the batter in the greased baking pan and bake for about 40 minutes, or until the top is golden and solid. Serve hot!

Nutritional information: Calories 395; Total Carbs 12g; Net Carbs 10g; Protein 7g; Fat 40g; Sugar 2g; Fiber 3g

Egg and Avocado Toasts

Prep Time: 17 minutes. | Cook Time: 0 minutes. | Servings: 4

4 eggs
4 slices of hearty whole grain bread
1 avocado, mashed
½ teaspoon salt, optional
¼ teaspoon black pepper
¼ cup Greek yogurt, non-fat

To pour each egg, fill ½ cup water into 1 cup bowl suitable for microwave. Slowly break the eggs into water and make sure they are completely submerged. Cover at high temperature for about 1 minute with a container and microwave, or before the egg whites solidify and the yolk begins to solidify, but still soft (not running). Toast the bread and use ¼ of the mashed avocado to sprinkle on each toast. Sprinkle salt (optional) and pepper. Place a piece of porched egg on top. Pour a tablespoon of Greek yogurt and serve.

Nutritional information: Calories 230; Total Carbs 26g; Net Carbs 18g; Protein 17g; Fat 13g; Sugar 2g; Fiber 5g

Banana Stuffed Muffin

Prep time: 5 minutes. | Cooking time: 0 minutes. | Servings: 1

1 English muffin toasted
1 tablespoon peanut butter
½ sliced banana
1 pinch ground cinnamon

Peanut butter, cinnamon, and banana go on top of such an English muffin.

Nutritional information: Calories 344; Total Carbs 56.2; Net Carbs 1.2g; Protein 10g; Fat 9.7g; fibers: 3g; Sugars: 6g

Trail Mix Hot Cereal

Prep time: 10 minutes. | Cooking time: 0 minutes. | Servings: 1

½ cup cooked cereal
2 tablespoons fruit bits mixed
2 tablespoons mixed nuts
2 teaspoons flaxseed

Inside the serving dish, place the cereal. Fruit pieces, nuts, and flaxseed must be sprinkled on top.

Nutritional information: Calories 227; Total Carbs 28.2; Net Carbs 2g; Protein 6g; Fat 11g; fibers: 3g; Sugars: 6g

Chicken and Egg Salad

Prep Time: 5 minutes. | Cook Time: 25 minutes. | Servings: 2

2 cooked chicken breasts
3 hard-boiled eggs
2 tablespoons fat-free mayo
1 tablespoon curry powder
Chives or basil (optional)
Salt (optional)

Bake the chicken for 15 minutes in the oven around 360° F. Cook the eggs for 8 minutes. Cut the eggs and chicken into a small-bite size piece. Combine the cream cheese with curry powder. In a large bowl, combine everything and mix. Allow a minimum of 10 minutes to chill in the refrigerator. Serve with chives on toast or muffins.

Nutritional information: Calories 139; Total Carbs 23g; Net Carbs 20g; Protein 18g; Fat 9g; Sugar 1g; Fiber 3g

Breakfast Salad

Prep Time: 5 minutes. | Cook Time: 15 minutes. | Servings: 3

1 cup finely diced kale
1 cup cabbage, red and Chinese
2 tablespoons coconut oil
1 cup spinach
2 moderate avocados
1.2kg of chickpeas sprout
2 tablespoons sunflower seed sprouts
pure sea salt (seasoning)
bell pepper (seasoning)
lemon juice (seasoning)

In a bowl, add spinach, Chinese and red cabbage, kale, coconut oil, and mix well. Add seasoning to taste and mix adequately. Add other Ingredients in salad and mix. Serve and enjoy.

Nutritional information: Calories 112; Total Carbs 14g; Net Carbs 10g; Protein 28g; Fat 8g; Sugar 4g; Fiber 6g

Pineapple Smoothie

Prep time: 5 minutes. | Cooking time: 0 minutes. | Servings: 1

1 cup frozen strawberries
1 cup pineapple chopped
¾ cup part-skim almond milk chilled
1 tablespoon almond butter

Inside the blender, mix the strawberries, almond butter, almond milk, and pineapple. Blend till smooth, adding additional almond milk if necessary to get the required consistency. Serve right away.

Nutritional information: Calories 255; Total Carbs 39.2; Net Carbs 5g; Protein 5.6g; Fat 11.1g; fibers: 3g; Sugars: 6g

Hite Sandwich

Prep Time: 10 minutes. | Cook Time: 20 minutes. | Servings: 1

1 cup warm water
1 cup warm unsweetened almond milk
2 tablespoons active dry yeast
4 tablespoons oil
2 ½ teaspoons salt
2 tablespoons splenda
6 cups all-purpose flour

In a bowl, add warm water, yeast, and sugar and stir. Set aside for 5 minutes or until lots of tiny bubbles are formed, sort of frothy. Add flour and salt into a mixing bowl and stir. Pour the oil, yeast mix and milk and mix into dough. Knead the dough until soft and supple. Use hands or hook attachment of the stand mixer. Keep the bowl covered with a towel. Let it rest until it doubles in size. Remove the dough from the bowl and place on your countertop. Punch the dough. Line a loaf pan with parchment paper. You can also grease with some oil if you prefer. Place the dough in the loaf pan. Keep the loaf pan covered rest until the dough doubles in size. Bake in a preheated oven at 370 ° F for about 40 to 50 minutes. Let it cool to room temperature. Cut into 16 equal slices and use as required. Store in a breadbox at room temperature.

Nutritional information: Calories 209; Total Carbs 11g; Net Carbs 6g; Protein 1g; Fat 4g; Sugar 0.6g; Fiber 0.2g

Spinach Rolls

Prep Time: 15 minutes. | Cook Time: 40 minutes. | Servings: 4

16 ounces frozen spinach leaves
3 eggs
2 and ½ ounce of onion
2 ounces carrot
1 ounce of low-fat mozzarella cheese
4 ounce of fat-free cottage cheese
½ cup parsley
1 clove of garlic
1 teaspoon curry powder
¼ teaspoon chili flakes
1 teaspoon salt
1 teaspoon pepper

Cooking spray

Preheat the oven to 400 ° F. Thaw the spinach and squeeze out the water. You can cook the spinach in the microwave for a few minutes to speed up the defrosting process. In an ovenproof dish, combine the spinach, 2 eggs, mozzarella, ginger, ½ salt, and pepper together. Place parchment paper on a baking sheet and coat with cooking spray. Turn the spinach mixture about ½ inch thick and about 10 to 12 inches high into a leaf and press it down. Bake for 15 minutes, then place on a wire rack to cool. Finely chop the onion and parsley. Grate the carrots. Brown the onion in a pan with a little oil for 1 minute. Add the carrots and parsley to the pan and simmer for 2 minutes. Add cottage cheese, curry, chili, salt, and pepper to the other half. Put the pan on fire, add the eggs and mix everything together. Spread the filling over the cooled spinach. Gently roll the spinach mat to the filling and bake for 25 minutes. When the time is up, remove the roll and let cool for 5-10 minutes, then cut into pieces and serve.

Nutritional information: Calories 149; Total Carbs 26g; Net Carbs 15g; Protein 17g; Fat 11g; Sugar 0.5g; Fiber 2g

Fruity Parfait

Prep time: 5 minutes. | Cooking time: 10 minutes. | Servings: 1

1 cup mixed berries
Greek yogurt non-fat
1 tablespoon flaxseed
1 teaspoon vanilla extract
½ Kiwi
¼ cup blueberries
3 tablespoons nut clusters and healthy fruit grains

Blend the frozen berries, yogurt, flaxseed, and vanilla extract till smooth inside the food processor or blender. Toss the yogurt mix with the kiwi, blueberries, and fruit and nut cluster in a suitable bowl.

Nutritional information: Calories 220; Total Carbs 17.2; Net Carbs 5g; Protein 11g; Fat 6g; fibers: 3g; Sugars: 6g

Creamy Smoked Salmon Wraps

Prep Time: 12 minutes. | Cook Time: 15 minutes. | Servings: 2

1 8-inch low carb flour tortilla
2 ounces smoked salmon
2 teaspoons low-fat cream cheese
One and ½ ounce of red onion
Handful of arugulas
½ teaspoon fresh or dried basil
A pinch of pepper

In the oven or microwave, warm the tortillas. In a bowl, mix the cream cheese, basil, and pepper and then scattered over the tortilla. Place the salmon, arugula, and finely sliced onion on top of cream mix. Roll the tortilla up and enjoy the wrap!

Nutritional information: Calories 138; Total Carbs 19g; Net Carbs 15g; Protein 14g; Fat 6g; Sugar 1.5g; Fiber 3.2g

Easy Rib-Eye Steak

Prep time: 5 minutes. | Cooking time: 14 minutes. | Servings: 2

2 medium-sized lean rib-eye steaks
salt and black pepper, to taste

At 400 degrees F, preheat your Air Fryer. Pat dry steaks with paper towels. Rub the steaks with the seasonings generously on both sides of the steak. Place the prepared steaks in the air fryer basket. Cook according to the rareness you want. Or cook for 14 minutes and flip after halftime. Take it out from the air fryer basket and let it rest for almost 5 minutes. Serve with microgreen salad.

Nutritional information: Calories: 470; Fat: 31g; Total Carbs: 23g; Net Carbs 1g; Proteins: 47 g; fibers: 3g; Sugars: 6g

Beef Kabobs with Vegetables

Prep time: 30 minutes. | Cooking time:10 minutes. | Servings: 4

2 tablespoons soy sauce
4 cups beef chuck ribs, sliced into one-inch pieces
⅓ cup low-fat sour cream
half onion
8 skewers: 6 inches
1 bell pepper, diced

In a suitable mixing bowl, add soy sauce and sour cream, mix well. Add the beef chunks, mix well, and let it marinate for half an hour or more. Cut onion and bell pepper into one-inch pieces. In water, soak skewers for ten minutes. Thread bell peppers, onions, and beef on skewers; alternatively, sprinkle with black pepper Let it cook for almost 10 minutes in a preheated air fryer at 400 degrees F, flip halfway through. Serve with yogurt dipping sauce.

Nutritional information: Calories 268; Total Carbs 15g; Net Carbs 1g; Proteins 20g; Fat 10g; fibers: 3g; Sugars: 6g

Steak with Asparagus

Prep time: 20 minutes. | Cooking time:30 minutes. | Servings: 2

olive oil spray
2 pounds flank steak, cut into 6 pieces
Kosher salt and black pepper, to taste
2 minced garlic cloves
4 cups asparagus
½ cup tamari sauce
3 bell peppers, sliced
⅓ cup beef broth, low-sodium
1 tablespoon of unsalted butter
¼ cup balsamic vinegar

Rub salt and pepper on steak liberally. In a Ziploc bag, mix garlic and tamari sauce, then place steak in it, toss well and seal the bag. Let it marinate in the refrigerator for 1 hour or up to overnight. Divide the bell peppers and asparagus in the center of the steak.

Roll the steak to seal the vegetables inside and secure well with toothpicks. Preheat the air fryer. Spray the steak with olive oil spray. And place steaks in the air fryer. Cook for almost 15 minutes at 400 degrees F or more till steaks are cooked Take the cooked steak out from the air fryer basket and let it rest for five minutes Remove prepared steak bundles and allow them to rest for almost 5 minutes before serving/slicing. Meanwhile, add butter, balsamic vinegar, and broth over medium flame. Mix well and reduce it by half. Add salt and black pepper to taste. 1pour over steaks right before serving.

Nutritional information: Calories 471; Total Carbs 20g; Net Carbs 1g; Proteins 29g; Fat 15g; fibers: 3g; Sugars: 6g

Beef Broccoli Noodle Stir-Fry

Prep time: 10 minutes. | Cooking time: 15 minutes. | Servings: 4

¾ pound beef top sirloin steak, boneless
⅓ teaspoon red pepper, crushed
½ red onion, wedges
3 cups napa cabbage, shredded
2 cups broccoli florets
3 ounces Buckwheat noodles or multigrain spaghetti
2 tablespoons teriyaki sauce
3 tablespoons orange marmalade, low-sugar
2 tablespoons of water
2 teaspoons canola oil
Cooking spray

Bring together the teriyaki sauce, red pepper, marmalade, and water in a suitable bowl. Keep aside. Cook the spaghetti as per the box's directions on the pack. In the meantime, apply cooking spray on your skillet. Preheat. Now add the red onion and broccoli to your skillet. Cook covered for 3 minutes. Add the carrots and cook for 3 more minutes. The vegetables should become tender. Take out the vegetables. Now add oil and the beef strips. Cook for 3 minutes until the Centre is slightly pink. Return the vegetables to your skillet with the cabbage and sauce. Cook, while stirring, for 1 minute.

Nutritional information: Calories: 279; Fats: 4g; Net Carbs 1g; Proteins: 25g; Total Carbs 30g fibers: 5g; Sugars: 1g

Spicy Pulled Beef

Prep time: 10 minutes. | Cooking time: 35 minutes. | Servings: 2

1-pound lean steak
1 cup gravy
2 tablespoon mixed spices

Mix all the recipe ingredients in your instant pot. Cook on stew for 35 minutes. Release the pressure naturally. Shred the beef.

Nutritional information: Calories: 200; Net Carbs 1g; Proteins: 48g; Total Carbs 2g; Fats: 9g; fibers: 1g; Sugars: 16g

Beef Hamburgers

Prep time: 5 minutes. | Cooking time: 13 minutes. | Servings: 4

4 buns
4 cups lean ground beef chuck
Salt to taste
4 slices of any cheese, low-fat
Black pepper, to taste

At 350 degrees F, preheat your Air Fryer. In a suitable bowl, add lean ground beef, pepper, and salt. Mix well and make patties out of it. Put them in the air fryer in one layer only, cook for almost 6 minutes, flip them halfway through. Add cheese on top. When cheese is melted, take it out from the air fryer. Add ketchup any dressing to your buns, add tomatoes, lettuce and patties. Serve hot.

Nutritional information: Calories: 520; Total Carbs 22g; Net Carbs 2g; Protein: 31g; Fat: 34g; fibers: 3g; Sugars: 6g

Beef Mushroom Empanadas

Prep time: 10 minutes. | Cooking time: 20 minutes. | Servings: 2

8 pieces square gyoza wrappers
1 tablespoon olive oil
¼ cup white onion, diced
¼ cup mushrooms, diced
½ cup lean ground beef
2 teaspoons chopped garlic
¼ teaspoon paprika
¼ teaspoon ground cumin
6 green olives, diced
⅛ teaspoon ground cinnamon
½ cup diced tomatoes
1 egg, lightly beaten

In a suitable skillet, over a medium heat, add oil, onions, mushrooms, and beef and cook for 3 minutes, until beef turns brown. Add mushrooms and cook for 6 minutes until it starts to brown. Then add paprika, cinnamon, olives, cumin, and garlic and cook for 3 minutes or more. Add in the tomatoes and sauté together for 1 minute. Turn off the heat; let it cool for five minutes. Lay gyoza wrappers on a flat surface; add 1 and a half tablespoons of beef filling in each wrapper. Brush edges with water or egg, fold wrappers, pinch edges. Put four empanadas in an even layer in an air fryer basket, and cook for 7 minutes at 400 degrees F until nicely browned. Serve with sauce and salad greens.

Nutritional information: Calories 343; Total Carbohydrate 12.9g; Net Carbs 2g; Protein 18g; Fat 19g; fibers: 3g; Sugars: 6g

Pork Chops with Vegetables

Prep time: 9 minutes. | Cooking time: 24 minutes. | Servings: 4

4 pork head chops
2 red tomatoes
1 large green pepper
4 mushrooms
1 onion

4 slices of cheese, non-fat
Salt to taste
Black pepper, to taste
olive oil

Put the four chops on a plate and salt and pepper. Put 2 of the chops in the air fryer basket. Place tomato slices, cheese slices, black pepper, onion slices and mushroom slices. Add some threads of oil. Take the air fryer and select 350 degrees F, 20 minutes. Repeat the same operation with the other 2 pork chops.

Nutritional information: Calories: 106; Fat: 3.41 g; Total Carbs 0 g; Net Carbs 1g; Proteins: 20.9 g; fibers: 3g; Sugars: 6g

Cheesy Brisket Cauliflower Meal

Prep time: 5 minutes. | Cooking time: 15 minutes. | Servings: 4

1 cup water
2 cups chopped cauliflower
3 tablespoons butter
¼ diced onion
¼ cup pickled jalapeno slices
2 cups cooked brisket
2 ounces softened cream cheese, low-fat
1 cup shredded sharp cheddar cheese, non-fat
¼ cup heavy cream
¼ cup cooked crumbled bacon
2 tablespoons sliced green onions

Add water to the instant pot. Steam the cauliflower on a steamer basket for 1 minute. Do a quick release and set aside. Pour out water and press sauté. Add butter, jalapeno slices, and onion. Sauté for 4 minutes, add cream cheese and cooked brisket. Cook 2 minutes more. Add cauliflower, heavy cream, and sharp cheddar. Press cancel and gently mix until mixed well. Sprinkle with green onions and crumbled bacon. Serve.

Nutritional information: Calories: 574; Fats: 40g; Net Carbs 1.2g; Net Carbs 1g; Proteins: 33g; Total Carbs 8g; Fibers: 2g; Sugars: 3g

Steak Topped with Tomato and Herbs

Prep time: 30 minutes. | Cooking time: 30 minutes. | Servings: 2

8 ounces Beef loin steak, sliced in half
salt and black pepper, to taste
Cooking spray
1 teaspoon basil, snipped
¼ cup green onion, sliced
½ cup tomato, chopped

Season the steak with salt and pepper. Spray oil on your pan. Put the pan over medium-high heat. Once hot, add the steaks. Reduce heat to medium. Cook for almost 10 to 13 minutes for medium, turning once. Add the basil and green onion. Cook for almost 2 minutes. Add the tomato. Cook for almost 1 minute. Let cool a small before slicing.

Nutritional information: Calories: 170; Fats: 6g; Net Carbs 1g; Proteins: 25g; Total Carbs 3g fibers: 1g; Sugars: 5g

Mushroom, Beef, and Cauliflower Rice in Lettuce

Prep Time: 5 minutes. | Cook Time: 20 minutes. | Servings: 4

1 tablespoon avocado oil
1 cup portobello mushrooms, chopped
½ cup white onion, chopped
1 pound (454 g) 93% lean ground beef
½ teaspoon garlic powder
Salt, to taste
1 (10-ounce / 284-g) bag frozen cauliflower rice
¾ cup Cheddar cheese, shredded
12 iceberg lettuce leaves

Heath the avocado oil in a nonstick skillet over medium heat. Add the mushrooms and onion to the skillet and sauté for 5 minutes until the mushrooms are soft and the onion starts to become translucent. Add the beef, garlic powder, and salt to the skillet and sauté for another 5 minutes to brown the beef. Increase the heat to medium-high, then add the cauliflower rice and sauté for an additional 5 minutes. Divide the mixture and cheese on all lettuce leaves with a spoon, then roll up the lettuce to seal the wrap and serve warm.

Nutritional information: Calories 289; Total Carbs 6.9g; Net Carbs 3g; Protein 31g; Fat 14g; Sugar 3.8g; Fiber 3.1g

Asparagus & Beef Rolls

Prep Time: 20 minutes. | Cook Time: 20 minutes. | Servings: 4

1 bunch scallions, trimmed & halved crosswise
1 tablespoon canola oil
¼ teaspoon salt
¼ teaspoon freshly ground pepper
1 ¼ pounds of skirt steak, trimmed
2 teaspoons toasted sesame seeds
3 tablespoons hoisin sauce
3 tablespoons water
1 tablespoon tomato paste
1 tablespoon rice vinegar
1 teaspoon toasted sesame oil
½ teaspoon crushed red pepper
1 bunch asparagus (about 1 pound), trimmed

Preheat one side of the grill to medium-high. Leave the other side unheated. Mix the vinegar, hoisin, sesame oil, water, tomato paste, and crushed red pepper in a bowl until smooth. Spoon 2 tablespoons the mixture into a small bowl. Set the rest aside. Place the canola oil, scallions, salt, asparagus, and pepper in a large bowl. Cut the steak in ½ lengthwise, then cut each long strip in ½ crosswise to make 4 2-by-6-inch (15cm) pieces Brush the top side of the steak pieces with the 2 tablespoons sauce. Divide the asparagus and scallions among the steak pieces, placing the bundles in the center. Fold and roll the steak over the top of the bundles Thread a skewer through the overlapping ends of the steak and hold the rolls together through the bundle. Place the rolls seam side down on the hot side of the grill for 5-7 minutes. Turn and grill until the second side begins to char, about 5 minutes longer. Move the rolls to the unheated side, cover, and cook for about 5 more minutes. Remove from grill. Brush steak with some of the reserved sauce and sprinkle with sesame seeds. Serve with the remaining sauce for dipping.

Nutritional information: Calories 220; Total Carbs 11.6g; Net Carbs 8g; Protein 35.2g; Fat 13.8g; Sugar 5g; Fiber 2.5g

Cauliflower and Beef Fajita

Prep Time: 10 minutes. | Cook Time: 15 minutes. | Servings: 4

4 tablespoons extra-virgin olive oil, divided
1 head cauliflower, riced
1 pound (454 g) sirloin steak, cut into ¼-inch-thick strips
1 red bell pepper, seeded and sliced
1 onion, thinly sliced
2 garlic cloves, minced
Juice of 2 limes
1 teaspoon chili powder

In a large skillet over medium-high heat, heat 2 tablespoons olive oil until it shimmers. Add the cauliflower. Cook, stirring occasionally, until it softens, about 3 minutes. Set aside. Wipe out the skillet with a paper towel. Add the remaining 2 tablespoons oil to the skillet, and heat it on medium-high until it shimmers. Add the steak and cook, stirring occasionally, until it browns, about 3 minutes. Use a slotted spoon to remove the steak from the oil in the pan and set aside. Add the bell pepper and onion to the pan. Cook, stirring occasionally, until they start to brown, about 5 minutes. Add the garlic and cook, stirring constantly, for 30 seconds. Return the beef along with any juices that have collected and the cauliflower to the pan. Add the lime juice and chili powder. Cook, stirring, until everything is warmed through, 2 to 3 minutes.

Nutritional information: Calories 311; Total Carbs 13.1g; Net Carbs 8g; Protein 27g; Fat 18g; Sugar 10g; Fiber 2.9g

Beef Tortillas

Prep Time: 15 minutes. | Cook Time: 0 minutes. | Servings: 6

6 whole wheat flour tortillas (10-inch)
6 large romaine lettuce leaves
12 ounces (340 g) cooked deli roast beef, thinly sliced
1 cup diced red bell peppers
1 cup diced tomatoes
1 tablespoon vinegar
1 teaspoon cumin
¼ teaspoon freshly ground black pepper
1 tablespoon olive oil

Unfold the tortillas on a clean work surface, then top each tortilla with a lettuce leaf. Divide the roast beef over the leaf. Combine the remaining Ingredients in a bowl. Stir to mix well. Pour the mixture over the beef. Fold the tortillas over the fillings, then roll them up. Serve immediately.

Nutritional information: Calories 295; Total Carbs 43g; Net Carbs 25g; Protein 19g; Fat 6g; Sugar 3g; Fiber 6g

Baked Basil Meatballs

Prep time: 09 minutes . | Cook Time: 12minutes | Serves 4

Non-stick cooking spray
½ lb. ground pork, lean
½ lb. ground beef, lean
1 onion, finely chopped
¼ cup breadcrumbs
2 tbsp. basil, chopped
2 tsp. garlic, minced
1 egg
Pinch Himalayan pink salt, ground
Pinch black pepper, ground
Marinara sauce
Vegetable of your choice

Preheat the oven to 350 degrees Fahrenheit (180 degrees Celsius). Set aside a baking tray that has been sprayed with nonstick cooking spray. Toss the ground pork, ground beef, chopped onion, breadcrumbs, chopped basil, minced garlic, egg, ground Himalayan pink salt, and ground black pepper together in a large mixing basin. Make medium-sized meatballs out of the ground beef. Place the meatballs on a baking pan and bake for 15 minutes, or until browned and well cooked. Serve the meatballs with marinara sauce and cooked green beans (or any other vegetable). Ingredient Tip: Serve with spaghetti squash or courgette noodles.

Nutritional information: Calories: 332; Net Carbs: 3g; Protein: 24g; Total Carbs: 13g; Total Fat: 19g

Pork Souvlakia with Tzatziki Sauce

Prep Time: 20 minutes. | Cook Time: 12 minutes. | Servings: 4

¼ cup lemon juice
1 tablespoon dried oregano
¼ teaspoon salt
¼ teaspoon ground black pepper
1 pound (454 g) pork tenderloin, cut into 1-inch cubes
1 tablespoon olive oil
Tzatziki Sauce:
½ cup plain Greek yogurt
1 large cucumber, peeled, deseeded and grated
1 tablespoon fresh lemon juice
4 cloves garlic, minced or grated
¼ teaspoon ground black pepper
8 bamboo skewers, soaked in water for at least 30 minutes

Combine the lemon juice, oregano, salt, and ground black pepper in a large bowl. Stir to mix well. Dunk the pork cubes in the bowl of mixture, then toss to coat well. Wrap the bowl in plastic and refrigerate to marinate for 10 minutes or overnight. Preheat the oven to 450ºF (235ºC) or broil. Grease a baking sheet with the olive oil. Remove the bowl from the refrigerator. Run the bamboo skewers through the pork cubes. Set the skewers on the baking sheet, then brush with marinade. Broil the skewers in the preheated oven for 12 minutes or until well browned. Flip skewers at least 3 times during the broiling. Meanwhile, combine the Ingredients for the tzatziki sauce in a small bowl. Remove the skewers from the oven and baste with the tzatziki sauce and serve immediately.

Nutritional information: Calories 260; Total Carbs 21g; Net Carbs 15g; Protein 28g; Fat 7g; Sugar 3g; Fiber 3g

Pork Wrapped in Ham

Prep time: 8 minutes. | Cooking time: 10-15 minutes. | Servings: 6

6 pieces serrano ham, sliced
1 pound pork, halved, with butter and crushed
Salt, to taste
Black pepper, to taste
7 ounces spinach leaves
4 slices mozzarella cheese
1 tablespoon sun-dried tomatoes
2 tablespoons olive oil

Place 3 pieces of ham on baking paper, slightly overlapping each other. Place 1 half of the pork in the ham. Repeat with the other half. Season the inside of the pork rolls with salt and pepper. Place half of the spinach, cheese, and sun-dried tomatoes on top of the pork loin, leaving a 13 mm border on all sides. Roll the fillet around the filling well and tie it with a kitchen cord to keep it closed. Repeat the process for the other pork steak and place them in the fridge. Warm in the air fryer and start cooking. Brush 5 ml of olive oil on each wrapped steak and place them in the preheated air fryer. Select steak. Set the timer to 9 minutes and press start/pause. Let it cool before cutting.

Nutritional information: Calories: 282; Fat: 23.41 g; Total Carbs 0 g; Net Carbs 1g; Proteins: 16.59 g; fibers: 3g; Sugars: 6g

Cabbage Stuffed Pork Rolls

Prep time: 5 minutes. | Cooking time: 28 minutes. | Servings: 4

1-pound white cabbage
1 onion
8 pork tenderloin steaks
2 carrots
4 tablespoons low-sodium soy sauce
1-ounce extra-virgin olive oil
salt to taste
8 sheets rice

Put the chopped cabbage in the thermo mix glass together with the onion and the chopped carrot. Select 5 seconds, speed 5. Add the olive oil. Select 5 minutes, left turn, and spoon speed. Cut the tenderloin steaks into thin strips. Add the meat to the thermo mix glass. Select 5 minutes, aroma temperature, left turn, spoon speed. Without beaker. Add the soy sauce. Select 5 minutes, aroma temperature, left turn, spoon speed. Hydrate the rice slices. Extend and distribute the filling between them. Make the rolls, folding so that the edges are completely closed. Set the rolls in the air fryer and paint with the oil. Select 10 minutes, 350 degrees F.

Nutritional information: Calories: 120; Fat: 3.41 g; Total Carbs 0 g; Net Carbs 1g; Proteins: 20.99 g; fibers: 3g; Sugars: 6g

Cauliflower Shepherd's Pie

Prep time: 15 minutes . | Cook Time: 20 minutes | Serves 4

1 cauliflower head, cored and cut into florets
1 tbsp. sea salt
2 tbsp. unsalted butter
1 tbsp. canola oil
1 onion, diced
2 carrots, cut into small cubes
1 celery stalk, diced
1 tbsp. fresh rosemary, minced
1 tsp. fresh thyme, minced
1 lb. ground beef
1 tbsp. tomato paste
¼ cup red wine
Salt and pepper

Preheat the oven to broil and position the oven rack at the top. In a large pot, add the salt, cauliflower, water that is enough to cover the cauliflower, boil them and cook for 15 minutes until the cauliflower is tender. Place the cauliflower in a food processor after draining it and allowing most of the liquid to drain. Purée in the butter until it is completely smooth. Remove from the equation. In a heavy-bottomed pan, heat the canola oil over medium-high heat. Stir in the chopped onions, carrots, celery, rosemary, thyme, and salt, and simmer for another 5 minutes, or until the veggies soften. Remove the pan from the heat. Add the ground beef and cook for 5 minutes, breaking up the ground beef with a fork as it cooks, or until no pink remains. Bring the vegetables, tomato paste, and wine to a low boil, then reduce to a low heat and cook for another 2 minutes to let the alcohol evaporate. To taste, mix with salt and pepper. Spread the cauliflower mash on top of the meat mixture in an oven-safe dish. Cook for 2 to 3 minutes under the broiler, or until browned. When done, serve and enjoy.

Nutritional information: Calories 337; Total Carbs 19g; Net Carbs 11g; Protein 18.1g; Fat 17.0g; Sugar 4.0g; Fiber 4 g

Beef with Vegetables

Prep time: 10 minutes. | Cooking time: 9-19 minutes. | Servings: 4

½ pound 96% lean ground beef
2 medium tomatoes, chopped
1 onion, chopped
2 garlic cloves, minced
2 cups baby spinach
2 tablespoons lemon juice
⅓ cup beef broth, low-sodium
2 tablespoons crumbled feta cheese, low-fat

In a baking pan, crumble the beef. Place in the air fryer basket. Air fry at 370 degrees F for 3 to 7 minutes, stirring once during cooking until browned. Drain off any fat or liquid. Swell the tomatoes, onion, and garlic into the pan. Air fry for 4 to 8 minutes more, or until the onion is tender. Add the spinach, lemon juice, and beef broth. Air fry for almost 2 to 4 minutes more, or until the spinach is wilted. Sprinkle with the feta cheese and serve immediately.

Nutritional information: Calories: 98; Fats: 1g; Net Carbs 1g; Proteins: 15g; Total Carbs 5g fibers: 1g; Sugars: 2g

Ribeye with Mushrooms and Onions

Prep time: 10minutes . | Cook Time: 25 minutes | Serves 4

4 (5 oz) rib-eye steaks, room temperature
Sea salt, ground
Black pepper, ground
2 tbsp. olive oil, divided
4 tbsp. plant-based butter
3 tsp. garlic, crushed
4 cups button mushrooms, sliced
1 medium red onion, thinly sliced
1 tbsp. Worcestershire sauce

Season the steaks with ground sea salt and ground black pepper after drying them with paper towels. In a large grill pan, heat 1 tablespoon olive oil over medium-high heat until hot. Cook for 2 minutes on each side, until the steaks are browned. Raise the heat to medium and add the plant-based butter, allowing it to thoroughly melt. Cook the steaks in the melted plant-based butter until done to your liking. Place the cooked steaks on a dish and drizzle with butter. Allow 10 minutes for rest. Cook the remaining 1 tbsp. olive oil and crushed garlic in the same pan over medium-high heat until fragrant. Cook for about 8 minutes, until the sliced mushrooms and onions are soft and caramelized. Cook for 2 minutes after adding the Worcestershire sauce. Add a bit of salt and black pepper to taste. Serve the steaks with onions and mushrooms that have been fried.

Nutritional information: Calories: 579; Total Fat: 49g; Protein: 28g; Total Carbs: 6g; Net Carbs: 5g

Slow Cooked Roast

Prep Time: 15 minutes. | Cook Time: 4 hours. | Servings: 4

1 tablespoon olive oil
2 medium celery stalks, halved lengthwise and cut into 3-inch pieces
4 medium carrots, scrubbed, halved lengthwise, and cut into 3-inch pieces
1 medium onion, cut in 8hs
1¼ pounds (567 g) lean chuck roast, boneless, trimmed of fat
2 teaspoons Worcestershire sauce
1 tablespoon balsamic vinegar
2 tablespoons water
1 tablespoon onion soup mix
½ teaspoon ground black pepper

Grease a slow cooker with olive oil. Put the celery, carrots, and onion in the slow cooker, then add the beef. Top them with Worcestershire sauce, balsamic vinegar, and water, then sprinkle with onion soup mix and black pepper. Cover and cook on high for 4 hours. Allow to cool for 20 minutes, then serve them on a large plate.

Nutritional information: Calories 250; Total Carbs 15g; Net Carbs 10g; Protein 33g; Fat 6g; Sugar 6g; Fiber 3g

Saucy Mushroom Beef

Prep time: 15 minutes. | Cooking time: 40 minutes. | Servings: 4

10 ½ ounces beef
6 ounces mushrooms
1 onion
1 teaspoon olive oil
3 ½ ounces vegetable broth, low-sodium
1 teaspoon basil
1 teaspoon chilli
½ ounce tomato juice

Take the beef and pierce the meat with a knife. Rub it with olive oil, basil, chilli and lemon juice. Chop the onion and mushrooms and pour them with vegetable broth. Cook the vegetables for almost 5 minutes. Take a big tray and put the meat in it. Add vegetable broth to the tray too. It will make the meat juicy. Preheat the air fryer oven to 350 degrees F and cook it for 35 minutes.

Nutritional information: Calories 175; Total Carbs 4.4 g; Net Carbs 1g; Proteins 24.9 g; Fats 6.2 g; Fibers: 2g; Sugars: 3g

Tortillas with Steak and Guacamole

Prep time: 10minutes . | Cook Time: 15 minutes | Serves 4

For The Guacamole
4 ripe avocados, peeled and pitted
Pinch of salt
1 tsp. garlic, minced
1 shallot or onion, minced
1 tomato chopped, remove the pulp
¼ tsp. chili flakes (optional)
1 tbsp. fresh lime juice
For The Filling
3 tbsp. olive oil, divided
1 tbsp. chili powder
2 tsp. ground coriander
2 tsp. ground cumin
1 tsp. salt
1 lb. frying steak, thinly sliced
1 onion, thinly sliced
1 finely sliced red and green bell pepper
8 lettuce leaves or low-carb tortillas
1 cup guacamole

To make the guacamole, mash the ripe avocados with a fork in a medium basin until slightly lumpy. Mix in the minced garlic, onion, diced tomato, chilli flakes (if using), and lime juice until everything is well combined. Salt & pepper to taste. Refrigerate until ready to use. Filling Ingredients In a medium bowl, whisk together 2 tablespoons olive oil, chilli powder, coriander, cumin, and 1 teaspoon salt. Add the thinly sliced steak and toss to coat. Heat a heavy-bottomed skillet over medium-high heat until it is smoking hot, then add the seasoned steak pieces and cook for 4 minutes. Take the object out of the room and put it away. Add the chopped onions and bell peppers to the pan with the remaining 1 tbsp. olive oil and sauté for 5 minutes, until lightly browned. To taste, mix with salt and pepper. Place the thinly cut steaks and vegetables in the center of the lettuce leaves or low-carb tortillas and top with homemade guacamole.

Nutritional information: Calories 547; Total Carbs 19g; Net Carbs 10g; Protein 18.1g; Fat 42.0g; Sugar 4.0g; Fiber 5 g

Beef Barley Stew

Prep time: 10 minutes. | Cooking time: 1 hour 5 minutes. | Servings: 2

¾ cup filtered water
¼ cup pearl barley
2 teaspoons olive oil
7 oz. lean ground beef
1 cup mushrooms, sliced
¾ cup onion, chopped
2 cups frozen green beans
¼ cup beef broth, low-sodium
2 tablespoons parsley, chopped

In a pan, add water, barley and a pinch of salt and bring to a boil over medium heat. Now, reduce its heat to low and simmer, covered for almost 30-40 minutes or until all the liquid is absorbed. Remove from heat and set aside. In a suitable skillet, heat oil over medium-high heat and cook beef for almost 8-10 minutes. Add the mushroom and onion and cook for about 6-7 minutes. Add the green beans and cook for almost 2-3 minutes. Stir in cooked barley and broth and cook for almost 3-5 minutes more. Stir in the parsley and serve hot. Transfer the beef mixture into a suitable bowl and set it aside to cool. Divide the mixture into 2 containers evenly. Cover the containers and refrigerate for almost 1-2 days. Reheat in the microwave before serving.

Nutritional information: Calories: 374; Fats: 11g; Net Carbs 1g; Proteins: 37g; Total Carbs 33g; fibers: 4g; Sugars: 1g

Mini Beef Meatloaf

Prep time: 15 minutes. | Cooking time: 25 minutes. | Servings: 6

1-lb. 80/20 ground beef
¼ yellow onion, peeled and chopped
1 large egg
3 tablespoons blanched ground almond flour
1 tablespoon Worcestershire sauce, low-sodium
½ green bell pepper, chopped
½ teaspoon garlic powder
1 teaspoon dried parsley
2 tablespoons tomato paste
¼ cup water
1 tablespoon powdered erythritol

In a suitable bowl, combine ground beef, onion, pepper, egg, and almond flour. Stir in the Worcestershire sauce, garlic powder and parsley to the bowl. Mix until fully combined. Divide the mixture into 2 and place into 2 (4") loaf baking pans. In a suitable bowl, mix the tomato paste, water, and erythritol. Spoon half the mixture over each loaf. Place meatloaf pans into the air fryer basket. Adjust the temperature to 350 degrees F and set the timer for almost 25 minutes or until the internal temperature is 180 degrees F. Serve warm.

Nutritional information: Calories: 170; Fats: 9g; Net Carbs 1g; Proteins: 15g; Total Carbs 3g; Fats: 9g; fibers: 1g; Sugars: 2g sodium: 85mg

Steak dipped in Mushroom Sauce

Prep time: 20 minutes. | Cooking time: 5 minutes. | Servings: 4

12 ounces Sirloin steak, sliced and trimmed
2 teaspoons grilling seasoning
2 teaspoons oil
6 ounces broccoli, trimmed
2 cups frozen peas
3 cups mushrooms, sliced
1 cup beef broth (unsalted)
1 tablespoon mustard
2 teaspoons cornstarch
Salt to taste

At 350 degrees F, preheat your oven. Season the sirloin steak with grilling seasoning. In a pan over medium-high heat, cook the meat and broccoli for 4 minutes. Sprinkle the peas around the steak. Put the pan inside the oven and bake for 8 minutes. Remove both meat and vegetables from the pan. Add the mushrooms to the pan. Cook for 3 minutes. Mix the broth, mustard, salt and cornstarch. Add to the mushrooms. Cook for almost 1 minute. Pour sauce over meat and vegetables before serving.

Nutritional information: Calories: 226; Fats: 6g; Net Carbs 1g; Proteins: 26g; Total Carbs 16g fibers: 5g; Sugars: 6g

Steak with Peanut Sauce

Prep time: 10 minutes. | Cooking time: 15 minutes. | Servings: 4

⅓ cup light coconut milk
1 teaspoon curry powder
1 teaspoon coriander powder
1 teaspoon low-sodium soy sauce
1 ¼-lb. skirt steak
Cooking spray
½ cup Asian peanut sauce

In a suitable bowl, whisk together the coconut milk, curry powder, coriander powder, and soy sauce. Add the steak and turn to coat. Cover the bowl and refrigerate for at least 30 minutes and no longer than 24 hours. Preheat the barbecue or coat a grill pan with cooking spray and place the steak over medium-high heat. Grill the prepared meat until it reaches an internal temperature of 145 º F, about 3 minutes per side. Remove the steak from the grill and let it rest for almost 5 minutes. Slice the steak into 5-ounce pieces and serve each with 2 tablespoons of the Asian peanut sauce. Refrigerate: store the cooled steak in a resealable container for up to 1 week. Reheat each piece in the microwave for almost 1 minute.

Nutritional information: Calories: 361; Fats: 22g; Net Carbs 5g; Net Carbs 1g; Proteins: 36g; Total Carbs 8g; Sugars: 1g; fibers: 5g

Beef Mushroom Stew

Prep Time: 40 minutes. | Cook Time: 4 hours. | Servings: 8

2 tablespoons mild-flavored molasses
½ teaspoon salt
½ teaspoon celery salt
¼ teaspoon ground black pepper
¼ a teaspoon ground ginger
12 ounces assorted fresh mushrooms, halved
¼ cup raisins
4 cups hot cooked noodles, rice, or mashed potatoes (Optional)
2 pounds of boneless beef chuck steak, trimmed and cut into 1-inch cubes
3 tablespoons all-purpose flour
2 tablespoons cooking oil
6 medium carrots, cut into ½ -inch-thick slices
2 medium onions, chopped
1 (14.5 ounces) can diced tomatoes, undrained
¼ cup cider vinegar

Mix the meat cubes with the flour in a bowl. Heat oil in an extra-large skillet over medium-high heat. Brown the meat cubes, ½ at a time, in the hot oil. Place the onions and carrots in a saucepan over low heat. Add the browned meat cubes. Combine the undrained tomatoes, pepper, celery salt, vinegar, molasses, salt, and ginger in a medium bowl. Pour over the meat. Cover and cook on low for 8 hours or on high for 4 hours. Add raisins and mushrooms, cover, and cook for 1 hour more over medium-high heat. Serve over hot cooked noodles, rice, or mashed potatoes, if desired. Enjoy!

Nutritional information: Calories 242; Total Carbs 21g; Net Carbs 15g; Protein 28.8g; Fat 8.5g; Sugar 8.9g; Fiber 2.6g

Beef and Sweet Potato Stew

Prep Time: 20 minutes. | Cook Time: 1 hour 40 minutes. | Servings: 8

2 tablespoons olive oil
1½ pounds (680 g) lean beef stew meat
2 carrots, cut ½ inch thick slices
2 celery stalks, diced
1 onion, diced
2½ cup low-sodium beef broth
½ cup prunes, diced
1 cup hot water
2 (6-ounce / 170-g) sweet potatoes, peeled and diced into 1-inch chunks
1½ teaspoon ground cinnamon
1 teaspoon salt
1 teaspoon black pepper
¼ teaspoon parsley, chopped

Heat the olive oil in a stockpot over high heat. Arrange the beef in a single layer in the pot and cook for 12 minutes or until browned on all sides. You may need to work in batches to avoid overcrowding. Transfer the beef to a plate and set aside. Add carrots, celery, and onions to the pot and sauté for 5 minutes or until the onions are translucent. Pour the beef broth over, then put the beef back to the pot. Simmer for 1 hour. Meanwhile, soak the prunes in hot water for 20 minutes, then pat dry with paper towels. Reserve ½ cup the prune water. Add the prunes, prune water, sweet potatoes, cinnamon, salt, and black pepper to the pot. Cover and simmer for 20 minutes until potatoes are soft. Spoon the stew in a large bowl, then serve with chopped parsley on top.

Nutritional information: Calories 196; Total Carbs 17g; Net Carbs 12g; Protein 19g; Fat 4g; Sugar 7g; Fiber 3g

Roasted Beef with Sherry and Pepper Sauce

Prep time: 10minutes . | Cook Time: 1 hr. 40 minutes | Serves 4

1½ lb. rump beef roast
Himalayan pink salt, fine
Black pepper, ground
3 tsp. olive oil, divided
3 small onions, minced
2 tsp. garlic, minced
1 tbsp. green peppercorns
2 tbsp. sherry
2 tbsp. almond flour
1 cup beef broth, no salt

Preheat the oven to 300 degrees Fahrenheit, gas mark 2. Season the beef roast liberally with fine Himalayan pink salt and freshly ground black pepper. Cook 2 tsp. olive oil in a cast-iron pan over medium-high heat until hot. Brown the beef on all sides for about 10 minutes, then transfer to a baking dish. Roast the meat until it's done to your liking, about 1½ hours for medium. Begin the pepper sauce after the roast has been in the oven for 1 hour. Fry the minced onion in the remaining 1 tsp. olive oil in the same skillet over medium-high heat for 4 minutes, or until tender. Cook for 1 minute after adding the minced garlic and green peppercorns. To deglaze the pan, whisk in the sherry. Cook for 1 minute, stirring frequently, after whisking in the almond flour to produce a thick paste. Whisk in the no-salt beef broth for 4 minutes, or until the sauce thickens and becomes glossy. Fine Himalayan pink salt and ground black pepper are used to season the sauce. Carve the steak and serve it with a large dollop of sauce.

Nutritional information: Calories: 330; Total Fat: 18g; Total Carbs: 4g; Net Carbs: 1g; Protein: 36g

Filet Mignon with Mushrooms and Peppercorns

Prep time: 10minutes . | Cook Time: 25 minutes | Serves 4

4 (5 oz) filet mignon steaks, room temperature
Sea salt, ground
Black pepper, ground
2 tbsp. avocado oil, divided
1 lb. Portobello mushrooms, sliced
½ medium yellow onion, sliced
3 tsp. garlic, finely chopped
4 tbsp. plant-based butter
6 sage leaves, finely chopped

Using paper towels, pat the filet mignon steaks dry Add a pinch of salt and black pepper to taste. 1 tbsp. avocado oil, heated in a big heavy bottom pan over medium-high heat Cook the steaks on both sides until they are cooked to your satisfaction. Remove the steaks from the pan and lay them aside on a platter. Reduce the heat to medium-low and stir in the remaining 1 tablespoon avocado oil. Cook for 5 to 7 minutes after adding the sliced mushrooms and onions. Cook for 2 minutes after adding the chopped garlic. Add it to the platter with the steaks and season with ground sea salt and ground black pepper. Add the plant-based butter and chopped sage leaves and cook for 3 to 5 minutes, until the plant-based butter has melted and browned. Remove the sage leaves and toss them out. Serve the steaks with the fried mushrooms and onions on top, drizzling the sage brown butter over top.

Nutritional information: Calories: 420; Total Fat: 28g; Protein: 36g; Total Carbs: 6g; Net Carbs: 4g

Sirloin Korma

Prep time: 10 minutes. | Cooking time: 17-20 minutes. | Servings: 4

1 pound sirloin steak, sliced
½ cup plain yogurt
1 tablespoon curry powder
1 tablespoon olive oil
1 onion, chopped
2 garlic cloves, minced
1 tomato, diced
½ cup frozen baby peas, thawed

In a suitable bowl, combine the steak, yogurt, and curry powder. Stir and set aside. In a metal bowl, combine the olive oil, onion, and garlic. Bake at 350 degrees F for 3 to 4 minutes or until crisp and tender. Add the steak along with the yogurt and the diced tomato. Bake for almost 12 to 13 minutes or until the steak is almost tender. Stir in the peas and bake for almost 2 to 3 minutes or until hot.

Nutritional information: Calories: 299; Fats: 11g; Net Carbs 1g; Proteins: 38g; Total Carbs 9g; Fibers: 2g; Sugars: 3g

Crusted Pork Chops with Gravy

Prep time: 15–20 minutes. | Cooking time: 60–75 minutes. | Servings: 6

¼ teaspoon salt
½ cup panko bread crumbs
¾ cup water
1 teaspoon dried rosemary, crushed
1 teaspoon ground ginger
10 ½ -ounce can fat cream of chicken soup
2 tablespoons flour
2 tablespoons vegetable oil
6 loin pork chops, ½-inch thick
dash black pepper to taste

Place oil in a good-sized frying pan. Mix flour, salt, and pepper in a shallow but wide dish. Dredge chops in the mixture one at a time. Place 2 or 3 chops in oil in a suitable frying pan at a time, being cautious not to crowd the frying pan. Brown chops over moderate to high heat, 3-4 minutes on each side, until a browned crust forms. As chops brown, place in thoroughly -oil-coated 7×11-inch baking dish. In a suitable vessel, mix soup, water, ginger, and rosemary. Pour over chops. Drizzle with half the panko bread crumbs. Cover. Bake at 350 degrees F for almost 50-60 minutes, or until chops are soft but not dry. Uncover. Drizzle with residual panko bread crumbs. Bake with an open lid for 10–15 minutes. Take out from the oven and serve.

Nutritional information: Calories: 215; Fats: 10g; Net Carbs 1g; Proteins: 18g fibers: 1g; Total Carbs 11g; Sugars: 1g

Roll from Mexico

Prep Time: 10 minutes. | Cook Time: 0 minutes. | Servings: 2

1 teaspoon olive oil
2 large heads 2 romaine lettuce leaves, large ribs removed
2 (8 inches) whole wheat 96% fat-free heart-healthy tortillas, such as Mission brand
8 ounces extra-lean ground beef (95% lean)
⅓ cup chopped tomato (1 small)
⅓ cup chopped red sweet pepper
1 tablespoon red wine vinegar
1 teaspoon ground cumin

In a skillet, cook ground beef over medium-high heat until golden brown, using a spoon to break up meat as it cooks. Drain off the fat. Stir the vinegar, tomato, cumin, sweet pepper, and oil into the meat in the skillet. Place a turbot leaf on each tortilla. Spoon ½ of the cooked ground meat mixture onto each lettuce leaf. Completely roll up each filled tortilla. If desired, secure roll-ups with skewers.

Nutritional information: Calories 296; Total Carbs 28g; Net Carbs 18g; Protein 28g; Fat 9g; Sugar g; Fiber 4g

Coffeed and Herbed Steak

Prep Time: 10 minutes. | Cook Time: 10 minutes. | Servings: 4

¼ cup whole coffee beans
2 teaspoons fresh rosemary, chopped
2 teaspoons fresh thyme, chopped
2 teaspoons garlic, minced
1 teaspoon freshly ground black pepper
2 tablespoons apple cider vinegar
2 tablespoons olive oil
1 pound (454 g) flank steak, trimmed of fat

Put the coffee beans, rosemary, thyme, garlic, and black pepper in a food processor. Pulse until well ground and combined. Pour the mixture in a large bowl, then pour the vinegar and olive oil in the bowl. Stir to mix well. Dunk the steak in the mixture, then wrap the bowl in plastic and refrigerate to marinate for 2 hours. Preheat the broiler to MEDIUM. Remove the bowl from the refrigerator, and discard the marinade. Place the marinated steak on a baking sheet lined with aluminum foil. Broil in the preheated broiler for 10 minutes or until the steak reaches your desired doneness. Flip the steak halfway through the cooking time. Remove the steak from the broiler. Allow to cool for a few minutes and slice to serve.

Nutritional information: Calories 316; Total Carbs 0g; Net Carbs 0g; Protein 31g; Fat 19g; Sugar 0g; Fiber 0g

Ritzy Beef Stew

Prep Time: 20 minutes. | Cook Time: 2 hours. | Servings: 6

2 tablespoons all-purpose flour
1 tablespoon Italian seasoning
2 pounds (907 g) top round, cut into ¾-inch cubes
2 tablespoons olive oil
4 cups low-sodium chicken broth, divided
1½ pounds (680 g) cremini mushrooms, rinsed, stems removed, and quartered
1 large onion, coarsely chopped
3 cloves garlic, minced
3 medium carrots, peeled and cut into ½-inch pieces
1 cup frozen peas
1 tablespoon fresh thyme, minced
1 tablespoon red wine vinegar
½ teaspoon freshly ground black pepper

Combine the flour and Italian seasoning in a large bowl. Dredge the beef cubes in the bowl to coat well. Heat the olive oil in a pot over medium heat until shimmering. Add the beef to the single layer in the pot and cook for 2 to 4 minutes or until golden brown on all sides. Flip the beef cubes frequently. Remove the beef from the pot and set aside, then add ¼ cup chicken broth to the pot. Add the mushrooms and sauté for 4 minutes or until soft. Remove the mushrooms from the pot and set aside. Pour ¼ cup chicken broth in the pot. Add the onions and garlic to the pot and sauté for 4 minutes or until translucent. Put the beef back to the pot and pour in the remaining broth. Bring to a boil. Reduce the heat to low and cover. Simmer for 45 minutes. Stir periodically. Add the carrots, mushroom, peas, and thyme to the pot and simmer for 45 more minutes or until the vegetables are soft. OPEN THE LID, DRIZZLE WITH RED WINE VINEGAR AND SEASON WITH BLACK PEPPER. STIR AND SERVE IN A LARGE BOWL.

Nutritional information: Calories 250; Total Carbs 24g; Net Carbs 18g; Protein 25g; Fat 7g; Sugar 5g; Fiber 3g

Beef and Mushroom Cauliflower Wraps

Prep Time: 5 minutes. | Cook Time: 20 minutes. | Servings: 4

Avocado oil cooking spray
½ cup chopped white onion
1 cup chopped portobello mushrooms
1 pound (454 g) 93% lean ground beef
½ teaspoon garlic powder
Pinch salt
1 (10-ounce / 283-g) bag frozen cauliflower rice
12 iceberg lettuce leaves
¾ cup shredded low-fat Cheddar cheese

Heat a large skillet over medium heat. When hot, coat the cooking surface with cooking spray and add the onion and mushrooms. Cook for 5 minutes, stirring occasionally. Add the beef, garlic powder, and salt, stirring and breaking apart the meat as needed. Cook for 5 minutes. Stir in the frozen cauliflower rice and increase the heat to medium-high. Cook for 5 minutes more, or until the water evaporates. For each portion, use 3 lettuce leaves. Spoon one-quarter of the filling onto the lettuce leaves, and top with one-quarter of the cheese. Then, working from the side closest to you, roll up the lettuce to close the wrap. Repeat with the remaining lettuce leaves and filling.

Nutritional information: Calories 290; Total Carbs 7.1g; Net Carbs 6g; Protein 31.1g; Fat 15g; Sugar 4g; Fiber 3.1g

Steak and Broccoli Bowls

Prep Time: 10 minutes. | Cook Time: 15 minutes. |
Servings: 4

2 tablespoons extra-virgin olive oil
1 pound (454 g) sirloin steak, cut into ¼-inch-thick
strips
2 cups broccoli florets
1 garlic clove, minced
1 teaspoon peeled and grated fresh ginger
2 tablespoons reduced-sodium soy sauce
¼ cup beef broth
½ teaspoon Chinese hot mustard
Pinch red pepper flakes

In a large skillet over medium-high heat, heat the
olive oil until it shimmers. Add the beef. Cook,
stirring, until it browns, 3 to 5 minutes. With a slotted
spoon, remove the beef from the oil and set it aside
on a plate. Add the broccoli to the oil. Cook, stirring,
until it is crisp-tender, about 4 minutes. Add the
garlic and ginger and cook, stirring constantly, for 30
seconds. Return the beef to the pan, along with any
juices that have collected. In a small bowl, whisk
together the soy sauce, broth, mustard, and red
pepper flakes. Add the soy sauce mixture to the
skillet and cook, stirring, until everything warms
through, about 3 minutes.

Nutritional information: Calories 230; Total Carbs
4.9g; Net Carbs 4g; Protein 27g; Fat 11g; Sugar 3g;
Fiber 1g

Steak Sandwich

Prep Time: 10 minutes. | Cook Time: 10 minutes. |
Servings: 4

2 tablespoons balsamic vinegar
2 teaspoons freshly squeezed lemon juice
1 teaspoon fresh parsley, chopped
2 teaspoons fresh oregano, chopped
2 teaspoons garlic, minced
2 tablespoons olive oil
1 pound (454 g) flank steak, trimmed of fat
4 whole-wheat pitas
1 tomato, chopped
1 ounce (28 g) low-sodium feta cheese
2 cups lettuce, shredded
1 red onion, thinly sliced

Combine the balsamic vinegar, lemon juice, parsley,
oregano, garlic, and olive oil in a bowl. Dunk the
steak in the bowl to coat well, then wrap the bowl in
plastic and refrigerate for at least 1 hour. Preheat the
oven to 450ºF (235ºC). Remove the bowl from the
refrigerator. Discard the marinade and arrange the
steak on a baking sheet lined with aluminum foil.
Broil in the preheated oven for 10 minutes for
medium. Flip the steak halfway through the cooking
time. Remove the steak from the oven and allow to
cool for 10 minutes. Slice the steak into strips.
Assemble the pitas with steak, tomato, feta cheese,
lettuce, and onion to make the sandwich, and serve
warm.

Nutritional information: Calories 345; Total Carbs
21g; Net Carbs 18g; Protein 28g; Fat 15g; Sugar 2g;
Fiber 3g

Blackberry Topped Pork Shoulder

Prep time: 15 minutes. | Cooking time: 8–10 hours. |
Servings: 10-12

¼ cup brown sugar
½ teaspoon red pepper
1 onion, chopped
1 teaspoon apple cider vinegar
1 teaspoon salt
2 pints blackberries
2 teaspoons garlic powder
2–3-lb. pork shoulder

Insert the pork shoulder your slow cooker and layer
the onion on top. Puree the blackberries and pass
them through a sieve or strainer to separate the puree from the seeds. Combine the residual ingredients
with the blackberry puree. Pour the blackberry puree
over the contents of the slow cooker. Cover and cook
on low for almost 8–10 hours. Take out the roast and
shred by pulling using 2 forks. Mix back into the liquid
in the slow cooker. Serve on buns.

Nutritional information: Calories: 218; Fats: 12g;
Net Carbs 1g; Proteins: 6g; Total Carbs 8g; fibers:
3g; Sugars: 6g

Garlicky Pork Chops

Prep time: 9 minutes. | Cooking time: 38 minutes. |
Servings: 2

3 ground garlic cloves
2 tablespoons olive oil
1 tablespoon marinade
4 thawed pork chops

Mix the cloves of ground garlic, marinade, and oil.
Then apply this mixture on the chops. Put the chops
in the air fryer at 360 degrees F and cook for 35
minutes. Serve.

Nutritional information: Calories: 118; Fat: 3.41 g;
Total Carbs 0 g; Net Carbs 1g; Proteins: 22 g; fibers:
3g; Sugars: 6g

Pork Flamingos

Prep time: 8 minutes. | Cooking time: 10-15
minutes. | Servings: 4

14 ounces very thin sliced pork fillets
2 boiled and chopped eggs
3 ½ ounces chopped Serrano ham, low-sodium
1 beaten egg
1 cup breadcrumbs

Make a roll with the pork fillets. Add half-cooked egg
and serrano ham. So that the roll does not lose its
shape, fasten with a string or chopsticks. Pass the
rolls through the beaten egg and then through the
breadcrumbs until it forms a good layer. Warm the air
fryer for a few minutes at 350 degrees F. Insert the
rolls in the basket and set the timer for almost 8
minutes at 350 degrees F.

Nutritional information: Calories: 482; Fat: 23.41
g; Total Carbs 0 g; Net Carbs 1g; Proteins: 16.59 g;
fibers: 3g; Sugars: 6g

Salisbury Steak in Mushroom Sauce

Prep time: 10 minutes. | Cooking time: 15 minutes. | Servings: 4

1 pound 85% lean ground beef
1 teaspoon steak seasoning
1 egg
2 tablespoons unsalted butter
½ sliced onion
½ cup sliced button mushrooms
1 cup beef broth
2 ounces cream cheese
¼ cup heavy cream
¼ teaspoon Xanthan gum

Mix egg, steak seasoning, and ground beef in a suitable bowl. Make 4 patties and set them aside. Press sauté and melt the butter. Add mushrooms and onion and stir-fry for 3 to 5 minutes. Press cancel and add beef patties, broth, and cream cheese to the instant pot. Close the lid and press the manual cook. Cook 15 minutes on high. Do a natural release when done. Remove the patties and set them aside. Add xanthan gum and heavy cream. Whisk to mix. Reduce the sauce on sauté for almost 5 to 10 minutes. Press cancel and add patties back to the instant pot. Serve.

Nutritional information: Calories: 420; Fats: 30g; Net Carbs 2g; Net Carbs 1g; Proteins: 25g; Total Carbs 2g; Fibers: 2g; Sugars: 3g

Taco-Stuffed Bell Peppers

Prep time: 10 minutes. | Cooking time: 15 minutes. | Servings: 4

1-pound 80/20 ground beef
1 tablespoon chilli powder
2 teaspoons cumin
1 teaspoon garlic powder
1 teaspoon salt
¼ teaspoon black pepper
1 (10-ounce) can diced tomatoes, drained
4 medium green bell peppers
1 cup shredded Monterey jack cheese

In a suitable skillet over medium heat, brown the ground beef for about 7–10 minutes. When no pink remains, drain the fat from the skillet. Return the beef skillet to the stovetop and add chilli powder, cumin, garlic powder, salt, and black pepper. Add drained can have diced tomatoes and chiles to the skillet. Continue cooking 3–5 minutes. While the mixture is cooking, cut each bell pepper in half. Remove the seeds and white membrane. Spoon the cooked mixture evenly into each bell pepper and top with a ¼ cup cheese. Place stuffed peppers into the air fryer basket. Adjust the temperature to 350 degrees F and set the timer for almost 15 minutes. Serve.

Nutritional information: Calories: 346; Fats: 19g; Net Carbs 1g; Proteins: 28g; Total Carbs 111g fibers: 4g; Sugars: 5g

Saucy Beef with Broccoli

Prep time: 10 minutes. | Cooking time: 14 minutes. | Servings: 4

2 tablespoons olive oil

2 garlic cloves, minced
1-lb. beef sirloin steak, sliced into thin strips
¼ cup chicken broth, low-sodium
2 teaspoons ginger, grated
1 tablespoon ground flax seeds
½ teaspoon red pepper flakes, crushed
Salt and black pepper, to taste
1 large carrot, peeled and sliced thinly
2 cups broccoli florets 1 scallion, sliced thinly

In a suitable skillet, heat 1 tablespoon of oil over medium-high heat and sauté the garlic for almost 1 minute. Add the beef and cook for almost 4-5 minutes or until browned. With a slotted spoon, transfer the beef into a suitable bowl. Remove the excess liquid from the skillet. In a suitable bowl, add the broth, ginger, flax seeds, red pepper flakes, salt and black pepper. In the same skillet, heat the remaining oil over medium heat. Add the carrot, broccoli and ginger mixture and cook for almost 3-4 minutes or until desired doneness. Stir in beef and scallion and cook for almost 3-4 minutes. Transfer the beef mixture into a suitable bowl and set it aside to cool. Divide the mixture into 4 containers evenly. Cover the containers and refrigerate for 1-2 days. Reheat in the microwave before serving.

Nutritional information: Calories: 211; Fats: 15g; Net Carbs 1g; Proteins: 36g; Total Carbs 7g fibers: 2g; Sugars: 2g

Low-Fat Pork Shoulder Slaw

Prep time: 15 minutes . | Cook Time: 5 hours | Serves 4

1½ tbsp. chili powder, divided
2 tbsp. ground cumin, divided
1½ tsp. salt, divided
2½ tsp. black pepper, divided
2 tbsp. orange zest, divided
3–4 lbs. pork shoulder, fat trimmed
6 tsp. chopped garlic, divided
Juice of 2 oranges, divided
4 cups green or red cabbage, julienned
½ tbsp. extra-virgin olive oil

Mix up 1 tbsp. chilli powder, 1 tbsp. cumin, 1 tsp. salt, 2 tsp. black pepper, and 1 tbsp. orange zest in a small bowl. Season the pork shoulder with the seasoning. Remove from the equation. Add 5 tsp. chopped garlic and 1 orange's juice to a slow cooker and stir to combine. Cook on low heat for 8 hours or high for 5 hours after placing the seasoned pork shoulder inside. Remove the cooked pork shoulder from the pan and set it aside in a dish that will gather the juices. Return the shredded meat to the slow cooker, along with the liquids. Toss with salt and pepper to taste. Preheat the broiler in the oven. Place the shredded pork on a baking pan and broil for 3 to 4 minutes, or until crispy. Combine the remaining orange juice, chilli powder, cumin, garlic, salt, black pepper, and orange zest in a large mixing bowl. Mix in the julienned cabbage and olive oil until thoroughly mixed. Serving Tip: Substitute any protein of your choosing for the protein. Tip: If you don't like the citrus flavour, step 2 can be replaced with sliced apples.

Nutritional information: Calories: 920; Total Fat: 72g; Protein: 59g; Net Carbs: 5g; Total Carbs: 9g

Mustard Glazed Pork Chops

Prep time: 20 minutes. | Cooking time: 3-4 hours. | Servings: 2

¼ cup hot water
½ pound boneless pork chops
¾ teaspoon bouillon granules
2 small onions
2 tablespoons mustard
ground pepper, to taste
parsley sprigs, or lemon slices

Chop off ends of onions and peel. Chop onions in half crosswise to make 4 thick wheels. Place in the bottom of the crock pot. Sear both sides of frozen chops in a heavy frying pan. Place in the cooker on top of on-ions. Drizzle with pepper. Dissolve bouillon in hot wa-ter. Mix in mustard. Pour into crock pot. Cover. Cook on high heat for almost 3-4 hours. Serve topped with parsley sprigs or lemon slices, if desired.

Nutritional information: Calories: 204; Fats: 8g; Net Carbs 1g; Proteins: 22g fibers: 2g; Total Carbs 11g; Sugars: 7g

Pork Topped with Cranberry Relish

Prep time: 30 minutes. | Cooking time: 30 minutes. | Servings: 4

12 ounces pork tenderloin, fat sliced crosswise
Salt and black pepper, to taste
¼ cup all-purpose flour
2 tablespoons olive oil
1 onion, sliced thinly
¼ cup dried cranberries
¼ cup chicken broth
1 tablespoon balsamic vinegar

Flatten each slice of pork using a mallet. In a dish, mix the salt, pepper and flour. Dip each pork slice into the flour mixture. Add oil to a pan over medium-high heat. Cook pork for 3 minutes per side or until golden crispy. Transfer to a serving plate and cover with foil. Cook the onion in the pan for 4 minutes. Stir in the rest of the ingredients. Simmer until the sauce has thickened.

Nutritional information: Calories: 211; Fats: 9g; Net Carbs 1g; Proteins: 18g; Total Carbs 15g fibers: 1g; Sugars: 6g

Mustard Sauce Glazed Sesame Pork

Prep time: 25 minutes. | Cooking time: 25 minutes. | Servings: 4

2 tablespoons low-sodium teriyaki sauce
¼ cup chilli sauce
2 garlic cloves, minced
2 teaspoons ginger, grated
2 pork tenderloins
2 teaspoons sesame seeds
¼ cup sour cream
1 teaspoon Dijon mustard
Salt to taste
Scallion, chopped

At 425 degrees F, preheat your oven Mix the teriyaki sauce, chili sauce, garlic and ginger. Put the pork on a roasting pan. Brush the prepared teriyaki sauce on both sides of the pork. Bake in the oven for almost 15 minutes. Brush with more sauce. Top with sesame seeds. Roast for almost 10 more minutes. Mix the rest of the ingredients. Serve the pork with mustard sauce.

Nutritional information: Calories: 135; Fats: 3g; Net Carbs 1g; Proteins: 20g; Total Carbs 7g fibers: 1g; Sugars: 15g

Roasted Pork Tenderloin & Apple Slaw

Prep time: 10minutes . | Cook Time: 20 minutes | Serves 4

2 tbsp. avocado oil, divided
1 (1¼ lb.) pork tenderloin, boneless and patted dry
Himalayan pink salt, ground
Black pepper, ground
1 tbsp. rosemary, chopped
1 Granny Smith apple, cored, seeded cut into wedges
½ red cabbage, thinly sliced and core removed
½ red onion, thinly sliced
1 tbsp. apple cider vinegar
½ cup parsley, roughly chopped
1 tbsp. mint, chopped

Preheat the oven to 425 degrees F. In a large cast-iron pan, heat 1 tablespoon avocado oil over medium heat until hot. Rub the ground Himalayan pink salt, ground black pepper, and finely chopped rosemary all over the dried pork. Place the pork in the pan and sear for about 10 minutes, or until both sides are browned. Combine the apple wedges, sliced cabbage, and sliced onion in a large mixing bowl with the re-maining 1 tablespoon avocado oil. In the cast iron pan, scatter the mixture around the meat. Arrange the pan to the oven and roast the pan for 10 minutes, or until the pork is fully cooked and the vegetables are soft. Set aside the cooked pork on a chopping board to cool. Mix the apple wedges and cabbage with the apple cider vinegar, chopped mint, and chopped parsley in the pan. Serve the pork slices with the slaw.

Nutritional information: Calories: 263; Net Carbs: 10g; Protein: 28g; Total Carbs: 15g; Total Fat: 11g

Mustard Pork Chops

Prep Time: 5 minutes. | Cook Time: 25 minutes. | Servings: 4

¼ cup Dijon mustard
1 tablespoon pure maple syrup
2 tablespoons rice vinegar
4 bone-in, thin-cut pork chops

Preheat the oven to 400ºF (205ºC). In a small saucepan, combine the mustard, maple syrup, and rice vinegar. Stir to mix and bring to a simmer over medium heat. Cook for about 2 minutes until just slightly thickened. In a baking dish, place the pork chops and spoon the sauce over them, flipping to coat. Bake, uncovered, for 18 to 22 minutes until the juices run clear.

Nutritional information: Calories 258; Total Carbs 6.9g; Net Carbs 4g; Protein 39g; Fat 7.1g; Sugar 4g; Fiber 0g

Hungarian Pork Goulash

Prep Time: 35 minutes. | Cook Time: 3 hours. | Servings: 6

2 stalks celery, thinly sliced (1 cup)
2 medium carrots, thinly sliced (1 cup)
2 medium parsnips, halved lengthwise if large & thinly sliced (1 cup)
1 large onion, chopped (1 cup)
1 (14.5 ounces) can no-salt-added diced tomatoes, undrained
½ cup water
4 ounces dried wide whole-grain noodles (2 cups dried)
6 tablespoons light sour cream
1 pinch of Paprika
1 ½ to 2-pound pork sirloin roast
1 tablespoon Hungarian paprika or Spanish paprika
1 teaspoon caraway seeds, crushed
½ teaspoon garlic powder
½ teaspoon black pepper
¼ teaspoon salt
1 tablespoon canola oil

Trim the fat from the roast. Cut roast into 2-inch (5cm) cubes. In a bowl, combine cumin seeds, paprika, garlic powder, pepper, and salt. Add pork cubes and toss to coat. In another skillet, cook pork, ½ at a time, in hot oil over medium heat until golden brown, turning occasionally. Transfer pork to a saucepan over low heat. Add onion, parsnips, carrots, celery, and tomatoes. Pour the total water into the pot. Cover and cook on low heat for about 5-6 hours or for 2-3 hours. Stir the noodles into the pork mixture in the pot. Cover and cook over high heat until noodles are tender for about 30 minutes, stirring once halfway through cooking. Add 1 tablespoon sour cream to each serving. If desired, sprinkle each serving with paprika. Serve

Nutritional information: Calories 224; Total Carbs 23g; Net Carbs 20g; Protein 27g; Fat 7.6g; Sugar 6g; Fiber 5.3g

Sweet & Sour Pork with Cabbage

Prep Time: 35 minutes. | Cook Time: 20 minutes. | Servings: 4

2 teaspoons rice vinegar
4 teaspoons canola oil
1 medium green sweet pepper, seeded & cut into 1-inch pieces
1 (8 ounces) can bamboo shoots, drained
1 tablespoon packed brown sugar or brown sugar substitute equivalent to 1 tablespoon brown sugar
1 tablespoon cornstarch
12 ounces boneless pork loin, bias-sliced across the grain into strips
4 cups shredded Napa cabbage
1 large red sweet pepper, quartered and seeded
1 teaspoon water
1 (8 ounces) can pineapple chunks (juice pack)
2 tablespoons reduced-sodium soy sauce
2 teaspoons grated fresh ginger
2 cloves garlic

Place red sweet pepper quarters, cut sides down, in a microwave-safe dish. Add the water. Cover with plastic wrap—microwave on 100 percent power (high) for

4 to 5 minutes or until tender. Let stand for about 10 minutes or until the skin easily peels from the flesh; remove and discard skin. Place red sweet pepper in a food processor—cover & process until smooth. Drain pineapple chunks, reserving ⅓ cup the juice. Set pineapple chunks aside. Add the reserved ⅓ cup pineapple juice, cornstarch, ginger, garlic, soy sauce, brown sugar, and rice vinegar to red sweet pepper in a food processor. Cover & process until combined; set aside. In a skillet, heat 1 teaspoon the oil over medium-high heat. Add sweet green pepper. Stir-fry for about 2 minutes or until crisp-tender. Add bamboo shoots—Stir-fry for 30 seconds. Remove vegetables from skillet. Add the 3 teaspoons oil to the pan with the pork strips and sauté for 2-3 minutes Next, add the red bell pepper mixture, cook, and stir for about 30 seconds. Cook and stir for an additional 2 minutes. Add the pineapple chunks and green bell pepper mixture; heat through. Serve over Napa cabbage and enjoy!

Nutritional information: Calories 256; Total Carbs 23g; Net Carbs 18g; Protein 21g; Fat 10g; Sugar 11g; Fiber 3.6g

Sumptuous Lamb and Pomegranate Salad

Prep Time: 8 hours 35 minutes. | Cook Time: 30 minutes. | Servings: 8

1½ cups pomegranate juice
4 tablespoons olive oil, divided
1 tablespoon ground cinnamon
1 teaspoon cumin
1 tablespoon ground ginger
3 cloves garlic, chopped
Salt and freshly ground black pepper, to taste
1 (4-pound / 1.8-kg) lamb leg, deboned, butterflied, and fat trimmed
2 tablespoons pomegranate balsamic vinegar
2 teaspoons Dijon mustard
½ cup pomegranate seeds
5 cups baby kale
4 cups fresh green beans, blanched
¼ cup toasted walnut halves
2 fennel bulbs, thinly sliced
2 tablespoons Gorgonzola cheese

Mix the pomegranate juice, 1 tablespoon olive oil, cinnamon, cumin, ginger, garlic, salt, and black pepper in a large bowl. Stir to mix well. Dunk the lamb leg in the mixture, press to coat well. Wrap the bowl in plastic and refrigerate to marinate for at least 8 hours. Remove the bowl from the refrigerate and let sit for 20 minutes. Pat the lamb dry with paper towels. Preheat the grill to high heat. Brush the grill grates with 1 tablespoon olive oil, then arrange the lamb on the grill grates. Grill for 30 minutes or until the internal temperature of the lamb reaches at least 145ºF (63ºC). Flip the lamb halfway through the cooking time. Remove the lamb from the grill and wrap with aluminum foil. Let stand for 15 minutes. Meanwhile, combine the vinegar, mustard, salt, black pepper, and remaining olive oil in a separate large bowl. Stir to mix well. Add the remaining Ingredients and lamb leg to the bowl and toss to combine well. Serve immediately.

Nutritional information: Calories 380; Total Carbs 16g; Net Carbs 8g; Protein 32g; Fat 21g; Sugar 6g; Fiber 5g

Parmesan Golden Pork Chops

Prep Time: 10 minutes. | Cook Time: 25 minutes. | Servings: 4

Nonstick cooking spray
4 bone-in, thin-cut pork chops
2 tablespoons butter
½ cup grated low-fat Parmesan cheese
3 garlic cloves, minced
¼ teaspoon salt
¼ teaspoon dried thyme
Freshly ground black pepper, to taste

Preheat the oven to 400ºF (205ºC). Line a baking sheet with parchment paper and spray with nonstick cooking spray. Arrange the pork chops on the prepared baking sheet so they do not overlap. In a small bowl, combine the butter, cheese, garlic, salt, thyme, and pepper. Press 2 tablespoons the cheese mixture onto the top of each pork chop. Bake for 18 to 22 minutes until the pork is cooked through and its juices run clear. Set the broiler to high, then broil for 1 to 2 minutes to brown the tops.

Nutritional information: Calories 333; Total Carbs 1.1g; Net Carbs 0.9g; Protein 44g; Fat 16.1g; Sugar 0g; Fiber 0g

Pulled Pork Sandwiches with Apricot Jelly

Prep Time: 5 minutes. | Cook Time: 15 minutes. | Servings: 4

Avocado oil cooking spray
8 ounces (227 g) store-bought pulled pork
½ cup chopped green bell pepper
2 slices reduced fat provolone cheese
4 whole-wheat sandwich thins
2½ tablespoons apricot jelly

Heat the pulled pork according to the package instructions. Heat a medium skillet over medium-low heat. When hot, coat the cooking surface with cooking spray. Put the bell pepper in the skillet and cook for 5 minutes. Transfer to a small bowl and set aside. Meanwhile, tear each slice of cheese into 2 strips, and halve the sandwich thins so you have a top and bottom. Reduce the heat to low, and place the sandwich thins in the skillet cut-side down to toast, about 2 minutes. Remove the sandwich thins from the skillet. Spread one-quarter of the jelly on the bottom ½ of each sandwich thin, then place one-quarter of the cheese, pulled pork, and pepper on top. Cover with the top ½ of the sandwich thin.

Nutritional information: Calories 250; Total Carbs 34.1g; Net Carbs 20.8g; Protein 16.1g; Fat 8.1g; Sugar 8g; Fiber 6g

Chipotle Chili Pork

Prep Time: 4 hours 20 minutes. | Cook Time: 20 minutes. | Servings: 4

4 (5-ounce / 142-g) pork chops, about 1 inch thick
1 tablespoon chipotle chili powder
Juice and zest of 1 lime
2 teaspoons minced garlic
1 teaspoon ground cinnamon
1 tablespoon extra-virgin olive oil

Pinch sea salt
Lime wedges, for garnish

Combine all the Ingredients, except for the lemon wedges, in a large bowl. Toss to combine well. Wrap the bowl in plastic and refrigerate to marinate for at least 4 hours. Preheat the oven to 400ºF (205ºC). Set a rack on a baking sheet. Remove the bowl from the refrigerator and let sit for 15 minutes. Discard the marinade and place the pork on the rack. Roast in the preheated oven for 20 minutes or until well browned. Flip the pork halfway through the cooking time. Serve immediately with lime wedges.

Nutritional information: Calories 204; Total Carbs 1g; Net Carbs 0g; Protein 30g; Fat 9g; Sugar 1g; Fiber g

Roasted Pork with Apples

Prep time: 15 minutes. | Cooking time: 30 minutes. | Servings: 4

salt and black pepper, to taste
½ teaspoon dried, crushed
1 pound pork tenderloin
1 tablespoon canola oil
1 onion, sliced into wedges
3 cooking apples, sliced into wedges
½ cup apple cider
Sprigs sage

In a suitable bowl, mix salt, pepper and sage. Season both sides of pork with this mixture. Place a pan over medium heat. Brown both sides. Transfer to a roasting pan. Add the onion on top and around the pork. Drizzle oil on top of the pork and apples. Roast in the oven at 425 degrees F for almost 10 minutes. Add the apple roast for another 15 minutes. In a pan, boil the apple cider and then simmer for almost 10 minutes. Pour the apple cider sauce over the pork before serving.

Nutritional information: Calories: 239; Fats: 6g; Net Carbs 1g; Proteins: 24g; Total Carbs 22g fibers: 3g; Sugars: 16g

Butter Glazed Lamb Chops

Prep time: 10 minutes. | Cooking time: 5 minutes. | Servings: 4

4 lamb chops
1 teaspoon rosemary, diced
1 tablespoon unsalted butter
Black pepper, to taste
salt to taste

Season lamb chops with pepper and salt. Place the dehydrating tray in the air fryer basket and place the basket in the instant pot. Place lamb chops on dehydrating tray. Seal the Instant pot with its air fryer lid and select "Air Fry" mode, then set the cooking temperature to 400 degrees F and timer for almost 5 minutes. Mix butter and rosemary and spread over air-fried lamb chops. Serve fresh.

Nutritional information: Calories 278; Total Carbs 0.2 g; Sugar 0 g; Net Carbs 2g; Protein 38 g; Fat 12.8 g; Sugar 1g; Fiber 2g

Pork Carnitas

Prep Time: 15 minutes. | Cook Time: 4 hours. | Servings: 6

2 teaspoons finely shredded lime peel
2 tablespoons lime juice
12 (16 inches) crisp corn tortillas
2 scallions, thinly sliced
⅓ cup light dairy sour cream (Optional)
⅓ cup purchased salsa (Optional)
1 (2 pounds) boneless pork shoulder roast, cut into 2-inch pieces
¼ teaspoon salt
¼ teaspoon ground pepper
1 tablespoon whole black peppercorns
2 teaspoons cumin seeds
4 cloves garlic, minced
1 teaspoon dried oregano, crushed
3 bay leaves
2 (14 ounces) cans of reduced-sodium chicken broth

Sprinkle pork with salt & pepper—place in a 3 ½ - or 4-quart slow cooker. To make a bouquet garni, cut a 6-inch square from a double thickness of cheesecloth. Place the garlic, peppercorns, cumin seeds, oregano, and bay leaves in the center of the cheesecloth square. Pull up the corners of the cheesecloth and tie it with kitchen twine. Add to the pot over low heat. Add the broth. Cover and cook on low for 10-12 hours or on High for 4-5 hours. Remove meat from the pot. Discard the bouquet and cooking liquid. Using 2 forks, coarsely shred the meat. Discard fat. Sprinkle meat with lime juice and lime zest. Toss to mix. Serve over tortillas. Top with scallions and, if not cooked, sour cream and salsa. Enjoy!

Nutritional information: Calories 318; Total Carbs 24g; Net Carbs 15g; Protein 32g; Fat 10g; Sugar 1g; Fiber 4g

Pork Diane

Prep Time: 10 minutes. | Cook Time: 20 minutes. | Servings: 4

2 teaspoons Worcestershire sauce
1 tablespoon freshly squeezed lemon juice
¼ cup low-sodium chicken broth
2 teaspoons Dijon mustard
4 (5-ounce / 142-g) boneless pork top loin chops, about 1 inch thick
Sea salt and freshly ground black pepper, to taste
1 teaspoon extra-virgin olive oil
2 teaspoons chopped fresh chives
1 teaspoon lemon zest

Combine the Worcestershire sauce, lemon juice, broth, and Dijon mustard in a bowl. Stir to mix well. On a clean work surface, rub the pork chops with salt and ground black pepper. Heat the olive oil in a nonstick skillet over medium-high heat until shimmering. Add the pork chops and sear for 16 minutes or until well browned. Flip the pork halfway through the cooking time. Transfer to a plate and set aside. Pour the sauce mixture in the skillet and cook for 2 minutes or until warmed through and lightly thickened. Mix in the chives and lemon zest. Baste the pork with the sauce mixture and serve immediately.

Nutritional information: Calories 200; Total Carbs 1g; Net Carbs 0.5g; Protein 30g; Fat 8g; Sugar 1g; Fiber 0g

Tuscan Pork Loin

Prep Time: 5 minutes. | Cook Time: 1 hour. | Servings: 6

2 tablespoons chopped fresh rosemary
1 tablespoon freshly grated lemon zest
¾ cup dry vermouth or white wine
2 tablespoons white wine vinegar
1 3-pound pork loin, trimmed
1 teaspoon kosher salt
3 cloves garlic, crushed and peeled
2 tablespoons extra-virgin olive oil

Tie kitchen string around pork in 3 places so it doesn't flatten while roasting. Place salt & garlic in a small bowl & mash with the back of a spoon to form a paste. Stir in oil, rosemary & lemon zest. Rub the mixture into the pork. Refrigerate, uncovered, for about an hour. Preheat oven to 375 degrees F. Place pork in a roasting pan. Roast, turning from time to time, 40 to 50 minutes. Transfer to a cutting board. Let rest for about 10 mins. Meanwhile, add vermouth (or wine) and vinegar to the roasting pan and place over medium-high heat. Bring to a simmer and cook, scraping up any browned bits, until the sauce is reduced by half, 2 to 4 minutes. Remove the string and slice the roast. Add any accumulated juices to the sauce and serve with the pork.

Nutritional information: Calories 182; Total Carbs 0.6g; Net Carbs 0g; Protein 20.7g; Fat 8.3g; Sugar 1.4g; Fiber 0.1g

Baked Fruity Bacon & Veggies

Prep time: 10minutes . | Cook Time: 15 minutes | Serves 4

Non-stick cooking spray
6 cups brussels sprouts, halved
¼ lb. bacon, chopped
1 onion, sliced
½ red apple, peeled, cored, and chopped
4 tsp. garlic, chopped
2 tbsp. olive oil, divided
2½ tsp. sea salt, ground and divided
1½ tsp. black pepper, ground and divided
2–2½ lb. pork tenderloin

Preheat the oven to 425°F. Using nonstick cooking spray, coat a roasting pan. Combine the brussels sprout halves, chopped bacon, sliced onion, diced apple, chopped garlic, and 1 tbsp. olive oil in a large mixing bowl and mix well. Mix in the 12 tsp. ground sea salt and ½ tsp. ground black pepper. Rub the remaining ground sea salt, ground black pepper, and olive oil into the pork tenderloin. Place it in the roasting pan's center. Surround the pork with the fruit and vegetable combination. Bake for 30 minutes, or until the pork is fully cooked. Serve immediately. You can use any vegetables you wish in this recipe as a substitute.

Nutritional information: Calories: 544; Net Carbs: 12g; Protein: 63g; Total Carbs: 19g; Total Fat: 24g

Lettuce Wraps with Pickled Onions and Pork

Prep time: 14 minutes . | Cook Time: 16 minutes | Serves 4

½ red onion, thinly sliced
2 tbsp. red wine vinegar
Pinch of sea salt
1 tbsp. olive oil
1 tbsp. fresh ginger, minced
1 tbsp. garlic, minced
¼ tsp. chili flakes
1½ lb. ground pork
1 red bell pepper, in thin slices
1 green bell pepper, in thin slices
Fresh black pepper
4–8 lettuce leaves
2 carrots, julienned
1 cup cilantro, coarsely chopped

Toss the thinly sliced red onion, red wine vinegar, and sea salt together in a small bowl. In a heavy bottom pan, heat the olive oil over medium-high heat until it is hot; add the minced ginger, garlic, and chilli flakes and cook for 30 seconds, or until aromatic. As for the ground pork, cook it for 7 to 8 minutes, breaking up the ground pork with a fork as it cooks. Place the bell pepper slices on top. Toss with salt and pepper to taste. Place the lettuce leaves flat on your work area and evenly distribute the pork filling on each leaf. Add the julienned carrots, cilantro, and pickled onion to the top of the salad. Fold the bottom of the lettuce leaf over the filling, then draw the edges over and roll. Serve and enjoy. Substitution Tip: Substitute cabbage leaves for lettuce leaves by cooking the cabbage for 2 to 3 minutes, or until al dente.

Nutritional information: Calories: 413; Net Carbs: 7g; Protein: 31g; Total Fat: 12g; Total Carbs: 9g

Lamb Stuffed Pita

Prep time: 15 minutes. | Cooking time: 5-7 minutes. | Servings: 4

Dressing
1 cup plain Greek yogurt
1 tablespoon lemon juice
1 teaspoon dried dill weed, crushed
1 teaspoon ground oregano
½ teaspoon salt
Meatballs
½ pound ground lamb
1 tablespoon diced onion
1 teaspoon dried parsley
1 teaspoon dried dill weed, crushed
¼ teaspoon oregano
¼ teaspoon coriander
¼ teaspoon ground cumin
¼ teaspoon salt
4 pita halves
Toppings
red onion, slivered
seedless cucumber, sliced
crumbled feta cheese, low-fat
sliced black olives
chopped peppers

Stir all the dressing recipe ingredients together and refrigerate while preparing lamb. Combine all meatball ingredients in a suitable bowl and stir to distribute seasonings. Shape the meat mixture into 12 meatballs. Air fry at 390 degrees F for almost 5 to 7 minutes, until well done. Remove and drain on paper towels. To serve, add meatballs and toppings in pita pockets and drizzle with dressing. Serve.

Nutritional information: Calories: 270; Net Carbs 4g; Total Carbs: 18g Protein: 18g; Fat: 14g fiber: 2g; Sugar: 2g

Lime Lamb Cutlets

Prep Time: 4 hours 20 minutes. | Cook Time: 8 minutes. | Servings: 4

¼ cup freshly squeezed lime juice
2 tablespoons lime zest
2 tablespoons chopped fresh parsley
Sea salt and freshly ground black pepper, to taste
1 tablespoon extra-virgin olive oil
12 lamb cutlets (about 1½ pounds / 680 g in total)

Combine the lime juice and zest, parsley, salt, black pepper, and olive oil in a large bowl. Stir to mix well. Dunk the lamb cutlets in the bowl of the lime mixture, then toss to coat well. Wrap the bowl in plastic and refrigerate to marinate for at least 4 hours. Preheat the oven to 450ºF (235ºC) or broil. Line a baking sheet with aluminum foil. Remove the bowl from the refrigerator and let sit for 10 minutes, then discard the marinade. Arrange the lamb cutlets on the baking sheet. Broil the lamb in the preheated oven for 8 minutes or until it reaches your desired doneness. Flip the cutlets with tongs to make sure they are cooked evenly. Serve immediately.

Nutritional information: Calories 297; Total Carbs 1g; Net Carbs 0.2g; Protein31g; Fat 18g; Sugar 0g; Fiber 0g

Herbed Lamb Chops

Prep time: 30 minutes. | Cooking time: 20 minutes. | Servings: 2 to 3

2 teaspoons oil
½ teaspoon ground rosemary
½ teaspoon lemon juice
1 pound lamb chops, almost 1-inch thick
salt and black pepper, to taste
cooking spray

Toss the rosemary, oil, and lemon juice in a small bowl and rub on lamb chops. Season to taste with salt and pepper. Cover lamb chops and refrigerate for 15 to 20 minutes. Spray air fryer basket with nonstick spray and place lamb chops in it. Air fry at 360 degrees F for almost 20 minutes. Air fry for 1 to 2 minutes longer for well-done chops. For rare chops, stop cooking after about 12 minutes and check for doneness. Serve.

Nutritional information: Calories: 237; Fat: 13g; Net Carbs 1.2g; Protein: 30g; Total Carbs: 0g fiber: 0g; Sugar 0g

Lamb Lettuce Cups with Garlic Yogurt

Prep time: 08 minutes . | Cook Time: 14 minutes | Serves 4

1 lb. ground lamb
1 tbsp. garlic, chopped and divided
½ tbsp. oregano, finely chopped
1 lemon, juiced and divided
3 tsp. olive oil, divided
¾ tsp. sea salt, ground
¾ tsp. black pepper, ground
½ cup low-fat yogurt, plain
8 crisp lettuce leaves
2 cups romaine lettuce, shredded
½ cup ricotta cheese, crumbled

Mix the ground lamb, ½ tablespoons chopped garlic, chopped oregano, half of the lemon juice, 2 teaspoons of olive oil, ground sea salt, and ground black pepper in a large mixing basin. In a heavy bottomed pan, heat the remaining olive oil until it is hot. Add the ground lamb and cook for 8 minutes, or until the ground lamb mixture is browned. Turn off the heat. Combine the plain yoghurt, the remaining minced garlic, and the lemon juice in a small mixing bowl, and season with ground sea salt and ground black pepper. Place 2 crisp lettuce leaves on each plate and create the lettuce cup according to the following order: ground lamb, shredded lettuce, crumbled ricotta cheese, yoghurt, and garlic sauce.

Nutritional information: Calories: 463; Total Fat: 35g; Protein: 31g; Total Carbs: 6g; Net Carbs: 5g

Lentil Shepherd's Pie with Lamb

Prep Time: 25 minutes. | Cook Time: 3 hours. | Servings: 8

1 can reduced-fat and reduced-sodium condensed tomato soup
1 cup dry brown lentils, rinsed and drained
¼ teaspoon crushed red pepper
2-⅔ cups prepared mashed potatoes
1 sprig Snipped fresh mint
1-pound lean ground lamb or beef
1 large onion, chopped (1 cup)
1 package frozen mixed vegetables
1 can lower-sodium beef broth
1 can no-salt-added diced tomatoes with basil, garlic, and oregano, undrained

In a large skillet, cook ground lamb and onion until meat is brown & onion is tender. Drain off fat. In a 3 ½ or 4-quart slow cooker, combine the meat mixture, frozen vegetables, tomato soup, lentils, broth, tomatoes, and crushed red pepper. Cover and cook on a low-heat setting for about 6 to 8 hours or on a high-heat setting for about 3 to 4 hours. Serve meat and lentil mixture over potatoes. If desired, sprinkle each serving with snipped fresh mint.

Nutritional information: Calories 317; Total Carbs 43g; Net Carbs 28g; Protein 24g; Fat 6g; Sugar 8g; Fiber 1g

Spiced Lamb Vegetable Casserole

Prep time: 10minutes . | Cook Time: 2 hr. 15 minutes | Serves 4

2 tbsp. canola oil
1½ lb. organic lamb shoulder, cut into chunks
½ sweet onion, finely chopped
1 tbsp. ginger, grated
2 tsp. garlic, minced
1 tsp. cinnamon, ground
1 tsp. cumin, ground
¼ tsp. cloves, ground
2 white sweet potatoes, peeled and diced
2 cups beef broth, low sodium
Himalayan pink salt, fine
Black pepper, ground
2 tsp. parsley, chopped for garnish
2 tsp. mint, finely chopped

Preheat the oven to 300 degrees Fahrenheit. Heat the canola oil in a big heavy-bottomed pan over medium-high heat. Cook for 6 minutes, tossing periodically, until the lamb chunks are browned. Fry for 5 minutes with the chopped onion, grated ginger, minced garlic, ground cinnamon, ground cumin, and ground cloves. Bring the stew to a boil with the diced sweet potatoes and low sodium beef stock. Place the lamb mixture in an oven-safe casserole dish and cover with a lid or aluminum foil before baking. Cook for 2 hours, stirring occasionally, or until the meat is cooked. Remove the stew from the oven and season with ground black pepper and fine Himalayan pink salt. Garnish with chopped parsley.and serve hot. Ingredient Tip: Mint goes well with almost any lamb dish. Mint can also assist with dyspepsia.

Nutritional information: Calories: 545; Total Fat: 35g; Total Carbs: 16g; Net Carbs: 4g; Protein: 32g

Lamb Chops with Lime

Prep time: 10minutes . | Cook Time: 10 minutes | Serves 4

¼ cup olive oil
¼ cup lime juice
2 tbsp. lime zest
2 tbsp. mint, chopped
2 tbsp. parsley, chopped
Pinch of Himalayan pink salt, ground
Pinch black pepper, ground
12 lamb chops

Combine the olive oil, lime juice, lime zest, chopped parsley, chopped mint, ground Himalayan pink salt, and ground black pepper in a small mixing dish. Pour the mixture into a lidded marinating dish. Cover the marinating dish with the lid and add the lamb chops. To blend, stir everything together. Refrigerate the dish with the marinated lamb for 4 hours, flipping it many times. Preheat the broiler in the oven. Remove the chops from the dish and place them on a baking sheet lined with aluminum foil. Remove the rest of the marinade and discard it. Cook the lamb chops for 4 minutes on each side under the broiler. Before serving, let the lamb chops rest for 5 minutes. Ingredient tip: Mint pairs well with lamb. You may thicken the remaining marinade by cooking it down.

Nutritional information: Calories: 413; Net Carbs: 0g; Protein: 31g; Total Carbs: 1g; Total Fat: 29g

Lamb Tagine from Morocco

Prep Time: 40 minutes. | Cook Time: 4 hours. | Servings: 6

2 tablespoons quick-cooking tapioca
2 tablespoons finely shredded lemon peel
½ teaspoon lemon zest
1 tablespoon lemon juice
2 cloves of garlic, minced
1 (14.5 ounces) can reduced-sodium chicken broth
2 cups hot, cooked whole-wheat couscous
¼ cup sliced almonds, toasted
¼ teaspoon ground cinnamon
1-½ pounds of boneless lamb shoulder or lamb stew meat, cut into 1-inch pieces
1-½ cups coarsely chopped, peeled sweet potato
1 medium of plum tomato, chopped
2 medium carrots, cut into 1-inch pieces
1 medium of onion, chopped
½ teaspoon ground ginger
½ teaspoon ground cumin
½ teaspoon salt
¼ teaspoon ground turmeric
¼ cup pitted dates, quartered
¼ cup green olives, halved

In a large bowl, combine salt, turmeric, ginger, cumin, and cinnamon. Add lamb to the bowl. Toss to coat in spices. In a 3 ½ to a 4-quart slow cooker, place the lamb, sweet potato, tomato, carrots, tapioca, lemon peel, lemon juice, onion, dates, olives, and garlic. Pour broth over all. Cover; cook on low-heat setting for about 8 to 10 hours or on high-heat setting for about 4 to 5 hours. Serve over couscous and top with almonds.

Nutritional information: Calories 343; Total Carbs 39.5g; Net Carbs 25g; Protein 28g; Fat 8.5g; Sugar 11g; Fiber 5.8g

Autumn Pork Chops

Prep Time: 15 minutes. | Cook Time: 30 minutes. | Servings: 4

¼ cup apple cider vinegar
2 tablespoons granulated sweetener
4 (4-ounce / 113-g) pork chops, about 1 inch thick
Sea salt and freshly ground black pepper, to taste
1 tablespoon extra-virgin olive oil
½ red cabbage, finely shredded
1 sweet onion, thinly sliced
1 apple, peeled, cored, and sliced
1 teaspoon chopped fresh thyme

In a small bowl, whisk together the vinegar and sweetener. Set it aside. Season the pork with salt and pepper. Place a large skillet over medium-high heat and add the olive oil. Cook the pork chops until no longer pink, turning once, about 8 minutes per side. Transfer the chops to a plate and set aside. Add the cabbage and onion to the skillet and sauté until the vegetables have softened, about 5 minutes. Add the vinegar mixture and the apple slices to the skillet and bring the mixture to a boil. Reduce the heat to low and simmer, covered, for 5 additional minutes. Return the pork chops to the skillet, along with any accumulated juices and thyme, cover, and cook for 5 more minutes.

Nutritional information: Calories 224; Total Carbs 12g; Net Carbs 8g; Protein 26g; Fat 8g; Sugar 8g; Fiber 3.1g

Oven Barbecued Pork Chops

Prep Time: 15 minutes. | Cook Time: 20 minutes. | Servings: 4

1 clove garlic, minced
⅓ cup orange juice
½ cup barbecue sauce
1 ½ -1 ¾ pounds of bone-in, ¾-inch-thick pork rib chops, trimmed of fat
¼ teaspoon salt
¼ teaspoon freshly ground pepper
3 teaspoons canola oil, divided
1 medium onion, diced

Preheat oven to 425 ° F. Sprinkle pork chops with pepper and salt. Heat 2 teaspoons oil in an ovenproof skillet over high heat. Add pork chops and cook until they begin to brown, 1 to 2 minutes per side. Transfer to a plate. Add 1 teaspoon oil to the skillet. Add onion and cook, stirring, until softened, 3 to 4 minutes. Add the garlic and cook, stirring, until fragrant, 30 seconds. Add orange juice and cook until most of the liquid has evaporated, 30 seconds to 1 minute. Add the barbecue sauce. Return the pork chops to the skillet, turning several times to coat them with the sauce. Transfer the skillet to the oven and bake until the pork chops are pink in the center, about 8 to 10 minutes. Serve the sauce over the pork chops and enjoy!

Nutritional information: Calories 196; Total Carbs 15.1g; Net Carbs 10g; Protein 20g; Fat 9.9g; Sugar 9g; Fiber 0.22g

Lamb and Mushroom Cheese Burgers

Prep Time: 15 minutes. | Cook Time: 15 minutes. | Servings: 4

8 ounces (227 g) grass-fed ground lamb
8 ounces (227 g) brown mushrooms, finely chopped
¼ teaspoon salt
¼ teaspoon freshly ground black pepper
¼ cup crumbled goat cheese
1 tablespoon minced fresh basil

In a large mixing bowl, combine the lamb, mushrooms, salt, and pepper, and mix well. In a small bowl, mix the goat cheese and basil. Form the lamb mixture into 4 patties, reserving about ½ cup the mixture in the bowl. In each patty, make an indentation in the center and fill with 1 tablespoon the goat cheese mixture. Use the reserved meat mixture to close the burgers. Press the meat firmly to hold together. Heat the barbecue or a large skillet over medium-high heat. Add the burgers and cook for 5 to 7 minutes on each side, until cooked through. Serve.

Nutritional information: Calories 172; Total Carbs 2.9g; Net Carbs 1.8g; Protein 11.7g; Fat 13.1g; Sugar 1g; Fiber g

Aubergine with Lamb and Pine Nuts

Prep time: 10minutes . | Cook Time: 25 minutes | Serves 4

2 medium aubergines, cut into thick slices
5 tbsp. olive oil, divided
Sea salt
Black pepper
1 small onion, minced
1 lb. ground lamb or pork
1 tbsp. tomato paste
1 tsp. garlic, minced
⅛ tsp. ground allspice
½ cup plain yogurt
¼ cup pine nuts
¼ cup parsley, minced

Preheat the oven to 375 degrees Fahrenheit. Toast the pine nuts in a small heavy bottom pan over medium heat until brown and aromatic. Remove from the equation. Toss the aubergine slices with 4 tablespoons olive oil in a large mixing bowl and spread them out on a baking sheet. Season with salt and pepper, then bake for 25 minutes, or until tender and gently browned. Meanwhile, heat the remaining 1 tablespoon olive oil in a large pan over medium-high heat; add the onion and cook for 3 minutes, or until the onion is gently browned. Add the ground lamb or pork and cook for about 5 minutes, breaking it up with a fork as it cooks, then add the tomato paste. Cook for 2 minutes, or until the paste's acidity has dissipated. Season the meat mixture to taste with the minced garlic and spices. Cook for another minute to fully integrate the Ingredients. On each plate, arrange the cooked aubergine slices and top with the ground lamb or beef mixture. Drizzle with yoghurt and top with parsley and toasted pine nuts. Substitution Tip: Put a can of coconut cream in the fridge overnight to substitute the yoghurt with a dairy-free alternative. Skim the cream that has developed on top and use it in place of the yoghurt when ready to use.

Nutritional information: Calories: 625; Net Carbs: 9g; Protein: 24g; Total Fat: 60g; Total Carbs: 20g

Lamb Kofta with Cucumber Salad

Prep Time: 10 minutes. | Cook Time: 15 minutes. | Servings: 4

¼ cup red wine vinegar
Pinch red pepper flakes
1 teaspoon sea salt, divided
2 cucumbers, peeled and chopped
½ red onion, finely chopped
1 pound (454 g) ground lamb
2 teaspoons ground coriander
1 teaspoon ground cumin
3 garlic cloves, minced
1 tablespoon fresh mint, chopped

Preheat the oven to 375ºF (190ºC). Line a rimmed baking sheet with parchment paper. In a medium bowl, whisk together the vinegar, red pepper flakes, and ½ teaspoon salt. Add the cucumbers and onion and toss to combine. Set aside. In a large bowl, mix the lamb, coriander, cumin, garlic, mint, and remaining ½ teaspoon salt. Form the mixture into 1-inch meatballs and place them on the prepared baking sheet. Bake until the lamb reaches 140ºF (60ºC) internally, about 15 minutes. Serve with the salad on the side.

Nutritional information: Calories 346; Total Carbs 6g; Net Carbs 3g; Protein 20g; Fat 27g; Sugar 5g; Fiber 1.1g

Herbed Meatballs

Prep Time: 10 minutes. | Cook Time: 15 minutes. | Servings: 4

½ pound (227 g) lean ground pork
½ pound (227 g) lean ground beef
1 sweet onion, finely chopped
¼ cup bread crumbs
2 tablespoons chopped fresh basil
2 teaspoons minced garlic
1 egg
Pinch sea salt
Pinch freshly ground black pepper

Preheat the oven to 350ºF (180ºC). Line a baking tray with parchment paper and set it aside. In a large bowl, mix together the pork, beef, onion, bread crumbs, basil, garlic, egg, salt, and pepper until very well mixed. Roll the meat mixture into 2-inch meatballs. Transfer the meatballs to the baking sheet and bake until they are browned and cooked through, about 15 minutes. Serve the meatballs with your favorite marinara sauce and some steamed green beans.

Nutritional information: Calories 33; Total Carbs 12g; Net Carbs 12g; Protein 24.7g; Fat 19g; Sugar 2.9g; Fiber 0.9g

Sloppy Joes

Prep Time: 10 minutes. | Cook Time: 15 minutes. | Servings: 4

1 tablespoon extra-virgin olive oil
1 pound (454 g) 93% lean ground beef
1 medium red bell pepper, chopped
½ medium yellow onion, chopped
2 tablespoons low-sodium Worcestershire sauce
1 (15-ounce / 425-g) can low-sodium tomato sauce
2 tablespoons low-sodium, sugar-free ketchup
4 whole-wheat sandwich thins, cut in ½
1 cup cabbage, shredded

Heat the olive oil in a nonstick skillet over medium heat until shimmering. Add the beef, bell pepper, and onion to the skillet and sauté for 8 minutes or until the beef is browned and the onion is translucent. Pour the Worcestershire sauce, tomato sauce, and ketchup in the skillet. Turn up the heat to medium-high and simmer for 5 minutes. Assemble the sandwich thin halves with beef mixture and cabbage to make the sloppy Joes, then serve warm.

Nutritional information: Calories 329; Total Carbs 35g; Net Carbs 20g; Protein 31.7g; Fat 8.9g; Sugar 10g; Fiber 7g

Alfredo Sausage and Vegetables

Prep Time: 10 minutes. | Cook Time: 15 minutes. | Servings: 6

1 package smoked sausage, cut in ¼-inch slices
1 cup half-and-½
½ cup zucchini, cut in matchsticks
½ cup carrots, cut in matchsticks
½ cup red bell pepper, cut in matchsticks
½ cup peas, frozen
¼ cup plant-based butter
¼ cup onion, diced
2 tablespoons fresh parsley, diced
1 cup whole-wheat pasta, cooked and drained
1/3 cup reduced fat Parmesan cheese
1 clove garlic, diced fine
Salt and ground black pepper, to taste

Melt plant-based butterbutter in a large skillet over medium heat. Add onion and garlic and cook, stirring occasionally, 3 to 4 minutes or until onion is soft. Increase heat to medium-high. Add sausage, zucchini, carrots, and red pepper. Cook, stirring frequently, 5 to 6 minutes, or until carrots are tender crisp. Stir in peas and half-and-half, cook for 1 to 2 minutes until heated through. Stir in cheese, parsley, salt, and pepper. Add pasta and toss to mix. Serve.

Nutritional information: Calories 285; Total Carbs 18g; Net Carbs 12g; Protein 21g; Fat 15g; Sugar 8g; Fiber 4g

Tangy Pork Chops

Prep time: 8 minutes. | Cooking time: 11 minutes. | Servings: 2

2 boneless pork chops
15 ml vegetable oil
½ ounce dark brown sugar, packaged
½ teaspoon Hungarian paprika
½ teaspoon ground mustard
½ teaspoon black pepper
½ teaspoon onion powder
½ teaspoon garlic powder
Salt and black pepper, to taste

Warm the air fryer for a few minutes at 350 degrees F. Cover the pork chops with oil. Put all the spices and season the pork chops abundantly, almost as if you were making them breaded. Place the pork chops in the preheated air fryer. Select steak and set the time to 10 minutes. Remove the pork chops when it has finished cooking. Let it stand and serve.

Nutritional information: Calories: 118; Fat: 6.85 g; Total Carbs 0.3 g; Net Carbs 1g; Proteins: 13.12 g; fibers: 3g; Sugars: 6g

Grilled Lamb Racks

Prep Time: 15 minutes. | Cook Time: 20 minutes. | Servings: 4

1 tablespoon olive oil, plus more for brushing the grill grates
1 tablespoon garlic, minced
½ teaspoon salt
Freshly ground black pepper, to taste
2 (1-inch) sprig fresh rosemary

2 (1½-pounds / 680-g) French lamb racks, trimmed of fat, cut into 4 pieces with 2 bones, and leave one bone with an equal amount of meat

Combine all the Ingredients in a large bowl. Toss to coat the lamb racks well. Wrap the bowl in plastic and refrigerate to marinate for at least 2 hours. Preheat the grill over medium heat. Brush the grill grates with olive oil. Remove the bowl from the refrigerator, and arrange the lamb racks on the grill grates, bone side down. Grill for 3 minutes until lightly browned, then flip the lamb racks, and cover and grill for 15 minutes or until it reaches your desired doneness. Remove the lamb racks from the grill grates and serve hot.

Nutritional information: Calories 192; Total Carbs 1g; Net Carbs 0.2g; Protein 22g; Fat 9g; Sugar 0g; Fiber 0g

Parmesan Topped Chicken

Prep time: 10 minutes. | Cooking time: 30 minutes. | Servings: 4

2 tablespoons olive oil
1 garlic clove, minced
1 cup dry bread crumbs
½ cup grated parmesan cheese, non-fat
1 teaspoon dried basil leaves
¼ teaspoon black pepper
6 skinless, boneless chicken breast halves

At 350 degrees F, preheat your oven. Lightly grease a 9x13 inch baking pan. In a suitable bowl, blend the garlic with olive oil. In another bowl, toss bread crumbs with parmesan cheese, basil, and pepper. Coat each chicken breast in the oil mixture, then coat with the bread crumb mixture. Place the coated chicken breasts in the prepared baking dish, and top with any remaining bread crumb mixture. Bake 30 minutes in the preheated oven, or until chicken is no longer pink and juices run clear.

Nutritional information: Calories 281; Total Carbs 14g; Net Carbs 2g; Protein 30g; Fat 11g; fibers: 3g; Sugars: 6g

Creamy and Aromatic Chicken

Prep time: 15 minutes. | Cooking time: 30 minutes. | Servings: 4

4 (4-ounce) boneless chicken breasts
Salt and black pepper, to taste
1 tablespoon olive oil
½ sweet onion, chopped
2 teaspoons chopped thyme
1 cup chicken broth
¼ cup heavy whipping cream
1 scallion, white and green parts, chopped

At 375 degrees F, preheat your oven. Rub the chicken liberally with salt and pepper. Heat the olive oil in an oven-safe skillet over medium-high heat until shimmering. Put the chicken in the skillet and cook for almost 10 minutes or until well browned. Flip halfway through. Transfer onto a platter and set aside. Toss in the onion to the same skillet and sauté for 3 minutes or until translucent. Add the thyme and broth and simmer for 6 minutes or until the liquid reduces in half. Mix in the cream, then put the chicken back to the skillet. Arrange the skillet in the oven and bake for 10 minutes almost. Remove the skillet from the oven and serve them with scallion. Garnish the chicken with black olives, sliced cherry tomatoes, or parsley for more flavor.

Nutritional information: Calories: 287; Fats: 14.0g; Net Carbs 2g; Protein: 34.0g; Total Carbs: 4.0g fiber: 1.0g; Sugar: 1.0g

Turkey Kabob with Pitas

Prep time: 25 minutes. | Cooking time: 15 minutes. | Servings: 4

1 teaspoon whole cumin seeds, crushed
1 cup shredded cucumber
⅓ cup Roma tomato, chopped
¼ cup slivered red onion
¼ cup shredded radishes
¼ cup snipped cilantro
¼ teaspoon black pepper
1 pound turkey breast, julienned
¼ cup plain Greek yogurt
4 whole wheat pita bread rounds (6-inch)

Toast the cumin seeds for 1 minute and transfer them to a suitable bowl. Add shredded cucumber, Roma tomato, slivered red onion, radishes, cilantro, and black pepper to the bowl. Mix well. To make the curry blend, combine ½ teaspoon olive oil, 1 teaspoon curry powder, ½ teaspoon ground turmeric, ½ teaspoon ground cumin, ½ teaspoon ground coriander, ¼ teaspoon ground ginger, ⅛ teaspoon of salt, and cayenne pepper. In another bowl, combine curry blend and turkey. Stir to coat. Thread turkey onto skewers. Grill kabobs, uncovered for 6 to 8 minutes or until turkey is no longer pink. Turning kabobs occasionally. Remove turkey from skewers. Spread Greek yogurt on pita bread. Spoon cucumber mixture over yogurt. Top with grilled turkey. Serve.

Nutritional information: Calories: 343; Total Carb: 40g; Net Carbs 5g; Protein: 35g; Fat: 6g; fibers: 3g; Sugars: 6g

Chicken Enchilada with Spaghetti Squash

Prep time: 5 minutes. | Cooking time: 40 minutes. | Servings: 4

1 (3-pound) spaghetti squash, halved
1 ½ teaspoons ground cumin
Avocado oil cooking spray
4 (4-ounce) boneless chicken breasts
1 large zucchini, diced
¾ cup canned red enchilada sauce
¾ cup shredded cheddar or mozzarella cheese

At 400 degrees F, preheat your oven. Season both halves of the squash with ½ teaspoon of cumin, and place them cut-side down on a baking sheet. Bake for almost 25 to 30 minutes.
Meanwhile, heat a suitable skillet over medium-low heat. When hot, spray the cooking surface with cooking spray and add the chicken breasts, zucchini, and 1 teaspoon of cumin. Cook the prepared chicken for 4 to 5 minutes per side. Stir the zucchini when you flip the chicken. Transfer the zucchini to a suitable bowl and set aside. Remove the chicken from the skillet, and let it rest for almost 10 minutes or until it's cool enough to handle. Shred or dice the cooked chicken. Place the chicken and zucchini in a suitable bowl, and add the enchilada sauce. Remove the squash from the oven, flip it over, and comb through it with a fork to make thin strands. Scoop the chicken mixture on top of the squash halves and top with the cheese. Return the cooked squash to the oven and broil for almost 2 to 5 minutes, or until the cheese is bubbly.

Nutritional information: Calories: 331; Fats: 11g; Net Carbs 1g; Proteins: 35g; Total Carbs 27g fibers: 2g; Sugars: 4g

Turkey Burgers

Prep Time: 10 minutes. | Cook Time: 20 minutes. | Servings: 4

1½ pounds (680 g) lean ground turkey
½ cup bread crumbs
½ sweet onion, chopped
1 carrot, peeled, grated
1 teaspoon minced garlic
1 teaspoon chopped fresh thyme
Sea salt and freshly ground black pepper, to taste
Nonstick cooking spray

In a large bowl, combine the turkey, breadcrumbs, onion, carrot, garlic and thyme until well combined. Season gently with salt and pepper. Make the turkey mixture into 4 equal patties. Place a large saucepan over medium heat and spray lightly with cooking spray. Cook the turkey patties until golden brown, about 10 minutes per side. Serve with a white burger or top with your favorite whole grain toppings.

Nutritional information: Calories 320; Total Carbs 11g; Net Carbs 7g; Protein 32g; Fat 15g; Sugar 2g; Fiber g

Coconut Crusted Chicken Tenders

Prep time: 10 minutes. | Cooking time: 20 minutes. | Servings: 6

4 chicken breasts each cut lengthwise into 3 strips
½ teaspoon salt
¼ teaspoon black pepper
½ cup coconut flour
2 eggs, beaten
2 tablespoons unsweetened plain almond milk
1 cup unsweetened coconut flakes

At 400 degrees F, preheat your oven. Layer a suitable baking sheet with parchment paper. Season the sliced chicken pieces with black pepper and salt. Place the coconut flour in a suitable bowl. In another bowl, mix the eggs with the almond milk. Spread the coconut flakes on a plate. One by one, roll the chicken pieces in the flour, then dip the floured chicken in the egg mixture and shake off any excess. Roll in the coconut flakes and transfer to the prepared baking sheet. Bake for almost 15 to 20 minutes, flipping once halfway through until cooked through and browned.

Nutritional information: Calories: 216; Fats: 13g; Net Carbs 1g; Proteins: 20g; Total Carbs 9g fibers: 6g; Sugars: 2g

Cheesy Chicken Casserole

Prep time: 25 minutes. | Cooking time: 32 minutes. | Servings: 4

1 tablespoon olive oil
4 eggs, beaten
3 tablespoons softened cream cheese, low-fat
¾ cup heavy whipping cream, part-skim
1 teaspoon cumin
½ garlic powder
½ teaspoon salt
½ teaspoon black pepper

2 (6- to 8-ounce) chicken breast, cooked and shredded
4 large whole green chiles, rinsed and patted dry, flattened
1 cup shredded jack cheese, low-fat
1 cup shredded cheddar cheese, low-fat
¼ teaspoon red pepper flakes

At 350 degrees F, preheat your oven. Grease a casserole dish with olive oil. Combine the eggs, cream cheese, cream, cumin, garlic powder, salt, and black pepper in a suitable bowl. Stir to mix well. Dunk the chicken in the mixture. Press to coat well. Set aside. Lay 2 chiles on the casserole dish, then flatten to cover the bottom. Pour half of the creamy chicken mixture over the chiles. Scatter jack cheese and cheddar cheese on the cream chicken, then top them with the remaining 2 flattened chiles. Pour the remaining cream chicken mixture over, then scatter the remaining cheeses and sprinkle them with red pepper flakes. Arrange the casserole dish in the preheated oven and bake for almost 30 minutes, then turn the oven to broil for almost 2 minutes until the top of the casserole is well browned. Remove the casserole from the oven. Allow to cool for almost 15 minutes, then serve warm.

Nutritional information: Calories: 412; Fats: 30.0g; Net Carbs 2g; Protein: 30.0g; Total Carbs: 4.0g fiber: 1.0g; Sugar: 1.0g

Ritzy Chicken Cacciatore

Prep Time: 20 minutes. | Cook Time: 1 hour. | Servings: 6

¼ cup all-purpose flour
1 (2-pound / 907-g) chicken, cut into 4 breasts, 2 drumsticks, 2 wings, and 2 thighs
Salt and freshly ground black pepper, to taste
2 tablespoons olive oil
3 slices bacon, chopped
4 ounces (113 g) button mushrooms, halved
1 sweet onion, chopped
2 teaspoons garlic, minced
½ cup red wine
1 (15-ounce / 425-g) can low-sodium stewed tomatoes
Pinch red pepper flakes
2 teaspoons fresh oregano, chopped

In a large bowl, put the flour, dip all the chicken in the flour and sprinkle with salt and pepper. Heat olive oil in a large skillet over medium-high heat. Place the chicken in the pan and cook for 20 minutes or until both sides are golden brown. Turn the chicken halfway through the cooking time. Transfer the grilled chicken to a plate. Place the bacon in the pan and cook for 5 minutes, until curls. Stir from time to time while cooking. Transfer the bacon to the same plate. Add the mushrooms, onion, and garlic to the pan and sauté for 4 minutes until tender. Combine red wine, tomatoes, pepper flakes, and oregano. Stir to mix. Bring to a boil. Return the chicken and bacon to the pan. Reduce heat and simmer for 30 minutes or until chicken is 74ºC (165ºF). Pour them into a large bowl. Cool 10 minutes, then serve.

Nutritional information: Calories 232; Total Carbs 13.7g; Net Carbs 9g; Protein 8.2g; Fat 16.8g; Sugar 4.8g; Fiber 2.2g

Lettuce Salad with Turkey

Prep time: 10 minutes. | Cooking time: 0 minutes. | Servings: 4

1 bibb or butterhead lettuce head, quartered
2 cups shredded cooked turkey breast
1 cup halved grape or cherry tomatoes
2 hard-cooked eggs, chopped
4 slices low-sodium and less-fat bacon, crisp-cooked, and crumbled
¼ cup chopped red onion
Black pepper, to taste

Arrange 1 lettuce quarter on each plate. Drizzle half of the dressing over wedges. Top with turkey, eggs, and tomatoes. Drizzle with the remaining dressing. Sprinkle with onion, bacon and pepper. Serve.

Nutritional information: Calories: 228; Total Carb: 8g; Net Carbs 1.2g; Fat: 9g Protein: 29g; fibers: 3g; Sugars: 6g

Stuffed Chicken Breasts

Prep Time: 15 minutes. | Cook Time: 30 minutes. | Servings: 4

1 cup chopped roasted red pepper
2 ounces (57 g) low-fat goat cheese
4 Kalamata olives, pitted, finely chopped
1 tablespoon chopped fresh basil
4 (5-ounce / 142-g) boneless, skinless chicken breasts
1 tablespoon extra-virgin olive oil

Preheat the oven to 400 ºF. In a small bowl, combine the peppers, goat cheese, olives, and basil until blended. Put the container in the refrigerator for 15 minutes to harden. Cut the chicken breast horizontally and make a pocket in the middle. Distribute the filling evenly between the chicken breast pouches and secure with a wooden toothpicks. Place a large saucepan over medium-high heat and pour in the olive oil. Cook chicken for a total of 10 minutes on both sides. Transfer to the oven. Cook the chicken until cooked through, about 20 minutes. Let the chicken sit for 10 minutes, then remove the toothpicks before eating.

Nutritional information: Calories 246; Total Carbs 3g; Net Carbs 2g; Protein 35g; Fat 9g; Sugar 2g; Fiber 1g

Spatchcock with Lime Aioli

Prep time: 15 minutes . | Cook Time: 45 minutes | Serves 6

4 pounds (1.8 kg) chicken, spatchcocked
3 tablespoons blackened seasoning
2 tablespoons olive oil
Lime Aioli:
½ cup lite mayonnaise
Juice and zest of 1 lime
¼ teaspoon kosher salt
¼ teaspoon ground black pepper

Heat the grill to a medium-high heat in advance. Rub the chicken with blackened seasoning and olive oil on a clean work surface. Cook the chicken for 45 minutes on a hot grill, skin side up, or until the internal temperature reaches 165°F (74°C). Meanwhile, in a small mixing bowl, add all of the aioli Ingredients and swirl well to combine. Transfer the chicken to a large platter and baste with the lime aioli after it's finished grilling. Allow to cool before serving. Serving Tip: Serve this dish with roasted Brussels sprouts or radish soup to make it a complete dinner.

Nutritional information: Calories 436; Total Carbs 6.8g; Net Carbs 4.6g; Protein 61.1g; Fat 8.0g; Sugar 1.5g; Fiber 0.7 g

Savory Bread Pudding

Prep Time: 15 minutes. | Cook Time: 20 minutes. | Servings: 6

2 cups low-fat (1%) milk
3 large egg whites
1 cup diced onion
9 small links (6 ounces) fully cooked chicken, apple, and maple breakfast sausage, thinly sliced
8 slices of whole wheat or multigrain bread, cut into 1-inch squares
1 tablespoon olive or vegetable oil
1 red bell pepper, diced
½ cup low-fat sharp Cheddar cheese, shredded

Preheat the oven to 350 º F. Coat a 11 by 7-inch baking dish or shallow pan with nonstick spray. Heat a large saucepan over medium heat until heated through. Add the oil, pepper and onion. Stir occasionally, for 6 to 8 minutes or until tender. Remove from the heat and set aside. Meanwhile, combine the milk and egg whites in a large bowl. Combine sausage and bread. Mix well. Add the cooked vegetables. Mix again. Transfer the mixture to the prepared baking dish and press gently. Bake for 40 to 45 minutes, or until puffed and centered. Remove from the oven. Sprinkle cheese over the pudding. Return to the oven; Bake for about 2 minutes or until the cheese is slightly melted. Cut into 6 equal parts. Help yourself and enjoy!

Nutritional information: Calories 215; Total Carbs 22g; Net Carbs 14g; Protein 14g; Fat 7g; Sugar 2g; Fiber 3g

Black Beans Chicken Stew

Prep time: 10 minutes. | Cooking time: 30 minutes. | Servings: 4

1 tablespoon vegetable oil
4 boneless chicken breast halves
1 (10 oz.) can tomatoes with chile peppers, diced
1 (15 oz.) can black beans, rinsed
1 (8.75 oz.) can kernel corn, drained
1 pinch ground cumin

In a suitable skillet, heat oil over medium-high heat. Brown chicken breasts on both sides. Add tomatoes with green chile peppers, beans and corn. Reduce heat and let simmer for almost 25 to 30 minutes or until chicken is cooked through and juices run clear. Add a dash of cumin and serve.

Nutritional information: Calories 310; Fat 6g; Total Carbs 28g; Net Carbs 2g; Protein 35g; fibers: 3g; Sugars: 6g

Carrots and Kale with Chicken

Prep time: 15 minutes . | Cook Time: 27 minutes | Serves 2

½ cup couscous
1 cup water, divided
⅓ cup basil pesto
3 teaspoons olive oil, divided
3 (2-ounce / 57-g) whole carrots, rinsed, thinly sliced
Salt and ground black pepper, to taste
1 (about 6-ounce / 170-g) bunch kale, rinsed, stems removed, chopped
2 cloves garlic, minced
2 tablespoons dried currants
1 tablespoon red wine vinegar
2 (6-ounce / 170-g) boneless, skinless chicken breasts, rinsed
1 tablespoon Italian seasoning

In a pot, combine the couscous and ¾ cup of water. On high heat, bring to a boil. Reduce the heat to a low setting. Cook for 7 minutes, or until the liquid has almost completely evaporated.Mix in the basil pesto and fluff with a fork. In a nonstick skillet, heat 1 teaspoon olive oil over medium-high heat until it shimmers. Season with salt and pepper after adding the carrots Sauté the vegetables for 3 minutes, or until they are tender. Sauté the kale and garlic for 2 minutes, or until the kale has wilted somewhat. Add the currents and the remaining water to the pan and cook for 3 minutes, or until most of the liquid has evaporated. Remove the pan from the heat and add the red wine vinegar, stirring constantly. Place them in a large mixing bowl and cover with plastic wrap to keep warm. Rub the chicken with Italian seasoning, salt, and pepper on a clean work surface. Clean the skillet and heat 2 teaspoons olive oil until it shimmers over medium-high heat. Sear the chicken for 12 minutes, or until it is thoroughly browned. Rotate the chicken midway through the cooking time. Place the chicken on a big platter with the vegetables and couscous on top. To serve, cut into slices. Tip: Serve with beef stew or a leafy green salad to make it a complete dinner.

Nutritional information: Calories 461; Total Carbs 9g; Net Carbs 0g; Protein 57.0g; Fat 5.0g; Sugar 5g; Fiber 6.5 g

Turkey Meatball and Vegetable Kabobs

Prep time: 50 minutes . | Cook Time: 20 minutes | Serves 6

20 ounces (567 g) lean ground turkey (93% fat-free)
2 egg whites
2 tablespoons grated low-fat cheese
2 cloves garlic, minced
½ teaspoon salt, or to taste
¼ teaspoon ground black pepper
1 tablespoon olive oil
8 ounces (227 g) fresh cremini mushrooms, cut in half to make 12 pieces
24 cherry tomatoes
1 medium onion, cut into 12 pieces
¼ cup balsamic vinegar
Special Equipment:
12 bamboo skewers, soaking for at least 30 minutes in water

In a large mixing bowl, combine the ground turkey, egg whites, Parmesan, garlic, salt, and pepper. Stir everything together thoroughly. Make 12 meatballs out of the mixture and lay them on a baking sheet. At the very least, chill for 30 minutes. Preheat the oven to 375 degrees Fahrenheit (190 degrees Celsius) before beginning. 1 tablespoon olive oil is used to grease a second baking sheet. Take the meatballs out of the fridge. Alternate between 2 meatballs, 1 mushroom, 2 cherry tomatoes, and 1 onion piece on the bamboo skewers. Brush the kabobs with balsamic vinegar and place them on a prepared baking sheet. Grill for 20 minutes in a preheated oven, or until an instant-read thermometer placed in the center of the meatballs registers 165°F (74°C). Halfway during the cooking period, flip the kabobs. Allow 10 minutes for the kabobs to cool before serving heated. Tips: Grape tomatoes can be used in place of cherry tomatoes. When brushing the kabobs, set aside half of the balsamic vinegar; when turning, brush the kabobs with the reserved balsamic vinegar and extra olive oil. This will aid in evenly grilling the kabobs.

Nutritional information: Calories 200; Total Carbs 7g; Net Carbs 2g; Protein 22.0g; Fat 8.0g; Sugar 4g; Fiber 1 g

Jerked Chicken Breasts

Prep time: 4 hours 10 minutes . | Cook Time: 15 minutes | Serves 4

2 habanero chile peppers, halved lengthwise, seeded
½ sweet onion, cut into chunks
1 tablespoon minced garlic
1 tablespoon ground allspice
2 teaspoons chopped fresh thyme
¼ cup freshly squeezed lime juice
½ teaspoon ground nutmeg
¼ teaspoon ground cinnamon
1 teaspoon freshly ground black pepper
2 tablespoons extra-virgin olive oil
4 (5-ounce / 142-g) boneless, skinless chicken breasts
2 cups fresh arugula
1 cup halved cherry tomatoes

In a blender, combine the habanero peppers, onion, garlic, allspice, thyme, lime juice, nutmeg, cinnamon, black pepper, and olive oil. Toss everything into the blender and give it a good pulsing. Place the mixture in a large mixing basin or two medium mixing bowls, then submerge the chicken in the bowl and press to thoroughly coat it. Place the bowl in the refrigerator for at least 4 hours to marinate. Preheat the oven to 400 degrees Fahrenheit (205 degrees Celsius) before beginning. Take the bowl out of the fridge and toss out the marinade. Place the chicken on a baking sheet and roast for 15 minutes, or until golden brown and faintly charred in the oven. Midway through the cooking time, rotate the chicken. Allow 5 minutes after removing the baking sheet from the oven. Serve the chicken with arugula and cherry tomatoes on a big platter. Tip: To serve with the chicken, replace the arugula with the same amount of blanched spinach.

Nutritional information: Calories 226; Total Carbs 3g; Net Carbs 2g; Protein 33.0g; Fat 9.0g; Sugar 1g; Fiber 0 g

Strawberry and Peach Chicken

Prep Time: 20 minutes. | Cook Time: 40 minutes. | Servings: 4

For the barbecue sauce:
1 cup frozen peaches
1 cup frozen strawberries
¼ cup tomato purée
½ cup white vinegar
1 tablespoon yellow mustard
1 teaspoon mustard seeds
1 teaspoon turmeric
1 teaspoon sweet paprika
1 teaspoon garlic powder
½ teaspoon cayenne pepper
½ teaspoon onion powder
½ teaspoon freshly ground black pepper
1 teaspoon celery seeds
For the Chicken:
4 boneless, skinless chicken thighs

To Make the Barbecue Sauce In a saucepan, combine the peaches, strawberries, tomato puree, vinegar, mustard, mustard seeds, turmeric, paprika, garlic powder, cayenne pepper, onion powder, black pepper, and celery seeds. Cook over low heat for 15 minutes or until the flavors are well mixed. Remove the sauce from the heat and let cool for 5 minutes. Transfer the sauce to a blender and blend to a smooth puree. To Make the Chicken Preheat the oven to 350 ºF (180 ºC). Place chicken in a medium bowl. Coat well with ½ cup of BBQ sauce. Place the chicken on a rimmed baking sheet. Place a baking sheet on the rack in the middle of the oven and bake for 20 minutes (depending on the thickness of the chicken) or until the juice runs out. Pour the sauce over the chicken, return to the oven and cook over high heat for 3 to 5 minutes or until the crust is light brown. Serve immediately.

Nutritional information: Calories 190; Total Carbs 11g; Net Carbs 8g; Protein 23g; Fat 5g; Sugar 7g; Fiber 3g

Chicken Sandwiches with Caesar Dressing

Prep Time: 5 minutes. | Cook Time: 0 minutes. | Servings: 4

For the Dressing:
4 tablespoons plain low-fat Greek yogurt
4 teaspoons Dijon mustard
4 teaspoons freshly squeezed lemon juice
4 teaspoons shredded reduced-fat Parmesan cheese
¼ teaspoon freshly ground black pepper
⅛ teaspoon garlic powder
For the Sandwiches:
2 cups shredded rotisserie chicken
1½ cups chopped romaine lettuce
12 cherry tomatoes, halved
4 whole-wheat sandwich thins
¼ cup thinly sliced red onion (optional)

To Make the Dressing In a small bowl, combine the yogurt, mustard, lemon juice, Parmesan, pepper, and garlic powder. To Make the Sandwiches In a large bowl, combine the chicken, lettuce, and tomatoes. Add dressing and toss until evenly coated. Divide the filling into 4 equal parts. Cut the sandwiches thinly so that the top and bottom are ½ for each. Put some of the fillings in each of the bottom halves and cover with the top half.

Nutritional information: Calories 243; Total Carbs 24g; Net Carbs 1g; Protein 28g; Fat 5g; Sugar 4g; Fiber 8g

Turkey Spaghetti

Prep time: 5 minutes. | Cooking time: 20 minutes. | Servings: 4

1 (10-ounce) package zucchini noodles
2 tablespoons olive oil
1 pound 93% lean ground turkey
½ teaspoon dried oregano
2 cups spaghetti sauce
½ cup shredded sharp cheddar cheese

Pat zucchini noodles dry between 2 paper towels. In an oven-safe suitable skillet, heat 1 tablespoon of olive oil over medium heat. When hot, add the zucchini noodles. Cook for 3 minutes, stirring halfway through. Add the remaining 1 tablespoon of oil, ground turkey, and oregano. Cook for 7 to 10 minutes, stirring and breaking apart, as needed. Add the prepared spaghetti sauce to the skillet and stir. Place the turkey skillet on the oven rack in the center position. Set the broiler on high. Top the turkey mixture with the cheese, and broil for almost 5 minutes or until the cheese is bubbly.

Nutritional information: Calories: 335; Fats: 21g; Net Carbs 1g; Proteins: 28g; Total Carbs 12g fibers: 3g; Sugars: 4g

Turkey Stuffed Red Bell Peppers

Prep Time: 15 minutes. | Cook Time: 50 minutes. | Servings: 4

1 teaspoon extra-virgin olive oil, plus more for greasing the baking dish
1 pound (454 g) ground turkey breast
½ sweet onion, chopped
1 teaspoon minced garlic
1 tomato, diced
½ teaspoon chopped fresh basil
Sea salt and freshly ground black pepper, to taste
4 red bell peppers, tops cut off, seeded
2 ounces (57 g) low-sodium feta cheese

Preheat the oven to 350 ºF (180 ºC). Grease a baking dish with a little olive oil and set it aside. Put a large saucepan over medium heat and add 1 teaspoon of olive oil. Place the turkey in the pan and cook until it is not red. Shred the meat, stirring occasionally, and simmer for about 6 minutes until evenly browned. Add onion and garlic and sauté until tender and translucent, about 3 minutes. Combine the tomatoes and basil. Season with salt and pepper. Place the chopped peppers on a baking sheet. Divide the meat filling into 4 equal parts and fill in the peppers. Sprinkle feta cheese over the filling. Add ¼ cup of water to the plate and cover with foil. Bake for about 40 minutes until the peppers are tender and hot.

Nutritional information: Calories 282; Total Carbs 14g; Net Carbs 10g; Protein 24g; Fat 14g; Sugar 9g; Fiber 4g

Roasted Chicken Breast with Vegetables

Prep time: 08 minutes . | Cook Time: 20 minutes | Serves 4

1 seeded red bell pepper, cut into 1-inch-wide strips
½ small eggplant, cut into ¼-inch-thick slices
½ small red onion, sliced
1 medium zucchini, cut lengthwise into strips
1 tablespoon extra-virgin olive oil
Salt, to taste
ground black pepper, to taste
4 whole-wheat tortilla wraps
2 (8-ounce / 227-g) cooked chicken breasts, sliced

Preheat the oven to 400 degrees Fahrenheit (205 degrees Celsius) before beginning. A baking pan should be lined with aluminium foil. In a large mixing bowl, combine the bell pepper, eggplant, red onion, zucchini, and olive oil. Toss well to coat. Sprinkle salt and pepper over the vegetables before placing them on the baking pan. Roast for 20 minutes or until tender and browned in a preheated oven. On a clean work area, unfold the tortillas and divide the vegetables and chicken slices among them. Wrap and serve right away. Tip: Cooking Instructions for Chicken Breasts: Preheat the oven to 400 degrees Fahrenheit (205 degrees Celsius) before beginning. 1 tablespoon olive oil is used to grease a baking sheet. Place the chicken on the baking pan and bake for 24 minutes, or until the internal temperature of the chicken reaches 165 degrees Fahrenheit (74 degrees Celsius). Allow for cooling time before utilising the combination.

Nutritional information: Calories 483; Total Carbs 9g; Net Carbs 2g; Protein 20.0g; Fat 25.0g; Sugar 4g; Fiber 3 g

Chicken Pappardelle

Prep Time: 15 minutes. | Cook Time: 15 minutes. | Servings: 4

¾ pound (340 g) chicken breast, sliced lengthwise into ⅛-inch strips
1 small onion, sliced thin
8 cups spinach, chopped fine
4 cups low sodium chicken broth
1 cup fresh basil
2 quarts water
¼ cup reduced fat Parmesan cheese, divided
6 cloves garlic, diced
1 tablespoon walnuts, chopped
¼ teaspoon cinnamon
¼ teaspoon paprika
¼ teaspoon red pepper flakes
Salt, to taste
Olive oil cooking spray

Boil 2 liters of water in a medium saucepan. Sprinkle cooking spray lightly on a medium frying pan and place over medium-high heat. Add the garlic and cook until golden brown. Add the cinnamon, paprika, red pepper flakes, basil leaves, and onion. Simmer until onion is tender, about 2 minutes. Add the spinach and cook for another 2 minutes, until wilted and tender. Add the broth and bring to a boil, cover and cook until tender, about 5 minutes. Now add a pinch of salt to the boiling water. Turn the heat off, add the chicken and stir to separate all the strips.

Cook until the strips turn white. They will be half cooked. Using a spoon, transfer the strips to a plate to cool. Check the spinach mixture. Boil until the broth is almost evaporated. Add ½ cheese, mix, and season with salt. Add the chicken and toss into the batter and cook until the chicken strips are all cooked through about 90 seconds. Divide the mixture among 4 plates, top with cheese and serve.

Nutritional information: Calories 175; Total Carbs 7.1g; Net Carbs 4g; Protein 24.2g; Fat 5g; Sugar 2g; Fiber 2g

Worcestershire Turkey Meatballs

Prep Time: 10 minutes. | Cook Time: 20 minutes. | Servings: 4

¼ cup tomato paste
1 tablespoon honey
1 tablespoon Worcestershire sauce
½ cup milk
½ cup whole-wheat bread crumbs
1 pound (454 g) ground turkey
1 onion, grated
1 tablespoon Dijon mustard
1 teaspoon dried thyme
½ teaspoon sea salt

Preheat the oven to 375 °F (190 °C). Line the baking sheets with parchment paper. In a small saucepan over medium-low heat, combine the tomato paste, honey, and Worcestershire sauce. Bring to a boil and remove from heat. In a large bowl, combine the milk and breadcrumbs. Rest for 5 minutes. Add the ground turkey, onion, mustard, thyme, and salt. Mix well by hand without overdoing it. Make 1-inch meatballs and place them on a baking sheet. Brush the top with tomato paste. Bake in the oven until meatballs reach 165 °F (74 °C), about 15 minutes.

Nutritional information: Calories 286; Total Carbs 21g; Net Carbs 17g; Protein 24g; Fat 11g; Sugar 13.6g; Fiber 2.1g

Mexican Turkey Sliders

Prep Time: 15 minutes. | Cook Time: 6 minutes. | Servings: 7

1 pound (454 g) lean ground turkey
1 tablespoon chili powder
½ teaspoon garlic powder
¼ teaspoon ground black pepper
7 mini whole-wheat hamburger buns
7 tomato slices
3½ slices reduced-fat pepper Jack cheese, cut in ½
½ mashed avocado

Preheat the grill to high heat. Place turkey, pepper, garlic powder, chili powder, and black pepper in a large bowl. Stir to combine well. Divide the mixture into 7 patties evenly, then place the patties on a preheated grill. Bake for 6 minutes or until golden brown. Turn the patties in half. Place the patties with the buns, tomato slices, cheese slices, and mashed avocado in sliders, then serve immediately.

Nutritional information: Calories 225; Total Carbs 21g; Net Carbs 18g; Protein 17g; Fat 9g; Sugar 6g; Fiber 4g

Sesame Chicken and Cucumber Soba

Prep Time: 10 minutes. | Cook Time: 15 minutes. | Servings: 6

8 ounces (227 g) soba noodles
2 boneless, skinless chicken breasts, halved lengthwise
¼ cup tahini
1 tablespoon tamari
1 (1-inch) piece fresh ginger, finely grated
2 tablespoons rice vinegar
1 teaspoon toasted sesame oil
1/3 cup water
1 large cucumber, deseeded and diced
1 scallions bunch, green parts only, cut into 1-inch segments
1 tablespoon sesame seeds

Preheat the broiler to a high setting. Add the soba noodles to the salted boiling water and cook for 5 minutes or until al dente. Transfer to a plate and pat dry with a paper towel. Place the chicken in a layer on a baking sheet. Cook on preheated grill for 6 to 7 minutes or until chicken is tender. Transfer the chicken to a bowl and finely chop with a fork. In a small bowl, put the tahini, tamari, ginger, rice vinegar, sesame oil, and water. Stir to combine well. Place soba, chicken, cucumber, and scallions in a large bowl. Sprinkle with tahini sauce and toss to combine. Put the sesame seeds on it.

Nutritional information: Calories 253; Total Carbs 34.8g; Net Carbs 28g; Protein 16.1g; Fat 7.8g; Sugar 1.8g; Fiber 2.2g

Chicken Thighs with Dandelion Greens

Prep Time: 10 minutes. | Cook Time: 30 minutes. | Servings: 4

4 boneless, skinless chicken thighs
Juice of 1 lime
½ cup white vinegar
2 garlic cloves, smashed
1 cup frozen peaches
½ cup water
Pinch ground cinnamon
Pinch ground cloves
Pinch ground nutmeg
1/8 teaspoon vanilla extract
½ cup low-sodium chicken broth
1 bunch dandelion greens, cut into ribbons
1 medium onion, thinly sliced

Preheat your oven to get ready for broil. In a bowl, put the chicken, lime juice, vinegar, and garlic to coat the chicken well. Meanwhile, prepare the peach frosting by mixing the peach, water, cinnamon, cloves, nutmeg, and vanilla in a small saucepan. Cook over medium heat, stirring frequently, for 10 minutes or until the peaches are tender. In a large cast-iron skillet, bring the broth to a boil over medium heat. Add the dandelion greens and sauté for 5 minutes or until the vegetables are tender. Add the onions and cook for 3 minutes or until soft, stirring occasionally. Add the chicken and cover with the peach frosting. Transfer the pan to the oven and cook for 10 to 12 minutes or until the chicken is golden brown.

Nutritional information: Calories 201; Total Carbs 13g; Net Carbs 9g; Protein 24g; Fat 4.9g; Sugar 6g; Fiber 4.1g

Chicken and Veggies Roast

Prep Time: 10 minutes. | Cook Time: 40 minutes. | Servings: 6

¼ cup olive oil, divided
½ head cabbage, cut into 2-inch chunks
1 sweet potato, peeled and cut into 1-inch chunks
1 onion, peeled and cut into eighths
4 garlic cloves, peeled and lightly crushed
2 teaspoons fresh thyme, minced
Salt and freshly ground black pepper, to taste
2½ pounds (1.1 kg) bone-in chicken thighs and drumsticks

Preheat the oven to 450 ºF (235 ºC). Grease 1 tablespoon of olive oil in a roasting pan. Place the cabbage, potatoes, onions, and garlic in a roasting pan. Sprinkle with thyme, salt, and pepper and pour 1 tablespoon of olive oil on top. Separate. On a clean work surface, rub the chicken with salt and pepper. Heat 2 tablespoons of olive oil in a large skillet over medium heat. Place the chicken in the pan and cook for 10 minutes or until lightly browned on both sides. Turn the chicken halfway through the cooking time. Place the chicken over the vegetables in a roasting pan and bake in a preheated oven for 30 minutes until the internal temperature of the chicken reaches 165 ºF (74 ºC).
Remove from the oven and serve hot on a large plate.

Nutritional information: Calories 542; Total Carbs 13g; Net Carbs 8g; Protein 43g; Fat 33g; Sugar 4g; Fiber 4.1g

Indian Creamy Curry Chicken

Prep Time: 15 minutes. | Cook Time: 35 minutes. | Servings: 4

2 teaspoons olive oil
3 (5-ounce / 142-g) boneless, skinless chicken breasts, cut into 1-inch chunks
1 tablespoon garlic, minced
2 tablespoons curry powder
1 tablespoon fresh ginger, grated
1 cup unsweetened coconut milk
2 cups low-sodium chicken broth
1 sweet potato, diced
1 carrot, peeled and diced
2 tablespoons fresh cilantro, chopped

Heat olive oil in a saucepan over medium-high heat. Place the chicken in the saucepan and sauté for 10 minutes until all sides are golden. Add the garlic, curry powder, and ginger to the pan and sauté for 3 minutes until fragrant. Pour the coconut milk and the chicken into the pot and add the sweet potatoes and carrots to the pot. Stir to combine well. Bring to a boil. Reduce heat to low and simmer for 20 minutes until tender. Stir from time to time. Pour it into a large bowl and sprinkle cilantro over it before eating.

Nutritional information: Calories 328; Total Carbs 14g; Net Carbs 9g; Protein 29g; Fat 16.9g; Sugar 3.9g; Fiber 1.1g

Herbed Turkey and Vegetable Roast

Prep Time: 20 minutes. | Cook Time: 2 hours. | Servings: 6

1 tablespoon fresh parsley, chopped
1 teaspoon fresh rosemary, chopped
1 teaspoon fresh thyme, chopped
2 teaspoons garlic, minced
Salt and freshly ground black pepper, to taste
2 pounds (907 g) boneless, skinless whole turkey breast
3 teaspoons extra-virgin olive oil, divided
2 carrots, peeled and cut into 2-inch chunks
1 sweet onion, peeled and cut into eighths
2 parsnips, peeled and cut into 2-inch chunks
2 sweet potatoes, peeled and cut into 2-inch chunks

Preheat the oven to 350 ºF (180 ºC). Combine parsley, rosemary, thyme, garlic, salt, and pepper in a bowl. Arrange the chicken breasts in a roasting pan with foil. Take 1 teaspoon of olive oil on each side. Rub with the parsley mixture. Bake in preheated oven for 30 minutes. Meanwhile, pour additional olive oil into a large bowl. Place the carrots, onions, parsnips, and sweet potatoes in a bowl. Mix well. Place the vegetables around the turkey, return the pan to the oven and cook for another half hour until the turkey has reached a temperature of 165 ºF (74 ºC). Serve hot and enjoy.

Nutritional information: Calories 274; Total Carbs 19.7g; Net Carbs 12g; Protein 38g; Fat 2.8g; Sugar 5.8g; Fiber 4.2g

Golden Chicken Tenders

Prep Time: 10 minutes. | Cook Time: 15 minutes. | Servings: 4

1 cup whole-wheat bread crumbs
1 tablespoon dried thyme
1 teaspoon garlic powder
1 teaspoon paprika
½ teaspoon sea salt
3 large eggs, beaten
1 tablespoon Dijon mustard
1 pound (454 g) chicken, cut into ½-inch-thick pieces and pounded to even thickness

Preheat the oven to 375 ºF (190 ºC). Line the baking pan with parchment paper edges. In a large bowl, combine the breadcrumbs, thyme, garlic powder, paprika, and salt. Beat together eggs and mustard in another bowl. Put each chicken in the egg mixture and then in the breadcrumb mixture. Place on a prepared baking sheet. Bake for 15 minutes until the chicken has reached a temperature of 165ºF (74ºC) and the breadcrumbs are golden brown.

Nutritional information: Calories 277; Total Carbs 16.9g; Net Carbs 12g; Protein 34.1g; Fat 6.1g; Sugar 8g; Fiber 3g

Yogurt Chicken Salad Sandwiches

Prep Time: 10 minutes. | Cook Time: 10 minutes. | Servings: 4

2 (4-ounce / 113-g) boneless, skinless chicken breasts
⅛ teaspoon freshly ground black pepper
1½ tablespoons plain low-fat Greek yogurt
¼ cup halved purple seedless grapes
¼ cup chopped pecans
2 tablespoons chopped celery
4 whole-wheat sandwich thins
Avocado oil cooking spray

Heat a small saucepan over medium-low heat. When hot, shake the sides with cooking spray. Sprinkle pepper on the chicken. Put the chicken in a pan and cook for 6 minutes. Flip and cook for another 3 to 5 minutes, or until cooked through. Remove the chicken from the pan and let it cool for 5 minutes. Chop or mash the chicken. Serve with chicken, yogurt, berries, pecans, and celery. Cut the sandwich in half finely so that it is on the top and bottom. Divide the chicken salad into 4 equal parts and thinly pour half of the sandwiches, then cover with the top half.

Nutritional information: Calories 251; Total Carbs 23g; Net Carbs 15g; Protein 23g; Fat 8g; Sugar 4g; Fiber 6g

Chicken with Couscous

Prep Time: 15 minutes. | Cook Time: 27 minutes. | Servings: 2

½ cup couscous
1 cup water, divided
⅓ cup basil pesto
3 teaspoons olive oil, divided
3 (2-ounce / 57-g) whole carrots, rinsed, thinly sliced
Salt and ground black pepper, to taste
1 (about 6-ounce / 170-g) bunch kale, rinsed, stems removed, chopped
2 cloves garlic, minced
2 tablespoons dried currants
1 tablespoon red wine vinegar
2 (6-ounce / 170-g) boneless, skinless chicken breasts, rinsed
1 tablespoon Italian seasoning

Pour the couscous and ¾ cup of water into the pot. Bring to a boil over high heat. Reduce the heat to low. Boil for 7 minutes or until most of the water is absorbed. Crisp with a fork and stir in the basil pesto. Add 1 teaspoon of olive oil to a nonstick skillet and heat over medium-high heat until cooked through. Add the carrots, then season with salt and pepper. Cook for 3 minutes or until tender. Add kale and garlic and sauté for 2 minutes or until onions are lightly wilted. Add water and sauté for 3 minutes or until most of the water is cooked through. Lower the heat and stir in the red wine vinegar. Transfer them to a large bowl and cover to keep warm. On a clean surface, sauté the chicken with Italian seasoning, salt, and pepper. Clean the pan and heat over medium-high heat until 2 teaspoons of olive oil boil. Add the chicken and cook for 12 minutes or until golden brown. Turn the chicken halfway through the cooking time. Transfer the chicken to a large plate and sprinkle with vegetables and couscous.

Nutritional information: Calories 461; Total Carbs 26g; Net Carbs 18g; Protein 57g; Fat 14g; Sugar 5g; Fiber 6g

Chicken with Balsamic Kale

Prep Time: 5 minutes. | Cook Time: 15 minutes. | Servings: 4

4 (4-ounce / 113-g) boneless, skinless chicken breasts
¼ teaspoon salt
1 tablespoon freshly ground black pepper
2 tablespoons unsalted butter
1 tablespoon extra-virgin olive oil
8 cups stemmed and roughly chopped kale, loosely packed (about 2 bunches)
½ cup balsamic vinegar
20 cherry tomatoes, halved

Season both sides of the chicken breast with salt and pepper. Heat a large saucepan over medium heat. Heat the butter and oil. Add the chicken and cook for 8 to 10 minutes, turning halfway through cooking. When finished cooking, remove the chicken from the pan and set it aside. Increase the heat to medium-high heat. Place the peppers in the pan and cook for 3 minutes, stirring every minute. Add the vinegar and tomatoes and cook for another 3 minutes to 5 minutes. Combine kale and tomatoes into 4 equal pieces and place 1 chicken breast in each.

Nutritional information: Calories 294; Total Carbs 17g; Net Carbs 12g; Protein 31g; Fat 11g; Sugar 4g; Fiber 3g

Asian Chicken and Edamame Stir-Fry

Prep Time: 10 minutes. | Cook Time: 10 minutes. | Servings: 4

3 tablespoons extra-virgin olive oil
1 pound (454 g) chicken breasts or thighs, cut into ¾-inch pieces
2 cups edamame or pea pods
3 garlic cloves, chopped
1 tablespoon peeled and grated fresh ginger
2 tablespoons reduced-sodium soy sauce
Juice of 2 limes
1 teaspoon sesame oil
2 teaspoons toasted sesame seeds
1 tablespoon chopped fresh cilantro

Heat olive oil in a large saucepan over medium-high heat until cooked through. Add the chicken to the oil and cook, stirring occasionally, until opaque, about 5 minutes. Add the peas and cook, stirring occasionally, until tender and crisp, 3 to 5 minutes. Add the garlic and ginger and cook for 30 seconds, stirring constantly. Combine soy sauce, lemon juice, and sesame oil in a small bowl. Add the sauce mixture to the pan. Bring to a boil over low heat, stirring, and simmer for 2 minutes. Remove from heat and garnish with sesame seeds and cilantro.

Nutritional information: Calories 332; Total Carbs 10g; Net Carbs 5g; Protein 31.1g; Fat 17.1g; Sugar 5g; Fiber 5g

Pecan Chicken Enchiladas

Prep Time: 20 minutes. | Cook Time: 45 minutes. | Servings: 12

1 onion, diced

4 cups chicken breast, cooked and cubed
1 cup fat free sour cream
1 cup skim milk
4 ounces (113 g) low fat cream cheese
½ cup reduced fat cheddar cheese, grated
2 tablespoons cilantro, diced
12 (6-inch) flour tortillas, warm
1 can low fat condensed cream of chicken soup
¼ cup pecans, toasted
2 tablespoons green chilies, diced
1 tablespoon water
1 teaspoon cumin
¼ teaspoon pepper
⅛ teaspoon salt
Nonstick cooking spray

Preheat the oven to 350 ºF (180 ºC). Spray the baking dish with cooking spray. Sprinkle a little cooking spray on a nonstick skillet and place it over medium heat. Add the onions and cook until tender. In a large bowl, whisk cream cheese, water, cumin, salt, and pepper until smooth. Stir in the onions, chicken, and pecans. Place ⅓ cup of the chicken mixture in the center of each tortilla. Roll it in a baking dish and lay it seam-side down. In a medium bowl, combine the soup, sour cream, milk, and pepper and pour over the enchiladas. Cover with foil and bake for 40 minutes. Open the lid, sprinkle the cheese on top, and cook for another 5 minutes until the cheese is melted. Sprinkle with cilantro and serve.

Nutritional information: Calories 321; Total Carbs 2g; Net Carbs 18g; Protein 21.2g; Fat 13g; Sugar 4g; Fiber 2g

Turkey and Cabbage Broth

Prep Time: 15 minutes. | Cook Time: 30 minutes. | Servings: 4

1 tablespoon olive oil
2 celery stalks, chopped
2 teaspoons fresh garlic, minced
1 sweet onion, chopped
1 sweet potato, peeled, diced
4 cups green cabbage, finely shredded
8 cups low-sodium chicken broth
2 bay leaves
1 cup cooked turkey, chopped
2 teaspoons fresh thyme, chopped
Salt and freshly ground black pepper, to taste

Place olive oil in a large saucepan and heat over medium heat. Add the celery, garlic, and onion to the pot and sauté for 3 minutes until the onions are translucent. Put the sweet potatoes and cabbage in the pan and cook for 3 minutes until the vegetables are slightly soft. Pour the chicken broth into the pan and add the bay leaves. Bring to a boil. Reduce the heat to low and simmer for 20 minutes until the vegetables are tender. Add the turkey and thyme to the pan and cook for 4 minutes until the turkey is heated through. Pour the chicken broth into a large bowl and discard the leafy greens. Season with salt and pepper to taste before cooking.

Nutritional information: Calories 328; Total Carbs 29.8g; Net Carbs 18.8g; Protein 24.1g; Fat 10g; Sugar 12g; Fiber 4.2g

Chicken Leg Roast

Prep Time: 10 minutes. | Cook Time: 35 minutes. | Servings: 6

1 teaspoon ground paprika
1 teaspoon garlic powder
½ teaspoon ground coriander
½ teaspoon ground cumin
½ teaspoon salt
¼ teaspoon ground cayenne pepper
6 chicken legs
1 teaspoon extra-virgin olive oil

Preheat the oven to 400 °F (205 °C). In a bowl, put the cilantro, cumin, paprika, garlic powder, salt, and cayenne pepper. Dip the chicken thighs in the mixture to coat them well. Heat olive oil in a pan over medium heat. Add the chicken and cook for 9 minutes or until golden brown and crisp. Turn the thighs halfway through cooking. Place the skillet in the oven and bake for 14 minutes or until the chicken reaches a temperature of 165 °F (74 °C). Take the chicken out of the oven and serve hot.

Nutritional information: Calories 278; Total Carbs 0.8g; Net Carbs 0.1g; Protein 30g; Fat 15g; Sugar 0g; Fiber 0g

Creamy Chicken with Quinoa and Broccoli

Prep Time: 5 minutes. | Cook Time: 15 minutes. | Servings: 4

½ cup uncooked quinoa
4 (4-ounce / 113-g) boneless, skinless chicken breasts
1 teaspoon garlic powder, divided
¼ teaspoon salt
¼ teaspoon freshly ground black pepper
1 tablespoon avocado oil
3 cups fresh or frozen broccoli, cut into florets
1 cup half-and-half

Put the quinoa in a saucepan with salted water. Bring to a boil. Reduce the heat and simmer for 15 minutes or until the quinoa is tender and the "tails" are white. Leave it for 5 minutes. In a clean area, rub the chicken with ½ teaspoon of garlic powder, salt, and pepper. Heat avocado oil in a nonstick skillet over medium-low heat. Place the chicken and broccoli in a skillet and cook for 9 minutes or until the chicken is golden brown and the broccoli is tender. Turn the chicken over and shake the pan halfway through cooking. Pour half-and-half into the pan and sprinkle with added garlic powder. Increase heat and simmer until creamy, about 2 minutes. Serve hot with rice, chicken breast, and florets of broccoli with the rest of the sauce.

Nutritional information: Calories 305; Total Carbs 21.8g; Net Carbs 15g; Protein 33g; Fat 9.8g; Sugar 3.9g; Fiber 9.8g

Herbed Chicken and Artichoke Hearts

Prep Time: 10 minutes. | Cook Time: 20 minutes. | Servings: 4

2 tablespoons olive oil, divided

4 (6-ounce / 170-g) boneless, skinless chicken breast halves
½ teaspoon dried thyme, divided
1 teaspoon crushed dried rosemary, divided
½ teaspoon ground black pepper, divided
2 (14-ounce / 397-g) cans water-packed, low-sodium artichoke hearts, drained and quartered
½ cup low-sodium chicken broth
2 garlic cloves, chopped
1 medium onion, coarsely chopped
¼ cup low-fat shredded Parmesan cheese
1 lemon, cut into 8 slices
2 green onions, thinly sliced

Preheat the oven to 375 °F (190 °C). Use 1 teaspoon of olive oil on a baking sheet. Place the chicken on a baking sheet and toss with ¼ teaspoon of thyme, ½ teaspoon of rosemary, 1 teaspoon of pepper and 1 teaspoon of olive oil. Add the artichoke heart, chicken broth, garlic, onion, remaining thyme, rosemary, black pepper and olive oil. Mix well. Use artichokes around the chicken breast and sprinkle with Parmesan and lemon slices. Place the baking sheet in a preheated oven and bake for 20 minutes or until the chicken breast has reached a temperature of 165 °F (74 °C). Take the form out of the oven. Let cool for 10 minutes, then place the green onions on top.

Nutritional information: Calories 339; Total Carbs 18g; Net Carbs 12g; Protein 42g; Fat 9g; Sugar 2g; Fiber 1g

Ritzy Jerked Chicken Breasts

Prep Time: 4 hours 10 minutes. | Cook Time: 15 minutes. | Servings: 4

2 habanero chile peppers, halved lengthwise, seeded
½ sweet onion, cut into chunks
1 tablespoon minced garlic
1 tablespoon ground allspice
2 teaspoons chopped fresh thyme
¼ cup freshly squeezed lime juice
½ teaspoon ground nutmeg
¼ teaspoon ground cinnamon
1 teaspoon freshly ground black pepper
2 tablespoons extra-virgin olive oil
4 (5-ounce / 142-g) boneless, skinless chicken breasts
2 cups fresh arugula
1 cup halved cherry tomatoes

Combine the habanero, onion, garlic, allspice, thyme, lemon juice, nutmeg, cinnamon, pepper, and olive oil in a blender. Mix well in a blender. Transfer mixture to 2 large or medium bowls, place chicken in a bowl, and coat well. Put the chicken in the refrigerator and let marinate for at least 4 hours. Preheat the oven to 400 °F (205 °C). Take the bowl out of the refrigerator and discard the marinade. Place the chicken on a baking sheet and bake in a preheated oven for 15 minutes or until golden brown and lightly charred. Turn the chicken halfway through the cooking time. Remove the foil from the oven and let stand for 5 minutes. Transfer the chicken to a large plate and serve with arugula and tomatoes.

Nutritional information: Calories 226; Total Carbs 3g; Net Carbs 1g; Protein 33g; Fat 9g; Sugar 1g; Fiber 0g

Chicken Lettuce Salad

Prep time: 10 minutes. | Cooking time: 15 minutes. | Servings: 2

1 garlic clove
½ teaspoon anchovy paste
Juice of ½ lemon
2 tablespoons olive oil
1 (8-ounce) boneless chicken breast
¼ teaspoon salt
Black pepper, to taste
2 romaine lettuce hearts, cored and chopped
1 red bell pepper, julienned
¼ cup grated parmesan cheese

Preheat the broiler to high. In a blender jar, combine the garlic, anchovy paste, lemon juice, and olive oil. Process until smooth and set aside. Cut the chicken breast lengthwise into 2 even cutlets of similar thickness. Season the sliced chicken with some black pepper and salt, and place on a baking sheet. Broil the chicken for almost 5 to 7 minutes on each side until cooked through and browned. Julienned. In a suitable mixing bowl, toss the lettuce, bell pepper, and cheese. Add the dressing and toss to coat. Divide the prepared salad between 2 plates and top with the chicken.

Nutritional information: Calories: 292; Total Carbs 6g; Net Carbs 1g; Proteins: 28g; Fats: 18g; fibers: 2g; Sugars: 3g

Chicken Breast with Artichoke Hearts

Prep time: 08 minutes . | Cook Time: 18 minutes | Serves 4

2 tablespoons olive oil, divided
4 boneless, skinless chicken breast halves (6 oz / 170-g)
½ teaspoon dried thyme, divided
1 teaspoon crushed dried rosemary, divided
½ teaspoon ground black pepper, divided
2 (14-ounce/397-g) cans water-packed, low-sodium artichoke hearts, drained and quartered
½ cup low-sodium chicken broth
2 garlic cloves, chopped
1 medium onion, coarsely chopped
¼ cup shredded low-fat Parmesan cheese
1 lemon, cut into 8 slices
2 green onions, thinly sliced

Preheat the oven at 375 degrees Fahrenheit (190 degrees Celsius) before beginning. Oil the baking sheet with 1 teaspoon of the olive oil. Rub ¼ teaspoon thyme, ½ teaspoon rosemary, 14 teaspoon black pepper, and 1 tablespoon olive oil into the chicken breasts on the baking sheet. Combine the artichoke hearts, chicken broth, garlic, onion, and the rest of the thyme, rosemary, black pepper, and olive oil in a large mixing bowl. Toss well to coat. Arrange the artichokes around the chicken breasts, then top with Parmesan cheese and lemon wedges. Place the baking sheet in a preheated oven and roast for 20 minutes, or until the chicken breasts reach an internal temperature of 165°F (74°C). Take the baking sheet out of the oven. Allow 10 minutes to cool before serving with green onions on top. Tip: You can use the same quantity of white wine in place of the chicken broth.

Nutritional information: Calories 339; Total Carbs 18g; Net Carbs 15g; Protein 42.0g; Fat 9.0g; Sugar 2g; Fiber 1 g

Limey Grilled Chicken

Prep time: 10 minutes. | Cooking time: 25 minutes. | Servings: 8

8 boneless chicken breast halves (4 ounces)
½ cup lime juice
⅓ cup olive oil
4 green onions, chopped
4 garlic cloves, minced
3 tablespoons chopped dill
¼ teaspoon black pepper

Flatten the chicken breasts into ¼-inch. Mix together the 2-tablespoon pepper and dill, garlic, onions, oil and lime juice in a Ziploc plastic bag, then add the chicken. Seal the bag securely and flip to coat, then let it chill in the fridge for almost 2-4 hours. Drain and get rid of the marinade. Grill the chicken for 6-7 minutes per side on medium-hot heat without a cover or until a thermometer reads 170 degrees F. Sprinkle the leftover dill on top.

Nutritional information: Calories: 235; Total Carbs 3g; Net Carbs 1g; Proteins: 27g Sodium: 66 mg Fat 10g; Sugar 1g; Fiber 2g

Cashew Chicken

Prep Time: 10 minutes. | Cook Time: 10 minutes. | Servings: 4

1 pound (454 g) skinless boneless chicken breast, cut in cubes
½ onion, sliced
2 tablespoons green onion, diced
½ teaspoon fresh ginger, peeled and grated
1 cup whole blanched cashews, toasted
1 clove garlic, diced fine
4 tablespoons oil
2 tablespoons dark soy sauce
2 tablespoons hoisin sauce
2 tablespoons water
2 teaspoons cornstarch
2 teaspoons dry sherry
1 teaspoon Splenda
1 teaspoon sesame seed oil

Place the chicken in a large bowl and add the cornstarch, sherry, and ginger. Stir until well mixed. In a small bowl, combine the sauce, hoisin, Splenda, and water and stir until smooth. Heat the oil in a wok or large saucepan over high heat. Add the garlic and onion and simmer until the garlic sizzles, about 30 seconds. Add the chicken and cook, stirring frequently, until the chicken is almost cooked through, about 2 minutes. Reduce the heat to medium and stir in the sauce. Continue to cook and stir until combined. Add the cashews and cook for 30 seconds. Drizzle with sesame oil and cook for another 30 seconds, stirring constantly. Garnish with green onions.

Nutritional information: Calories 484; Total Carbs 19g; Net Carbs 15g; Protein 33g; Fat 32g; Sugar 6.1g; Fiber 2.2g

Greek Chicken Sandwiches

Prep Time: 10 minutes. | Cook Time: 0 minutes. | Servings: 3

3 slices 100% whole-wheat bread, toasted
3 tablespoons red pepper hummus
3 cups arugula
¾ cup cucumber slices
1 cup rotisserie chicken, shredded
¼ cup sliced red onion
Oregano, for garnish (optional)

Place the toast on a clean baking sheet and sprinkle 1 tablespoon of red pepper hummus on each slice of bread. Place each arugula, cucumber slices, chicken, and red onion evenly on each slice of bread. Garnish with oregano, if desired, and serve.

Nutritional information: Calories 227; Total Carbs 24g; Net Carbs 19g; Protein 23g; Fat 6.1g; Sugar 4.1g; Fiber 4g

Turkey Zoodles with Spaghetti Sauce

Prep Time: 5 minutes. | Cook Time: 20 minutes. | Servings: 4

1 (10-ounce / 284-g) package zucchini noodles, rinsed and patted dry
2 tablespoons olive oil, divided
1 pound (454 g) 93% lean ground turkey
½ teaspoon dried oregano
2 cups low-sodium spaghetti sauce
½ cup low-fat Cheddar cheese, shredded

Preheat the broiler to a high temperature. Heat 1 tablespoon of olive oil in an ovenproof skillet over medium heat. Place the noodles in the pan and cook for 3 minutes until tender. Stir the noodles several times. Drizzle with additional olive oil, then add the ground turkey and oregano to the pan. Cook 8 minutes until the turkey is golden brown. Pour the spaghetti sauce over the turkey and stir to combine. Spread cheddar cheese on top and cook in preheated grills for 5 minutes until cheese is melted and foamy. Remove from the grill and serve hot.

Nutritional information: Calories 337; Total Carbs 20g; Net Carbs 18g; Protein 27g; Fat 20g; Sugar 3.8g; Fiber 3.2g

Blackened Spatchcock with Lime Aioli

Prep Time: 15 minutes. | Cook Time: 45 minutes. | Servings: 6

4 pounds (1.8 kg) chicken, spatchcocked
3 tablespoons blackened seasoning
2 tablespoons olive oil
Lime Aioli:
½ cup mayonnaise
Juice and zest of 1 lime
¼ teaspoon kosher salt
¼ teaspoon ground black pepper

Preheat the grill to medium high heat. Rub the chicken with the blackened seasoning and olive oil on a clean work surface. Place the chicken in a preheated oven and bake on the skin side up for 45 minutes or until the chicken is 74ºC (165ºF).

Meanwhile, put the Ingredients for the aioli in a small bowl and stir to combine well. When the chicken is completely browned, transfer it to a large plate and sprinkle with lime aioli. Cool and help.

Nutritional information: Calories 436; Total Carbs 6.8g; Net Carbs 2g; Protein 61.7g; Fat 16.3g; Sugar 1.4g; Fiber 0.7g

Arroz Con Pollo

Prep Time: 10 minutes. | Cook Time: 25 minutes. | Servings: 4

1 onion, diced
1 red pepper, diced
2 cup chicken breast, cooked and cubed
1 cup cauliflower, grated
1 cup peas, thaw
2 tablespoons cilantro, diced
½ teaspoon lemon zest
14½ ounces (411 g) low-sodium chicken broth
¼ cup black olives, sliced
¼ cup sherry
1 clove garlic, diced
2 teaspoons olive oil
¼ teaspoon salt
¼ teaspoon cayenne pepper

Heat the oil in a large saucepan over medium-high heat. Add the pepper, onion, and garlic and cook for 1 minute. Add the cauliflower and cook, stirring frequently, until light brown, 4 to 5 minutes. Stir in the broth, sherry, zest, and seasonings. Bring to a boil. Lower the heat, cover, and simmer for 15 minutes. Stir in the chicken, peas, and olives. Cover and simmer for 3 to 6 minutes or until completely heated through. Garnish with cilantro and serve.

Nutritional information: Calories 162; Total Carbs 13g; Net Carbs 9g; Protein 14g; Fat 5g; Sugar 5g; Fiber 4.2g

Roasted Vegetable and Chicken Tortillas

Prep Time: 10 minutes. | Cook Time: 20 minutes. | Servings: 4

1 red bell pepper, seeded and cut into 1-inch-wide strips
½ small eggplant, cut into ¼-inch-thick slices
½ small red onion, sliced
1 medium zucchini, cut lengthwise into strips
1 tablespoon extra-virgin olive oil
Salt and freshly ground black pepper, to taste
4 whole-wheat tortilla wraps
2 (8-ounce / 227-g) cooked chicken breasts, sliced

Preheat the oven to 400 ºF (205 ºC). Prepare the baking sheet with foil. In a large bowl, put the bell peppers, eggplant, red onion, zucchini, and olive oil. Mix well. Pour the vegetables on the baking sheet and sprinkle with salt and pepper. Bake in preheated oven for 20 minutes or until tender and charred. Spread the tortillas out on a clean surface, then divide the vegetables and chicken into tortillas.Wrap and serve immediately.

Nutritional information: Calories 483; Total Carbs 45g; Net Carbs 28g; Protein 20g; Fat 25g; Sugar 4g; Fiber 4g

Coconut-Encrusted Chicken

Prep Time: 10 minutes. | Cook Time: 20 minutes. | Servings: 6

4 chicken breasts, each cut lengthwise into 3 strips
½ teaspoon salt
¼ teaspoon freshly ground black pepper
2 eggs
2 tablespoons unsweetened plain almond milk
½ cup coconut flour
1 cup unsweetened coconut flakes

Preheat the oven to 400 ºF (205 ºC). On a clean work surface, rub the chicken with salt and pepper. Combine the eggs and almond milk in a bowl. Put the coconut powder in another bowl. Place the coconut flakes in the third bowl. Place the chicken in a bowl of flour, then dredge the egg mixture and dip it in the coconut flakes. Shake excess off. Arrange the chicken well coated in an ovenproof dish lined with parchment paper. Bake in preheated oven for 16 minutes. Turn the chicken for half the cooking time or until golden brown. Take the chicken out of the oven and place it on a plate.

Nutritional information: Calories 218; Total Carbs 8.8g; Net Carbs 4g; Protein 20g; Fat 12g; Sugar 1.8g; Fiber 6.1g

Chicken Zucchini Patties with Salsa

Prep Time: 10 minutes. | Cook Time: 10 minutes. | Servings: 8

2 cup chicken breast, cooked, divided
1 zucchini, cut in ¾-inch pieces
¼ cup cilantro, diced
1/3 cup bread crumbs
1/3 cup lite mayonnaise
2 teaspoons olive oil
½ teaspoon salt
¼ teaspoon pepper
Roasted Tomato Salsa:
6 plum tomatoes
1¼ cups cilantro
2 teaspoons olive oil
1 teaspoon adobo sauce
½ teaspoon salt, divided
Nonstick cooking spray

Place 1½ cups of chicken and zucchini in a food processor. Cover and mix until coarsely chopped. Add the breadcrumbs, mayonnaise, pepper, cilantro, remaining chicken, and salt. Cover and pulse until chunky. Heat the oil in a large saucepan over medium-high heat. Shape the chicken into 8 patties and cook 4 minutes for each side or until golden brown. Meanwhile, combine the salsa Ingredients in a small bowl. Serve the patties topped with salsa.

Nutritional information: Calories 147; Total Carbs 10g; Net Carbs 6g; Protein 12.2g; Fat 7g; Sugar 5g; Fiber 2g

Roasted Duck Legs with Balsamic Mushrooms

Prep Time: 15 minutes. | Cook Time: 1 hour. | Servings: 4

4 bone-in, skin-on duck legs
½ pound (227 g) cremini mushrooms, remove stems and cut caps into thick slices
1 green onion, sliced thin
1 small shallot, sliced thin
3 to 4 fresh thyme sprigs, crushed lightly
5 tablespoons extra-virgin olive oil
5 tablespoons balsamic vinegar
2 cloves garlic, sliced thin
½ teaspoon fresh thyme, chopped
Kosher salt and freshly ground pepper

Rinse the duck and dry it with a paper towel. In a shallow bowl large enough for the ducks, put 3 tablespoons of oil, 3 tablespoons of vinegar, garlic, shallots, thyme sprigs, ½ teaspoon of salt and a little pepper. Add the ducks and toss to coat. Cover the lid and turn the thighs 1 to 2 times to cool for 3 to 4 hours. Remove the duck from the marinade. Pour the marinade into a saucepan and bring to a boil over high heat. Place the rack with the base at the bottom of the pot large enough that your duck feet stand 2 inches off the ground. Add about 1 inch of water. Place the ducks on the grill, skin side down. Cover with a lid and cook over medium-high heat. Steam until the skin is translucent, about 20 minutes. While the duck cooks, preheat the oven to 450 ºF (235 ºC). Line a skillet large enough to hold the duck in foil. Place the counter flat on the platter. When the duck is ready, transfer it to a ready-to-use oven, skin side down. Glaze the skin and bake for 20 minutes until the skin is golden and crisp. Take out of the oven and reglaze the duck. Rest for 5 minutes. Heat the oil in a large saucepan over medium-high heat. Add the mushrooms and green onions and simmer for 2 minutes, stirring frequently. Add the remaining vinegar, minced thyme, salt and pepper to taste. Cook until mushrooms are tender and most of the liquid has evaporated. To serve, place the duck legs on a plate and spoon in the mushrooms.

Nutritional information: Calories 375; Total Carbs 4.1g; Net Carbs 2g; Protein 26.7g; Fat 28.2g; Sugar 1g; Fiber 1g

Broiled Garlicky Chicken

Prep Time: 15 minutes. | Cook Time: 30 minutes. | Servings: 4

2 ½ pounds chicken, quartered
6 cloves garlic
¾ teaspoon powdered rosemary
Salt & pepper to taste
Chicken bouillon

Rub the chicken with 2 cloves of garlic and rosemary. Also add pepper and salt. Rest the chicken for 30 minutes. Place the chicken on the grill pan and coat with the bouillon. Add a little broth to the pan. When half cooked, turn over and cook. Add the broth and add 2 or more garlic cloves to cover the top. Season with leftover sauce. Serve and enjoy!

Nutritional information: Calories 324; Total Carbs 7.7g; Net Carbs 4.8g; Protein 27g; Fat 22g; Sugar 6.1g; Fiber 2g

Turkey Taco

Prep Time: 10 minutes. | Cook Time: 20 minutes. | Servings: 4

3 tablespoons extra-virgin olive oil
1 pound (454 g) ground turkey
1 onion, chopped
1 green bell pepper, seeded and chopped
½ teaspoon sea salt
1 small head cauliflower, grated
1 cup corn kernels
½ cup prepared salsa
1 cup shredded pepper Jack cheese

In a large non-stick skillet, heat over medium-high heat until the olive oil is shiny. Add the turkey. Mix with a spoon until browned, about 5 minutes. Add the onion, pepper, and salt. Cook, stirring occasionally, for 4 to 5 minutes, until the vegetables are tender. Add the cauliflower, corn, and salsa. Cook, stirring constantly, until the cauliflower rice is tender, about 3 minutes more. Sprinkle with cheese. Reduce the heat to low, cover, and let the cheese melt for 2-3 minutes.

Nutritional information: Calories 449; Total Carbs 17g; Net Carbs 12g; Protein 30g; Fat 30g; Sugar 8.7g; Fiber 4.1g

Chicken Tuscany

Prep Time: 10 minutes. | Cook Time: 15 minutes. | Servings: 4

1½ pounds (680 g) chicken breasts, boneless, skinless and sliced thin
1 cup spinach, chopped
1 cup half-and-half
½ cup reduced fat Parmesan cheese
½ cup low sodium chicken broth
½ cup sun dried tomatoes
2 tablespoons olive oil
1 teaspoon Italian seasoning
1 teaspoon garlic powder

Heat the oil in a large saucepan over medium-high heat. Add the chicken and cook for 3 to 5 minutes for each side or until golden brown and cooked through. Transfer to a plate. Add half and half, broth, cheese, and seasoning to the pan. Continue until the sauce begins to thicken. Add the spinach and tomatoes and cook, stirring frequently, until the spinach begins to wilt, about 2-3 minutes. Return the chicken to the pan and cook long enough to heat through.

Nutritional information: Calories 463; Total Carbs 6.1g; Net Carbs 4g; Protein 55g; Fat 23g; Sugar 0g; Fiber 1.0g

Cheesy Chicken Cauliflower Casserole

Prep Time: 10 minutes. | Cook Time: 40 minutes. | Servings: 6

4 slices bacon, cooked and crumbled
3 cups cauliflower
3 cups chicken, cooked and chopped
3 cups broccoli florets
2 cups reduced fat cheddar cheese, grated
1 cup fat free sour cream

4 tablespoons olive oil
1 teaspoon salt
½ teaspoon black pepper
½ teaspoon garlic powder
½ teaspoon paprika
Nonstick cooking spray

Put 4 to 5 cups of water in a large saucepan and bring to a boil. Add the cauliflower and drain well, then cook 4 to 5 minutes or until tender. Repeat with the broccoli. Preheat the oven to 350 ºF (180 ºC). Spray the baking dish with cooking spray. In a large bowl, mash the cauliflower with olive oil, sour cream, and seasonings. Add ½ more cheese and mix well. Spread the mixture on a prepared baking sheet and sprinkle with the rest cheese. Bake for 20-25 minutes or until heated through and cheese is melted.

Nutritional information: Calories 345; Total Carbs 10g; Net Carbs 8g; Protein 28.7g; Fat 15g; Sugar 4g; Fiber 2.2g

Cheesy Chicken and Spinach

Prep Time: 10 minutes. | Cook Time: 45 minutes. | Servings: 6

3 chicken breasts, boneless, skinless and halved lengthwise
6 ounces (170 g) low fat cream cheese, soft
2 cup baby spinach
1 cup low-fat Mozzarella cheese, grated
2 tablespoons olive oil, divided
3 cloves garlic, diced fine
1 teaspoon Italian seasoning
Nonstick cooking spray

Preheat the oven to 350 ºF (180 ºC). Spray cooking spray on a baking sheet. Place the chicken cutlets on the baking sheet. Pour 1 tablespoon of cooking oil over the chicken. Sprinkle evenly with garlic and Italian seasoning. Spread cream cheese over the chicken. Heat the remaining oil in a saucepan over medium heat. Add the spinach and simmer until the spinach is wilted, for about 3 minutes. Spread evenly over the layer of cream cheese. Sprinkle the top with mozzarella. Bake for 35-40 minutes or until the chicken is cooked through. provided.

Nutritional information: Calories 362; Total Carbs 3.1g; Net Carbs 1.8g; Protein 31g; Fat 25g; Sugar 0g; Fiber 0g

Baked Spiced Chicken

Prep Time: 20 minutes. | Cook Time: 1 hour 20 minutes. | Servings: 4

11 (3 ounces of) chicken breast, boned & skinned
2 tablespoons (any brand) bottled diet Italian dressing

Marinate chicken in dressing overnight in a covered casserole in a refrigerator. Bake the marinated chicken for one hour at 350 ºF. After baking, it will be very tender and juicy. Serve and enjoy!

Nutritional information: Calories 240; Total Carbs 1.8g; Net Carbs 0.2g; Protein 29.5g; Fat 12.2g; Sugar 8.2g; Fiber 0.3g

Creole Chicken

Prep Time: 15 minutes. | Cook Time: 25 minutes. | Servings: 2

2 chicken breast halves, boneless and skinless
1 cup cauliflower rice, cooked
1/3 cup green bell pepper, julienned
1/4 cup celery, diced
1/4 cup onion, diced
14½ ounces (411 g) stewed tomatoes, diced
1 teaspoon sunflower oil
1 teaspoon chili powder
½ teaspoon thyme
⅛ teaspoon pepper

Heat the oil in a small skillet over medium heat. Add the chicken and cook 5 to 6 minutes per side or until cooked through. Transfer to a plate and keep warm. Add the bell pepper, celery, onion, tomato, and seasoning. Bring to a boil. Reduce the heat, cover, and simmer for 10 minutes or until the vegetables start to soften. Return the chicken to the pan and heat through. Serve over cauliflower rice.

Nutritional information: Calories 361; Total Carbs 14g; Net Carbs 10g; Protein 45.2g; Fat 14g; Sugar 8g; Fiber 4g

Duck Breasts with Grilled Plums

Prep Time: 10 minutes. | Cook Time: 20 minutes. | Servings: 6

4 (12- to 14-ounce / 340- to 397-g) boneless duck breast halves, trim off excess fat
6 firm purple plums, halved, pitted
4 teaspoons fresh thyme, chopped.
1 tablespoon extra-virgin olive oil
2 teaspoons fresh ground black pepper, divided
1½ teaspoons salt, divided
½ teaspoon Splenda

Heat the grill over medium-high heat. Cut the duck skin in a cross shape with a sharp knife, being careful not to cut the meat. Sprinkle 1 teaspoon of thyme, 1 teaspoon of pepper, and 1 teaspoon of salt on both sides. Cover and cool. In a large bowl, put olive oil, Splenda, 1 teaspoon of thyme, add black pepper and ½ teaspoon of salt and mix with the plums. Cut the plums one side at a time on the grill and cook until the grill marks appear and the plums begin to soften about 4 minutes. Flip and cook another 4 minutes until tender. Transfer to a bowl and cover with foil. Heat 2 large saucepans over medium-high heat. Add 2 breasts to a saucepan, skin side down. Cook for about 7 minutes until the skin is crisp and most of the fat is gone. Turn and cook until desired. Cook the ducks to rare, about 6-8 minutes. Transfer the duck to a cutting board and let stand for 5 minutes. Cut the duck into thin slices and place them on a plate. Place 2 plum halves next to the duck. Sprinkle the juice from the bowl over the duck and sprinkle with the added thyme. Serve.

Nutritional information: Calories 345; Total Carbs 9.1g; Net Carbs 4g; Protein 50.7g; Fat 12g; Sugar 7g; Fiber 1.2g

Lemon Pepper Wings

Prep Time: 25 minutes. | Cook Time: 35 minutes. | Servings: 4

2 tablespoons grated lemon zest
2 tablespoons freshly squeezed lemon juice
1 tablespoon freshly ground black pepper
Large baking sheet, lined with foil, with a wire rack set on top
2 pounds of free-range chicken wings
1 teaspoon sea salt

Preheat the oven to 375 degrees ° F. Pat the chicken with a paper towel. Bake in preheated oven for 30 to 35 minutes, flipping halfway when chicken is pierced and juices are translucent. Meanwhile, in a large bowl, combine the lemon juice, pepper, lemon zest and salt. Add the wings to the lemon juice. Coat evenly in juices. Serve hot and enjoy!

Nutritional information: Calories 286; Total Carbs 2.2g; Net Carbs 1.8g; Protein 27g; Fat 15g; Sugar 2.8g; Fiber 1g

Chicken Stew

Prep Time: 10 minutes. | Cook Time: 1 hour 15 minutes. | Servings: 4

4 chicken breasts, stewed
1 (6 ounces of) can mushrooms
½ medium head cabbage, chopped
2 medium onions, chopped
Salt, pepper, and garlic to taste
1 (12 ounces of) tomato juice

To cook the chicken, cover with water and pressure for 15 minutes. Remove the chicken from the water and add the cabbage, mushrooms and onions. Add pepper, salt and garlic to taste. Add tomato juice and shredded chicken. Simmer for about 1 hour. Serve.

Nutritional information: Calories 284; Total Carbs 18g; Net Carbs 10g; Protein 17g; Fat 4g; Sugar 5g; Fiber 1g

Onion Fried Chicken

Prep Time: 15 minutes. | Cook Time: 30 minutes. | Servings: 12

1 broiler (2 ½ to 3 pounds cut up)
1 teaspoon salt
½ teaspoon pepper
2 onions, peeled and sliced
½ cup water

Place the chicken in a nonstick skillet. Sprinkle with salt and pepper and put the onions on top. Cover with a lid and cook over low heat for 30 minutes. Tilt the lid so that the liquid evaporates. Continue cooking for 20 minutes or until tender. Place the chicken on a plate. Return the onions, add water and cook until thickened. Serve warm and enjoy.

Nutritional information: Calories 280; Total Carbs 13.5g; Net Carbs 13.5g; Protein 25g; Fat 9g; Sugar 1.5g; Fiber 1g

Kung Pao Chicken

Prep Time: 20 minutes. | Cook Time: 15 minutes. | Servings: 4

Sauce:
1 tablespoon rice vinegar
1 tablespoon hoisin sauce
1 teaspoon chili sauce
1 tablespoon cornstarch
1 tablespoon tamari or soy sauce
1 tablespoon ketchup
½ cup low-sodium chicken or vegetable broth (chilled in the refrigerator for at least 1 hour)
Chicken:
1 tablespoon dry sherry
1 red bell pepper (seeded and cut into 1-inch chunks)
2 scallions (white part thinly sliced and green part cut into 1-inch lengths)
2 tablespoons roasted cashews
2 boneless chicken breasts (about 1 pound)
ground white pepper
1 tablespoon peanut oil (can use coconut or canola oil)
4 dried red chilies

Put the cornstarch and cold broth in a glass jar with a lid. Shake vigorously until the corn is mixed. Add the ketchup, vinegar, hoisin sauce, tamari or soy sauce and gravy to the jar. Replace the cover. Shake again until well combined. Cut each chicken breast in half lengthwise, then into ½ inch pieces horizontally. Place the chicken in a bowl and season with white pepper. Heat a large pot or skillet over medium heat and add the oil. Season with pepper and sauté for a few minutes, then add the chicken. Sauté for 2-3 minutes or until the chicken is opaque, then add the sherry and mix well. Shake the sauce bottle and pour it into the pan. Bring everything to a boil, then add the pepper. Fry another 2 to 3 minutes until the chicken is cooked through and the sauce thickens. Remove from the heat and stir in the green onions and cashews. Serve and enjoy.

Nutritional information: Calories 154; Total Carbs 14.1g; Net Carbs 10g; Protein 31.7g; Fat 8g; Sugar 6g; Fiber 3.9g

Sweet 'n Sour Chicken

Prep Time: 25 minutes. | Cook Time: 30 minutes. | Servings: 12

½ cup chopped green pepper
½ cup chopped carrots
½ cup chopped onion
¾ cup lite ketchup
2 tablespoons Vinegar
2 tablespoons low sodium soy sauce
1 cup pineapple juice
1 teaspoon brown Sugar Twin
½ teaspoon garlic powder
¼ teaspoon freshly ground pepper
Dash ground ginger
1 cup pineapple chunks, drained

Heat the margarine in a large saucepan until it melts. Add the green peppers, carrots and onions. Cook for 5 minutes and stir. Add the ketchup, pineapple juice, vinegar, soy sauce, Sugar twin, garlic powder, black pepper and ginger. Stir and cook until boiling. Add

the pineapple pieces. Prepare the chicken meat in a 9 "x 13" dish. Pour the sauce over it. Cover tightly with foil. Bake at 400 degrees F for 45 minutes. Open the lid and bake for 30 minutes or until cooked through. Serve with rice.

Nutritional information: Calories 298; Total Carbs 48g; Net Carbs 28g; Protein 2g; Fat 15g; Sugar 6g; Fiber 12g

Curried Apple Chicken

Prep Time: 15 minutes. | Cook Time: 30 minutes. | Servings: 4

1 pound (454 g) chicken breasts, boneless, skinless, cut in 1-inch cubes
2 tart apples, peel and slice
1 sweet onion, cut in ½ and slice
1 jalapeno, seeded and diced
2 tablespoons cilantro, diced
½ teaspoon ginger, grated
14½ ounces (411 g) tomatoes, diced and drained
½ cup water
3 cloves garlic, diced
2 tablespoons sunflower oil
1 teaspoon salt
1 teaspoon coriander
½ teaspoon turmeric
¼ teaspoon cayenne pepper

Heat oil in a large skillet over medium-high heat. Add chicken and onion, and cook until onion is tender. Add garlic and cook 1 more minute. Add apples, water and seasonings and stir to combine. Bring to a boil. Reduce heat and simmer 12 to 15 minutes, or until chicken is cooked through, stirring occasionally. Stir in tomatoes, jalapeno, and cilantro and serve hot.

Nutritional information: Calories 372; Total Carbs 23.1g; Net Carbs 18g; Protein 34.2g; Fat 16.0g; Sugar 15g; Fiber 2g

Cumin Chicken Salad

Prep time: 10 minutes. | Cook Time: 0 minute. | Servings: 6

2 cups chicken, cooked and shredded
1 red bell pepper, diced fine
¼ cup red onion, diced fine
¼ cup mayonnaise
1 ½ teaspoon ground cumin
1 teaspoon garlic powder
½ teaspoon coriander
Salt and Black pepper, to taste

Combine all the recipe ingredients in a suitable bowl and mix to thoroughly combine. Taste and adjust seasonings as desired. Cover and chill good before serving.

Nutritional information: Calories 117; Total Carbs 4g; Net Carbs 0g; Protein 14g; Fat 5g; Sugar 2g; Fiber 0g

Turkey Stuffed Zucchini

Prep Time: 25 minutes. | Cook Time: 15 minutes. | Servings: 4

4 medium zucchini, halved lengthwise
1 pound ground turkey
¼ cup onion, chopped
1 garlic clove, minced
1 tablespoon olive oil
1 small tomato, chopped (½ cup)
1 tablespoon chopped parsley
½ teaspoon salt
¼ teaspoon basil
⅛ teaspoon pepper
½ cup crunchy nut (cereal nuggets or Grape nuts)
1 (8 ounces of) container plain low-fat yogurt

Remove the pulp from the zucchini. Cut and set aside. Immerse the zucchini shells in boiling water to blanch, for 2 minutes. Remove and place in a shallow bowl. In a skillet with the margarine, brown the turkey, onion and garlic for 2 minutes. Add the chopped pulp, parsley, tomatoes, salt, basil and pepper. Cook for 5 minutes or more, or until zucchini is tender. Add the cereal and ½ cup yogurt. Fill the filling in the zucchini shells with a spoon. Bake at 350 degrees F for 10-15 minutes or until the skin is soft. Serve with the rest of the yogurt. If desired, add to sprinkle with chopped parsley.

Nutritional information: Calories 214; Total Carbs 11g; Net Carbs 6g; Protein 31.7g; Fat 4.6g; Sugar 3.6g; Fiber 2.9g

Turkey Chili

Prep Time: 10 minutes. | Cook Time: 45 minutes. | Servings: 4

1 pound (454 g) lean ground turkey
2 carrots, peeled and diced
2 stalks of celery, diced
1 onion, diced
1 zucchini, diced
1 red pepper, diced
1 (14-ounce / 397-g) can tomato sauce
1 can black beans, drained and rinsed
1 can kidney beans, drained and rinsed
3 cups water
3 garlic cloves, diced fine
1 tablespoon chili powder
1 tablespoon olive oil
2 teaspoons salt
1 teaspoon pepper
1 teaspoon cumin
1 teaspoon coriander
1 bay leaf

Heat the oil in a heavy-bottomed pan over medium-high heat. Add the turkey and onions and cook, 5 to 10 minutes, until they are no longer pink. Add the vegetables and cook for 5 minutes, stirring occasionally. Add the garlic and spices and cook,

stirring, for 2 minutes. Add the leftovers and bring them to a boil. Lower the heat to low and simmer for 30 minutes.

Nutritional information: Calories 220; Total Carbs 14.1g; Net Carbs 14g; Protein 25.2g; Fat 9g; Sugar 6g; Fiber 4g

Chicken Guacamole

Prep time: 10 minutes. | Cooking time: 20 minutes. | Servings: 6

1 lb. Chicken breast, boneless and skinless
2 avocados
1-2 jalapeno peppers, diced
⅓ cup onion, diced
3 tablespoon Cilantro, diced
2 tablespoon lime juice
2 garlic cloves, diced
1 tablespoon Olive oil
Salt and pepper, to taste

At 400 degrees F, preheat your oven. Line a baking sheet with foil. Season the chicken breast liberally with black pepper and salt and place on a prepared pan. Bake 20 minutes, or until chicken is cooked through. Let cool completely. Once the chicken has cooled, shred or dice and add to a suitable bowl. Add remaining ingredients and mix well, mashing the avocado as you mix it in. Serve immediately.

Nutritional information: Calories 324; Total Carbs 12g; Net Carbs 5g; Protein 23g; Fat 22g; Sugar 1g; Fiber 7g

Chicken Casserole

Prep Time: 20 minutes. | Cook Time: 20 minutes. | Servings: 12

¼ cup margarine
⅓ cup flour
1 cup turkey
2 cups skim milk
1 ½ teaspoon salt
½ cup blanched almonds, slivered & toasted
1 cup brown rice
2 ½ cups diced, cooked turkey
1 (3 or 4 ounces of) can mushroom, drained
½ cup chopped pimiento
⅓ cup chopped green pepper

Melt the margarine in a large saucepan and stir in the flour. Mix the broth and the milk. Cook over low heat until thickened, stirring constantly. Combine all the Ingredients except the almonds. Pour into 9 "x 13" mold. Garnish with almonds and bake at 350 degrees F uncovered. You can eliminate salt for no-salt, less cholesterol diet. Serve and enjoy!

Nutritional information: Calories 324; Total Carbs 19g; Net Carbs 12g; Protein 32g; Fat 21g; Sugar 7g; Fiber 3g

Salmon Zucchini Salad

Prep time: 10 minutes. | Cooking time: 10 minutes. | Servings: 1

For dressing
½ tablespoon olive oil
½ tablespoon balsamic vinegar
⅛ tablespoon Dijon mustard
pinch of red pepper flakes, crushed
For salad
3 ounces smoked salmon
½ of zucchinis, spiralized with blade c
1 teaspoon basil, chopped

For the dressing: in a small blender, add all the recipe ingredients and pulse until smooth. For the salad: in a suitable bowl, add all the recipe ingredients and mix. Place the dressing over salad and toss to coat well. Serve immediately.

Nutritional information:
Calories: 179; Fat: 11g; Total Carbs 3.6g; Fiber: 1.2g; Sugar: 1.8g; Net Carbs 1.2g; Protein: 15.9g

Salmon Mozzarella Salad

Prep time: 10 minutes. | Cooking time: 10 minutes. | Servings: 1

2 tablespoons part-skim mozzarella cheese, cubed
3 tablespoons tomato, chopped
½ tablespoon dill, chopped
1 cup baby spinach
½ teaspoon lemon juice
Salt, as required
3 ounces cooked salmon, chopped

In a salad bowl, add all the recipe ingredients and stir to combine. Serve immediately.

Nutritional information: Calories: 268; Fat: 11.4g; Total Carbs 5.3g; Fiber: 1.3g; Sugar: 1.1g; Net Carbs 2g; Protein: 36.8g

Salmon Avocado Salad

Prep time: 10 minutes. | Cooking time: 10 minutes. | Servings: 1

3 ounces cooked salmon, flaked
3 tablespoons cucumber, chopped
3 tablespoons avocado, peeled, pitted and chopped
½ cup lettuce, chopped
¼ tablespoon olive oil
¼ tablespoon lemon juice
salt and black pepper, to taste

In a salad bowl, add all the recipe ingredients and stir to combine. Serve immediately.

Nutritional information: Calories: 206; Fat: 14.2g; Total Carbs 4g; Fiber: 2.1g; Sugar: 0.8g; Net Carbs 2g; Protein: 17.3g

Greens Shrimp Salad

Prep time: 10 minutes. | Cooking time: 6 minutes. | Servings: 1

1 tablespoon olive oil
½ of garlic clove, crushed
¼ pound shrimp, peeled and deveined
Salt and black pepper, to taste
¾ cup baby arugula
¾ cup baby spinach
¼ tablespoon lime juice

In a suitable wok, heat the oil over medium heat and sauté garlic for almost 1 minute. Add the shrimp with salt and black pepper and cook for almost 3-5 minutes. Remove it from the heat and set it aside to cool. In a salad bowl, add the shrimp, arugula, spinach, remaining oil, lime juice, salt and black pepper and gently toss to coat. Serve immediately.

Nutritional information: Calories: 266; Fat: 14.5g; Total Carbs 3.6g; Fiber: 0.8g; Sugar: 0.4g; Net Carbs 2g; Protein: 27g

Corn Shrimp Salad

Prep time: 10 minutes. | Cooking time: 10 minutes. | Servings: 1

¼ pound cooked shrimp
1 cup lettuce, torn
2 tablespoons onion, sliced
¼ tablespoon olive oil
Salt and black pepper, to taste

In a salad bowl, add shrimp, corn, onion, oil, salt and black pepper and toss to coat well. Serve immediately.

Nutritional information: Calories: 180; Fat: 5.5g; Total Carbs 5.1g; Fiber: 0.8g; Sugar: 1.4g; Net Carbs 2g; Protein: 26.3g

Salmon Caper Burger

Prep time: 10 minutes. | Cooking time: 6 minutes. | Servings: 1

2 ounces skinless, boneless salmon, cut into large chunks
½ teaspoon Dijon mustard
½ shallot, peeled and cut into chunks
¼ tablespoon capers, drained
2 tablespoons whole-wheat breadcrumbs
Salt and black pepper, to taste
½ tablespoon olive oil

In a mini food processor, add ½ ounce of salmon chunks and mustard until the mixture becomes pasty. Add the remaining salmon and shallot and pulse until chopped Transfer the salmon mixture into a suitable bowl. Add the capers, breadcrumbs, salt and black pepper and stir to combine. Shape the mixture into a patty. In a suitable frying pan, heat the oil over medium-high heat and cook the patty for almost 2-3 minutes per side or until desired doneness. Serve hot.

Nutritional information: Calories: 198; Fat: 10.5g; Total Carbs 10.1g; Fiber: 0.7g; Sugar: 1g; Net Carbs 4g; Protein: 13.4g

Tuna Egg Salad

Prep time: 10 minutes. | Cooking time: 10 minutes. | Servings: 1

For dressing
½ tablespoon dill, minced
½ tablespoon olive oil
¼ tablespoon lime juice
Salt and black pepper, to taste
For salad
1 cup spinach, torn
3 ounces canned water-packed tuna, drained and flaked
1 hard-boiled egg, peeled and sliced
¼ cup tomato, chopped

For the dressing: place dill, oil, lime juice, salt, and black pepper in a suitable bowl and beat until well combined. Place the torn spinach onto a serving plate and top with tuna, egg and tomato. Drizzle with dressing and serve.

Nutritional information: Calories: 241; Fat: 12.4g; Total Carbs 4.1g; Fiber: 1.4g; Sugar: 1.7g; Net Carbs 2g; Protein: 28.8g

Avocado Shrimp Salad

Prep time: 10 minutes. | Cooking time: 10 minutes. | Servings: 1

½ tablespoon olive oil
½ tablespoon lime juice
¼ teaspoon ground cumin
Salt, as required
¼ pound cooked shrimp
½ of a small avocado, peeled, pitted and cubed
½ of scallion, chopped

For the dressing: in a salad bowl, add oil, lime juice, cumin and salt and beat until well combined. In the salad bowl, add shrimp, avocado and scallion and gently toss to coat well. Serve immediately.

Nutritional information: Calories: 285; Fat: 15.5g; Total Carbs 7.5g; Fiber: 4.1g; Sugar: 0.5g; Net Carbs 5g; Protein: 27.1g

Easy Crab Cakes

Prep time: 10 minutes. | Cooking time: 10 minutes. | Servings: 1

¾ tablespoon olive oil
2 tablespoons onion, chopped
¾ tablespoon blanched almond flour
1 tablespoon egg white
½ tablespoon low-fat mayonnaise
¼ tablespoon dried parsley, crushed
¼ teaspoon yellow mustard
¼ teaspoon Worcestershire sauce, low-sodium
¼ tablespoon old bay seasoning
black pepper, to taste
¼ lb. lump crabmeat, drained

Heat up a teaspoon of olive oil in a wok over medium heat and sauté onion for almost 8-10 minutes. Remove the frying pan from heat and set it aside to cool slightly. Place cooked onion and remaining ingredients except for crabmeat in a suitable mixing bowl

and mix until well combined. In the bowl of onion mixture, add the crabmeat and gently stir to combine. Make 2 equal-sized patties from the mixture. Arrange the patties onto a foil-lined tray and refrigerate for almost 30 minutes. In a large frying pan, heat the remaining oil over medium-low heat and cook the crab patties for almost 3-4 minutes per side or until desired doneness. Serve hot.

Nutritional information: Calories: 253; Fat: 19g; Total Carbs 5.1g; Fiber: 1.1g; Sugar: 1.9g; Net Carbs 5g; Protein: 15.6g

Tuna Cucumber Salad

Prep time: 10 minutes. | Cooking time: 10 minutes. | Servings: 1

For vinaigrette
1 tablespoon extra-virgin olive oil
½ tablespoon lime juice
¼ teaspoon Dijon mustard
⅛ teaspoon lime zest, grated
Salt and black pepper, to taste
For salad
3 ounces canned water-packed tuna, drained and flaked
¼ of cucumber, sliced
1 tablespoon red onion, chopped
¼ of tomato, sliced
1 cup lettuce leaves, torn

For the vinaigrette: in a suitable bowl, add all the recipe ingredients and beat until well combined. For the salad: in a large serving bowl, add all the recipe ingredients and mix. Place the dressing over the salad and gently toss to coat. Refrigerate, covered for almost 30-40 minutes before serving.

Nutritional information: Calories: 246; Fat: 15g; Total Carbs 6.1g; Fiber: 1.2g; Sugar: 2.7g; Net Carbs 5g; Protein: 22.6g

Crusted Tuna Burger

Prep time: 10 minutes. | Cooking time: 5 minutes. | Servings: 1

3¾ ounces canned wild tuna, drained
½ tablespoon olive oil
1 tablespoon whole-wheat breadcrumbs
½ of small egg, beaten
¼ tablespoon garlic, minced
½ teaspoon chives, minced
½ teaspoon dried parsley
¼ teaspoon paprika
Salt and black pepper, to taste

In a suitable bowl, add the tuna, ¼ tablespoon of oil, breadcrumbs, egg, garlic, chives, parsley, paprika, salt and black pepper and mix until well combined. Shape the mixture into a patty. In a suitable frying pan, heat the remaining oil over medium-high heat and cook the patty for almost 3-5 minutes per side or until desired doneness. Serve hot.

Nutritional information: Calories: 316; Fat: 17.5g; Total Carbs 6.1g; Fiber: 0.6g; Sugar: 0.7g; Net Carbs 2g; Protein: 31.7g

Shrimp Olives Salad

Prep time: 10 minutes. | Cooking time: 3 minutes. | Servings: 1

¼ pound shrimp, peeled and deveined
1 lemon slice
½ tablespoon olive oil
½ teaspoon lemon juice
Salt and black pepper, to taste
½ of tomato, sliced
1 tablespoon onion, sliced
1 tablespoon green olives
1 teaspoon parsley, chopped

In a small pan of lightly salted boiling water, add the lemon slice. Then, add the shrimp and cook for almost 2-3 minutes or until pink and opaque. With a slotted spoon, transfer the shrimp into a suitable bowl of ice water to stop the cooking process. Drain the shrimp completely, and then pat dry with paper towels. In a suitable bowl, add the oil, lemon juice, salt, and black pepper, and beat until well combined. Place the shrimp, tomato, onion, olives, and parsley onto a serving plate. Drizzle with oil mixture and serve.

Nutritional information: Calories: 215; Fat: 9.9g; Total Carbs 4.5g; Fiber: 0.9g; Sugar: 1.3g; Net Carbs 4g; Protein: 26.3g

Scallops Egg Salad

Prep time: 10 minutes. | Cooking time: 10 minutes. | Servings: 1

For dressing
2 tablespoons plain Greek yogurt
½ teaspoon Dijon mustard
Salt and black pepper, to taste
For salad
¼ pound cooked scallops
1 hard-boiled egg, peeled and sliced
½ of apple, cored and sliced
2-3 tablespoons purple cabbage, chopped

For the dressing: in a suitable bowl, add all the recipe ingredients and beat until well combined. For the salad: in a salad bowl, add all the salad ingredients and mix. Drizzle with dressing and serve immediately.

Nutritional information: Calories: 183; Fat: 5.4g; Total Carbs 5.4g; Fiber: 0.4g; Sugar: 1.1g; Net Carbs 2g; Protein: 26.1g

Smoked Salmon Lettuce Wraps

Prep time: 10 minutes. | Cooking time: 10 minutes. | Servings: 1

2 tablespoons part-skim mozzarella cheese, cubed
2 tablespoons tomato, chopped
½ teaspoon fresh dill, chopped
¼ teaspoon fresh lemon juice
Salt, as required
2 lettuce leaves
2 smoked salmon slices

In a suitable bowl, combine mozzarella, tomato, dill, lemon juice, and salt until well combined. Arrange the 2 lettuce leaves onto a serving plate. Divide the salmon slices and tomato mixture over each lettuce leaf and serve immediately.

Nutritional information: Calories: 1237; Fat: 12.5g; Total Carbs 3.5g; Fiber: 0.4g; Sugar: 0.7g; Net Carbs 2g; Protein: 27.3g

Tilapia dipped in Caper Sauce

Prep time: 10 minutes. | Cooking time: 8 minutes. | Servings: 1

½ tablespoon lemon juice
½ tablespoon olive oil
1 garlic clove, minced
¼ teaspoon lemon zest, grated
1 teaspoon caper, drained
2 teaspoons basil, minced and divided
1 (6-ounce) tilapia fillet
Salt and black pepper, to taste

Preheat the broiler of the oven. Arrange an oven rack about 4-inch from the heating element. Grease a broiler pan. In a suitable bowl, add the lemon juice, oil, garlic and lemon zest and beat until well combined. Add the capers and half of the basil and stir to combine. Reserve about ½ of the tablespoon of mixture in a suitable bowl. Coat the fish fillet with the remaining capers mixture and sprinkle with salt and black pepper. Place the tilapia fillet onto the broiler pan and broil for almost 3-4 minutes side. Remove from the oven and place the fish fillet onto a serving plate. Drizzle with reserved capers mixture and serve with the garnishing of remaining basil.

Nutritional information: Calories: 208; Fat: 8.5g; Total Carbs 1.4g; Net Carbs 2g; Protein: 32g; Fiber: 0.2g; Sugar: 0.2g

Strawberry Shrimp Salad

Prep time: 10 minutes. | Cooking time: 6 minutes. | Servings: 1

For dressing
½ tablespoon olive oil
½ tablespoon balsamic vinegar
½ tablespoon lemon juice
Salt and black pepper, to taste
For salad
¼ pound shrimp, peeled and deveined
1 cup baby spinach
¼ cup strawberries, hulled and chopped
1 tablespoon almonds, chopped

In a suitable mason jar, add vinegar, olive oil, lemon juice, salt and black pepper. Seal the jar tightly and shake for almost 30 seconds. In a Ziploc bag, add half of the dressing and shrimp and seal it tightly. Shake the bag to mix well. Refrigerate to marinate for almost 30 minutes. Heat a small cast-iron skillet over medium-high heat and cook the shrimp for almost 2-3 minutes per side. In a salad bowl, add cooked shrimp, spinach, strawberries and almonds and mix. Drizzle with reserved dressing and serve immediately.

Nutritional information: Calories: 216; Fat: 9.2g; Total Carbs 5.8g; Fiber: 1.4g; Sugar: 2.1g; Net Carbs 1.2g; Protein: 27g

Saucy Tomato Cod

Prep time: 10 minutes. | Cooking time: 35 minutes. | Servings: 1

¼ teaspoon dried dill weed
¼ teaspoon sumac
¼ teaspoon ground coriander
¼ teaspoon ground cumin
⅛ teaspoon ground turmeric
½ tablespoon olive oil
¼ of onion, chopped
1 garlic clove, chopped
½ of jalapeño pepper, chopped
1 tomato, chopped
1 tablespoon tomato paste
½ tablespoon lime juice
2-3 tablespoons water
Salt and black pepper, to taste
1 (6-ounce) cod fillet

For spice mixture: in a suitable bowl, add the dill weed and spices and mix well. In a suitable, deep skillet, heat the oil over medium-high heat and sauté the onion for almost 2 minutes. Add the garlic and jalapeno and sauté for almost 2 minutes. Stir in the tomatoes, tomato paste, lime juice, water, half of the spice mixture, salt and pepper and bring to a boil. Then reduce its heat to medium-low and cook, covered for almost 10 minutes, with occasional stirring. Meanwhile, season the cod fillet with the remaining spice mixture, salt and pepper evenly. Place the fish fillet into the skillet and gently press into the tomato mixture. Increase the heat to medium-high and cook for almost 2 minutes. Reduce its heat to medium and cook, covered for almost 10-15 minutes or until the desired doneness of the fish. Serve hot.

Nutritional information: Calories: 244; Fat: 9g; Total Carbs 9.1g; Net Carbs 2g; Protein: 32.4g; Fiber: 2.7g; Sugar: 4g

Poached Orange Salmon

Prep time: 10 minutes. | Cooking time: 15 minutes. | Servings: 1

1 garlic clove, crushed
¼ teaspoon ginger, grated
2 tablespoons orange juice
1 tablespoon low-sodium soy sauce
1 (6-ounce) salmon fillet, skinless

In a suitable bowl, mix together all the recipe ingredients except for salmon. In the bottom of a pan, place the salmon fillet. Place the ginger mixture over the salmon and set aside for almost 15 minutes. Place the pan over high heat and bring to a boil. Reduce its heat to low and simmer, covered for almost 10-12 minutes or until desired doneness. Serve hot.

Nutritional information: Calories: 249; Fat: 10.5g; Total Carbs 5.3g; Fiber: 0.1g; Sugar: 3.3g; Net Carbs 2g; Protein: 34.4g

Gingered Dill Salmon

Prep time: 10 minutes. | Cooking time: 10 minutes. | Servings: 1

½ tablespoon scallion, chopped

½ teaspoon ginger, minced
½ of garlic clove, minced
¼ teaspoon dried dill weed, crushed
½ tablespoon olive oil
½ tablespoon balsamic vinegar
½ tablespoon soy sauce, low-sodium
1 (5-ounce) boneless, salmon fillet

Add all the recipe ingredients except for salmon in a suitable bowl and mix well. Add salmon and coat with marinade generously. Cover and refrigerate the salmon to marinate for at least 4-5 hours. Preheat the grill to medium heat. Grease the grill grate. Place the salmon fillet onto the grill and cook for almost 5 minutes per side. Serve hot.

Nutritional information: Calories: 255; Fat: 15.5g; Total Carbs 1.6g; Net Carbs 2g; Protein: 28.2g; Fiber: 0.2g; Sugar: 0.6g

Zesty Salmon

Prep time: 10 minutes. | Cooking time: 10 minutes. | Servings: 1

½ tablespoon olive oil
⅓ tablespoon lime juice
¼ teaspoon Worcestershire sauce
¼ teaspoon lime zest, grated finely.
1 (6-ounce) salmon fillet
Salt and black pepper, to taste

In a small baking dish, place oil, lemon juice, Worcestershire sauce and lemon zest and mix well. Coat the fillet with the mixture and then arrange skin side-up in the baking dish. Set aside for almost 15 minutes. Preheat the broiler of the oven. Arrange the oven rack about 6-inch from the heating element. Line a broiler pan with a piece of foil. Remove the salmon fillet from the baking dish and season with salt and black pepper. Arrange the salmon fillet onto the prepared broiler pan, skin side down. Broil for almost 8-10 minutes. Serve hot.

Nutritional information: Calories: 287; Fat: 17.5g; Total Carbs 0.4g; Fiber: 0.1g; Sugar: 0.3g; Net Carbs 4g; Protein: 33g

Paprika Rubbed Salmon

Prep time: 5 minutes. | Cooking time: 10 minutes. | Servings: 1

¼ teaspoon ground cumin
¼ teaspoon ground coriander
¼ teaspoon red chilli powder
⅛ teaspoon paprika
Salt and black pepper, to taste
1 (6-ounce) salmon fillet
½ tablespoon olive oil

In a suitable bowl, mix together the spices. Coat the salmon fillet with spice mixture evenly. In a non-stick skillet, heat the oil over medium-high heat and cook salmon fillet for almost 3-4 minutes. Flip and cook for almost 4-5 minutes or until desired doneness. Serve hot.

Nutritional information: Calories: 290; Fat: 17.5g; Total Carbs 0.7g; Fiber: 0.4g; Sugar: 0.1g; Net Carbs 1.2g; Protein: 33.2g

Zesty Dill Salmon

Prep time: 10 minutes. | Cooking time: 15 minutes. | Servings: 1

1 tablespoon dill, chopped and divided
¼ teaspoon lemon zest
¼ teaspoon smoked paprika
¼ teaspoon fennel seeds, crushed lightly
Salt and black pepper, to taste
1 (6-ounce) skinless, boneless salmon fillet
½ tablespoon lemon juice
½ tablespoon olive oil

In a suitable bowl, place ½ tablespoon of dill, lemon zest, paprika, fennel seeds, salt and black pepper and mix well. Season the salmon fillet with dill mixture evenly and then drizzle with lemon juice. In a small wok, heat oil over medium heat. Place the salmon fillet and immediately reduce its heat to the low. Cook for almost 10 minutes. Flip and cook for almost 5 minutes more. With a slotted spoon, transfer the salmon fillet onto a paper towel-lined plate to drain. Serve immediately with the topping of the remaining dill.

Nutritional information: Calories: 290; Fat: 17.5g; Total Carbs 0.8g; Net Carbs 2g; Protein: 33.2g; Fiber: 0.5g; Sugar: 0.2g

Parmesan Shrimp Scampi

Prep time: 10 minutes. | Cooking time: 10 minutes. | Servings: 1

¼ pound medium shrimp, peeled and deveined
Salt and black pepper, to taste
1 tablespoon olive oil
1 garlic clove, minced
⅓ cup chicken broth
½ tablespoon lemon juice
⅛ teaspoon dried thyme
⅛ teaspoon dried rosemary
Pinch of dried oregano
Pinch of dried basil
¼ tablespoon parsley, chopped
1 tablespoon low-fat parmesan cheese, grated freshly

Rub the shrimp with salt and black pepper. Heat olive oil in a small cast-iron skillet over medium-high heat. Cook the shrimp for almost 2-3 minutes, with occasional stirring. With a slotted spoon, transfer the shrimp onto a plate and set aside. In the same skillet, add the garlic and sauté for almost 1 minute. Stir in white broth and lemon juice and bring to a boil. Reduce its heat to low and simmer for almost 4-5 minutes. Add the dried herbs and stir to combine. Sir in the cooked shrimp, parsley, salt and black pepper and remove from the heat. Serve immediately with the garnishing of parmesan.

Nutritional information: Calories: 281; Fat: 17.1g; Total Carbs 3.6g; Net Carbs 1.2g; Protein: 27.8g; Fiber: 0.3g; Sugar: 0.2g

Lemony Tuna Burger

Prep time: 10 minutes. | Cooking time: 10 minutes. | Servings: 1

4 ounces canned tuna, drained

2 tablespoons almond meal
1 egg
½ tablespoon olive oil
½ tablespoon soy sauce, low-sodium
½ tablespoon lemon juice
1 tablespoon cilantro, chopped
¼ tablespoon ginger root, grated
Black pepper, to taste

In a suitable bowl, add the tuna, almond meal, egg, ¼ tablespoon of oil, soy sauce, lemon juice, cilantro, ginger and black pepper and mix until well combined. Shape the mixture into a patty. In a suitable frying pan, heat the remaining oil over medium-high heat and cook the patty for almost 4-5 minutes per side or until desired doneness. Serve hot.

Nutritional information: Calories: 370; Fat: 20.5g; Total Carbs 2.7g; Fiber: 0.9g; Sugar: 1.2g; Net Carbs 1.2g; Protein: 36.9g

Shrimp Lettuce Wraps

Prep time: 10 minutes. | Cooking time: 10 minutes. | Servings: 1

¼ pound cooked shrimp
2-3 tablespoons tomato, chopped
2 tablespoons onion, chopped
1 teaspoon parsley, chopped
2 lettuce leaves

In a suitable bowl, mix together shrimp, tomato, onion, and parsley. Arrange the 2 lettuce leaves onto a serving plate. Divide the shrimp mixture over lettuce leaves evenly. Serve immediately.

Nutritional information: Calories: 149; Fat: 2g; Total Carbs 4.9g; Fiber: 0.8g; Sugar: 1.6g; Net Carbs 1.2g; Protein: 26.3g

Halibut Baked with Veggies

Prep time: 10 minutes. | Cooking time: 20 minutes. | Servings: 1

1 teaspoon olive oil
2 tablespoons yellow onion, minced
¼ cup zucchini, chopped
1 garlic clove, minced
½ teaspoon basil, chopped
2-3 tablespoons tomato, chopped
Salt and black pepper, to taste
1 (6-ounce) halibut fillet

At 450 degrees F, preheat your oven. Grease a suitable shallow baking dish with cooking spray. In a suitable skillet, heat the oil over medium heat and sauté the onion, zucchini and garlic for almost 4-5 minutes. Stir in the basil, tomato, salt and black pepper and immediately remove from heat. Place the halibut steak into prepared baking dish and top with the tomato mixture evenly. Bake for almost 15 minutes or until desired doneness. Serve hot.

Nutritional information: Calories: 246; Fat: 8.5g; Total Carbs 3.7g; Net Carbs 2g; Protein: 36.6g; Fiber: 1g; Sugar: 1.9g

Parsley Topped Salmon

Prep time: 5 minutes. | Cooking time: 20 minutes. | Servings: 1

1 (4-ounce) salmon fillet
½ tablespoon olive oil
1 teaspoon parsley, minced
Salt and black pepper, to taste

At 400 degrees F, preheat your oven. Grease a baking dish. In a suitable bowl, place all the recipe ingredients and mix well. Arrange the salmon fillet into the prepared baking dish. Bake for almost 15-20 minutes or until the desired doneness of salmon. Serve hot.

Nutritional information: Calories: 210; Fat: 14g; Total Carbs 0.1g; Fiber: 0g; Sugar: 0g; Net Carbs 2g; Protein: 22g

Scallops Tomato Salad

Prep time: 10 minutes. | Cooking time: 10 minutes. | Servings: 1

¼ pound cooked scallops
1 cup mixed baby greens
¼ cup grape tomatoes, halved
½ tablespoon olive oil
½ tablespoon lemon juice
Salt and black pepper, to taste

In a salad bowl, add all the recipe ingredients and stir to combine. Serve immediately.

Nutritional information: Calories: 173; Fat: 8g; Total Carbs 5.1g; Fiber: 0.9g; Sugar: 1.7g; Net Carbs 1.2g; Protein: 19.8g

Yogurt Marinated Salmon

Prep time: 10 minutes. | Cooking time: 12 minutes. | Servings: 1

1 tablespoon plain Greek yogurt
¼ tablespoon olive oil
¼ tablespoon lemon juice
¼ tablespoon dill, minced
⅛ teaspoon ground cumin
⅛ teaspoon ground coriander
Salt and black pepper, to taste
1 (6-ounce) salmon fillet

In a suitable bowl, add all the recipe ingredients except the salmon and mix well. Add the salmon fillet and coat with the mixture well. Refrigerate for almost 25-30 minutes, flipping once halfway through. Preheat the grill to medium-high heat. Lightly grease the grill grate. Remove the salmon fillet from the bowl, and with the paper towels, discard the excess yogurt mixture. Place the salmon fillet onto the grill and cook for almost 4-6 minutes per side. Serve hot.

Nutritional information: Calories: 266; Fat: 14.1g; Total Carbs 1.7g; Net Carbs 2g; Protein: 33.9g; Fiber: 0.2g; Sugar: 0.1g

Greek Salmon Burger

Prep time: 10 minutes. | Cooking time: 8 minutes. | Servings: 1

5 ounces boneless salmon fillet, diced
¾ tablespoon parsley, chopped
½ tablespoon plain Greek yogurt
¼ tablespoon lemon juice
Salt and black pepper, to taste
½ tablespoon olive oil

In a suitable bowl, add salmon, parsley, yogurt, lemon juice, salt and black pepper and mix until well combined. Shape the mixture into a patty. In a suitable frying pan, heat the oil over medium-high heat and cook the patty for almost 4 minutes per side or until desired doneness. Serve hot.

Nutritional information: Calories: 253; Fat: 15.8g; Total Carbs 0.8g; Fiber: 0.1g; Sugar: 0.1g; Net Carbs 2g; Protein: 27.9g

Salmon Burger

Prep time: 10 minutes. | Cooking time: 6 minutes. | Servings: 1

3-ounce cooked salmon
2 tablespoons almond flour
½ of a large egg, beaten
½ tablespoon dill
½ tablespoon parsley
¼-½ tablespoon lemon juice
Salt, as required
1 teaspoon olive oil

In a suitable mixing bowl, add all of the ingredients except for oil and mix until well combined. Shape the mixture into a patty. In a suitable frying pan, heat the oil over medium-high heat and cook the patty for almost 2-3 minutes per side or until desired doneness. Serve hot.

Nutritional information: Calories: 280; Fat: 18g; Total Carbs 2.9g; Fiber: 1.6g; Sugar: 0.8g; Net Carbs 2g; Protein: 19.7g

Chimichurri-Dipped Tuna

Prep time: 10 minutes. | Cooking time: 30 minutes. | Servings: 1

¼ cup parsley
1 garlic clove, chopped
1 tablespoon olive oil
1 tablespoon lemon juice
⅛ teaspoon red pepper flakes
Salt and black pepper, to taste
1 (6-ounce) tuna steak

In a mini food processor, add parsley, garlic, olive oil and lemon juice and pulse until smooth. Transfer the parsley mixture into a suitable bowl. Add the red pepper flakes, salt, and black pepper and stir to combine. Refrigerate for almost 2 hours before cooking. At 350 degrees F, preheat your oven. Arrange the tuna steak into a small glass baking dish. Place the parsley mixture over tuna steak evenly. Bake for almost 25-30 minutes. Serve hot.

Nutritional information: Calories: 313; Fat: 14.5g; Total Carbs 2.4g; Net Carbs 3g; Protein: 40.6g; Fiber: 0.7g; Sugar: 0.5g

Pea Paella

Prep time: 22 minutes. | Cook Time: 34 minutes. | Serves: 6

1 lb. chicken thighs, skinless & boneless
1 lb. medium shrimp, raw, peel & devein
1 dozen mussels, cleaned
2 chorizo sausages, cut into pieces
1 medium head cauliflower, grated
1 yellow onion, diced fine
1 green bell pepper, sliced into strips
1 cup frozen peas
What you'll need from store cupboard:
15 oz. can tomatoes, diced, drain well
2 tbsp. extra-virgin olive oil
2 tsp. garlic, diced fine
2 tsp. salt
1 tsp. saffron
½ tsp. pepper
¼ tsp. paprika
Nonstick cooking spray

Preheat oven to broil. Applying cooking spray, coat a baking dish. Season the chicken on both sides with salt and pepper before placing it in a baking tray. Bake for about 4 minutes per side, or until the middle is no longer pink. Allow to cool completely before serving. Heat 1 tablespoon of oil in a medium skillet over medium heat. Combine the onion, pepper, and garlic in a mixing bowl. Cook, turning regularly, for about 4-5 minutes, or until peppers begin to soften. Place in a mixing basin. Cook, stirring often, for 2 minutes with the chorizo in the skillet. Drain the fat and toss it in with the vegetables. Cut the chicken into small pieces and toss it with the vegetables once it has cooled. Add the remaining oil to a large saucepot and heat over medium heat. Add the cauliflower and seasonings once it's hot. Cook, stirring regularly, for 8-10 minutes, or until cauliflower is almost soft. Cook the mussels and shrimp until the mussels open and the shrimp turn pink. Stir the mixture into the tomatoes and peas in the mixing bowl to incorporate everything. Cook for another 5 minutes, or until the mussels have all opened and everything is hot. Serve.

Nutritional information: Calories 423 Total Carbs 21g Net Carbs 15g Protein 46g Fat 18g Sugar 9g Fiber 6g

Lemony Cod

Prep time: 10 minutes. | Cooking time: 10 minutes. | Servings: 1

1 (5-ounce) boneless cod fillet
Salt and black pepper, to taste
½ tablespoon olive oil
½ tablespoon lemon juice
1 teaspoon rosemary, minced
¼ teaspoon lemon zest, grated

Rub the cod fillet with salt and black pepper evenly. In a nonstick wok, heat olive oil over medium heat. In the wok, place the cod fillet, skin side down and cook for almost 3-5 minutes, without stirring. Flip the cod fillet and cook for almost 2 minutes. Add the lemon juice, rosemary and lemon zest and cook for almost 2 minutes, spooning the sauce over the fillet occasionally. Serve hot.

Nutritional information: Calories: 180; Fat: 8.5g; Total Carbs 1g; Net Carbs 1.2g; Protein: 25.4g; Fiber: 0.6g; Sugar: 0.2g

Easy Baked Haddock

Prep time: 5 minutes. | Cooking time: 8 minutes. | Servings: 1

1 (6-ounce) haddock fillet
salt and black pepper, to taste
½ tablespoon olive oil

Season the haddock fillet with salt and black pepper evenly. In a small non-stick skillet, heat the olive oil over medium-high heat and cook the haddock fillet for almost 3-4 minutes per side or until desired doneness. Serve hot.

Nutritional information: Calories: 251; Fat: 8.5g; Total Carbs 0g; Net Carbs 1.2g; Protein: 41.2g; Fiber: 0g; Sugar: 0g

Citrus Glazed Salmon

Prep time: 10 minutes. | Cooking time: 14 minutes. | Servings: 1

1 garlic clove, minced
¼ tablespoon lemon zest, grated
½ tablespoon olive oil
½ tablespoon lemon juice
Salt and black pepper, to taste
1 (6-ounce) boneless, salmon fillet

Preheat the grill to medium-high heat. Grease the grill grate. In a suitable bowl, place all the recipe ingredients except for salmon fillet and mix well. Add the salmon fillet and coat with garlic mixture generously. Place the salmon fillet onto the grill and cook for almost 6-7 minutes per side. Serve hot.

Nutritional information: Calories: 292; Fat: 17.5g; Total Carbs 1.5g; Net Carbs 2g; Protein: 33.3g; Fiber: 0.2g; Sugar: 0.3g

Thyme Rubbed Tuna

Prep time: 10 minutes. | Cooking time: 8 minutes. | Servings: 1

½ tablespoon lemon juice
¼ tablespoon olive oil
½ teaspoon thyme, minced
½ of garlic clove, minced
Salt and black pepper, to taste
1 (6-ounce) tuna steak

Add the oil, lemon juice, thyme, garlic, salt and black pepper to a Ziploc plastic bag, Place the tuna steak in the bag, shake and seal the bag. Shake to coat well. Refrigerate for almost 30 minutes, shaking the bag occasionally. Preheat the grill to medium-high heat. Grease the grill grate. Remove tuna from the bag and discard the excess marinade. Place the tuna steak over direct heat and cook for almost 3-4 minutes per side. Serve hot.

Nutritional information: Calories: 215; Fat: 5.1g; Total Carbs 1g; Net Carbs 2g; Protein: 40g; Fiber: 0.3g; Sugar: 0.2g

Salmon with Capers

Prep time: 10 minutes. | Cooking time: 8 minutes. | Servings: 1

½ tablespoon olive oil
1 (6-ounce) salmon fillet
½ tablespoon capers
Salt and black pepper, to taste

In a suitable skillet, heat oil over high heat and cook the salmon fillet for almost 3 minutes. Sprinkle the salmon fillet with capers, salt and black pepper. Flip the salmon fillet and cook for almost 5 minutes or until browned. Serve hot.

Nutritional information: Calories: 286; Fat: 17.5g; Total Carbs 0.2g; Net Carbs 5g; Protein: 33.1g; Fiber: 0.1g; Sugar: 0g

Nut-Topped Salmon

Prep time: 10 minutes. | Cooking time: 20 minutes. | Servings: 1

2 tablespoons walnuts
¼ tablespoon dill, chopped
¼ tablespoon lemon rind, grated
Salt and black pepper, to taste
½ tablespoon olive oil
1 tablespoon Dijon mustard
2 (3-ounce) salmon fillets
2 teaspoons lemon juice

At 350 degrees F, preheat your oven. Layer a suitable baking sheet with parchment paper. Place the walnuts in a mini food processor and pulse until chopped roughly. Add the dill, lemon rind, garlic salt, black pepper, and oil and pulse until a crumbly mixture forms. Place the salmon fillet onto the prepared baking sheet in a single layer, skin-side down. Coat the top of each salmon fillet with Dijon mustard. Place the walnut mixture over each fillet and gently press into the surface of the salmon. Bake for almost 15 to 20 minutes. Remove the salmon fillets from the oven and transfer them onto the serving plates. Drizzle with the lemon juice and serve.

Nutritional information: Calories: 324; Fat: 18.5g; Total Carbs 2.3g; Net Carbs 1.2g; Protein: 33.6g; Fiber: 1g; Sugar: 0.5g

Baked Herbed Sea Bass

Prep time: 10 minutes. | Cooking time: 20 minutes. | serves: 2

1 (1¼-pound) whole sea bass, gutted
Salt and black pepper, to taste
3 bay leaves
1 thyme sprig
1 parsley sprig
1 rosemary sprig
1 tablespoon olive oil
1 tablespoon lemon juice

Season the cavity and outer side of fish with salt and black pepper evenly. With plastic wrap, cover the fish and refrigerate for almost 1 hour. At 450 degrees F, preheat your oven. Lightly grease a baking dish. Arrange 2 bay leaves in the bottom of the prepared baking dish. Divide herb sprigs and the remaining bay leaf inside the cavity of the fish. Arrange the fish over bay leaves in a baking dish and drizzle with oil. Roast for almost 15-20 minutes or until fish is cooked through. Remove the baking dish from the oven and place the fish onto a platter. Serve the fish with the drizzling of lemon juice.

Nutritional information: Calories: 343; Fat: 8.4g; Total Carbs 0.8g; Net Carbs 2g; Protein: 56g; Fiber: 0.4g; Sugar: 0.2g

BBQ Tilapia

Prep time: 10 minutes. | Cooking time: 8 minutes. | Servings: 1

1 (5-ounce) tilapia fillet
¼ tablespoon BBQ seasoning
salt and black pepper, to taste
1 teaspoon olive oil

Season the tilapia fillet with BBQ seasoning, salt and black pepper. In a suitable non-stick pan, heat oil over medium-high heat and cook the tilapia fillet for almost 3-4 minutes per side. Serve hot.

Nutritional information: Calories: 159; Fat: 6g; Total Carbs 0.3g; Net Carbs 2g; Protein: 26.4g; Fiber: 0g; Sugar: 0g

Easy Baked Tuna

Prep time: 5 minutes. | Cooking time: 6 minutes. | Servings: 1

1 (6-ounce) tuna steak
¼ tablespoon olive oil
Salt and black pepper, to taste

Preheat the grill to high heat. Grease the grill grate. Coat the tuna steak with ¼ tablespoon of the oil and sprinkle with salt and black pepper. Set aside for almost 5 minutes. Place the tuna steak over direct heat and cook for almost 2-3 minutes per side. Serve hot.

Nutritional information: Calories: 209; Fat: 5g; Total Carbs 0g; Net Carbs 1.2g; Protein: 39.8g; Fiber: 0g; Sugar: 0g

Almond Topped Tilapia

Prep time: 10 minutes. | Cooking time: 15 minutes. | Servings: 1

2 tablespoons almonds, chopped
1 tablespoon ground flaxseed
1 (6-ounce) tilapia fillet
Salt, as required
½ tablespoon olive oil

In a shallow bowl, mix together the almonds and ground flaxseed. Season the tilapia fillet with the salt evenly. Now, coat the fillet with the almond mixture evenly. In a small heavy skillet, heat the oil over medium heat and cook the tilapia fillet for almost 4 minutes per side. Serve hot.

Nutritional information: Calories: 299; Fat: 16.5g; Total Carbs 4.6g; Net Carbs 5g; Protein: 35.6g; Fiber: 2.6g; Sugar: 0.5g

Garlicky Tilapia

Prep time: 10 minutes. | Cooking time: 5 minutes. | Servings: 1

½ tablespoon olive oil
1 (5-ounce) tilapia fillet
1 garlic clove, minced
¼ tablespoon ginger, minced
2 tablespoons chicken broth, low-sodium
Salt and black pepper, to taste

Heat some oil in a suitable sauté pan over medium heat and cook the tilapia fillet for almost 3 minutes. Flip the side and stir in the garlic and ginger. Cook for almost 2 minutes. Add the broth and cook for almost 2-3 more minutes. Serve hot.

Nutritional information: Calories: 155; Fat: 7.5g; Total Carbs 5.1g; Net Carbs 2g; Protein: 15.6g; Fiber: 0.6g; Sugar: 3.3g

Herb Seasoned Halibut

Prep time: 10 minutes. | Cooking time: 8 minutes. | serves:1

¼ teaspoon dried oregano, crushed
¼ teaspoon dried basil, crushed
¼ teaspoon dried rosemary, crushed
Salt and black pepper, to taste
½ tablespoon olive oil
½ tablespoon lemon juice
1 (4-ounce) halibut fillet

In a suitable bowl, add all the recipe ingredients except for halibut fillet and mix well. Add the halibut fillet and coat with marinade generously. Cover the halibut in the bowl and refrigerate to marinate for at least 1 hour. Preheat the grill to medium-high heat. Grease the grill grate. Place the halibut fillet onto the grill and cook for almost 4 minutes per side. Serve hot.

Nutritional information: Calories: 190; Fat: 9.5g; Total Carbs 0.6g; Net Carbs 2g; Protein: 24g; Fiber: 0.3g; Sugar: 0.2g

Baked Mackerel

Prep time: 10 minutes. | Cooking time: 20 minutes. | Servings: 1

1 (6-ounce) mackerel fillet
½ tablespoon olive oil
Salt and black pepper, to taste

At 350 degrees F, preheat your oven. Arrange the rack in the middle portion of the oven lightly greases a baking dish. Brush the fish fillet with oil and then season with salt and black pepper. Arrange the fish fillet into the prepared baking dish. Bake for almost 16-20 minutes. Serve hot.

Nutritional information: Calories: 330; Fat: 17.5g; Total Carbs 0g; Net Carbs 1.2g; Protein: 29.9g; Fiber: 0g; Sugar: 0g

Oregano Seasoned Tuna

Prep time: 10 minutes. | Cooking time: 4 minutes. | Servings: 1

⅛ teaspoon dried oregano
⅛ teaspoon paprika
⅛ teaspoon cayenne pepper
⅛ teaspoon fennel seeds, crushed
Salt and black pepper, to taste
1 (5-ounce) tuna steak
½ tablespoon olive oil

In a suitable bowl, mix together the oregano and spices. Rub the tuna steak with spice mixture generously. In a cast-iron wok, heat oil over medium-high heat and sear the tuna steak for almost 1½-2 minutes per side. Serve hot.

Nutritional information: Calories: 212; Fat: 8.1g; Total Carbs 0.5g; Net Carbs 2g; Protein: 33.3g; Fiber: 0.3g; Sugar: 0.1g

Halibut Packets

Prep time: 10 minutes. | Cooking time: 40 minutes. | Servings: 1

¼ of onion, chopped
¼ of tomato, chopped
1-ounce kalamata olives, pitted
1 tablespoon capers
½ tablespoon olive oil
¼ tablespoon lemon juice
Salt and black pepper, to taste
1 (5-ounce) halibut fillet
¼ tablespoon Greek seasoning

At 350 degrees F, preheat your oven. In a suitable bowl, add the onion, tomato, onion, olives, capers, oil, lemon juice, salt and black pepper and mix well. Season the halibut fillet with the Greek seasoning and arrange it onto a large piece of foil. Top the fillet with the tomato mixture. Carefully fold all the edges of to create a large packet. Arrange the packet onto a baking sheet. Bake for almost 30 to 40 minutes. Serve hot.

Nutritional information: Calories: 267; Fat: 12.5g; Total Carbs 5.1g; Net Carbs 3g; Protein: 30.8g; Fiber: 2g; Sugar: 1.7g

Baked Cod

Prep time: 5 minutes. | Cooking time: 9 minutes. | Servings: 1

1 (6-ounce) cod fillet
½ tablespoon olive oil
Salt and black pepper, to taste

At 450 degrees F, preheat your oven Rub the cod fillet with oil and then season with salt and black pepper generously. Heat an oven-proof sauté pan over medium heat and cook the cod fillet for almost 2 minutes without stirring. Flip the fillet and immediately transfer the pan into the oven. Bake for almost 5-7 minutes or until the desired doneness of salmon. Serve hot.

Nutritional information: Calories: 197; Fat: 7.5g; Total Carbs 0g; Net Carbs 2g; Protein: 33.4g; Fiber: 0g; Sugar: 0g

Citrus Glazed Trout

Prep time: 10 minutes. | Cooking time: 25 minutes. | serves: 4

1 (1½-pound) wild-caught trout, gutted and cleaned
Salt and black pepper, to taste
½ of lemon, sliced
1 tablespoon dill, minced
1 tablespoon olive oil
½ tablespoon lemon juice

At 475 degrees F, preheat your oven. Arrange a suitable wire rack onto a foil-lined baking sheet. Rub the trout with salt and black pepper from inside and outside generously. Fill the cavity of each fish with lemon slices and dill. Place the trout onto a prepared baking sheet and drizzle with the oil and lemon juice. Bake for almost 25 minutes. Remove the baking sheet from the oven and transfer the trout onto a serving platter. Serve hot.

Nutritional information: Calories: 356; Fat: 18g; Total Carbs 0.5g; Net Carbs 2g; Protein: 45.1g; Fiber: 0.1g; Sugar: 0g

Shrimp with Kale

Prep time: 10 minutes. | Cooking time: 11 minutes. | Servings: 1

½ tablespoon olive oil
¼ pound medium shrimp, peeled and deveined
1 tablespoon onion, chopped
1 garlic clove, chopped
¼ of red chili, sliced
3 ounces kale, tough ribs removed and chopped
2-3 tablespoons chicken broth

In a small non-stick wok, heat 1 tablespoon of the oil over medium-high heat and cook the shrimp for almost 2 minutes per side. With a slotted spoon, transfer the shrimp onto a plate. In the same wok, heat the remaining 2 tablespoons of oil over medium heat and sauté the garlic and red chili for almost 1 minute. Add the kale and broth and cook for almost 4 to 5 minutes, with occasional stirring. Stir in the cooked shrimp and cook for almost 1 minute. Serve hot.

Nutritional information: Calories: 243; Fat: 8.5g; Total Carbs 8.2g; Net Carbs 2g; Protein: 29g; Fiber: 2.1g; Sugar: 0.4g

Shrimp Stir Fry

Prep time: 10 minutes. | Cooking time: 10 minutes. | Servings: 1

1 tablespoon low-sodium soy sauce
¼ tablespoon balsamic vinegar
1 teaspoon erythritol
¼ tablespoon arrowroot starch
¼ tablespoon ginger, minced
⅛ teaspoon red pepper flakes, crushed
½ tablespoon olive oil
½ of small bell pepper, julienned
¼ of a small onion, julienned
¼ of red chili, chopped
¼ pound shrimp, peeled and deveined
¼ of scallion, chopped

Place soy sauce, vinegar, erythritol, arrowroot starch, ginger, and red pepper flakes in a suitable bowl and mix well. Set aside. Heat the oil in a small high-sided wok over high heat and stir-fry the bell peppers, onion, and red chili for almost 1-2 minutes. With the spoon, push the pepper mixture to the edge of the wok to create a space in the center. In the center of wok, place the shrimp in a single layer and cook for almost 1 to 2 minutes. Stir the shrimp with bell pepper mixture and cook for almost 2 minutes. Stir in the sauce and cook for almost 2 to 3 minutes, stirring frequently. Stir in the scallion and remove from the heat. Serve hot.

Nutritional information: Calories: 225; Fat: 8.2g; Total Carbs 8g; Net Carbs 2g; Protein: 27.5g; Fiber: 1.3g; Sugar: 2.3g

Mustard Seasoned Shrimp

Prep time: 10 minutes. | Cooking time: 20 minutes. | Servings: 1

¼ tablespoon olive oil
¼ lb. medium shrimp, peeled and deveined
¼ teaspoon dry mustard
¼ teaspoon dried thyme
¼ teaspoon dried oregano
¼ teaspoon cayenne pepper
¼ teaspoon paprika
¼ teaspoons ground cumin
Salt and black pepper, to taste

At 400 degrees F, preheat your oven. In a small baking dish, place the oil and then place the pan in the oven while preheating. In a suitable bowl, mix together the mustard, dried herbs and spices. Remove the baking dish from the oven. In the baking dish, place the shrimp and spice mixture and mix with oil well. Then arrange the seasoned shrimp in a single layer. Bake for almost 15 minutes. Serve hot.

Nutritional information: Calories: 173; Fat: 6g; Total Carbs 3g; Net Carbs 2g; Protein: 26.2g; Fiber: 0.7g; Sugar: 0.2g

Lemony Dill Tuna

Prep time: 10 minutes. | Cooking time: 12 minutes. | Servings: 1

½ tablespoon olive oil
½ tablespoon lemon juice
¼ teaspoon lemon zest, grated
¼ teaspoon dried dill
Salt and black pepper, to taste
1 (6-ounce) tuna steak

At 400 degrees F, preheat your oven. Line a suitable baking sheet with a piece of foil. In a suitable bowl, combine the oil, lemon juice, zest, dill, salt and black pepper. Place the tuna steak and coat with the mixture generously. Arrange the tuna steak onto the prepared baking sheet and top with any remaining oil mixture from the bowl. Bake for almost 10-12 minutes. Serve hot.

Nutritional information: Calories: 242; Fat: 8.5g; Total Carbs 0.4g; Net Carbs 2g; Protein: 39.9g; Fiber: 0.1g; Sugar: 0.2g

Lemony Shrimp Scampi

Prep time: 10 minutes. | Cooking time: 7 minutes. | Servings: 1

½ tablespoon olive oil
¼ lb. medium shrimp, peeled and deveined
1 garlic clove, minced
¼ of lemon, sliced
⅛ teaspoon red pepper flakes, crushed
Salt, as required
1 tablespoon water
¼ tablespoon lemon juice
1 teaspoon parsley, chopped

In a suitable skillet, heat the oil over medium heat and cook the shrimp, garlic, lemon slices, red pepper flakes and salt for almost 3 minutes per side. Stir in the water, lemon juice and parsley and immediately, remove from the heat. Serve hot.

Nutritional information: Calories: 175; Fat: 8.5g; Total Carbs 1.3g; Net Carbs 2g; Protein: 24.6g; Fiber: 0.2g; Sugar: 0.1g

Saucy Shrimp

Prep time: 10 minutes. | Cooking time: 6 minutes. | Servings: 1

½ tablespoon olive oil
1 garlic clove, minced
¼ lb. raw jumbo shrimp, peeled and deveined
1 tablespoon soy sauce, low-sodium
Black pepper, to taste

In a suitable skillet, heat the oil over medium heat and sauté the garlic for almost 1 minute. Stir in the shrimp, soy sauce and black pepper and cook for almost 4-5 minutes or until done completely. Serve hot.

Nutritional information: Calories: 151; Fat: 7g; Total Carbs 2.1g; Net Carbs 2g; Protein: 21.5g; Fiber: 0.1g; Sugar: 3.1g

Shrimp Bell Peppers Soup

Prep time: 10 minutes. | Cooking time: 22 minutes. | Servings: 1

½ tablespoon olive oil
¼ pound medium shrimp, peeled and deveined
1 garlic clove, minced
¼ teaspoon ginger, minced
¼ teaspoon red curry paste
½ of bell pepper, chopped
¾ cup chicken broth
¼ cup unsweetened coconut milk
¼ tablespoon lime juice
Salt and black pepper, to taste
1 teaspoon scallion, chopped

In a suitable saucepan, heat oil over medium-high heat and cook the shrimp for almost 2 to 3 minutes. With a slotted spoon, transfer the shrimp onto a plate. In the same pan, add garlic and ginger and sauté for almost 30 seconds. Stir in curry paste and sauté for almost 30 seconds more. Add chopped bell peppers and sauté for 2 minutes almost. Stir in the broth and coconut milk and bring to a boil over high

heat. Reduce its heat to low and simmer for 8-10 minutes. Stir in shrimp, lime juice, scallion, salt and black pepper and cook for almost 1-2 minutes. Serve hot.

Nutritional information: Calories: 235; Fat: 10.4g; Total Carbs 6g; Net Carbs 2g; Protein: 27.9g; Fiber: 1.3g; Sugar: 1.5g

Shrimp Kabobs

Prep time: 10 minutes. | Cooking time: 8 minutes. | Servings: 1

½ tablespoon olive oil
½ tablespoon lime juice
¼ teaspoon paprika
Pinch of ground cumin
Salt and black pepper, to taste
¼ pound medium raw shrimp, peeled and deveined

In a small glass baking dish, add all the recipe ingredients except for shrimp and mix well. Add the shrimp and coat with the herb mixture generously. Refrigerate to marinate for at least 30 minutes. Preheat the grill to medium-high heat. Grease the grill grate. Thread the shrimp onto pre-soaked wooden skewers. Place the prepared skewers onto the hot grill and cook for almost 2-4 minutes per side. Serve.

Nutritional information: Calories: 198; Fat: 9g; Total Carbs 2.2g; Net Carbs 2g; Protein: 26g; Fiber: 0.2g; Sugar: 0.1g

Garlick Mixed Shrimp

Prep time: 10 minutes. | Cooking time: 6 minutes. | Servings: 1

½ tablespoon olive oil
¼ pound medium shrimp, peeled and deveined
1 large garlic clove, minced
Salt and black pepper, to taste

Heat ½ tablespoon of the oil in a sauté pan over medium heat and cook the shrimp, garlic, salt, and black pepper for almost 3 minutes per side, with occasional stirring. Serve hot.

Nutritional information: Calories: 172; Fat: 8.4g; Total Carbs 1g; Net Carbs 3g; Protein: 24.5g; Fiber: 0.1g; Sugar: 0g

Glazed Scallops

Prep time: 10 minutes. | Cooking time: 6 minutes. | Servings: 1

¼ pound sea scallops, side muscles removed
Salt and black pepper, to taste
½ tablespoon olive oil
1 garlic clove, minced

Sprinkle the scallops evenly with salt and black pepper. Heat ½ tablespoon of the oil in a suitable sauté pan over medium-high heat and then sauté the garlic, for almost 1 minute. Add the scallops and cook for almost 2 to 3 minutes per side. Serve hot.

Nutritional information: Calories: 164; Fat: 7.9g; Total Carbs 2g; Net Carbs 2g; Protein: 19.2g; Fiber: 0.1g; Sugar: 0g

Shrimp Zucchini Kabobs

Prep time: 10 minutes. | Cooking time: 6 minutes. | Servings: 1

1 tablespoon olive oil
½ tablespoon lemon juice
¼ tablespoon garlic, minced
½ teaspoon thyme
½ teaspoon oregano
⅛ teaspoon dried Italian seasoning
⅛ teaspoon ground cumin
⅛ teaspoon red pepper flakes
Salt and black pepper, to taste
¼ pound large shrimp, peeled deveined
½ of zucchini, sliced

Preheat the grill to medium-high heat. Grease the grill grate. In a suitable bowl, blend together all the recipe ingredients except for shrimp and zucchini. Add the shrimp and zucchini slices and coat with mixture evenly. Thread the shrimp and zucchini onto pre-soaked wooden skewers. Place the prepared skewers onto the hot grill and cook for almost 2-3 minutes per side. Serve.

Nutritional information: Calories: 283; Fat: 16.5g; Total Carbs 7g; Net Carbs 3g; Protein: 27.4g; Fiber: 1.8g; Sugar: 2g

Salmon Cabbage Soup

Prep time: 10 minutes. | Cooking time: 30 minutes. | Servings: 1

½ tablespoon olive oil
¼ of onion, chopped
¼ cup cabbage, chopped
1 cup low-sodium chicken broth
1 (4-ounce) boneless salmon fillet, cubed
1 teaspoon cilantro, minced
¼ tablespoon lemon juice
Salt and black pepper, to taste

In a suitable saucepan, heat the oil over medium heat and sauté the onion for almost 5 to 6 minutes. Add the cabbage and sauté for almost 5 to 6 minutes. Add the broth and bring to a boil over high heat. Reduce its heat to medium-low and simmer for almost 10 minutes. Add the salmon and cook for almost 5 to 6 minutes. Stir in the cilantro, lemon juice, salt and black pepper and cook for almost 1 to 2 minutes. Serve hot.

Nutritional information: Calories: 241; Fat: 12.5g; Total Carbs 4.7g; Net Carbs 2g; Protein: 24.6g; Fiber: 1.1g; Sugar: 1.8g

Spicy Grouper Curry

Prep time: 10 minutes. | Cooking time: 15 minutes. | Servings: 1

½ tablespoon olive oil
¼ of small yellow onion, chopped
1 garlic clove, minced
¼ teaspoon ginger, minced
½ of a small tomato, peeled and chopped
¼ tablespoon curry powder
¼ cup water
2 tablespoons unsweetened coconut milk
¼ pound grouper fillet, cubed into 2-inch size
Salt, as required
1 teaspoon parsley, chopped

In a suitable wok, heat the ½ tablespoon oil over medium heat. Sauté the onion, garlic, and ginger for almost 5 minutes. Add the tomato and curry powder and cook for almost 2-3 minutes, crushing with the back of a spoon. Add the water and coconut milk and bring to a gentle boil. Stir in grouper pieces and cook for almost 4-5 minutes. Stir in the salt and basil leaves and serve hot.

Nutritional information: Calories: 226; Fat: 9.4g; Total Carbs 6g; Net Carbs 2g; Protein: 29.2g; Fiber: 1.6g; Sugar: 2g

Salmon Pepper Kabobs

Prep time: 10 minutes. | Cooking time: 8 minutes. | Servings: 1

½ tablespoon lime juice
½ tablespoon olive oil
¼ tablespoon Dijon mustard
¼ pound salmon, cut into 1-inch-thick cubes
½ of small bell pepper, cubed
¼ of a small onion, cut into wedges

In a suitable bowl, combine the lime juice, oil, and mustard. Add fish cubes and coat with marinade generously. Cover the fish bowl and refrigerate to marinate for almost 15 minutes, flipping occasionally. Preheat the broiler of the oven. Arrange a rack about 4-inches from the heating element. Remove the salmon cubes from the bowl, reserving the remaining marinade. Thread the salmon cubes, bell pepper and onion onto pre-soaked wooden skewers. Place the skewers onto a broiler pan and broil for almost 6-8 minutes, flipping and coating with reserved marinade once halfway through. Serve hot.

Nutritional information: Calories: 228; Fat: 14.2g; Total Carbs 3.6g; Net Carbs 2g; Protein: 22.6g; Fiber: 1.1g; Sugar: 1.7g

Salmon with Maple and Orange Glaze

Prep time: 03 minutes. | Cook Time: 18 minutes. | Serves: 4

1 ½ lb. salmon fillet
1 tbsp. orange juice
What you'll need from store cupboard:
2 tbsp. sugar-free maple syrup
2 tbsp. grainy Dijon mustard
2 tsp. garlic, diced fine
Nonstick cooking spray

Preheat the oven to 375 degrees Fahrenheit. Coat a baking dish with cooking spray and place the salmon skin side down in it. Combine orange juice, syrup, mustard, and garlic in a small mixing basin. Cover the fish with foil and pour the sauce over it. Bake for 15 minutes in the oven; uncover and bake for another 5 minutes, or until the top of the fish is caramelized and the fish readily flakes with a fork. When done, serve and enjoy.

Nutritional information: Calories 247 Total Carbs 6g Protein 33g Fat 11g Sugar 1g Fiber 0g

Tangy Snapper Kabobs

Prep time: 10 minutes. | Cooking time: 10 minutes. | Servings: 1

½ tablespoon lemon juice
½ tablespoon olive oil
¼ tablespoon cilantro, minced
1 garlic clove, crushed
⅛ teaspoon paprika
⅛ teaspoon cayenne pepper
⅛ teaspoon ground cumin
Pinch of ground turmeric
Salt, as required
¼ pound snapper fillet, cut into 1½-inch chunks

In a suitable glass baking dish, whisk lemon juice, oil, cilantro, garlic and spices. Place fish chunks and coat with marinade generously. With a plastic wrap, cover the baking dish and refrigerate to marinate for almost 30 minutes. Preheat the grill to medium heat. Grease the grill grate. Thread the fish chunks onto pre-soaked wooden skewers. Place the prepared skewers onto the grill and cook for almost 10 minutes, flipping once halfway through. Serve hot.

Nutritional information: Calories: 217; Fat: 9.2g; Total Carbs 1.7g; Net Carbs 1.2g; Protein: 29.8g; Fiber: 0.4g; Sugar: 0.3g

Halibut Kabobs

Prep time: 10 minutes. | Cooking time: 8 minutes. | Servings: 1

1 teaspoon cilantro leaves, chopped
1 garlic clove, chopped
½ tablespoon olive oil
½ tablespoon lemon juice
⅛ teaspoon ground coriander
⅛ teaspoon ground cumin
Salt and black pepper, to taste
¼ lb. halibut fillet, cut into ½-inch cubes
4 cherry tomatoes

In a suitable bowl, combine the cilantro, garlic, oil, lemon juice and spices. Add fish cubes and coat with marinade generously. Cover this bowl and refrigerate to marinate for almost 1 hour, flipping occasionally. Preheat the grill to medium heat. Grease the grill grate. Thread the fish chunks and tomatoes onto pre-soaked wooden skewers. Place the prepared skewers onto the hot grill and cook for almost 6-8 minutes, flipping occasionally. Serve hot.

Nutritional information: Calories: 201; Fat: 9.9g; Total Carbs 3g; Net Carbs 2g; Protein: 24.6g; Fiber: 0.7g; Sugar: 1.4g

Shrimp Mushroom Soup

Prep time: 10 minutes. | Cooking time: 35 minutes. | Servings: 1

1 cup chicken broth, low-sodium
½ of red chili, sliced
¼ tablespoon ginger, sliced
3 ounces canned straw mushrooms, halved
¼ tablespoon red boat fish sauce
¼ pound large shrimp, peeled and deveined
¼ tablespoon lime juice

1 teaspoon cilantro, chopped

In a suitable saucepan, pour broth over medium-high heat and bring to a boil. Add the red chiles and ginger and stir to combine. Adjust the heat to medium-low and simmer, covered for almost 15 minutes. Stir in mushrooms and fish sauce and simmer, uncovered for almost 5 to 7 minutes. Stir in shrimp and cook for almost 8 minutes. Stir in remaining ingredients, and immediately remove from the heat. Serve hot.

Nutritional information: Calories: 177; Fat: 2.2g; Total Carbs 5g; Net Carbs 2g; Protein: 31.6g; Fiber: 1g; Sugar: 1.5g

Salmon Bell Pepper Stew

Prep time: 18 minutes. | Cooking time: 10 minutes. | Servings: 1

¼ pound salmon fillet, cut into 2-inch pieces
Salt and black pepper, to taste
½ tablespoon olive oil
½ of small bell pepper, sliced
¼ of small white onion, chopped
½ garlic clove, minced
1 bay leaf
¼ teaspoons smoked paprika
1 tomato, chopped
⅓ cup water
1 teaspoon cilantro, chopped

In a suitable bowl, add salmon and sprinkle with a small salt and black pepper. Set aside. In a suitable skillet, heat oil over medium-high heat and sauté bell peppers and onion for almost 4-5 minutes. Add garlic, bay leaf and paprika and sauté for almost 1 minute. Stir in tomatoes and cook, covered for almost 5 minutes. Add water and bring to a boil. Stir in salmon and reduce its heat to medium-low. Cover and simmer for almost 5-7 minutes. Stir in cilantro, salt and black pepper and remove from heat. Discard bay leaf and serve hot.

Nutritional information: Calories: 243; Fat: 14.3g; Total Carbs 7g; Net Carbs 3g; Protein: 23.4g; Fiber: 2.1g; Sugar: 3.3g

Tuna Steaks on the Grill

Prep time: 04 minutes. | Cook Time: 08 minutes. | Serves: 6

6 6 oz. tuna steaks
3 tbsp. fresh basil, diced
What you'll need from store cupboard:
4 ½ tsp. olive oil
¾ tsp. salt
¼ tsp. pepper
Nonstick cooking spray

Preheat the grill to medium. Using cooking spray, coat the rack. Drizzle oil on all sides of the tuna. Mix in the basil and season to taste with salt and pepper. Cook for 5 minutes per side on the grill; the tuna should be slightly pink in the center. Serve.

Nutritional information: Calories 343; Total Carbs 0g; Net Carbs 0g; Protein 51.0g; Fat 14.0g; Sugar 0g; Fiber 0 g

Cakes of Crab

Prep time: 10 minutes. | Cook Time: 10 minutes. | Serves: 8 (2 crab cakes per serving)

1 lb. lump blue crabmeat
1 tbsp. red bell pepper, diced fine
1 tbsp. green bell pepper, diced fine
1 tbsp. fresh parsley, chopped fine
2 eggs
¼ tsp. fresh lemon juice
What you'll need from store cupboard:
¼ cup + 1 tbsp. lite mayonnaise
¼ cup Dijon mustard
2 tbsp. sunflower oil
1 tbsp. baking powder
1 tbsp. Worcestershire sauce
1 ½ tsp. Old Bay

¼ cup mayonnaise, Dijon mustard, Worcestershire sauce, and lemon juice, whisked together in a small bowl Refrigerate until ready to serve. Mix crab, bell peppers, parsley, eggs, 1 tablespoon mayonnaise, baking powder, and Old Bay flavour in a large mixing basin until everything is well blended. In a large skillet, heat the oil over medium-high heat. Drop 2 teaspoons crab mixture into heated skillet once oil is hot. They'll be a little loose at first, but they'll stick together as the egg cooks. Cook for 2 minutes, or until firm, then flip and cook for an additional minute. Place on a serving dish. With a mustard dipping sauce on the side.

Nutritional information: Calories 96; Total Carbs 3g; Net Carbs 2g; Protein 12.0g; Fat 4.0g; Sugar 1g; Fiber 0 g

Catfish in the Cajun style

Prep time: 5 minutes. | Cook Time: 15 minutes. | Serves: 4

4 (8 oz.) catfish fillets
What you'll need from store cupboard:
2 tbsp. olive oil
2 tsp. garlic salt
2 tsp. thyme
2 tsp. paprika
½ tsp. cayenne pepper
½ tsp. red hot sauce
¼ tsp. black pepper
Nonstick cooking spray

Preheat the oven to 450 degrees Fahrenheit. Using cooking spray, coat a 9x13-inch baking dish. Everything except the catfish goes into a small bowl and is whisked together. Brush both sides of the fillets with the spice mixture. Bake for 10-13 minutes, or until the fish easily flakes with a fork. Serve.

Nutritional information: Calories 366; Total Carbs 0g; Net Carbs 0g; Protein 35.0g; Fat 24.0g; Sugar 0g; Fiber 0g

Tomatoes & Cajun Flounder

Prep time: 10 minutes. | Cook Time: 15 minutes. | Serves: 4

4 flounder fillets
2 ½ cups tomatoes, diced
¾ cup onion, diced
¾ cup green bell pepper, diced
What you'll need from store cupboard:
2 cloves garlic, diced fine
1 tbsp. Cajun seasoning
1 tsp. olive oil

In a large skillet, heat the oil over medium-high heat. Cook for 2 minutes, or until onion and garlic are tender. Cook for 2-3 minutes, or until tomatoes soften, before adding tomatoes, peppers, and seasonings. Place the fish on top. Cook for 5-8 minutes, covered, on medium heat, or until fish flakes easily with a fork. Place the fish on serving dishes and drizzle with the sauce.

Nutritional information: Calories 194; Total Carbs 6g; Net Carbs 0g; Protein 32.0g; Fat 3.0g; Sugar 5g; Fiber 2 g

Cajun Shrimp & Roasted Vegetables

Prep time: 04 minutes. | Cook Time: 14 minutes. | Serves: 4

1 lb. large shrimp, peeled and deveined
2 zucchinis, sliced
2 yellow squash, sliced
½ bunch asparagus, cut into thirds
2 red bell pepper, cut into chunks
What you'll need from store cupboard:
2 tbsp. olive oil
2 tbsp. Cajun Seasoning
Salt & pepper, to taste

Preheat the oven to 400 degrees Fahrenheit. In a large mixing basin, combine the shrimp and vegetables. To coat, toss in the oil and spices. Bake for 15-20 minutes, or until vegetables are soft, on a large baking sheet. Serve.

Nutritional information: Calories 251; Total Carbs 13g; Net Carbs 9g; Protein 30.0g; Fat 9.0g; Sugar 6g; Fiber 4 g

Salmon Shrimp Stew

Prep time: 10 minutes. | Cooking time: 18 minutes. | Servings: 1

⅓ cup tomatoes, peeled, chopped
½ cup chicken broth
2 ounces salmon fillet, cubed
¼ pound shrimp, peeled and deveined
½ tablespoon lime juice
Salt and black pepper, to taste
1 teaspoon parsley, chopped

In a suitable saucepan, add the tomatoes and broth and bring to a boil. Reduce its heat to medium and simmer for almost 5 minutes. Add the salmon and simmer for almost 3 to 4 minutes. Stir in the shrimp and cook for almost 4 to 5 minutes. Stir in lemon juice, salt, and black pepper, and remove from heat. Serve hot with the garnishing of parsley.

Nutritional information: Calories: 229; Fat: 5.6g; Total Carbs 4.7g; Net Carbs 2g; Protein: 38.4g; Fiber: 0.8g; Sugar: 1.6g

Grilled Shrimp with Cilantro and Lime

Prep time: 5 minutes. | Cook Time: 5 minutes. | Serves: 6

12-pound uncooked, peeled, deveined big shrimp with tails
Juice and zest of 1 lime
2 tbsp. fresh cilantro chopped
What you'll need from store cupboard:
¼ cup olive oil
2 cloves garlic, diced fine
1 tsp. smoked paprika
¼ tsp. cumin
½ teaspoon salt
¼ tsp. cayenne pepper

In a big Ziploc bag, place the shrimp. In a small bowl, combine the other Ingredients and pour over the shrimp. Allow 20-30 minutes for marinating. Preheat the grill. Cook the shrimp on skewers for 2-3 minutes per side, or until they turn pink. Make sure you don't overcook them. Serve with cilantro on top.

Nutritional information: Calories 317; Total Carbs 4g; Net Carbs 4g; Protein 39.0g; Fat 15.0g; Sugar 0g; Fiber 0 g

Frittata with Crab

Prep time: 10 minutes. | Cook Time: 50 minutes. | Serves: 4

4 eggs
2 cups lump crabmeat
1 cup half-n-half
1 cup green onions, diced
What you'll need from store cupboard:
1 cup reduced fat parmesan cheese, grated
1 tsp. salt
1 tsp. pepper
1 tsp. smoked paprika
1 tsp. Italian seasoning
Nonstick cooking spray

Preheat the oven to 350 degrees Fahrenheit. Using cooking spray, coat the suitable springform pan or pie dish. Whisk together the eggs and half-n-half in a large mixing bowl. Stir in the Ingredients and parmesan cheese. Combine the onions and crab meat in a mixing bowl. Bake 35-40 minutes, or until eggs are set and top is gently browned, in prepared pan. Allow 10 minutes to cool before slicing and serving warm or at room temperature.

Nutritional information: Calories 276; Total Carbs 5g; Net Carbs 4g; Protein 25.0g; Fat 17.0g; Sugar 1g; Fiber 1 g

Fish & Tomatoes in the Crock Pot

Prep time: 10 mins. | Cook Time: 2 hours 30 mins. | Serves: 4

1 lb. cod
1 bell pepper, diced
1 small onion, diced
What you'll need from store cupboard:
15 oz. can tomatoes, diced
1/3 cup low-sodium vegetable broth
1 clove garlic, diced fine

½ tsp. basil
½ tsp. oregano
½ tsp. salt
¼ tsp. pepper

In the crock pot, combine the onion, bell pepper, tomatoes, and garlic. To blend, stir everything together. Arrange the fish on top. Season with herbs and seasonings before serving. Pour the broth on top. Cook on high for 1-2 hours or low for 2-4 hours, covered.

Nutritional information: Calories 165; Total Carbs 11g; Net Carbs 8g; Protein 28.0g; Fat 1.0g; Sugar 6g; Fiber 3 g

Lemon Shrimp with a Crunch

Prep time: 5 minutes. | Cook Time: 10 minutes. | Serves: 4

1 lb. raw shrimp, peeled and deveined
2 tbsp. Italian parsley, roughly chopped
2 tbsp. lemon juice, divided
What you'll need from store cupboard:
⅔ cup panko bread crumbs
2½ tbsp. olive oil, divided
Salt and pepper, to taste

Preheat the oven to 400 degrees Fahrenheit. Sprinkle salt and pepper equally over the shrimp in a baking dish. 1 tablespoon lemon juice and 1 tablespoon olive oil, drizzled on top. Remove from the equation. Combine parsley, remaining lemon juice, bread crumbs, remaining olive oil, and ¼ teaspoons salt and pepper in a medium mixing bowl. On top of the shrimp, equally distribute the panko mixture. Bake for 8-10 minutes, or until the shrimp are done and the panko is golden brown.

Nutritional information: Calories 283; Total Carbs 15g; Net Carbs 14g; Protein 28.0g; Fat 12.0g; Sugar 1g; Fiber 1 g

Fish Fillet Crusted with Cumin

Prep Time: 10 minutes. | Cook Time: 4 minutes. | Servings: 4

1 tablespoon Cumin (ground)
¼ teaspoon thyme
1 teaspoon Paprika
½ teaspoon Lemon pepper
1 pound Halibut fish fillets
½ tablespoon Canola oil
2 tablespoons Parsley (chopped)
4 Lime wedges

Prepare a shallow bowl and add the cumin, paprika, lemon pepper, and thyme. Mix well to combine. Rub both sides of the fillet evenly with the prepared spice blend. Prepare a suitable cooking skillet and place it over a medium flame. Pour in the canola oil and heat. Place the fish fillet in the pan and cook 4 minutes per side or until the fish is opaque. Transfer to a plate and sprinkle with parsley. Serve with lemon wedges.

Nutritional information: Calories 130; Total Carbs 1g; Net Carbs 0.4g; Protein 22g; Fat 4g; Sugar 0g; Fiber 0g

Sun-Dried Tomatoes with Garlic Shrimp

Prep time: 08 minutes. | Cook Time: 28 minutes. | Serves: 4

½ lb. shrimp, peeled and deveined
4 oz. sun-dried tomatoes
1 cup half-n-half
What you'll need from store cupboard:
1 cup reduced fat parmesan cheese
4 cloves garlic, diced fine
2 tbsp. olive oil
1 teaspoon dried basil
¼ tsp. salt
¼ tsp. paprika
¼ teaspoon crushed red pepper
½ recipe homemade pasta, cook and drain, (chapter 14)

Heat the oil in a large pan over medium heat. Cook for 1 minute after adding the garlic and tomatoes. Cook for 2 minutes after adding the shrimp, seasoning with salt and paprika. Bring to a boil with the half-n-half, basil, and crushed red pepper. Reduce the heat to a low simmer. On low heat, whisk the parmesan cheese into the hot cream and stir to melt the cheese. Remove the pan from the heat. Toss in the spaghetti and coat with the sauce. Serve.

Nutritional information: Calories 353; Total Carbs 23g; Net Carbs 20g; Protein 22.0g; Fat 22.0g; Sugar 3g; Fiber 3 g

Steamed Mussels in Italy

Prep time: 08 minutes. | Cook Time: 08 minutes. | Serves: 4

2 lbs. mussels, cleaned
2 plum tomatoes, peeled, seeded and diced
1 cup onion, diced
2 tbsp. fresh parsley, diced
What you'll need from store cupboard:
¼ cup dry white wine
3 cloves garlic, diced fine
3 tbsp. olive oil
2 tbsp. fresh breadcrumbs
¼ teaspoon crushed red pepper flakes

In a large sauce saucepan over medium heat, heat the oil. Cook, stirring occasionally, until the onions are tender, about 2-3 minutes. After adding the garlic, cook for another minute. Combine the wine, tomatoes, and pepper flakes in a mixing bowl. Bring to a boil, stir to combine. Cook for 3 to 4 minutes, or until all of the mussels have opened. Mussels that do not open should be thrown away. Transfer the mussels to a serving basin once they have opened. Cook, stirring regularly, until the mixture thickens, then add the bread crumbs to the sauce. Stir in the parsley and pour over the mussels evenly. Serve and enjoy.

Nutritional information: Calories 340; Total Carbs 18g; Net Carbs 16g; Protein 29.0g; Fat 8.0g; Sugar 4g; Fiber 2 g

Pasta with Mediterranean Shrimp

Prep time: 14 minutes. | Cook Time: 18 minutes. | Serves: 4

1 lb. med. shrimp, peel & devein
1 lb. Trimmed asparagus, cut into 1-inch segments
½ cup sun dried tomatoes
½ cup green onions, sliced thin
What you'll need from store cupboard:
½ recipe Homemade Pasta, (chapter 15) cook & drain
8 oz. tomato sauce
1 cup boiling water
2 cloves garlic, diced
2 tbsp. clam juice
2 tbsp. apple juice, unsweetened
1 tbsp. olive oil
1 tsp. curry powder
¼ tsp. pepper

Fill a small bowl halfway with boiling water and add the tomatoes. Drain after 5 minutes of standing. Combine tomato sauce, clam juice, apple juice, and seasonings in a small bowl. Heat the oil in a large skillet over medium-high heat. Cook for 2 minutes after adding the asparagus. Cook for another minute after adding the green onions and garlic. Add the shrimp and mix well. Cook for 3 minutes, stirring occasionally, or until shrimp turn pink. Heat through the tomato mixture and the sun dried tomatoes. Cook, stirring constantly, until the pasta is hot. Serve.

Nutritional information: Calories 296 Total Carbs 20g Net Carbs 15g Protein 37g Fat 9g Sugar 9g Fiber 5g

Halibut from Spain

Prep time: 10 minutes. | Cook Time: 40 minutes. | Serves: 6

6 6 oz. halibut filets, pat dry
6 thick slices tomato
1 onion, sliced thin
1 cup mushrooms, sliced thin
4 ½ tsp. plant-based butter
What you'll need from store cupboard:
½ cup bread crumbs
¼ cup white wine
2 tbsp. pimientos, diced
1 tbsp. olive oil
1 ¼ tsp. salt
¼ tsp. mace
¼ tsp. cayenne pepper
¼ tsp. black pepper

Preheat the oven to 350 degrees Fahrenheit. Brush the oil into the bottom of a 13x9-inch baking dish. On the bottom of the prepared dish, place the onion and pimiento. Combine seasonings in a small bowl and sprinkle on both sides of the halibut. In a baking dish, place the halibut. Place a piece of tomato on top of each fillet, then top with mushrooms and green onions. Pour the wine over everything. In a skillet over medium heat, melt butter. Cook, stirring constantly, until the bread crumbs are light brown. Sprinkle on top of the fish. Bake for 20 minutes, covered in foil. Remove the lid and bake for another 20-25 minutes, or until the fish flakes easily with a fork. Serve.

Nutritional information: Calories 205 Total Carbs 13g Net Carbs 11g Protein 22g Fat 6g Sugar 4g Fiber 2g

Noodles with Dill Smoked Salmon

Prep time: 08 minutes. | Cook Time: 08 minutes. | Serves: 4

6 oz. smoked salmon, chopped
Juice from ½ a lemon
¼ cup half-n-half
3 tbsp. plant-based butter
2 tbsp. fresh dill, diced
What you'll need from store cupboard:
Homemade noodles
½ cup low sodium chicken broth
½ cup dry white wine
1 tbsp. olive oil
2 cloves garlic, diced fine
Salt & pepper, to taste

In a large frying pan, heat the oil and butter over moderate flame. Cook for another 30 seconds after adding the garlic. Combine the broth, wine, and lemon juice in a mixing bowl. Cook for about 4 minutes, or until the sauce has been reduced by half. Cook for 2 minutes, or until the noodles are done, stirring in the half-n-half. Season the salmon to taste with salt and pepper. Garnish with a sprig of fresh dill.

Nutritional information: Calories 273; Total Carbs 4g; Net Carbs 4g; Protein 14.0g; Fat 21.0g; Sugar 0g; Fiber 0 g

Skillet with Shrimp and Artichokes

Prep time: 04 minutes. | Cook Time: 08 minutes. | Serves: 4

1 ½ cups shrimp, peel & devein
2 shallots, diced
1 tbsp. plant-based butter
What you'll need from store cupboard
2 12 oz. jars artichoke hearts, drain & rinse
2 cups white wine
2 cloves garlic, diced fine

Melt butter in a large saucepan over moderate heat. Cook, stirring often, until the shallot and garlic begin to brown. Cook for 5 minutes after adding the artichokes. Remove the pan from the heat and add the wine. Cook, stirring occasionally, for 3 minutes. Cook for a few minutes, just until the shrimp turn pink. Serve.

Nutritional information: Calories 487 Total Carbs 26g Net Carbs 17g Protein 64g Fat 5g Sugar 3g Fiber 9g

Pasta with a Seafood Medley

Prep time: 5 minutes. | Cook Time: 3 hours 10 minutes. | Serves: 10

24 oz. seafood mix, thaw
1 lemon, cut in wedges
¼ cup fresh parsley, diced
1 onion, diced
What you'll need from store cupboard:
28 oz. can petite tomatoes, diced
2½ cup low-sodium chicken broth
⅔ cup dry white wine
4 cloves garlic, diced fine

2 tbsp. olive oil
1 tsp. paprika
¼ tsp. salt and
¼ tsp. black pepper
1 recipe Homemade Pasta, (chapter 15)

In a big, deep skillet, heat the oil over medium-high heat. Cook for 1 minute, or until garlic begins to smell fragrant. Cook until the liquid has mostly evaporated, then add the wine. Increase the heat to high and toss in the tomatoes, broth, and seasonings to bring to a boil. Reduce the heat to medium-low and cook, stirring periodically, for 7-9 minutes, or until the pasta is done. Cook for 3-4 minutes, or until the seafood is cooked through. Serve garnished with a lemon wedge and parsley.

Nutritional information: Calories 358 Total Carbs 24g Net Carbs 19g Protein 35g Fat 11g Sugar 11g Fiber 5g

Tilapia Fillet with Fruity Salsa

Prep Time: 30 minutes. | Cook Time: 0 minutes. | Servings: 4

½ lb. (quartered) raspberries
½ (peeled, cored and chopped) fresh pineapple
1 (peeled, seeded and diced) large mango
3 (peeled and diced) kiwifruit
2 tablespoons fresh parsley, finely chopped
½ cup grape tomatoes
1 ½ lbs. tilapia fillets
1 tablespoon balsamic vinegar
½ teaspoon seasoned pepper blend

Add the vinegar, parsley, tomatoes, mango, kiwi, strawberry, and pineapple to a bowl and wait until combined. Add avocado oil to a saucepan on medium-high heat. Coat the tilapia fillets with the pepper mixture. Put the caoted fish in a hot pan and fry for 2-3 minutes until the fish is opaque and white. Serve the salsa with the cooked tilapia.

Nutritional information: Calories 305; Total Carbs 35g; Net Carbs 25g; Protein 36g; Fat 3g; Sugar 5g; Fiber 6g

Lemon Trout Fillets

Prep time: 04 minutes. | Cook Time: 08 minutes. | Serves: 6

6 6 oz. trout fillets
6 lemon slices
What you'll need from store cupboard:
4 tbsp. olive oil
¾ tsp. salt
½ tsp. pepper
Italian-Style Salsa, (chapter 16)

Season the fillets with salt and pepper before serving. Heat the oil in a large nonstick skillet over medium-high heat. Cook 3 fillets at a time for 2-3 minutes per side, or until fish easily flakes with a fork. Continue with the remaining fillets. Serve with salsa and a lemon slice on top.

Nutritional information: Calories 320 Total Carbs 2g Protein 30g Fat 21g Sugar 1g Fiber 0g

Halibut with Vegetables

Prep Time: 25 minutes. | Cook Time: 20 minutes. | Servings: 4

1 pound green beans, trimmed
2 red bell peppers, seeded and cut into strips
1 onion, sliced
Zest and juice of 2 lemons
3 garlic cloves, minced
2 tablespoons extra-virgin olive oil
1 teaspoon dried dill
1 teaspoon dried oregano
4 halibut fillets
½ teaspoon salt
¼ teaspoon freshly ground black pepper

Preheat the oven to 400ºF (205ºC). Line a baking sheet with parchment paper. Toss the green beans, bell peppers, onion, lemon zest and juice, garlic, olive oil, dill, and oregano in a large bowl. Transfer the vegetables to the prepared baking sheet in a single layer, leaving the juice behind in the bowl. Gently place the halibut fillets in the bowl, and coat in the vegetable juice. Transfer the fillets to the baking sheet, nestled between the vegetables, and drizzle them with any juice left in
the bowl. Sprinkle the vegetables and halibut with the salt and pepper. Bake the fish for 15 to 20 minutes until the vegetables are just tender and the fish flakes apart easily. When done, serve and enjoy.

Nutritional information: Calories 235; Total Carbs 16g; Net Carbs 11g; Protein 23g; Fat 9g; Sugar 2g; Fiber 3g

Pasta with Sweet and Spicy Seafood

Prep time: 10 minutes. | Cook Time: 10 minutes. | Serves: 4

¼ lb. shrimp, peel & devein
¼ lb. scallops
6 oz. Chilean sea bass, cut in ½ -inch pieces
½ white onion, cut in strips
Juice of 1 lemon
½ cup fresh pineapple, diced
½ cup flat-leaf parsley, diced
What you'll need from store cupboard:
1½ cup white wine
¼ cup extra virgin olive oil
3 cloves garlic, diced fine
1½ tbsp. salt
¾ tsp. red pepper flakes
½ recipe Homemade Pasta,

In a big pot, heat the oil over high heat. Cook, stirring regularly, until the onion is tender, about 1 minute. Combine the garlic, shrimp, scallops, sea bass, and salt in a large mixing bowl. Cook for another minute, stirring occasionally. Toss the spaghetti in the pot, making sure that each strand is well-coated in oil. Reduce the heat to medium-low and stir in the wine, lemon juice, and pineapple until the pasta and fish are fully cooked, about 8 minutes. Take the pan off the heat and add the parsley and red pepper flakes. Serve right away.

Nutritional information: Calories 334 Total Carbs 13g Net Carbs 11g Protein 25g Fat 21g Sugar 6g Fiber 2g

Seafood & Broccoli Pasta

Prep time: 10 minutes. | Cook Time: 15 minutes. | Serves: 6

1 lb. shrimp, peel & devein
1 lb. sea scallops, pat dry
1 lb. broccoli florets, steamed
2 6.5 oz. cans clams, chopped
1 cup half-n-half
½ tablespoon olive oil
What you'll need from store cupboard:
1 cup clam juice
6 cloves garlic, diced fine
4 tbsp. reduced fat parmesan
3 tbsp. flour
1 recipe Homemade Pasta, cook & drain

In a large pot over medium heat, heat the oil. Cook, stirring constantly, for 2 minutes after adding the garlic. Cook for 5 minutes, or until shrimp turn pink, before adding the shrimp and scallops. Bring to a gentle boil with the clams, clam juice, and half-n-half. Cook, stirring constantly, until the sauce has thickened. Heat the broccoli until it is fully cooked. Serve with parmesan cheese on top of cooked spaghetti.

Nutritional information: Calories 519 Total Carbs 28g Net Carbs 23g Protein 50g Fat 23g Sugar 7g Fiber 5g

Curry with Shrimp and Coconut

Prep time: 08 minutes. | Cook Time: 24 minutes. | Serves: 4

1 lb. extra-large shrimp, peel & devein
1 onion, diced fine
1 ¾ cup coconut milk, unsweetened
2 tbsp. fresh lemon juice
1 tbsp. fresh ginger, grated
What you'll need from store cupboard:
14.5 oz. can tomatoes, diced
3 cloves garlic, diced fine
1 tbsp. coconut oil
2 tsp. coriander
1 tsp. curry powder
1 tsp. salt, or to taste
½ tsp. turmeric
¾ tsp. black pepper
¼ tsp. cayenne

Combine the lemon juice, ¼ teaspoon salt, ¼ teaspoon pepper, and the cayenne pepper in a medium mixing basin. Toss in the shrimp to coat. After covering, refrigerate for at least 10 minutes. Heat the oil in a large, deep skillet over medium-high heat. Cook, stirring periodically, for about 2-3 minutes, or until the onion begins to soften.Cook for another minute after adding the remaining Ingredients. Bring the tomatoes, juices, and coconut milk to a boil, stirring constantly. Cook for 5 minutes, stirring periodically. Cook, stirring occasionally, until the shrimp turn pink, about 2-3 minutes. Serve.:

Nutritional information: Calories 448 total Carbs 12g Net carbs 9g Protein 29g fat 30g Sugar 5g fiber 3g

Pasta with Shrimp in a Hot Pepper Sauce

Prep time; 08 minutes. | Cook Time: 22 minutes. | Serves: 4

¾ lb. shrimp, cooked
3 red bell peppers, chopped
1 onion, diced
8 oz. snow peas, steamed
2 tbsp. plant-based butter
What you'll need from store cupboard:
1 cup low sodium chicken broth
½ tsp. salt
½ tsp. chicken bouillon
¼ tsp. pepper
1 recipe Homemade Pasta, cook & drain

Melt butter in a large skillet over medium-high heat. Cook, stirring occasionally, until the onions are completely translucent. Bring to a simmer the peppers, broth, bouillon, salt, and pepper. Cover and cook for 5-10 minutes over low heat, or until peppers are tender. Blend the mixture until it is completely smooth. Return the liquid to the pan. Cook until the shrimp are fully cooked. Mix in the spaghetti and snow peas thoroughly. Serve.

Nutritional information: Calories 387 Total Carbs 27g Net Carbs 21g Protein 40g Fat 14g Sugar 14g Fiber 6g

Carbonara with tuna

Prep time: 5 minutes. | Cook Time: 25 minutes. | Serves: 4

½ lb. tuna fillet, cut in pieces
2 eggs
4 tbsp. fresh parsley, diced
What you'll need from store cupboard:
½ recipe Homemade Pasta, cook & drain, (chapter 15)
½ cup reduced fat parmesan cheese
2 cloves garlic, peeled
2 tbsp. extra virgin olive oil
Salt & pepper, to taste

In a small mixing bowl, whisk together the eggs, parmesan, and a pinch of pepper. Heat the oil in a large skillet over medium-high heat. Cook until the garlic is browned. Cook for another 2-3 minutes, or until the tuna is almost done. Garlic should be discarded. Reduce the heat to a low setting and toss in the pasta. Cook, stirring constantly, for 2 minutes after adding the egg mixture. If the sauce is too thick, add a little water at a time until it reaches a creamy consistency. Season with salt and pepper to taste, then top with parsley.

Nutritional information: Calories 409 Total Carbs 7g Net Carbs 6g Protein 25g Fat 30g Sugar 3g Fiber 1g

Risotto with Shrimp and Pumpkin

Prep time: 5 minutes. | Cook Time: 15 minutes. | Serves: 3

½ lb. raw shrimp, peel & devein
2 cups cauliflower, grated
¼ cup half-n-half

2 tbsp. plant-based butter
What you'll need from store cupboard:
½ cup low sodium vegetable broth
¼ cup pumpkin puree
¼ cup reduced fat parmesan cheese
2 cloves garlic, diced fine
¼ tsp. sage
¼ tsp. salt
¼ tsp. pepper

Melt butter in a large skillet over medium-high heat. Cook for 1-2 minutes after adding the garlic. Whisk together the broth, pumpkin, and half-and-half until smooth. Cook for 5 minutes, or until cauliflower is soft, with the cauliflower and parmesan. Cook until the Shrimp turn pink, stirring regularly. Season with a touch of salt and pepper before serving.

Nutritional information: Calories 236 Total Carbs 9g Net Carbs 7g Protein 21g Fat 13g Sugar 3g Fiber 2g

Sesame Tuna Steak

Prep Time: 21 minutes. | Cook Time: 21 minutes. | Servings: 2

2 (6-ounce) Tuna steaks
2 tablespoons reduced-sodium Soy sauce
1 tablespoon Sesame oil
1 teaspoon Sesame seeds
Salt as per taste
Pepper as per taste

Start by placing the tuna steak on a shallow plate and lightly season with pepper and salt. Place sesame oil and soy sauce in a small bowl. Mix well and pour over the tuna steak, coat well. Place the nonstick skillet over medium heat. When the pan is hot, add the seasoned tuna and cook for about 3 minutes. Flip and cook for another 3 minutes. When finished, transfer it to a cutting board and cut it into thin slices about ½-inch thick. Transfer to a platter and garnish with black and white sesame seeds. Serve hot!

Nutritional information: Calories 255; Total Carbs 1g; Net Carbs 0.2g; Protein 40g; Fat 9g; Sugar 0.1g; Fiber 0g

Shrimp Stewed in Curry Butter

Prep Time: 5 minutes. | Cook Time: 5 minutes. | Servings: 2

6 tablespoons (85 g) plant-based butter
2 teaspoons curry powder
1 teaspoon minced garlic or 2 cloves garlic, crushed
24 large, raw, "easy peel" shrimp

Melt the butter in a larger pan over the lowest heat. Mix with the curry powder and the garlic, then put the shrimp in a single layer. Cook for 3 to 5 minutes per side or until the shrimp are tender. Serve on a plate and scrape the extra curry butter.

Nutritional information: Calories 218; Total Carbs 2g; Net Carbs 1g; Protein 15g; Fat 8g; Sugar 0.2g; Fiber 1g

Cod Gratin

Prep Time: 30 minutes. | Cook Time: 22 minutes. | Servings: 4

½ cup olive oil, divided
1-pound fresh cod
1 cup black kalamata olives, pitted and chopped
4 leeks, trimmed and sliced
1 cup whole-wheat bread crumbs
¾ cup low-sodium chicken stock
Fine-grained kosher salt and freshly ground black pepper, to taste

Preheat the oven to 350 degrees F. Grease 4 gratin plates and the larger ovenproof dish with olive oil. Place the cod in a large bowl and bake for 5-7 minutes. Let cool and cut into 1-inch pieces. Add and heat the olive oil to a large saucepan. Add the olives and leeks and cook over medium-low heat until tender. Add breadcrumbs and chicken broth and mix. Gently fold the pieces of cod. Divide the mixture among 4 gratin plates and drizzle with olive oil. Season with salt and pepper. Bake for 15 minutes or until heated through. When done, serve and enjoy.

Nutritional information: Calories 578; Total Carbs 32g; Net Carbs 20g; Protein 25g; Fat 36g; Sugar 3g; Fiber 4g

Simple Salmon Patties

Prep Time: 15 minutes. | Cook Time: 10 minutes. | Servings: 4

2 cups flaked cooked salmon
6 soda crackers, crushed
1 egg
½ cup skim milk
1 small onion, chopped
1 tablespoon chopped fresh parsley
1 tablespoon unbleached all-purpose flour
1 tablespoon olive oil
Pure Rice Flour (optional)

Place the salmon in a bowl. Add the mashed crackers, eggs, milk, onion, parsley, and flour. Mix well. Make 5 patties. Heat oil in a medium-high nonstick skillet. Fry on both sides until golden, about 10 minutes. Serve hot with salad and enjoy.

Nutritional information: Calories 168; Total Carbs 3g; Net Carbs 1g; Protein 17g; Fat 9g; Sugar 1g; Fiber 0.5g

Milanese salmon

Prep time: 08 minutes. | Cook Time: 18minutes. | Serves: 6

2 ½ lb. salmon filet
2 tomatoes, sliced
½ cup olive oil
What you'll need from store cupboard:
½ cup basil pesto

Preheat the oven to 400 degrees Fahrenheit. Cover the edges and bottom of a 9x15-inch baking sheet with foil. Place a second large piece of foil on top of the salmon fillet on the baking sheet. Pulse the pesto and oil until smooth in a blender or food processor.

Distribute equally over the salmon. Top with tomato slices. Wrap the foil around the salmon, tenting it at the top to keep the foil from touching the salmon. Bake for 15-25 minutes, or until salmon easily flakes with a fork. Serve.

Nutritional information: Calories 444; Total Carbs 2g; Net Carbs 1g; Protein 55.0g; Fat 8.0g; Sugar 1g; Fiber 0 g

Shrimp Creole

Prep Time: 110 minutes. | Cook Time: 1 hour 25 minutes. | Servings: 8

1¾ lbs. raw shrimp, peeled
pepper, to taste
2 tablespoons canola oil
1 cup chopped onion
1 cup chopped celery
½ cup chopped bell pepper
1 8-oz. can low-sodium tomato paste
1 8-oz. can low-sodium tomato sauce
1 tablespoons Louisiana hot sauce
2½ cups water
3 cloves garlic, minced
1 cup chopped green onions
parsley

Peel the shrimp. Season with pepper to taste and set aside. In a suitable saucepan, heat oil. Sauté onion, celery, and pepper until cooked through. Add tomato paste and cook 5 minutes over low heat, stirring constantly. Add tomato sauce, hot sauce, and water. Cook for 1 hour, stirring occasionally. Stir in shrimp and garlic. Cook another 15 minutes. Sprinkle with green onions and parsley. Cook 2–3 more minutes. Serve with the allowd staples.

Nutritional information: Calories 150; Total Carbs 13g; Net Carbs 10g; Protein 15g; Fat 4g; Sugar 2g; Fiber 3g

Basil-Lime Shrimp

Prep Time: 10 minutes. | Cook Time: 10 minutes. | Servings: 2

½ cup (120 ml) lime juice
½ cup (120 ml) olive oil
¼ cup (10 g) fresh basil—Just compact sprigs into your measuring cup.
4 teaspoons (16 g) brown mustard
¼ teaspoon Splenda
4 scallions—thinly sliced, including the crisp part of the green
½ pound (225 g) shrimp

Add all the lemon juice to Splenda in a blender and mix for just 1 to 2 seconds. Pour the mixture into a saucepan and place at medium heat. Reduce the heat until it boils and when it begins to boil, simmer until reduced by half. Slice the scallions. When the lemon juice is reduced, place the shrimp in. Blanch for 2 minutes, then flip again and leave for a few more minutes until firm and pink. Serve drizzled with sauce and sprinkle with sliced scallion on top.

Nutritional information: Calories 438; Total Carbs 6g; Net Carbs 5g; Protein 35g; Fat 30g; Sugar 1g; Fiber g

Chipotle Spicy Fish Tacos

Prep Time: 20 minutes. | Cook Time: 17 minutes. | Servings: 4

2 tablespoons Olive oil
½ small yellow onion, diced
1 Jalapeño (chopped)
2 cloves Garlic (pressed)
4 ounces Chipotle peppers soaked in adobo sauce
2 tablespoons plant-based butter
2 tablespoons lite Mayonnaise
1 pound Haddock fillets
4 Tortillas (low carb)

Place a nonstick skillet over medium-high heat. Pour in the olive oil and let it hot. Add the chopped onion and stir constantly for 5 minutes to prevent the onions from turning brown. Reduce the heat and add the chopped garlic and jalapeno. Cook, stirring, about 2 minutes. Remove the chipotle pepper from the adobo sauce and finely chop it. Transfer the chopped chipotle and adobo sauce to a hot skillet. Add the mayonnaise, butter and the fish fillet to the pepper sauce and mix well. Cook the fish for 8 minutes or until completely cooked through. Divide into 4 equal parts. To prepare the taco shells, make tortillas and fry them over high flame for 2 minutes on both sides. Place the tacos on a plate and let the tacos cool if needed. Fill the shells with ¼ of the fish mixture. Serve hot with freshly chopped chives!

Nutritional information: Calories 300; Total Carbs 7g; Net Carbs 4g; Protein 24g; Fat 20g; Sugar 0.4g; Fiber 2g

Tuna Bake with Cheese Swirls

Prep Time: 55 minutes. | Cook Time: 25 minutes. | Servings: 8

½ cup diced green bell pepper
½ cup chopped onion
2 tablespoons canola oil
6 tablespoons flour
2 cups fat-free milk
6½- or 7-oz. tuna
Cheese Swirls:
1½ cups reduced-fat buttermilk biscuit mix
¾ cup grated 50%-less fat cheddar cheese
½ cup fat-free milk
2 chopped pimentos (from jar)

In the saucepan, sauté the peppers and onions in the oil until tender but not brown. Incorporate the flour and cook for a few minutes over low heat to remove the raw flour taste. Gently stir in the milk. Sauté over low heat, stirring constantly, until smooth. Add Tuna. Pour into a 9 x 13 inch pan and then set aside for later use. For cheese swirls, prepare the biscuit with milk according to the instructions on the package. Sprinkle with cheese and chopped pimento. Roll up Jelly roll fashion. Cut the roll into 8 pieces. Spread gently and place on top of the tuna mixture. Bake at 450°F for 25 minutes or until tuna mixture is foamy and cookies are golden brown. When done, serve and enjoy.

Nutritional information: Calories 215; Total Carbs 25g; Net Carbs 20g; Protein 13g; Fat 7g; Sugar 10g; Fiber 12g

Herbed Parmesan Crusted Fish

Prep Time: 15 minutes. | Cook Time: 12 minutes. | Servings: 4

⅓ cup Almonds (chopped)
¼ cup Dry bread crumbs (plain)
3 tablespoons low-fat Parmesan cheese (grated)
½ teaspoon Garlic powder
½ teaspoon Paprika
½ teaspoon Parsley flakes
¼ teaspoon Black pepper (freshly ground)
I pound Tilapia fillets
Olive oil

Start by preheating the oven to a temperature of 450 degrees F. Make a baking sheet and line it with foil. Prepare a shallow bowl and add the chopped almonds, parsley, breadcrumbs, garlic powder, paprika, black pepper, and parsley flakes in it. Mix well to combine. Place the fish on a plate and use a brush to lightly grease on both sides with olive oil. Coat the fish with the almond and the seasoning mix, make sure both sides of the fish are even coated. Place the coated fish on a baking sheet and bake for 12 minutes. When done, the fish should be flaked with a fork.

Nutritional information: Calories 225; Total Carbs 7g; Net Carbs 4g; Protein 29g; Fat 9g; Sugar 0.2g; Fiber 0.5g

Asparagus with Scallops

Prep Time: 25 minutes. | Cook Time: 15 minutes. | Servings: 4

3 teaspoons extra-virgin olive oil, divided
1 pound asparagus, trimmed and cut into 2-inch segments
1 tablespoon plant-based butter
1 pound sea scallops
¼ cup dry white wine
Juice of 1 lemon
2 garlic cloves, minced
¼ teaspoon freshly ground black pepper

In a large skillet, heat half of the oil over medium heat. Add the asparagus in it and sauté for 5 to 6 minutes until tender. Remove from the skillet and cover with aluminum foil to keep warm. Add the remaining oil and the butter to the skillet. When the butter is melted and sizzling, place the scallops in a single layer in the skillet. Cook for about 3 minutes on one side until nicely browned. Gently flip the scallops with the tongs, and cook on the other side for another 3 minutes until browned and cooked through. Remove and cover with foil to keep warm. In the same skillet, combine the wine, lemon juice, garlic,and pepper. Bring to a simmer for 1 to 2 minutes, stirring to mix in any browned pieces left in the pan. Return the asparagus and the cooked scallops to the skillet to coat with the sauce. Serve warm.

Nutritional information: Calories 253; Total Carbs 14g; Net Carbs 9g; Protein 26g; Fat 7g; Sugar 4g; Fiber 3g

Mediterranean Tuna Cups

Prep Time: 15 minutes. | Cook Time: 20 minutes. | Servings: 5

White albacore tuna in water, flaked and drained 10 ounces
0.25 teaspoon Garlic salt
2 tablespoons fresh Lemon juice
0.33 cups red onion, chopped
0.33 cups pitted and chopped Kalamata olives
0.66 cups Non-fat, plain Greek yogurt
3 medium cucumbers

Cut the cucumber into 10 pieces and discard the ends. Keep the cucumber shell and use a 0.5 teaspoon to scoop out the insides. Make sure there is a thin layer on the bottom of the slice to accommodate the tuna mixture. Combine the olives, garlic, yogurt, onion, and lemon juice. Mix until the mixture is smooth. Add the tuna and stir again until combined. Take about 1 tablespoon of the tuna mixture and put it in cucumber cup. Repeat this until all 10 cups of cucumber are filled with tuna. Refrigerate and serve.

Nutritional information: Calories 150; Total Carbs 2g; Net Carbs 1g; Protein 6g; Fat 1g; Sugar 0.9g; Fiber 1g

Saigon Shrimp

Prep Time: 10 minutes. | Cook Time: 5 minutes. | Servings: 3

½ teaspoon salt
½ teaspoon pepper
1 ½ teaspoons Splenda
3 scallions
4 tablespoons (60 ml) canola oil
1 pound (455 g) large shrimp, shelled and deveined
1 ½ teaspoons chili garlic paste
2 teaspoons minced garlic

Combine salt, pepper, and Splenda in a small bowl or mug. Thinly slice the scallions and set them aside. Collect all the Ingredients except for the scallions. On the highest heat, hot oil in a wok or large saucepan. Add the shrimp and fry for 2-3 minutes or until about ⅔ are pink. Add the chili, garlic paste, and garlic and contine to sauté. When the shrimp are fully cooked, sprinkle with salt, pepper, and Splendid and stir for only 10 seconds. Turn off the heat and divide the shrimp into 3 plates. Top each serving with a scattering of sliced scallion, serve and enjoy.

Nutritional information: Calories 288; Total Carbs 2g; Net Carbs 0.8g; Protein 25g; Fat 7g; Sugar 1g; Fiber 1g

Shrimp in Curried Coconut Milk

Prep Time: 10 minutes. | Cook Time: 15 minutes. | Servings: 3

½ onion
½ green pepper
2 tablespoons (28 ml) coconut oil
2 teaspoons cumin
2 teaspoons curry powder
1 ½ teaspoons ground coriander
1 ½ teaspoons chopped garlic
1 cup (235 ml) unsweetened coconut milk
½ teaspoon salt or Vege-Sal
¼ teaspoon chili garlic paste
3 cups (384) frozen cooked salad shrimp, thawed

Place the onions and green pepper in a food processor and pulse until finely chopped. Start sautéing them in coconut oil in a deep-bottomed pan. When the onions and peppers begin to soften, add the seasoning. Cook for a few more minutes, add the garlic and put one more minute. Add the coconut milk and stir. Also, stir in the salt and the garlic, and chili paste. Now add the thawed and drained shrimp, stir and turn up the burner slightly. Simmer for 1 to 2 minutes, thickening with a little guar, xanthan, or sugar if you feel it need it. When done, serve and enjoy with all of the sauce.

Nutritional information: Calories 235; Total Carbs 6g; Net Carbs 5g; Protein 28g; Fat 11g; Sugar 1g; Fiber 1g

Feta-Spinach Salmon Roast

Prep Time: 15 minutes. | Cook Time: 20 minutes. | Servings: 4

3 ounces low-fat cheese, softened
¾ cup crumbled low-fat feta
2 scallions, thinly sliced, including the crisp part of the green
½ cup fresh spinach, chopped
2 skinless salmon fillets of roughly equal size and shape, totaling ¾ pound
Olive oil

Preheat the oven to 350°F. Combine the cheese and feta, mashing and stirring with a fork until well blended. Add the scallions and spinach, and combine well. Spread the mixture evenly over one salmon fillet. (The filling will be about ¾ inch thick.) Top with the second salmon fillet. Brush both sides with olive oil, turning the whole thing over carefully with a spatula. Place the loaf on a shallow baking pan, and bake for 20 minutes. Slice carefully with a sharp, serrated knife.

Nutritional information: Calories 236; Total Carbs 24g; Net Carbs 18g; Protein 57g; Fat 9g; Sugar 6g; Fiber 4g

Tuna Salad

Prep Time: 5 minutes. | Cook Time: 0 minutes. | Servings: 2

1 cup (284 g) light tuna, in water, drained
¼ cup (25 g) celery, chopped
2 tablespoons (28 g) low-fat mayonnaise
3 tablespoons (12 g) fresh dill, chopped
2 tablespoons (20 g) white onions, diced
Pepper to taste

Mix all Ingredients in a large bowl. Serve and enjoy.

Nutritional information: Calories 66; Total Carbs 5g; Net Carbs 4g; Protein 5g; Fat 5g; Sugar 1g; Fiber 1g

Barbecued Sea-Bass

Prep Time: 10 minutes. | Cook Time: 10 minutes. | Servings: 2

1 pound (455 g) sea bass fillets
Barbecue Rub (sugar free)
4 slices nitrate-free & sugar-free bacon
2 tablespoons (30 ml) lemon juice

Cut your sea bass fillets into serving portions. Sprinkle both sides liberally with the barbecue rub. Spray your big, heavy skillet with nonstick cooking spray, and place over medium-low heat. Using a sharp kitchen shears, snip your bacon into small pieces, straight into the skillet. Stir it about for a moment. As soon as a little grease starts to cook out of the bacon, clear a couple of spaces for the fish, and put the fish in the pan. Cover and set your oven timer for 4 minutes. When time is up, flip the fish, and stir the bacon around a bit, so it will cook evenly. Re-cover the pan, and set the timer for another 3 to 4 minutes. Peek at your fish at least once; you don't want to overcook it! When the fish is flaky, remove to serving plates, and top with the browned bacon bits. Pour the lemon juice in the skillet, stir it around, and pour over the fish.

Nutritional information: Calories 357; Total Carbs 13g; Net Carbs 10g; Protein 58g; Fat 18g; Sugar 4g; Fiber 6g

Tasty Fish Cakes

Prep Time: 10 minutes. | Cook Time: 15 minutes. | Servings: 3

1-pound catfish fillet
2 green onions, minced
1 banana pepper, cored, seeded, and chopped
2 cloves garlic, minced
1 tablespoon grated or minced fresh ginger
1 tablespoon Bragg Liquid Aminos
1 tablespoon lemon juice
1 teaspoon grated lemon zest
Nonstick cooking spray

Preheat the oven to 375°F. Combine the fish with green onions, banana pepper, garlic, ginger, Bragg Liquid Aminos, lemon juice, and lemon zest in your food processor. Chop until combined. Add Old Bay Seasoning to it and stir to mix. Make patties of about 2 tablespoons of the fish mixture. Must have a total of 6 patties. Place the patties on a baking sheet a. Bake the patties for 12-15 minutes or until crispy. serve hot and enjoy.

Nutritional information: Calories 66; Total Carbs 1g; Net Carbs 0g; Protein 11g; Fat 2g; Sugar 0g; Fiber 0g

Buttered Salmon with Creole Seasonings

Prep Time: 10 minutes. | Cook Time: 10 minutes. | Servings: 3

12 ounces (340 g) salmon fillet, in 2 or three pieces
1 teaspoon purchased Creole seasoning
¼ teaspoon dried thyme
4 tablespoons (55 g) plant-based butter
1 teaspoon minced garlic or 2 cloves garlic, minced

Sprinkle Creole seasoning and thyme evenly over the salmon. Melt the butter in a pan over medium-low heat and add the salmon skin side down. Cook 4 to 5 minutes per side, turning gently. Transfer to a saucepan, skin side down, and toss the garlic with the additional butter in the saucepan. Cook for just a minute, then rub all the garlic butter over the salmon and serve.

Nutritional information: Calories 241; Total Carbs 2g; Net Carbs 0.1g; Protein 35g; Fat 14g; Sugar 0.2g; Fiber 0.4g

Glazed & Grilled Salmon

Prep Time: 10 minutes. | Cook Time:12 minutes. | Servings: 2

2 tablespoons (3 g) Splenda
1 ½ teaspoons dry mustard
1 tablespoon (15 ml) reduced-sodium soy sauce
1 ½ teaspoons vinegar
¼ teaspoon blackstrap molasses
12 ounces (340 g) salmon fillet, cut into 2 or 3 serving-size pieces

In a small bowl, combine the Splenda, mustard, soy sauce, vinegar, and molasses. Pour 1 tablespoon of this mixture and place it on a separate plate. Place the salmon on a plate, pour in the sauce mixture, and turn the fillets over so that both sides are coated with the sauce. rest the fish, skinless side down, for 2-3 minutes. Heat oil in the pan and cook the salmon for 5 minutes on both sides. When the salmon is cooked, transfer to a bowl and drizzle with the reserved seasoning mixture before serving.

Nutritional information: Calories 189; Total Carbs 3g; Net Carbs 1g; Protein 35g; Fat 8g; Sugar 0g; Fiber 0.2g

Salmon in Citrus Vinaigrette

Prep Time: 10 minutes. | Cook Time: 10 minutes. | Servings: 4

1 tablespoon (15 ml) coconut oil
24 ounces (680 g) salmon fillet in 4 servings
½ cup (120 ml) vinaigrette
½ cup (120 ml) lemon juice
2 ½ tablespoons (4 g) Splenda
¼ teaspoon orange extract
1 teaspoon brown mustard
1 teaspoon chili powder
2 tablespoons (28 ml) lime juice

Grease a nonstick pan with cooking spray and set it on medium heat. Add the coconut oil and when it melts, add the salmon in it. Put other Ingredients in a blender and blend well. Flip the salmon until tender. Now add the vinaigrette mixture to the salmon and turn the burner to medium. Cook for 5 minutes or until the salmon is cooked through. Place the salmon on a plate. Boil the vinaigrette dressing until harden into foamy syrup. Pour the sauce over the salmon and serve.

Nutritional information: Calories 384; Total Carbs 5g; Net Carbs 3g; Protein 34g; Fat 25g; Sugar 1g; Fiber 1.5g

Fish Cakes

Prep Time: 10 minutes. | Cook Time: 6 minutes. | Servings: 8

1 ½ lb (680 g) boneless, skinless salmon filet
2 tablespoon (30 ml) lite mayonnaise
1 tablespoon (15 ml) finely chopped green onion tops
1 tablespoon (15 ml) finely chopped fresh dill
1 tablespoon (15 ml) freshly squeezed lemon juice
¾ (3.7 ml) sea salt
freshly ground black pepper
2 tablespoon (30 ml) vegetable oil

Cut the fillet into ¼ inch pieces with a knife and place them in a bowl. Add mayonnaise, green onions, dill, lemon juice, salt, and pepper to taste. Stir quickly in the same direction for 1 minute. Make 8 patties with the mix. It can be refrigerated for up to 6 hours or until cooked through. Heat oil in a skillet over medium-high heat. Add the cake and cook 2-3 minutes until lightly browned. Flip and cook for another 2-3 minutes or until golden brown. Serve and enjoy.

Nutritional information: Calories 209; Total Carbs 0.3g; Net Carbs 0g; Protein 17g; Fat 15g; Sugar 0g; Fiber 0.1g

Fish with Lemon-Dill Dip

Prep Time: 5 minutes. | Cook Time: 14 minutes. | Servings: 4

2 (1-ounce) bags low-carb soy chips. finely ground
4 (8-ounce) fish fillets, about ¼ inch thick
2 tablespoons canola oil, divided
½ cup lite mayonnaise
3 tablespoons chopped fresh dill
2 teaspoons grated lemon zest
¼ teaspoon pepper

Sprinkle the ground chips on a plate. Dredge the fillet with fries to coat on both sides. Heat 1 tablespoon of oil in a non-stick pan. Add half of the fish and cook until opaque on the inside and golden on the outside for 3-4 minutes per side. Carefully transfer to the plate and cover with foil to keep them warm. Repeat with additional oil and fish. Mix mayonnaise, dill and zest in a small bowl. Serve with pepper and alongside sauce.

Nutritional information: Calories 520; Total Carbs 3g; Net Carbs 1g; Protein 51g; Fat 32g; Sugar 1g; Fiber 2g

Grilled Haddock with Peach-Mango Salsa

Prep Time: 10 minutes. | Cook Time: 10 minutes. | Servings: 4

2 tablespoons olive oil
2 tablespoons lime juice
½ teaspoon salt
½ teaspoon ground pepper
1-pound haddock, cut into 4 fillets
Nonstick cooking spray
2 cups Fresh Peach-Mango Salsa

Combine olive oil, lemon juice, salt, and pepper in a shallow bowl. Add the haddock. Turn the fish over and cover with the marinade. Prepare grill on high heat. Grease foil paper with cooking spray. Place the fillet on the foil. Cook, 7 to 8 minutes per side, or until fish is tender when pricked with a fork. Top each fish piece with ½ cup fresh peach-mango salsa and serve.

Nutritional information: Calories 204; Total Carbs 11g; Net Carbs 7g; Protein 22g; Fat 8g; Sugar 1.4g; Fiber 2g

Crusted Catfish

Prep Time: 10 minutes. | Cook Time: 25 minutes. | Servings: 8

8 catfish fillets
1 cup (115 g) bread crumbs
¾ cup (75 g) low-fat parmesan cheese, grated
¼ cup (15 g) fresh parsley, chopped
1 teaspoon paprika
½ teaspoon oregano
¼ teaspoon basil
½ teaspoon pepper
½ cup (112 g) melted butter

Pat dry fish Add the breadcrumbs, cheese, seasonings to a bowl. Mix well. Dip the catfish in the butter and roll it in the breadcrumb mixture. Arrange the fish in a well-greased 13 x 9 x 2-inch baking sheet. Bake at 375°F for about 25 minutes or until the fish is crisp and tender.

Nutritional information: Calories 412; Total Carbs 10g; Net Carbs 8g; Protein 30g; Fat 12g; Sugar 1g; Fiber 1g

Smoked Shrimp and Cheese Quesadillas

Prep Time: 10minutes. | Cook Time: 5 minutes. | Servings: 4

4 (8") flour tortillas
4 teaspoons olive oil
2 ounces part-skim mozzarella or other mild cheese (such as fontina or baby Swiss)
1 jalapeño or banana pepper, finely chopped
2 cloves garlic, crushed
4 ounces smoked shrimp
1 cup thinly sliced red onion
½ cup roughly chopped fresh cilantro

Preheat the oven to 375 ° F. Gentlygrease one side of the tortilla with olive oil. Combine the cheese, pepper, and garlic with additional olive oil. Sprinkle ½ of the cheese mixture in the middle of the oiled tortilla. Garnish with shrimp, red onion, and cilantro. Fold the tortilla in half to cover the Ingredients. Place the tortillas in a roasting pan greased with nonstick spray. Bake for 3-5 minutes or until golden brown and melted. Serve with the tomato sauce of your choice.

Nutritional information: Calories 272; Total Carbs 32g; Net Carbs 15g; Protein 11g; Fat 11g; Sugar 15g; Fiber 3g

Slow-Roasted Salmon

Prep Time:10 minutes. | Cook Time: 25 minutes. | Servings: 4

2 teaspoons extra-virgin olive oil
4 (5-ounce) salmon fillets with skin, at room temperature
1 cup finely minced fresh chives
Sea or kosher salt and freshly ground white pepper to taste (optional)
Nonstick cooking spray
Sage sprigs for garnish

Preheat the oven to 250°F. Rub ½ teaspoon of olive oil into the salmon fillet. Completely cover the fillet with chives. Gently press in chives. Season with salt and pepper if needed. Place fillets skin side down on a non-stick baking dish. Bake for 25 minutes or until tender. Decorate with sage sprigs.

Nutritional information: Calories 257; Total Carbs 1g; Net Carbs 1g; Protein 25g; Fat 16g; Sugar 0g; Fiber 0g

Spicy Fish Fillet

Prep Time: 5 minutes. | Cook Time: 10 minutes. | Servings:2

½ cup cornmeal
½ teaspoon salt
1 teaspoon chipotle seasoning
1 egg
2 tablespoons 1% milk
16 ounces flounder, cut into 4 pieces
2 tablespoons olive oil

In a shallow bowl, toast the corn, salt, and chipotle together. Place the eggs and milk in a shallow bowl. Dip the fish in the egg mixture. Place the fillet with the corn mixture. Heat the olive oil in a non-stick pan. cook fillets until golden and crispy, about 6-7 minutes per side.

Nutritional information: Calories 230; Total Carbs 9g; Net Carbs 6g; Protein 24g; Fat 10g; Sugar 1.4g; Fiber 1g

Tuna-Noodle Casserole

Prep Time: 15 minutes. | Cook Time: 15minutes. | Servings: 4

1 ½ cups egg noodles
1 recipe Condensed Cream of Mushroom Soup
1 teaspoon steamed chopped onion
1 tablespoon steamed chopped celery
½ cup skim milk
1 ounce shredded low-fat American, Cheddar, or Colby cheese
1 cup frozen mixed peas and carrots
1 cup steamed sliced fresh mushrooms
1 can water-packed tuna, drained

Cook egg noodles according to package instructions. Drain and return to the pan Add all the Ingredients to the pan. Stir to mix. Cook over medium heat, stirring occasionally until the cheese melts. Serve hot and enjoy.

Nutritional information: Calories 245; Total Carbs 33g; Net Carbs 20g; Protein 20g; Fat 4g; Sugar 12g; Fiber 15g

Honey-Soy Broiled Salmon

Prep Time: 35 minutes. | Cook Time: 20 minutes. | Servings: 4

1 scallion, minced
2 tablespoons reduced-sodium soy sauce
1 tablespoon vinegar
1 tablespoon honey
1 teaspoon minced fresh ginger
1-pound center-cut salmon fillet, skinned and cut into 4 portions
1 teaspoon toasted sesame seeds

Whisk scallion, soy sauce, vinegar, honey, and ginger in a medium bowl until the honey is dissolved. Place salmon in a sealable plastic bag, add 3 tablespoons of the sauce and refrigerate; let marinate for 15 minutes. Reserve the remaining sauce. Preheat broiler. Line a small baking pan with foil and coat with cooking spray. Transfer the salmon to the pan, skinned-side down. (Discard the marinade.) Broil the salmon 4 to 6 inches from the heat source until cooked through, 6 to 10 minutes.

Nutritional information: Calories 257; Total Carbs 23g; Net Carbs 18g; Protein 28g; Fat 18g; Sugar 6g; Fiber 4g

Shrimp Pie with Rice Crust

Prep Time: 10 minutes. | Cook Time: 35 minutes. | Servings: 4

1 ½ cups cooked white rice
2 teaspoons dried parsley
2 tablespoons grated onion
1 teaspoon olive oil
1 tablespoon plant-based butter
1 clove garlic, crushed
1 pound shrimp, peeled and deveined
1 recipe Condensed Cream of Mushroom Soup (see recipe in Chapter 4)
1 teaspoon lemon juice
1 cup sliced steamed mushrooms

Preheat the oven to 350°F. Add the rice, parsley, and onion. Mix well. Use olive oil to coat 10" pie plate; Combine the rice and press down the sides and bottom evenly. It works best if the rice is wet. Add 1 teaspoon of water if needed. Melt the butter in a non-stick pan at medium heat. saute garlic and shrimps, stir frequently, for 5 minutes, until pink. Add the soup and lemon juice to the pan. Stir until smooth and firm, about 5 minutes. Stir Mushrooms in a soup mixture; Pour over the rice "crust". Bake for 30 minutes or until the top is lightly browned. Serve hot.

Nutritional information: Calories 273; Total Carbs 27g; Net Carbs 18g; Protein 27g; Fat 6g; Sugar 2g; Fiber 12g

Shrimp with Zoodles

Prep time: 10 minutes. | Cooking time: 7 minutes. | Servings: 1

½ tablespoon olive oil
½ of small garlic clove, minced
⅛ teaspoon red pepper flakes, crushed
¼ pound medium shrimp, peeled and deveined
Salt and black pepper, to taste
2 to 3 tablespoons chicken broth
½ of small zucchini, spiralized with blade c
2 to 3 cherry tomatoes, quartered

Heat the oil in a small wok over medium heat and sauté garlic and red pepper flakes for almost 1 minute. Add shrimp, salt and black pepper and cook for almost 1 minute per side. Add broth and zucchini noodles and cook for almost 2 to 3 minutes. Stir in tomatoes and cook for almost 1 minute. Serve hot.

Nutritional information: Calories: 211; Fat: 9g; Total Carbs 4.8g; Net Carbs 2g; Protein: 27g; Fiber: 1g; Sugar: 1.6g

Tangy Prawn Curry

Prep time: 10 minutes. | Cooking time: 20 minutes. | Servings: 1

½ tablespoon olive oil
¼ of small onion, chopped
1 garlic clove, crushed
¼ teaspoon ginger, grated
¼ teaspoon red chili powder
¼ teaspoon ground turmeric
⅛ teaspoon ground cinnamon
⅛ teaspoon ground cardamom
⅛ teaspoon ground cloves
Salt and black pepper, to taste
¼ cup unsweetened coconut milk
¼ pound raw prawns, peeled and deveined
1 teaspoon basil, chopped

Heat ½ tablespoon of oil in a suitable sauté pan over medium heat and sauté the onion, garlic, and ginger for almost 5-8 minutes. Add the spices, salt, black pepper, and sauté for almost 1-2 minutes. Add the coconut milk and bring to a gentle simmer. Add in the prawns and simmer for almost 5 to 7 minutes almost. Toss in the basil and serve hot.

Nutritional information: Calories: 225; Fat: 10g; Total Carbs 5.2g; Net Carbs 1.2g; Protein: 26.5g; Fiber: 1.3g; Sugar: 0.9g

Basic Lemony Prawns

Prep time: 10 minutes. | Cooking time: 4 minutes. | Servings: 1

¼ pound large prawns, peeled and deveined, with tails intact
1 garlic clove, minced
½ tablespoon olive oil
½ tablespoon lemon juice
Salt and black pepper, to taste

Preheat the barbecue grill to high heat. Lightly grease the grill grate. In a suitable bowl, add all the recipe ingredients and toss to coat. Place the coated prawns

onto the grill and cook for almost 1 to 2 minutes per side. Serve hot.

Nutritional information: Calories: 201; Fat: 9g; Total Carbs 2.9g; Net Carbs 2g; Protein: 26.1g; Fiber: 0.1g; Sugar: 0.2g

Seafood Stew

Prep time: 10 minutes. | Cooking time: 30 minutes. | Servings: 1

½ tablespoon olive oil
¼ of small yellow onion, chopped
1 garlic clove, minced
¼ of serrano pepper, chopped
½ teaspoon dried herbs (rosemary, thyme, marjoram)
1 tomato, chopped
½ cup fish broth
2 ounces tilapia fillet, cubed
1 ounce shrimp, peeled and deveined
1-ounce mussels
¼ tablespoon lime juice
2 teaspoons basil, chopped
Salt and black pepper, to taste

In a suitable heavy-bottomed saucepan, heat the oil over medium heat. Sauté the onion for almost 5-6 minutes. Add the garlic, serrano peppers and dried herbs and sauté for almost 1 minute. Add the tomato and broth and bring to a gentle simmer. Adjust the heat and cook for almost 10 minutes. Add in the tilapia and cook for almost 2 minutes. Stir in the remaining seafood and cook for almost 6-8 minutes. Stir in the basil, lemon juice, salt and black pepper and remove from heat. Serve hot.

Nutritional information: Calories: 202; Fat: 8.9g; Total Carbs 6.6g; Net Carbs 2g; Protein: 22.5g; Fiber: 0.6g; Sugar: 3.2g

Avocado Citrus Shrimp Salad

Prep time: 10 minutes. | Cooking time: 5 minutes. | Servings: 4

1 lb. Medium shrimp, peeled and deveined, remove tails
8 cup salad greens
1 lemon, juiced
1 avocado, diced
1 shallot, diced
½ cup almonds, sliced and toasted
1 tablespoon olive oil
Salt and black pepper

Heat the oil in a suitable skillet over medium heat. Add lemon wedges and let cook for about 1 minute, to infuse the oil with the lemons. Add the shrimp and cook until the shrimp turn pink.
Discard the lemon wedges and let cool. Place the salad greens in a suitable bowl. Add the shrimp with the juices from the pan, and toss to coat. Add remaining ingredients and toss to combine. Serve.

Nutritional information: Calories 425; Total Carbs 17g; Net Carbs8g; Protein 35; Fat 26g; Sugar 2g; Fiber 9 g

Scallops Broccoli Meal

Prep time: 10 minutes. | Cooking time: 9 minutes. | Servings: 1

½ tablespoon olive oil
¼ cup broccoli, cut into small pieces
½ of garlic clove, crushed
¼ pound scallops, side muscles removed
½ teaspoon lemon juice
Salt, as required

Heat ½ tablespoon oil in a suitable sauté pan over medium heat and cook the broccoli and garlic for almost 3 to 4 minutes, with occasional stirring. Add in the sea scallops and cook for almost 3 to 4 minutes, flipping occasionally. Add the lemon juice and serve hot.

Nutritional information: Calories: 170; Fat: 8g; Total Carbs 4.7g; Fiber: 0.6g; Net Carbs 2g; Protein: 19.8g; Sugar: 0.5g

Parsley Mixed Scallops

Prep time: 10 minutes. | Cooking time: 7 minutes. | Servings: 1

¼ pound sea scallops, side muscles removed
Salt and black pepper, to taste
½ tablespoon olive oil
¼ tablespoon parsley, minced

Season the sea scallops with black pepper and salt. In a suitable skillet, heat the oil over medium-high heat and cook the scallops for almost 2-3 minutes per side. Stir in the parsley and remove from the heat. Serve hot.

Nutritional information: Calories: 160; Fat: 7.9g; Total Carbs 2.7g; Net Carbs 3g; Protein: 19.1g; Fiber: 0g; Sugar: 0g

Garlic Parmesan Topping on Baked Salmon

Prep time: 04 minutes. | Cook Time: 18 minutes. | Serves: 4

1 lb. wild caught salmon filets
2 tbsp. plant-based butter
What you'll need from store cupboard:
¼ cup reduced fat parmesan cheese, grated
¼ cup light mayonnaise
2-3 cloves garlic, diced
2 tbsp. parsley
Salt and pepper

Preheat the oven to 350 degrees Fahrenheit, and use a piece of parchment paper, line the baking tray. Season the salmon with salt and pepper and place it on the pan. In a medium skillet, warm the butter over medium heat for 1 minute, stirring constantly. Reduce to a low heat setting and add the other Ingredients. Stir until all of the Ingredients are melted and mixed. Spread equally over the salmon and bake for 15 minutes if the fish is thawed or 20 minutes if it is frozen. When a fork easily flakes the salmon, it's done. Serve.

Nutritional information: Calories 408; Total Carbs 4g; Net Carbs 3g; Protein 41.0g; Fat 24.0g; Sugar 1g; Fiber 0 g

Green Beans and Crispy Baked Flounder

Prep time: 10 minutes. | Cook Time: 20 minutes. | serves 4

1 lb. flounder
2 cups green beans
4 tbsp. plant-based butter
8 basil leaves
What you'll need from store cupboard:
1 ¾ oz. pork rinds
½ cup reduced fat parmesan cheese
3 cloves garlic
Salt and pepper to taste
Nonstick cooking spray

Preheat the oven to 350 degrees Fahrenheit. Using cooking spray, coat a baking dish. Green beans should be steamed until almost soft, around 15 minutes (less if using frozen or canned beans). Place the green beans in the dish that has been prepared. Season the fish fillets with salt and pepper and serve over the green beans. In a food processor, pulse the garlic, basil, pork rinds, and parmesan cheese until the mixture resembles crumbs. Sprinkle on top of the fish. Place the butter on top, cut into small pieces. Bake for 15-20 minutes, or until the fish readily flakes with a fork. Serve.

Nutritional information: Calories 358; Total Carbs 5g; Net Carbs 2g; Protein 39.0g; Fat 8.0g; Sugar 1g; Fiber 2 g

Tuna Casserole

Prep Time: 10 minutes. | Cook Time: 25 minutes. | Servings: 8

Sauce Ingredients:
1 cup sour cream
2 eggs
½ tablespoon minced onion, dried
1 teaspoon dill weed
½ teaspoon orange zest
½ teaspoon seasoning salt
Other Ingredients
1 pound cauliflower, cut into bite-sized pieces (may be fresh or frozen)
1 6-ounce can of tuna, drained
Cooking oil spray
1 ½ cups low-fat cheese, shredded (Monterey jack, Co-Jack, Cheddar, or a blend)

Combine the sauce Ingredients in a mixing bowl. Add the cauliflower into the sauce, then the tuna and coat well in sauce. Spray a 9" x 13" baking dish with cooking oil spray and pour the cauliflower tuna mixture into the baking dish. Top it with the cheese. Bake it at 350°F for about 25 minutes or until the cheese is thoroughly melted and starting to become golden brown. Serve hot and enjoy.

Nutritional information: Calories 390; Total Carbs 10g; Net Carbs 6g; Protein 27g; Fat 28g; Sugar 1.4g; Fiber 3g

Grilled Sesame Tofu

Prep time: 45 minutes. | Cooking time: 10 minutes. | Serving: 6

1½ tablespoons brown rice vinegar
1 scallion
1 tablespoon ginger root
1 tablespoon no-sugar-added applesauce
2 tablespoons naturally brewed soy sauce
¼ teaspoon dried red pepper flakes
2 teaspoons sesame oil, toasted
1 (14-ounce / 397-g) package extra-firm tofu
2 tablespoons cilantro
1 teaspoon sesame seeds

Combine the vinegar, scallion, ginger, applesauce, soy sauce, red pepper flakes, and sesame oil in a suitable bowl. Stir to mix well. Dunk the tofu pieces in the bowl, then refrigerate to marinate for almost 30 minutes. Preheat a grill pan over medium-high heat. Place the tofu on the grill pan with tongs, reserve the marinade, then grill for 8 minutes, flipping halfway through. Transfer the tofu to a large plate and sprinkle with cilantro leaves and sesame seeds. Serve with the marinade alongside.

Nutritional information: Calories: 189; Total Carbs 7.9g; Net Carbs 4.5g; Protein: 6g; Fat 10g; Sugars 1 g; Fiber 5g

Garlicky Kale Chips

Prep time: 5 minutes. | Cooking time: 15 minutes. | Serving: 1

¼ teaspoon garlic powder
Pinch cayenne to taste
1 tablespoon olive oil
½ teaspoon sea salt, or to taste
1 (8-ounce) bunch kale

At 355 degrees F, preheat your oven. Line 2 baking sheets with parchment paper. Toss the garlic powder, cayenne pepper, olive oil, and salt in a suitable bowl, then dunk the kale in the bowl. Situate kale in a single layer on 1 of the baking sheets. Arrange the sheet in the preheated oven and bake for 7 minutes. Remove the sheet from the oven and pour the kale into the single layer of the other baking sheet. Move the sheet of kale back to the oven and bake for another 7 minutes. Serve and enjoy.

Nutritional information: Calories: 116; Total Carbs 4 g; Net Carbs 3g; Protein: 12 g; Fat 12g; Sugars 0.5 g; Fiber 6g

Jewel Yams with Nutmeg

Prep time: 7 minutes. | Cooking time: 45 minutes. | Serving: 8

2 medium jewel yams
2 tablespoons unsalted butter
Juice of 1 large orange
1½ teaspoons ground cinnamon
¼ teaspoon ground ginger
¾ teaspoon ground nutmeg
⅛ teaspoon ground cloves

Set the oven at 355 degrees F. Arrange the yam dices on a rimmed baking sheet in a single layer. Set aside. Add the butter, orange juice, cinnamon, ginger, nutmeg, and garlic cloves to a medium saucepan over medium-low heat. Cook for 3 to 5 minutes, stirring occasionally. Spoon the sauce over the yams and toss to coat well. Bake in the preheated oven for 40 minutes. Let the yams cool for 8 minutes on the baking sheet before removing and serving.

Nutritional information: Calories: 129; Total Carbs 10g; Net Carbs 6g; Protein: 11g; Fat 9g; Sugars 1 g; Fiber 3g

Roasted Squash with Thyme

Prep time: 10 minutes. | Cooking time: 20 minutes. | Serving: 4

1 (1½-pound) delicata squash
1 tablespoon olive oil
½ teaspoon dried thyme
¼ teaspoon salt
¼ teaspoon black pepper

At 400 degrees F, preheat your oven. Line the baking sheet with parchment paper and set aside for later use. Add the squash strips, olive oil, thyme, salt, and pepper in a suitable bowl, and then toss to coat the squash strips well. Place the squash strips on the prepared baking sheet in a single layer. Roast for almost 20 minutes, flipping the strips halfway through. Remove from the oven and serve on plates.

Nutritional information: Calories: 80; Total Carbs 6.2g; Net Carbs 1.2g; Protein: 7g; Fat 13g; Sugars 2 g; Fiber 3.3g

Tasty Spinach Shrimp Salad

Prep time: 10 minutes. | Cooking time: 10 minutes. | Servings: 4

1 lb. Uncooked shrimp, peeled and deveined
2 tablespoons parsley, minced
¾ cup halved cherry tomatoes
1 lemon
4 cups baby spinach
2 tablespoons unsalted butter
3 minced garlic cloves
¼ teaspoon black pepper
¼ teaspoon salt

Melt the unsalted butter over the medium temperature in a nonstick skillet. Add the shrimp. Now cook the shrimp for 3 minutes until your shrimp becomes pink. Add the parsley, garlic and cook for 1 minute more. Take out from the heat. Keep the spinach in your salad bowl. Top with the shrimp mix and tomatoes. Drizzle lemon juice on the salad. Sprinkle pepper and salt. Serve and enjoy.

Nutritional information: Calories: 196; Total Carbs 8g; Net Carbs 5g; Protein: 10 g; Fat 7g; Sugars 5 g; Fiber 2g

Tomato Mozzarella Skewers

Prep time: 5 minutes. | Cooking time: 5 minutes. | Serving: 2

12 cherry tomatoes
8 (1-inch) pieces reduced-fat mozzarella cheese
12 basil leaves
¼ cup Italian vinaigrette, for serving

Thread the tomatoes, cheese and bay leave alternatively through the skewers. Place the Caprese skewers on a large plate and baste with the Italian vinaigrette. Serve immediately.

Nutritional information: Calories: 116; Total Carbs 4 g; Net Carbs 3g; Protein: 12 g; Fat 12g; Sugars 0.5 g; Fiber 6g

Sautéed Greens

Prep time: 10 minutes. | Cooking time: 10 minutes. | Serving: 4

2 tablespoons olive oil
1 lb. Swiss chard
1-lb. kale
½ teaspoon ground cardamom
1 tablespoon lemon juice

Heat up olive oil in a big skillet over medium-high heat. Stir in Swiss chard, kale, cardamom, lemon juice to the skillet, and stir to combine. Cook and stir the greens for about 10 minutes, or until the greens are wilted. Sprinkle with salt and pepper and stir well. Serve the greens on a plate while warm.

Nutritional information: Calories: 139; Total Carbs 7.9g; Net Carbs 4.5g; Protein: 6g; Fat 10g; Sugars 1 g; Fiber 5g

Sautéed Greens with Cabbage

Prep time: 10 minutes. | Cooking time: 10 minutes. | Serving: 8

2 tablespoons olive oil
1 collard greens bunch
½ small green cabbage
6 garlic cloves
1 tablespoon low-sodium soy sauce

Cook olive oil in a suitable skillet over medium-high heat. Sauté the collard greens in the oil for almost 2 minutes, or until the greens start to wilt. Toss in the cabbage and mix well. Decrease the heat to medium-low, cover and cook for almost 5 to 7 minutes. Fold in the garlic and soy sauce and stir to combine. Cook for almost 30 seconds more until fragrant. Remove from the heat to a plate and enjoy.

Nutritional information: Calories: 73; Total Carbs 8g; Net Carbs 2.4g; Protein: 9.5g; Fat 7g; Sugars 1.2g; Fiber 4g

Roasted Asparagus

Prep time: 5 minutes. | Cooking time: 15 minutes. | Serving: 4

1-lb. asparagus
2 red bell peppers, seeded

1 onion
2 tablespoons Italian dressing

At 425 degrees F, preheat your oven. Wrap baking sheet with parchment paper and set aside for later use. Combine the asparagus with the peppers, onion, dressing in a suitable bowl and then toss well. Arrange the vegetables on the baking sheet and roast for almost 15 minutes, flipping halfway through. Transfer to a large platter when done and enjoy.

Nutritional information: Calories: 92; Total Carbs 4 g; Net Carbs 1.2g; Protein: 12 g; Fat 12g; Sugars 0.5 g; Fiber 6g

Tarragon Peas Meal

Prep time: 10 minutes. | Cooking time: 12 minutes. | Serving: 6

1 tablespoon unsalted butter
½ Vidalia onion
1 cup vegetable broth
3 cups shelled peas
1 tablespoon minced tarragon

Melt the unsalted butter in a pan over medium heat. Add the onion to the pan and sauté for almost 3 minutes, stirring occasionally. Pour in the vegetable broth and whisk well. Add the peas and tarragon to the skillet and stir to combine. Reduce its heat to low, cover and cook for almost 8 minutes more, or until the peas are tender. Let the peas cool for almost 5 minutes and serve warm.

Nutritional information: Calories: 82; Total Carbs 8 g; Net Carbs 3g; Protein: 13g; Fat 11g; Sugars 1.5 g; Fiber 7g

Cheesy Broccoli Florets

Prep time: 10 minutes. | Cooking time: 35 minutes. | Serving: 6

2 tablespoons olive oil
2 heads broccoli, trimmed
1 egg
⅓ cup reduced-fat cheddar cheese, shredded
1 egg white
½ cup onion, chopped
⅓ cup bread crumbs
¼ teaspoon salt
¼ teaspoon black pepper

At 400 degrees F, preheat your oven. Coat a large baking sheet with olive oil. Arrange a colander in a saucepan, then place the broccoli in the colander. Pour the water into the saucepan to cover the bottom. Boil, and then reduce its heat to low heat. Close and simmer for 6 minutes. Allow cooling for almost 10 minutes. Blend broccoli and remaining ingredients in a food processor. Let sit for almost 10 minutes. To make the bites, drop 1 tablespoon of the mixture on the baking sheet. Repeat with the remaining mixture. Bake in the preheated oven for almost 25 minutes, flipping halfway through. Serve immediately.

Nutritional information: Calories: 106; Total Carbs 8 g; Net Carbs 3g; Protein: 13g; Fat 11g; Sugars 1.5 g; Fiber 7g

Roasted Brussels Sprouts

Prep time: 15 minutes. | Cooking time: 20 minutes. | Serving: 4

1-pound Brussels sprouts
1 tablespoon olive oil
½ cup sun-dried tomatoes
2 tablespoons lemon juice
1 teaspoon lemon zest

At 400 degrees F, preheat your oven. Line the baking sheet with aluminum foil. Mix the Brussels sprouts in the olive oil in a suitable bowl until well coated. Sprinkle with salt and pepper. Spread out the seasoned Brussels sprouts on the prepared baking sheet in a single layer. Roast for almost 20 minutes, shaking halfway through. Remove from the oven, then situate in a suitable bowl. Whisk tomatoes, lemon juice, and lemon zest to incorporate. Serve immediately.

Nutritional information: Calories: 112; Total Carbs 8g; Net Carbs 5g; Protein: 10 g; Fat 7g; Sugars 5 g; Fiber 2g

Barley Vegetable Salad

Prep time: 10 minutes. | Cooking time: 20 minutes. | Servings: 6

1 tomato, chopped
2 tablespoons parsley, minced
1 yellow pepper, chopped
1 tablespoon basil, minced
¼ cup almonds, toasted
1-¼ cups vegetable broth
1 cup barley
1 tablespoon lemon juice
2 tablespoons of white wine vinegar
3 tablespoons olive oil
¼ teaspoon black pepper
½ teaspoon salt
1 cup water

Boil the broth, barley and water in a saucepan. Reduce heat. Cover and let it simmer for almost 10 minutes. In the meantime, bring together the parsley, yellow pepper and tomato in a suitable bowl, the stir in the barley. Whisk the vinegar, oil, basil, lemon juice, water, pepper and salt in another suitable bowl. Pour this over your barley mix. Toss to coat well. Stir the almonds in before serving.

Nutritional information: Calories: 210; Total Carbs 4 g; Net Carbs 3g; Protein: 12 g; Fat 12g; Sugars 0.5 g; Fiber 6g

Mustard Deviled Eggs

Prep time: 5 minutes. | Cooking time: 8 minutes. | Serving: 12

6 large eggs
⅛ teaspoon mustard powder
2 tablespoons light mayonnaise

Sit the eggs in a saucepan, then pour in enough water to cover the egg. Bring to a boil, then boil the eggs for another 8 minutes. Turn off the heat and cover, then let the food stand for almost 15 minutes. Transfer the boiled eggs to a pot of cold water and peel under the water. Transfer the eggs to a large plate, then cut in half. Remove the egg yolks and place them in a suitable bowl, then use a fork to mash them. Add the mustard powder, mayo, salt, and pepper to the bowl of yolks, then stir to mix well. Spoon the yolk mixture in the egg white on the plate. Enjoy.

Nutritional information: Calories: 45; Total Carbs 7.2g; Net Carbs 2g; Protein: 9g; Fat 10g; Sugars 2.2 g; Fiber 1.3g

Baked Olive Chicken

Prep time: 15 minutes. | Cooking time: 25 minutes. | Serving: 4

2 (6-oz) bone-in chicken breasts
⅛ teaspoon salt
⅛ teaspoon black pepper
3 teaspoon olive oil
½ teaspoon dried oregano
7 pitted kalamata olives
1 cup cherry tomatoes
½ cup onion
1 (9-oz) package frozen artichoke hearts
1 lemon

At 400 degrees F, preheat your oven. Sprinkle the chicken with pepper, salt, and oregano. Heat oil in a skillet, add chicken and cook until it browned. Place chicken on the baking dish. Arrange tomatoes, coarsely chopped olives, and onion, artichokes and lemon cut into wedges around the chicken. Bake 20 minutes or until chicken is done and vegetables are tender. Serve and enjoy.

Nutritional information: Calories: 199; Total Carbs 6.2g; Net Carbs 1.2g; Protein: 7g; Fat 13g; Sugars 2 g; Fiber 3.3g

Fish Dipped in Tomato-Pepper Sauce

Prep time: 5 minutes. | Cooking time: 10 minutes. | Serving: 2

2 (4-oz) cod fillets
1 big tomato
⅓ cup red peppers (roasted)
3 tablespoon almonds
2 garlic cloves
2 tablespoons basil leaves
2 tablespoons extra-virgin olive oil
¼ teaspoon salt
⅛ teaspoon black pepper

Toast sliced almonds in a pan until fragrant. Grind almonds, basil, minced garlic, 1-2 teaspoons of oil in a food processor until ground. Add coarsely-chopped tomato and red peppers; grind until smooth. Season the cod fillets with salt and pepper. Cook in hot oil in a large pan over medium-high heat until fish is browned. Pour sauce around fish and cook for 6 minutes more. When done, serve and enjoy.

Nutritional information: Calories: 90; Total Carbs 8g; Net Carbs 5g; Protein: 10 g; Fat 7g; Sugars 5 g; Fiber 2g

Garlicky Button Mushrooms

Prep time: 10 minutes. | Cooking time: 12 minutes. | Serving: 4

1 tablespoon unsalted butter
2 teaspoons extra-virgin olive oil
2 pounds button mushrooms
2 teaspoons minced garlic
1 teaspoon chopped thyme

Heat the unsalted butter and olive oil in a suitable skillet over medium-high heat. Add the mushrooms and sauté for almost 10 minutes, with occasional stirring. Stir in the garlic and thyme and cook for an additional 2 minutes. Season and serve on a plate.

Nutritional information: Calories: 98; Total Carbs 4 g; Net Carbs 3g; Protein: 12 g; Fat 12g; Sugars 0.5 g; Fiber 6g

Baked Green Beans

Prep time: 5 minutes. | Cooking time: 17 minutes. | Serving: 3

12 oz. Green bean pods
1 tablespoon Olive oil
½ teaspoon Onion powder
⅛ teaspoon black pepper
⅛ teaspoon Salt

At 350 degrees F, preheat your oven. Mix up the green beans, onion powder, pepper and oil in a suitable bowl. Spread the mixture on the baking sheet. Bake 17 minutes or until you have a delicious aroma in the kitchen. Serve and enjoy.

Nutritional information: Calories: 39; Total Carbs 7.2g; Net Carbs 2g; Protein: 9g; Fat 10g; Sugars 2.2 g; Fiber 1.3g

Broiled Flounder

Prep time: 10 minutes. | Cooking time: 7 minutes. | Serving: 2

2 (4-oz) flounder
1,5 tablespoon reduced-fat parmesan cheese
1,5 tablespoon light mayonnaise
⅛ teaspoon soy sauce
¼ teaspoon chili sauce
⅛ teaspoon salt-free lemon-pepper seasoning

Heat your flounder in advance. Mix the parmesan cheese, mayonnaise, soy sauce, chili sauce, seasoning. Put fish on the baking sheet coated with cooking spray and then sprinkle with salt and pepper. Spread the mixture over flounder. Broil 6 to 8 minutes or until a crust appears on the fish. Serve and enjoy.

Nutritional information: Calories: 116; Total Carbs 4 g; Net Carbs 1.2g; Protein: 12 g; Fat 12g; Sugars 0.5 g; Fiber 6g

Fish with Herb Sauce

Prep time: 10 minutes. | Cooking time: 10 minutes. | Serving: 2

2 (4-oz) cod fillets
⅓ cup cilantro

¼ teaspoon cumin
1 tablespoon red onion
2 teaspoons olive oil
1 teaspoon red wine vinegar
1 garlic clove
⅛ teaspoon salt
⅛ black pepper

Combine chopped cilantro, chopped onion, oil, red wine vinegar, minced garlic, and salt. Sprinkle both sides of cod fillets with cumin and pepper. Cook fillets 4 minutes per side. Top each fillet with cilantro mixture. Serve an enjoy.

Nutritional information: Calories: 101; Total Carbs 8g; Net Carbs 5g; Protein: 10 g; Fat 7g; Sugars 5 g; Fiber 2g

Chicken Soaked in Coconut Sauce

Prep time: 15 minutes. | Cooking time: 20 minutes. | Serving: 2

½ lb. Chicken breasts
⅓ cup red onion
1 tablespoon paprika (smoked)
2 teaspoon cornstarch
½ cup light coconut milk
1 teaspoon olive oil
2 tablespoon cilantro
1 (10-oz) can tomatoes and green chilies
¼ cup water

Cut chicken into small cubes; sprinkle with 1.5 teaspoon of paprika. Heat oil, add chicken and cook 3 to 5 minutes. Remove from skillet, and fry finely-chopped onion 5 minutes. Return chicken to pan. Add tomatoes, 1.5 teaspoon of paprika, and water. Bring to a boil and then simmer 4 minutes. Mix cornstarch and coconut milk; stir into chicken mixture, and cook until it has done. Sprinkle with chopped cilantro.

Nutritional information: Calories: 116; Total Carbs 4 g; Net Carbs 3g; Protein: 12 g; Fat 12g; Sugars 0.5 g; Fiber 6g

Fish with Tomato Sauce

Prep time: 10 minutes. | Cooking time: 15 minutes. | Serving: 2

2 (4-oz) tilapia fillets
1 tablespoon basil, chopped
⅛ teaspoon salt
1 pinch of crushed red pepper
1 cup cherry tomatoes, chopped
2 teaspoons olive oil

At 400 degrees F, preheat your oven. Line the baking sheet with the foil. Arrange the rinsed and patted-dry tilapia fillets on foil. Sprinkle tilapia fillets with salt and red pepper. Bake for almost 12 - 15 minutes. Meanwhile, mix leftover ingredients in a saucepan and cook over medium-high heat, until the tomatoes are tender. Top fish fillets properly with tomato mixture. Enjoy.

Nutritional information: Calories: 129; Total Carbs 8g; Net Carbs 5g; Protein: 10 g; Fat 7g; Sugars 5 g; Fiber 2g

Cheesy Potato Casserole

Prep time: 10 minutes. | Cooking time: 40 minutes. | Serving: 3

1 tablespoon olive oil
¾ lb. Red potatoes
¾ cup green peas
½ cup red onion
¼ teaspoon dried rosemary
¼ teaspoon salt
⅛ teaspoon black pepper

At 350 degrees F, preheat your oven Heat 1 teaspoon of oil in a suitable skillet. Stir in thinly sliced onions and cook for a few seconds. Remove from pan. Situate half of the thinly sliced potatoes and onions in bottom of skillet; top with peas, crushed dried rosemary, pepper and ⅛ teaspoon of salt. Place remaining potatoes and onions on top. Season them with the remaining ⅛ teaspoon of salt. Bake 35 minutes, and then pour remaining 2 teaspoons of oil and sprinkle with cheese. When done, serve and enjoy.

Nutritional information: Calories: 80; Total Carbs 8g; Net Carbs 2.4g; Protein: 9.5g; Fat 7g; Sugars 1.2g; Fiber 4g

Oven-Baked Tilapia

Prep time: 7 minutes. | Cooking time: 15 minutes. | Serving: 2

2 (4-oz) tilapia fillets
¼ cup yellow cornmeal
2 tablespoon light ranch dressing
1 tablespoon canola oil
1 teaspoon dill (dried)
⅛ teaspoon salt

At 425 degrees F, preheat your oven. Brush both sides of rinsed and patted dry tilapia fish fillets with dressing. Combine cornmeal, oil, dill, and salt. Sprinkle fish fillets with cornmeal mixture. Put fish on a prepared baking sheet. Bake for almost 15 minutes. Serve.

Nutritional information: Calories: 96; Total Carbs 4 g; Net Carbs 1.2g; Protein: 12 g; Fat 12g; Sugars 0.5 g; Fiber 6g

Chicken Breasts with Roasted Vegetable Mixture

Prep time: 20 minutes. | Cooking time: 30 minutes. | Serving: 1

1 (8-oz) boneless, chicken breasts
¾ lb. Small Brussels sprouts
2 large carrots
1 large red bell pepper
1 red onion
2 garlic cloves halved
2 tablespoon olive oil
½ teaspoon dried dill
¼ teaspoon black pepper
¼ teaspoon salt

At 425 degrees F, preheat your oven Match Brussels sprouts cut in half, red onion cut into wedges, sliced carrots, bell pepper cut into pieces and halved garlic on the baking sheet. Sprinkle with 1 tablespoon oil, ⅛ teaspoon salt and ⅛ teaspoon black pepper. Bake until well-roasted, cool slightly. While baking, sprinkle chicken with dill, remaining ⅛ teaspoon salt and ⅛ teaspoon black pepper. Cook until chicken breasts are done. Put roasted vegetables with drippings over the chicken breasts. Enjoy.

Nutritional information: Calories: 170; Total Carbs 8 g; Net Carbs 3g; Protein: 13g; Fat 11g; Sugars 1.5 g; Fiber 7g

Crispy Chicken Salad

Prep time: 10 minutes. | Cooking time: 10 minutes. | Servings: 2

2 chicken breasts halved,
½ cup panko bread crumbs
4 cups spring mix salad greens
4 teaspoons of sesame seeds
½ cup mushrooms, sliced
1 teaspoon sesame oil
2 teaspoons of canola oil
2 teaspoons hoisin sauce
¼ cup sesame ginger salad dressing

Flatten the chicken breasts to half-inch thickness. Mix the sesame oil and hoisin sauce. Brush over the chicken. Combine the sesame seeds and panko in a suitable bowl. Now dip the chicken mix in it. Cook each side of the chicken for almost 5 minutes. In the meantime, divide the salad greens between 2 plates. Top with mushroom. Slice the chicken and keep on top. Drizzle the dressing. When done, serve and enjoy.

Nutritional information: Calories: 116; Total Carbs 4 g; Net Carbs 2g; Protein: 12 g; Fat 12g; Sugars 0.5 g; Fiber 6g

Turkey Meatloaf

Prep time: 10 minutes. | Cooking time: 50 minutes. | Serving: 2

½ lb. 93% lean ground turkey
⅓ cup panko breadcrumbs
½ cup green onion
1 egg
½ cup green bell pepper
1 tablespoon ketchup
¼ cup sauce (Picante)
½ teaspoon cumin (ground)

At 350 degrees F, preheat your oven. Mix lean ground turkey, 3 tablespoons Picante sauce, panko breadcrumbs, egg, chopped green onion, chopped green bell pepper and cumin in a suitable bowl. Put the mixture into a baking sheet; shape into an oval (about 1 ½ inches thick). Bake 45 minutes. Mix remaining Picante sauce and the ketchup; apply over the loaf. Bake 5 minutes longer. Let stand 5 minutes. Serve and enjoy.

Nutritional information: Calories: 170; Total Carbs 7.2g; Net Carbs 2g; Protein: 9g; Fat 10g; Sugars 2.2 g; Fiber 1.3g

Kale Pesto Pasta

Prep time: 10 minutes. | Cooking time: 0 minutes. | Servings: 1-2

1 bunch of kale
2 cups basil
¼ cup olive oil
½ cup walnuts
2 limes, freshly squeezed
Sea salt and chili pepper
1 zucchini, noodles
garnish with chopped asparagus, spinach leaves, and tomato (optional)

The night before, soak the walnuts in order to improve absorption. Blend all the recipe ingredients in a blender until the consistency of the cream is reached. Add the zucchini noodles and enjoy.

Nutritional information: Calories: 206; Total Carbs 8 g; Net Carbs 3g; Protein: 13g; Fat 11g; Sugars 1.5 g; Fiber 7g

Tomato Roasted Cod

Prep time: 10 minutes. | Cooking time: 35 minutes. | Serving: 2

2 (4-oz) cod fillets
1 cup cherry tomatoes
½ cup onion
2 teaspoon orange rind
1 tablespoon olive oil
1 teaspoon thyme (dried)
¼ teaspoon salt
¼ teaspoon black pepper

At 400 degrees F, preheat your oven. Mix in half tomatoes, sliced onion, grated orange rind, olive oil, dried thyme, ⅛ teaspoon of salt and pepper. Fry 25 minutes and then remove from the oven. Arrange fish on pan, and flavor with remaining ⅛ teaspoon of each salt and pepper. Put reserved tomato mixture over fish. Bake 10 minutes. When done, serve and enjoy.

Nutritional information: Calories: 129; Total Carbs 6.2g; Net Carbs 1.2g; Protein: 7g; Fat 13g; Sugars 2 g; Fiber 3.3g

Ground Turkey Mayo Salad

Prep time: 10 minutes. | Cooking time: 35 minutes. | Servings: 6

1 lb. lean ground turkey
½-inch ginger, minced
2 garlic cloves, minced
1 onion, chopped
1 tablespoon olive oil
1 bag lettuce leaves (for serving)
¼ cup cilantro, chopped
2 teaspoon coriander powder
1 teaspoon red chili powder
1 teaspoon turmeric powder
salt to taste
4 cups water
dressing:
2 tablespoon yogurt
1 tablespoon sour cream, non-fat

1 tablespoon mayonnaise
1 lemon, juiced
1 teaspoon red chili flakes
salt and Black pepper, to taste

In a suitable skillet, sauté the garlic and ginger in olive oil for almost 1 minute. Add onion and season with salt. Cook for almost 10 minutes over medium heat until soft. Add the ground turkey and sauté for 3 more minutes. Add the spices and 4 cups water and cook for 30 minutes, covered. Prepare the dressing by combining yogurt, sour cream, mayo, lemon juice, chilli flakes, salt and pepper. Arrange the salad leaves in the serving plates and place the cooked ground turkey on them. Top with the dressing. Serve and enjoy.

Nutritional information: Calories: 176; Total Carbs 4.7 g; Net Carbs 2g; Protein: 2 g; Fat 2g; Sugars 0.5 g; Fiber 3g

Broccoli Salad

Prep time: 10 minutes. | Cooking time: 10 minutes. | Servings: 10

8 cups broccoli florets
3 strips of bacon, cooked and crumbled
¼ cup sunflower kernels
1 bunch of green onion, sliced
3 tablespoons seasoned rice vinegar
3 tablespoons canola oil
½ cup dried cranberries

Combine the green onion, cranberries, and broccoli in a suitable bowl. Whisk the vinegar and oil in another bowl. Blend well. Now drizzle over the broccoli mix. Toss to coat well. Sprinkle bacon and sunflower kernels before serving.

Nutritional information: Calories: 178; Total Carbs 10g; Net Carbs 6g; Protein: 11g; Fat 9g; Sugars 1 g; Fiber 3g

Garden Salad Wraps

Prep time: 20 minutes. | Cooking time: 10 minutes. | Servings: 8

1 cucumber, chopped
1 sweet corn
1 cabbage, shredded
1 tablespoon lettuce, minced
1 tomato, chopped
3 tablespoons of rice vinegar
2 teaspoons peanut butter
⅓ cup onion paste
⅓ cup chili sauce
2 teaspoons of soy sauce

Cut corn from the cob. Keep in a suitable bowl. Add the tomato, cabbage, cucumber, and onion paste. Now whisk the vinegar, peanut butter, and chili sauce together. Pour this over the vegetable mix. Toss to coat well. Let this stand for almost 10 minutes. Take your slotted spoon and place ½ cup salad in every lettuce leaf. Fold the lettuce over your filling.

Nutritional information: Calories: 98; Total Carbs 8g; Net Carbs 2.4g; Protein: 9.5g; Fat 7g; Sugars 1.2g; Fiber 4g

Red Potato Salad

Prep time: 15 minutes. | Cooking time: 5 minutes. |
Servings: 14

4 red potatoes, peeled and cooked
1-½ cups kernel corn, cooked
½ cup green pepper, diced
½ cup red onion, chopped
1 cup carrot, shredded
½ cup olive oil
¼ cup vinegar
1-½ teaspoons chili powder
1 teaspoon salt
Dash of hot pepper sauce

Keep all the recipe ingredients together in a jar. Close
it and shake to coat well. Combine with the carrot,
onion, and corn in your salad bowl. Pour the dressing
over. Now toss lightly. Enjoy.

Nutritional information: Calories: 116; Total Carbs
4 g; Net Carbs 1.2g; Protein: 12 g; Fat 12g; Sugars
0.5 g; Fiber 6g

Strawberry Salsa

Prep time: 10 minutes. | Cooking time: 5 minutes. |
Servings: 4

4 tomatoes, chopped
1-pint strawberry, chopped
1 red onion, chopped
2 tablespoons of juice from a lime
1 jalapeno pepper, minced
1 tablespoon olive oil
2 garlic cloves, minced

Bring together the strawberries, tomatoes, jalapeno,
and onion in the bowl. Stir in the garlic, oil, and lime
juice. Refrigerate. Serve with separately cooked pork
or poultry.

Nutritional information: Calories: 206; Total Carbs
8 g; Net Carbs 3g; Protein: 13g; Fat 11g; Sugars 1.5
g; Fiber 7g

Mushroom Linguine

Prep time: 7 minutes. | Cooking time: 10 minutes. |
Serving: 4

4 oz. whole-grain linguine
1 teaspoon olive oil
½ cup light sauce
2 tablespoon green onion
1 (8-oz) package mushrooms
1 garlic clove
⅛ teaspoon salt
⅛ teaspoon black pepper

Cook pasta according to package directions, drain.
Fry sliced mushrooms 4 minutes. Stir in fettuccine
minced garlic, salt and pepper. Cook 2 minutes. Heat
light sauce until heated; top pasta mixture properly
with sauce and with finely-chopped green onion.
When done, serve and enjoy.

Nutritional information: Calories: 116; Total Carbs
4 g; Net Carbs 1.2g; Protein: 12 g; Fat 12g; Sugars
0.5 g; Fiber 6g

Broccoli Salad with Tahini Dressing

Prep time: 10 minutes. | Cooking time: 25 minutes. |
Servings: 1-2

1 slice stale sourdough, torn into chunks
1 oz. mixed seeds
1 teaspoon Cumin seeds
1 teaspoon Coriander seeds
1 oz. baby kale
75g long-stemmed broccoli, blanched and chopped
½ red onion, sliced
3 ½ oz. cherry tomatoes, halved
½ a small bunch parsley, torn
Dressing
100ml natural yogurt
1 tablespoon Tahini
1 lemon, juiced

At 425 degrees F, preheat your oven. Put the bread
into a food processor and pulse into very rough
breadcrumbs. Put into a suitable bowl with the mixed
seeds and spices, season, and spray well with oil. Tip
onto a non-stick baking tray and roast for almost 15-
20 minutes, stirring and tossing regularly, until deep
golden brown. Whisk together the dressing ingredients, some seasoning and a splash of water in a suitable bowl. Tip the baby kale, broccoli, red onion,
cherry tomatoes and flat-leaf parsley into the dressing, and mix well. Divide the prepared salad between
2 plates and top with the crispy breadcrumbs and
seeds.

Nutritional information: Calories: 89; Total Carbs
6.2g; Net Carbs 1.2g; Protein: 7g; Fat 13g; Sugars 2
g; Fiber 3.3g

Cucumber Tofu Salad

Prep time: 10 minutes. | Cooking time: 15 minutes. |
Servings: 4

2 cups cauliflower florets, blended
1 cucumber, diced
½ cup green olives, diced
⅓ cup red onion, diced
2 tablespoon toasted pine nuts
2 tablespoon raisins
⅓ cup feta, crumbled
½ cup pomegranate seeds
2 lemons (juiced, zest grated)
8 oz. tofu
2 teaspoon oregano
2 garlic cloves, minced
½ teaspoon red chili flakes
3 tablespoon olive oil
salt and Black pepper, to taste

Mix the processed cauliflower with salt and keep in a
strainer to drain. Prepare the tofu marinade by mixing all its ingredients in a bowl then toss in tofu. At
450 degrees F, preheat your oven. Spread tofu on a
baking sheet and bake for 12 minutes almost. In a
salad bowl mix the leftover marinade with cauliflower,
cucumber, onions, raisins and olives. Add in the leftover olive oil and grated lemon zest. Top with tofu,
pine nuts, and feta and pomegranate seeds. Enjoy.

Nutritional information: Calories: 216; Total Carbs
8g; Net Carbs 5g; Protein: 10 g; Fat 7g; Sugars 5 g;
Fiber 2g

Parsnip Kale Salad

Prep time: 10 minutes. | Cooking time: 0 minutes. | Servings: 4

Dressing:
⅓ cup olive oil
Juice of 1 lime
2 tablespoon Minced mint leaves
1 teaspoon Pure maple syrup
Pinch sea salt
For the salad
1 bunch kale, chopped
½ parsnip, grated
½ carrot, grated
2 tablespoon Sesame seeds

To make the dressing, mix all the dressing ingredients in a suitable bowl. To make the salad, add the kale to the dressing and massage the dressing into the kale for almost 1 minute. Add the parsnip, carrot, and sesame seeds. Toss to combine well, the you can serve and enjoy.

Nutritional information: Calories: 116; Total Carbs 4 g; Net Carbs 3g; Protein: 12 g; Fat 12g; Sugars 0.5 g; Fiber 6g

Tomato Avocado Toasts

Prep time: 5 minutes. | Cooking time: 5 minutes. | Servings: 4

4 slices of sprouted bread toasts
2 tomatoes, sliced
1 avocado, mashed
1 teaspoon olive oil
1 pinch of salt
¾ teaspoon black pepper

Blend together the olive oil, mashed avocado, salt, and black pepper. When the mixture is homogenous, spread it over the sprouted bread. Then place the sliced tomatoes over the toasts. Enjoy!

Nutritional information: Calories: 148; Total Carbs 8g; Net Carbs 2.4g; Protein: 9.5g; Fat 7g; Sugars 1.2g; Fiber 4g

Tabbouleh Salad

Prep time: 5 minutes. | Cooking time: 10 minutes. | Servings: 6

¼ cup chopped mint
1-⅔ cups boiling water
1 cucumber, peeled, chopped
1 cup bulgur
1 cup chopped parsley
1 cup chopped green onions
1 teaspoon salt
⅓ cup lemon juice
⅓ cup olive oil
3 tomatoes, chopped
Black pepper, to taste

In a suitable bowl, mix up the boiling water and bulgur. Let soak and set aside for an hour while covered. After 1 hour, toss in cucumber, tomatoes, mint, parsley, onions, lemon juice and oil. Then season with

black pepper and salt to taste. Toss well and refrigerate for another hour while covered before serving.

Nutritional information: Calories 158; Total Carbs 30g; Net Carbs 24g; Protein 4g; Fat 4g; Sugar 19g; Fiber 6g

Mushroom Tomato Salad

Prep time: 10 minutes. | Cooking time: 40 minutes. | Servings: 6

5 halved mushrooms
6 halved cherry (plum) tomatoes
6 rinsed lettuce leaves
10 olives
½ chopped cucumber
Juice from ½ key lime
1 teaspoon olive oil
Pure sea salt

Tear rinsed lettuce leaves into medium pieces and put them in a medium salad bowl. Add mushrooms halves, chopped cucumber, olives and cherry tomato halves into the bowl. Mix well. Pour olive and key lime juice over the salad. Add pure sea salt to taste. Mix it all till it is well combined. Serve and enjoy.

Nutritional information: Calories: 116; Total Carbs 4 g; Net Carbs 1.2g; Protein: 12 g; Fat 12g; Sugars 0.5 g; Fiber 6g

Mayo Caesar Salad

Prep time: 5 minutes. | Cooking time: 10 minutes. | Servings: 4

¼ cup olive oil
¾ cup mayonnaise
1 head romaine lettuce, torn into bite sized pieces
1 tablespoon Lemon juice
1 teaspoon Dijon mustard
1 teaspoon Worcestershire sauce
3 garlic cloves, peeled and minced
3 garlic cloves, peeled and quartered
4 cups day old bread, cubed
5 anchovy filets, minced
6 tablespoon Grated parmesan cheese
Black pepper, to taste
Salt to taste

In a suitable bowl, whisk well lemon juice, mustard, Worcestershire sauce, 2 tablespoons of Parmesan cheese, anchovies, mayonnaise, and minced garlic; season with the salt and black pepper. Set aside. On medium fire, place a large nonstick saucepan and heat oil. Sauté quartered garlic until browned around a minute or two. Remove and discard. Add bread cubes in the same pan, sauté until lightly browned. Season with pepper and salt. Transfer to a plate. In a suitable bowl, place lettuce and pour in the dressing. Toss well to coat. Top with remaining parmesan cheese. Garnish with bread cubes, serve and enjoy.

Nutritional information: Calories: 443.3g; Fat: 32.1g; Net Carbs 1.2g; Protein: 11.6g; Total Carbs: 27g; Sugar 19g; Fiber 6g

Roasted Portobello Salad

Prep time: 10 minutes. | Cooking time: 15 minutes. | Servings: 4

1 ½ lb. Portobello mushrooms stems trimmed
3 heads Belgian endive, sliced
1 red onion, sliced
4 oz. Blue cheese
8 oz. Mixed salad greens
Dressing:
3 tablespoon Red wine vinegar
1 tablespoon Dijon mustard
½ cup olive oil
Salt and Black pepper, to taste

At 450 degrees F, preheat your oven. Prepare the dressing by whisking all its ingredients into a bowl. Cut and arrange the mushrooms on a baking sheet. Coat the cut mushrooms with the dressing and bake for 15 minutes almost. In a salad bowl, toss the salad ingredients in a bowl. Sprinkle with the dressing. Add mushrooms to the salad bowl. Enjoy,

Nutritional information: Calories: 178; Total Carbs 10g; Net Carbs 6g; Protein: 11g; Fat 9g; Sugars 1 g; Fiber 3g

Greens with Avocado Cumin Dressing

Prep time: 10 minutes. | Cooking time: 0 minutes. | Servings: 1-2

For Avocado Cumin:
1 avocado
1 tablespoon cumin powder
2 limes,
1 cup filtered water
¼ seconds. sea salt
1 tablespoon olive oil
cayenne pepper dash
¼ teaspoon smoked pepper
For Tahini Lemon Dressing
¼ cup tahini
½ cup filtered water
½ lemon,
1 clove of minced garlic
¾ teaspoon sea salt
1 tablespoon olive oil
black pepper taste
For Salad
3 cups kale, chopped
½ cup broccoli flowers, chopped
½ zucchini (make spiral noodles)
½ cup kelp noodles, soaked and drained
⅓ cup cherry tomatoes, halved.
2 teaspoon hemp seeds

Gently steam the kale and the broccoli (flash the steam for 4 minutes), set aside. Mix the zucchini noodles and kelp noodles and toss with a generous portion of the smoked avocado cumin dressing. Add the cherry tomatoes and stir again. Place the steamed kale and broccoli and drizzle with the lemon tahini dressing. Top the kale and the broccoli with the noodles and tomatoes and sprinkle the whole dish with the hemp seeds. When done, serve and enjoy.

Nutritional information: Calories: 89; Total Carbs 7.2g; Net Carbs 2g; Protein: 9g; Fat 10g; Sugars 2.2 g; Fiber 1.3g

Grape and Bulgur Salad

Prep time: 10 minutes. | Cooking time: 15 minutes. | Servings: 6

1 cup bulgur
1 cup pecan, toasted and chopped
¼ cup scallions, sliced
½ cup parsley, chopped
2 cups California grapes, seedless and halved
2 tablespoons of olive oil
¼ cup juice from a lemon
Pinch of kosher salt
Pinch of black pepper
2 cups water

Boil 2 cups of water in a saucepan. Stir the bulgur in and ½ teaspoon of salt. Take out from the heat. Keep covered and drain out. Stir in the other ingredients, and then season with pepper and salt. Serve.

Nutritional information: Calories: 189; Total Carbs 7.9g; Net Carbs 4.5g; Protein: 6g; Fat 10g; Sugars 1 g; Fiber 5g

Mini Zucchini Pizzas

Prep time: 20 minutes. | Cooking time: 10 minutes. | Servings: 24

1 zucchini, cut into ¼ inch slices diagonally
½ cup pepperoni, small slices
1 teaspoon basil, minced
½ cup onion, chopped
1 cup tomatoes
⅛ teaspoon black pepper
⅛ teaspoon salt
¾ cup reduced-fat mozzarella cheese, shredded
⅓ cup pizza sauce

Preheat your broiler. Keep the zucchini in 1 layer on your greased baking sheet. Add the onion and tomatoes. Broil each side for almost 1 to 2 minutes till they become tender and crisp. Now sprinkle pepper and salt. Top with cheese, pepperoni, and sauce. Broil for a minute to melt the cheese after putting on the top. Sprinkle basil on top. Serve and enjoy.

Nutritional information: Calories: 116; Total Carbs 4 g; Net Carbs 3g; Protein: 12 g; Fat 12g; Sugars 0.5 g; Fiber 6g

Bacon Shrimps

Prep time: 10 minutes. | Cooking time: 6 minutes. | Serving: 10

20 shrimps, peeled and deveined
7 slices low-fat bacon
4 leaves romaine lettuce

At 400 degrees F, preheat your oven. Wrap each shrimp with each bacon strip, then arrange the wrapped shrimps in a single layer on a baking sheet, seam side down. Broil for 6 minutes, flipping halfway through. Take out from the oven and serve on lettuce leaves.

Nutritional information: Calories 158; Total Carbs 30g; Net Carbs 24g; Protein 4g; Fat 4g; Sugar 19g; Fiber 6g

Garlic Veggie Balls

Prep Time: 08 minutes. | Cook Time: 24 minutes | Serve: 2

½ of medium sweet potato, peeled and cubed into ½-inch size
½ tablespoon unsweetened coconut milk
¼ cup fresh spinach, chopped
¼ of medium shallot, chopped finely
¼ teaspoon ground cumin
⅛ teaspoon granulated garlic
Pinch of ground turmeric
Salt and ground black pepper, as required
1-2 tablespoons ground flax seeds

Preheat the oven to 400 degrees Fahrenheit. Utilizing parchment paper, line a large baking sheet.Place a steamer basket in a pan of boiling water. Steam the sweet potato for around 10-15 minutes in a steamer basket. Remove the sweet potato from the steamer basket and place it in a bowl. Mash in the coconut milk thoroughly. Mix in the remaining Ingredients, except the flax seeds, until thoroughly incorporated. From the mixture, make 1½-2-inch balls. Place the balls in a single layer on the prepared baking sheet and top with flax seeds. Pre - heat to 200 degrees Fahrenheit and bake for 20 to 25 minutes. Warm the dish before serving.

Nutritional information: Calories 63 Total Carbs 9g Net Carbs 12.8g Protein 1.6g Fat 7.5 g Sugar 2.5g Fiber 2.4g

Cranberry Brussels Sprouts Salad

Prep time: 10 minutes. | Cooking time: 0 minute. | Servings: 4

Dressing
⅓ cup olive oil
2 tablespoon apple cider vinegar
1 tablespoon pure maple syrup
juice of 1 orange
½ tablespoon dried rosemary
1 tablespoon scallion, whites only
1 pinch sea salt
Salad
1 bunch scallions, chopped
1 cup Brussels sprouts, stemmed, halved, and sliced
½ cup cranberries
4 cups baby spinach

To make the dressing: in a suitable bowl, whisk the dressing ingredients. To make the salad: add the scallions, Brussels sprouts, cranberries, and spinach to the bowl with the dressing. Combine well, serve and enjoy.

Nutritional information: Calories: 116; Total Carbs 4 g; Net Carbs 2g; Protein: 12 g; Fat 12g; Sugars 0.5 g; Fiber 6g

Italian Shrimp

Prep time: 15 minutes. | Cooking time: 10 minutes. | Servings: 30

16 oz. uncooked shrimp, peeled and deveined
1-½ teaspoons of juice from a lemon
½ teaspoon basil, chopped
1 teaspoon coriander, chopped
½ cup tomato
1 tablespoon of olive oil
½ teaspoon Italian seasoning
½ teaspoon paprika
1 sliced garlic clove
¼ teaspoon black pepper

Bring together everything except the shrimp in a dish or bowl. Add the shrimp and toss to coat well. Set aside for later use. Drain the shrimp and discard the marinade. Keep them on a baking sheet. It should not be greased. Broil each side for 4 minutes. The shrimp should become pink. When done, serve and enjoy.

Nutritional information: Calories: 199; Total Carbs 6.2g; Net Carbs 1.2g; Protein: 7g; Fat 13g; Sugars 2 g; Fiber 3.3g

Seared Turkey Patties

Prep time: 7 minutes. | Cooking time: 8 minutes. | Serving: 2

½ lb. Lean ground turkey
½ cup chicken broth
¼ cup red onion
½ teaspoon Worcestershire sauce
1 teaspoon olive oil
¼ teaspoon oregano (dried)
⅛ teaspoon black pepper

Combine turkey, chopped onion, Worcestershire sauce, dried oregano, and pepper; make 2 patties. Warm-up oil and cook patties 4 minutes per side; set aside. Add broth to skillet, bring to a boil. Boil 2 minutes, spoon sauce over patties.

Nutritional information: Calories: 189; Total Carbs 7.9g; Net Carbs 4.5g; Protein: 6g; Fat 10g; Sugars 1 g; Fiber 5g

Sesame Pumpkin Seeds

Prep time: 10 minutes. | Cooking time: 20 minutes. | Servings: 2

1 egg white
1 teaspoon onion, minced
½ teaspoon caraway seeds
2 cups pumpkin seeds
1 teaspoon sesame seeds
1 garlic clove, minced
1 tablespoon of canola oil
¾ teaspoon of kosher salt

Preheat your oven to 350 ºF. Whisk together the oil and egg white in a suitable bowl. Add pumpkin seeds and toss to coat well. Now stir in the onion, garlic, sesame seeds, caraway seeds, and salt. Spread in 1 layer in your parchment-lined baking pan. Bake for almost 15 minutes until it turns golden brown. When done, serve and enjoy.

Nutritional information: Calories: 116; Total Carbs 4 g; Net Carbs 1.2g; Protein: 12 g; Fat 12g; Sugars 0.5 g; Fiber 6g

Scallop Caesar Salad

Prep time: 5 minutes. | Cooking time: 2 minutes. | Servings: 2

8 sea scallops
4 cups romaine lettuce
2 teaspoon olive oil
3 tablespoon Caesar salad dressing
1 teaspoon lemon juice
salt and Black pepper, to taste

In a suitable frying pan, heat olive oil and cook the scallops in 1 layer for no longer than 2 minutes per both side, then season with the salt and black pepper. Spread the lettuce leaves on the serving plates and add scallops on top. Pour over the Caesar dressing and lemon juice. Serve and enjoy.

Nutritional information: Calories: 340; Total Carbs 4 g; Net Carbs 2g; Protein: 12 g; Fat 12g; Sugars 0.5 g; Fiber 6g

Pomegranate Cucumber Salad

Prep time: 10 minutes. | Cooking time: 0 minutes. | Servings: 1-2

1 big head of butter lettuce
½ of cucumber, sliced
1 pomegranate, seeds
1 avocado, 1 cubed
¼ cup shelled pistachio, chopped
Ingredients for Dressing:
¼ cup apple cider vinegar
½ cup olive oil
1 clove of garlic, minced

Put the butter lettuce in a salad bowl. Add the remaining ingredients and toss with the salad dressing. When done, serve and enjoy.

Nutritional information: Calories: 196; Total Carbs 8g; Net Carbs 5g; Protein: 10 g; Fat 7g; Sugars 5 g; Fiber 2g

Ham and Turkey Wraps

Prep time: 5 minutes. | Cooking time: 15 minutes. | Servings: 4

4 slices turkey breast, cooked
4 slices ham, cooked
4 lettuce leaves
4 slices tomato
4 slices avocado
1 teaspoon lime juice
a handful of watercress leaves
4 tablespoon ranch dressing

Top a lettuce leaf with turkey slice, ham slice and tomato. In a suitable bowl combine avocado and lime juice and place on top of tomatoes. Top with watercress and dressing. Repeat with the remaining ingredients for topping. Top lettuce leaf with a turkey slice, ham slice, tomato and dressing. When done, serve and enjoy.

Nutritional information: Calories: 116; Total Carbs 4 g; Net Carbs 2g; Protein: 12 g; Fat 12g; Sugars 0.5 g; Fiber 6g

Jalapeno Cucumber Salad

Prep time: 10 minutes. | Cooking time: 0 minutes. | Servings: 6

1 lb. cucumbers, sliced
2 scallions, sliced
2 tablespoon sliced pickled ginger, chopped
¼ cup cilantro
½ red jalapeño, chopped
3 tablespoon rice wine vinegar
1 tablespoon sesame oil
1 tablespoon sesame seeds

In a salad bowl combine all the recipe ingredients and toss together. You can serve directly.

Nutritional information: Calories: 116; Total Carbs 4 g; Net Carbs 1.2g; Protein: 12 g; Fat 12g; Sugars 0.5 g; Fiber 6g

Mayo Broccoli Bacon Salad

Prep time: 10 minutes. | Cooking time: 0 minutes. | Servings: 6

1 head broccoli, raw, florets only
½ cup red onion, chopped
12 oz. crisp Turkey bacon, chopped,
½ cup cherry tomatoes, halved
¼ cup sunflower kernels
¾ cup raisins
¾ cup mayonnaise
2 tablespoon White vinegar

In a salad bowl, combine the broccoli, tomatoes and onion. Mix mayo with vinegar and sprinkle over the broccoli. Add the sunflower kernels, raisins and bacon and toss well. You can serve directly.

Nutritional information: Calories: 148; Total Carbs 8g; Net Carbs 2.4g; Protein: 9.5g; Fat 7g; Sugars 1.2g; Fiber 4g

Shredded Chicken Peanut Salad

Prep time: 5 minutes. | Cooking time: 5 minutes. | Servings: 6

2 chicken breasts, boneless,
1 head iceberg lettuce, cut into strips
2 bell peppers, cut into strips
1 cucumber, quartered, sliced
3 scallions, sliced
2 tablespoon chopped peanuts
1 tablespoon peanut vinaigrette
Salt to taste
1 cup water

In a suitable skillet simmer, 1 cup salted water. Place the chicken breasts in it, cover and cook on low flame for almost 5 minutes. Then remove the chicken from the skillet and shred with a fork. In a salad bowl, mix the vegetables with the cooled chicken, season with salt and sprinkle with peanut vinaigrette and chopped peanuts.

Nutritional information: Calories: 116; Total Carbs 4 g; Net Carbs 3g; Protein: 12 g; Fat 12g; Sugars 0.5 g; Fiber 6g

Lettuce Salad with Olive Oil Dressing

Prep time: 10 minutes. | Cooking time: 0 minute. | Servings: 4

1 cup coarsely chopped iceberg lettuce
1 cup coarsely chopped romaine lettuce
1 cup baby spinach
1 large tomato, hulled and coarsely chopped
1 cup diced cucumber
2 tablespoons olive oil
¼ teaspoon of sea salt

In a suitable bowl, combine the spinach and lettuces. Add the tomato and cucumber. Drizzle with oil and sprinkle with sea salt. Mix well, then you can serve and enjoy.

Nutritional information: Calories: 159; Total Carbs 4 g; Net Carbs 1.2g; Protein: 12 g; Fat 12g; Sugars 0.5 g; Fiber 6g

Greek Olive Salad

Prep time: 10 minutes. | Cooking time: 0 minutes. | Servings: 1-2

1 romaine head, torn in bits
1 cucumber sliced
1 pint cherry tomatoes, halved
1 green pepper, sliced
1 onion sliced into rings
1 cup kalamata olives
1 ½ cups feta cheese, crumbled
For dressing
1 cup olive oil
¼ cup lemon juice
2 teaspoon Oregano
Salt and pepper

Lay ingredients on plate. Mix up the dressing ingredients and then drizzle dressing over salad Enjoy.

Nutritional information: Calories: 170; Total Carbs 7.2g; Net Carbs 2g; Protein: 9g; Fat 10g; Sugars 2.2 g; Fiber 1.3g

Chicken Tikka

Prep time: 5 minutes. | Cooking time: 15 minutes. | Serving: 2

½ lb. Chicken breasts
¼ cup onion
1.5 teaspoon olive oil
1 (14.5-oz) can tomatoes
1 teaspoon ginger
1 teaspoon lemon juice
⅓ cup plain Greek yogurt (fat-free)
1 tablespoon garam masala
¼ teaspoon salt
¼ teaspoon black pepper

Flavor chicken cut into 1-inch cubes with 1.5 teaspoon of garam masala, ⅛ teaspoon of salt and pepper. Cook chicken and diced onion 4 to 5 minutes. Add diced tomatoes, grated ginger, 1.5 teaspoon garam masala, ⅛ teaspoon salt. Cook 8 to 10 minutes. Add lemon juice and yogurt until blended. When done, serve and enjoy.

Nutritional information: Calories: 206; Total Carbs 8 g; Net Carbs 3g; Protein: 13g; Fat 11g; Sugars 1.5 g; Fiber 7g

Spinach Orange Salad

Prep time: 10 minutes. | Cooking time: 0 minutes. | Servings: 4

4 cups baby spinach
1 blood orange, chopped
½ red onion, sliced
½ shallot, chopped
2 tablespoon minced fennel fronds
Juice of 1 lemon
1 tablespoon olive oil
Pinch sea salt

In a suitable bowl, toss together the spinach, orange, red onion, shallot, and fennel fronds. Add the lemon juice, oil, sea salt and mix well. Serve.

Nutritional information: Calories: 79; Total Carbs 10g; Net Carbs 6g; Protein: 11g; Fat 9g; Sugars 1 g; Fiber 3g

Chicken Avocado Lettuce Salad

Prep time: 30 minutes. | Cooking time: 15 minutes. | Servings: 4

1 lb. chicken breast, cooked, shredded
1 avocado, pitted, peeled, sliced
2 tomatoes, diced
1 cucumber, peeled, sliced
1 head lettuce, chopped
3 tablespoons olive oil
2 tablespoons lime juice
1 tablespoon cilantro, chopped
salt and Black pepper, to taste

In a suitable bowl whisk together oil, lime juice, cilantro, salt, and 1 pinch of pepper. Combine tomatoes, lettuce, cucumber in a salad bowl and add half of the dressing. Toss chicken with the leftover dressing and combine with vegetable mixture. Top with avocado and enjoy.

Nutritional information: Calories: 189; Total Carbs 7.9g; Net Carbs 4.5g; Protein: 6g; Fat 10g; Sugars 1 g; Fiber 5g

Lettuce Cucumber Broccoli Salad

Prep time: 10 minutes. | Cooking time: 0 minutes. | Servings: 1-2

4 cups each of raw spinach and romaine lettuce
2 cups each of cherry tomatoes, sliced cucumber, chopped baby carrots and chopped red, orange and yellow bell pepper
1 cup each of chopped broccoli, sliced yellow squash, zucchini and cauliflower.

Wash all these vegetables. Mix in a suitable mixing bowl and top off with a non-fat or low-fat dressing of your choice. Enjoy.

Nutritional information: Calories: 206; Total Carbs 8 g; Net Carbs 3g; Protein: 13g; Fat 11g; Sugars 1.5 g; Fiber 7g

Basil Beet Salad

Prep time: 10 minutes. | Cooking time: 0 minutes. | Servings: 4

¼ cup blackberries
¼ cup olive oil
Juice of 1 lemon
2 tablespoons minced basil
1 teaspoon poppy seeds
1 pinch of sea salt
For the salad
2 celery stalks, chopped
4 cooked beets, peeled and chopped
1 cup blackberries
4 cups spring mix

To make the dressing, mash the blackberries in a suitable bowl. Whisk in the oil, lemon juice, basil, poppy seeds, and sea salt. To make the salad: add the celery, beets, blackberries, and spring mix to the bowl with the dressing. Combine and serve.

Nutritional information: Calories: 189; Total Carbs 7.9g; Net Carbs 4.5g; Protein: 6g; Fat 10g; Sugars 1 g; Fiber 5g

Walnut Gems Salad

Prep time: 10 minutes. | Cooking time: 0 minutes. | Servings: 1-2

4 cups seasonal greens
1 cup cherry tomatoes
¼ cup walnuts
¼ cup herbs
For the dressing
3-4 key limes
1 tablespoon sesame
Sea salt and cayenne pepper

First, get the juice of the key limes. In a suitable bowl, whisk together the key lime juice with the homemade raw sesame "tahini" butter. Add sea salt and cayenne pepper to taste. Cut the cherry tomatoes in half. In a suitable bowl, combine the greens, cherry tomatoes, and herbs. Pour the dressing on top and "massage" with your hands. Let the greens soak up the dressing. Add more sea salt, cayenne pepper and herbs on top as needed. Enjoy!

Nutritional information: Calories: 189; Total Carbs 7.9g; Net Carbs 4.5g; Protein: 6g; Fat 10g; Sugars 1 g; Fiber 5g

Chicken in Cucumber Cups

Prep time: 5 minutes. | Cooking time: 15 minutes. | Servings: 4

½ chicken breast, skinless, boiled and shredded
2 long cucumbers, cut into 8 thick rounds
1 teaspoon ginger, minced
1 teaspoon lime zest, grated
4 teaspoons olive oil
1 teaspoon sesame oil
1 teaspoon lime juice
salt and Black pepper, to taste

In a suitable bowl combine lime zest, juice, olive and sesame oils, ginger, and season with salt. Toss the chicken with the dressing and fill the cucumber cups with the salad. Enjoy.

Nutritional information: Calories: 116; Total Carbs 4 g; Net Carbs 3g; Protein: 12 g; Fat 12g; Sugars 0.5 g; Fiber 6g

Red Pepper Hummus

Prep Time: 10 minutes. | Cook Time: 10 minutes. | Servings: 8

1 tablespoon olive oil
1 can garbanzo beans
1 medium-sized bell pepper (red)
1 fresh lime
¼ teaspoon garlic powder
1 tablespoon tahini
1 ½ tablespoons water
¼ teaspoon ground black pepper
½ teaspoon salt

Add all Ingredients in a blender or food processor. Blend until completely smooth. Plate it top with olive oil and serve.

Nutritional information: Calories 216; Total Carbs 15.1g; Net Carbs 12g; Protein 3.4g; Fat 3.4g; Sugar 0.5g; Fiber 4.2g

Jicama Appetizer

Prep Time: 10 minutes. | Cook Time: 0 minutes. | Servings: 4

2 tablespoons chili powder
2 tablespoons lime juice
1 cut and peeled jicama

In a bowl, place jicama and toss it with the fresh lemon juice and some chili powder. Plate and serve right away.

Nutritional information: Calories 203; Total Carbs 17.3g; Net Carbs 15g; Protein 1.7g; Fat 0.8g; Sugar 0.9g; Fiber 4.2g

Green Herbed Hummus

Prep Time: 10 minutes. | Cook Time: 0 minutes. | Servings: 5

½ cup basil leaves
1 garbanzo beans rinsed and drained chickpeas
Salt and black pepper
1 clove of garlic
½ teaspoon balsamic vinegar
1 tablespoon olive oil
½ teaspoon soy sauce

In a hand blender, combine the basil, chickpeas, garbanozo beans, and garlic. Pulse several times. Use a spatula to push the mixture out of the edge of the processor container. When you mix the Ingredients again, drizzle with a little olive oil. Blend until the soy sauce and vinegar combine well. Salt and pepper to taste. Serve with toasted bread.

Nutritional information: Calories 298; Total Carbs 21g; Net Carbs 14g; Protein 4.7g; Fat 3.8g; Sugar 0.9g; Fiber 4.1g

Fruit Leather

Prep Time: 20 minutes. | Cook Time: 5 hours. | Servings: 2

4 cups pears
¼ cup lemon juice
1 cup sugar
4 cups apple

Preheat oven at 150 ℉. Line the baking sheet with wrap. In a blender, put the sugar, apples, lemon juice, and pears. Close and mix until the mixture is completely smooth. Using a spatula, distribute the mixture evenly in the prepared baking dish. Bake for 5 to 6 hours with the oven door half open. Whenever the edges of the fruit are not sticky and can be torn like leather. Remove it and place it to cool down. Serve and enjoy.

Nutritional information: Calories 243; Total Carbs 23.5g; Net Carbs 15g; Protein 0.3g; Fat 0.1g; Sugar 1.4g; Fiber 9.2g

Baked Tortilla Chips

Prep Time: 10 minutes. | Cook Time: 15 minutes. | Servings: 6

1 tablespoon vegetable oil
1 package corn tortillas
1 teaspoon salt
3 tablespoon lime juice
1 teaspoon chili powder
1 teaspoon ground cumin

Preheat your oven to 350 ° F. Cut all the tortillas into large 8 pieces and arrange them together in a thin layer on a baking sheet. Combine oil and lemon juice. Sprinkle all tortilla pieces with the mixture until slightly moist. In a small bowl, combine the pepper, cumin, and salt. Sprinkle the spice mix over the chips and bake for 7 minutes. Turn the pan halfway through and bake another 8 minutes until the chips are crispy but not completely golden. Serve with salsa, guacamole.

Nutritional information: Calories 298; Total Carbs 26g; Net Carbs 20g; Protein 3.3g; Fat 4.1g; Sugar 2g; Fiber 4g

Popcorn

Prep Time: 2 minutes. | Cook Time: 3 minutes. | Servings: 3

1 teaspoon vegetable oil
½ cup un-popped popcorn
½ teaspoon salt

In a mug, combine the popcorn with oil. Spread the salt over and the covered corn in a wrapping paper. Microwave on high for 2-3 minutes, or till pauses of approximately 2 seconds after pops are heard. To prevent steam, cautiously open your bag and put it into the serving dish.

Nutritional information: Calories 195; Total Carbs 24.6g; Net Carbs 20g; Protein 4.1g; Fat 3.1g; Sugar 0.4g; Fiber 6g

Salsa

Prep Time: 10 minutes. | Cook Time: 0 minutes. | Servings: 4

1 minced jalapeno pepper
1 chopped onion
4 large chopped tomatoes
½ cup fresh cilantro, chopped
Salt as per taste
1 tablespoon lime juice
3 minced cloves of garlic
1 diced tomatillo

In a bowl, combine onion, tomatoes, garlic, cilantro, tomatillo, lime juice, and salt until well incorporated. Taste after adding ½ of the jalapeño pepper. Mix the remaining ½ jalapeño if you want your salsa to be spicier. Cover and refrigerate the salsa until it is ready for serving.

Nutritional information: Calories 283; Total Carbs 11.7g; Net Carbs 7g; Protein 2.3g; Fat 0.5g; Sugar 1g; Fiber 5g

Fried Carrot Slices

Prep Time: 10 minutes. | Cook Time: 20 minutes | Serve: 1

3 ounces carrots, peeled and cut into thin slices diagonally
½ tablespoon extra-virgin olive oil
¼ teaspoon arrowroot starch
⅛ teaspoons red chili powder
⅛ teaspoon ground cinnamon
Salt and ground black pepper, as required

Preheat the oven to 425 degrees Fahrenheit. To use parchment paper, line a rimmed baking sheet. Combine all of the Ingredients in a mixing bowl. Arrange the carrot sticks to the baking sheet lined with a piece of parchment paper and bake for 20 minutes, tossing halfway through. When done, serve and enjoy.

Nutritional information: Calories 99 Total Carbs 8g Net Carbs 5.6g Protein 0.8g Fat 7.1 g Sugar 4g Fiber 2.4g

Baked Banana Chips

Prep Time: 10 minutes. | Cook Time: 2 hours. | Servings: 2

1 teaspoon lemon juice
2 bananas, just-ripe

Preheat the oven at 225 ℉. Line the baking sheet with baking paper. Distribute banana slices evenly over the baking sheet in an even layer. Brush lemon juice on the slices. Bake the chips for 90 minutes in a preheated oven. Allow bananas chips to cool for at least five minutes before eating.

Nutritional information: Calories 264; Total Carbs 27.2g; Net Carbs 20g; Protein 1.3g; Fat 0.4g; Sugar 11g; Fiber 12g

Mini Meatball with Apricot Dip

Prep Time: 15 minutes. | Cook Time: 25 minutes. | Servings: 1

¼ cup bread crumbs, seasoned and dry
1 lb. of ground beef
2 egg whites
¼ teaspoon salt
2 tablespoons mustard of Dijon-style
2 tablespoons water
⅛ teaspoon pepper
¾ cup barbecue sauce
¾ cup apricot preserves

Preheat the oven at 400 ℉. In a large bowl, combine the breadcrumbs, ground beef, water, egg whites, salt, and pepper and mix gently. Make 36 balls, ½ inches in diameter. Place on a steamed grill pan for cooking. Preheat the oven to 400 ° F and bake for 15-17 minutes. Meanwhile, heat a small skillet over medium heat to warm the jams, mustard, and barbecue sauce. Bring to a boil, then transfer to low heat and cook, uncovered, 3 to 5 minutes or until the sauce thickens slightly. place meatballs in the slow cooker until heated through and cook for another 2-3 minutes. Place the pork in a slow cooker set to the low heat option. Cover securely. Meatballs can be kept in it for up to 2-3 hours by mixing them regularly.

Nutritional information: Calories 128; Total Carbs 7g; Net Carbs 4g; Protein 3g; Fat 1g; Sugar 0g; Fiber 2.4g

Gazpacho with Avocados

Prep time: 10 minutes. | Cook Time: 00 minutes. | Serves: 1

½ of avocado, peeled, pitted and chopped
1 tablespoon fresh cilantro leaves
½ cup low-sodium vegetable broth
¼ tablespoon fresh lemon juice
⅛ teaspoon ground cumin
⅛ teaspoon cayenne pepper
Salt, as required

Combine all of the Ingredients in a high-powered blender and pulse until smooth. Place the soup in a large mixing bowl. Refrigerate with lid on for at least 2-3 hours. Enjoy.

Nutritional information: Calories 155 Total Carbs 7g Net Carbs 2.4g Protein 2.5g Fat 11g Sugar 0.5g Fiber 4.6g

Guacamole with Avocados

Prep time: 10 minutes. | Cook Time: 00 minutes. | Serves: 1

¼ of ripe avocados, peeled, pitted and chopped
1 tablespoon red onion, chopped
½ of small garlic clove, minced
¼ of Serrano pepper, seeded and chopped
¼ of tomato, seeded and chopped
½ tablespoon fresh cilantro leaves, chopped
¼ tablespoon fresh lime juice
Salt, as required

Add avocado to a bowl and mash it completely with a fork. Stir in the remaining Ingredients carefully to mix. Serve right away.

Nutritional information: Calories 68 Total Carbs 4.6g Net Carbs 2.2g Protein 0.9g Fat 5.6g Sugar 1.1g Fiber 2.4g

Guacamole

Prep Time: 10 minutes. | Cook Time: 0 minutes. | Servings: 2

⅛ to a quarter of teaspoon salt
1 tablespoon lemon juice
2 medium-sized ripe avocados
¼ cup chunky salsa

Peel avocados and chopped. Placed the avocado in a small bowl. Add lemon juice in it. Toss in the salsa and season with salt, then mash roughly with the fork. Chill until ready to serve.

Nutritional information: Calories 162; Total Carbs 3g; Net Carbs 2g; Protein g; Fat 5g; Sugar 0g; Fiber 2g

Tomato Mozzarella Salad

Prep time: 10 minutes. | Cooking time: 0 minutes. | Servings: 6

40 cherry tomatoes, cut in half
1 cup mozzarella balls, cut in half
1 cup green olives, sliced
1 can (6 oz.) Black olives, sliced
2 green onions, chopped
3 oz. Roasted pine nuts
Dressing:
½ cup olive oil
2 tablespoon Red wine vinegar
1 teaspoon Dried oregano
Salt and Black pepper, to taste

In a suitable salad bowl, toss the tomatoes, onions and olives. Prepare the dressing by combining all its recipe ingredients in a bowl. Pour the dressing over the salad and add the nuts. Refrigerate for 1 hour to marinate well before serving.

Nutritional information: Calories: 116; Total Carbs 4 g; Net Carbs 2g; Protein: 12 g; Fat 12g; Sugars 0.5 g; Fiber 6g

Salsa de Strawberry

Prep time: 10 minutes. | Cook Time: 00 minutes. | Serves: 1

¼ cup fresh strawberries, hulled and chopped
½ of small tomato, seeded and chopped
1 tablespoon red onion, finely chopped
½ of small garlic clove, minced
¼ tablespoon fresh lime juice
⅛ teaspoon olive oil

Combine all of the Ingredients in a mixing bowl and gently toss to combine. Serve right away.

Nutritional information: Calories 31 Total Carbs 6g Net Carbs 4.5g Protein 0.9g Fat 0.8g Sugar 3.3g Fiber 1.5g

Garlic Hummus

Prep Time: 10 minutes. | Cook Time: 0 minutes. | Servings: 2

½ teaspoon salt
¼ cup tahini
1 can chickpeas with no salt
¼ cup olive oil
½ teaspoon chili powder
1 clove of garlic
¼ cup lemon juice
1 teaspoon ground cumin

Add all Ingredients along chickpea liquid in a hand blender and blend until smooth. Scrape of the container edges and blend until all the Ingredients well combined. Serve top with olive oil and enjoy with bread.

Nutritional information: Calories 152; Total Carbs 9.7g; Net Carbs 6.2g; Protein 3.7g; Fat 11.9g; Sugar 0.2g; Fiber 4.6g

Gazpacho with Strawberries

Prep time: 10 minutes. | Cook Time: 00 minutes. | Serves: 1

1½ ounces fresh strawberries, hulled and sliced
2 tablespoons red bell pepper, seeded and chopped
¼ tablespoon onion, chopped
¼ tablespoon fresh basil leaves
¼ of small garlic clove, chopped
¼ teaspoon olive oil
¼ teaspoon balsamic vinegar

Add all Ingredients to a small blender and pulse until smooth. Place the gazpacho in a serving basin. Before serving, cover and refrigerate to chill.

Nutritional information: Calories 30 Total Carbs 5g Net Carbs 3.7g Protein 1g Fat 1.5g Sugar 2.3g Fiber 1.3g

Paprika Chickpeas

Prep Time: 5 minutes. | Cook Time: 45 minutes | Serve: 1

2 tablespoons cooked chickpeas
½ of small garlic clove, minced
⅛ teaspoon dried oregano, crushed
Pinch of ground cumin
Pinch of smoked paprika
Pinch of cayenne pepper
Salt, as required
½ teaspoon olive oil

Preheat the oven to 400 degrees Fahrenheit. Roast the chickpeas on the sprayed baking sheet for about 30 minutes, tossing them every 10 minutes. While cooking, add and mix up garlic, thyme, and spices in a small mixing bowl. When the time is up, take the baking sheet out of the oven, drizzle the oil over the chickpeas and sprinkle with the garlic mixture. Toss well and cook for another 10-15 minutes. Turn off the oven but leave the baking sheet in for another 10 minutes. Remove the chickpeas from the oven and set aside to cool completely before serving.

Nutritional information: Calories 59 Total Carbs 7.3g Net Carbs 5.7g Protein 1.6g Fat 2.8g Sugar 0.1g Fiber 1.6g

Roasted Cinnamon Almonds

Prep Time: 5 minutes. | Cook Time: 10 minutes | Serve: 1

2 tablespoons whole almonds
Pinch of ground cinnamon
Pinch of ground cumin
Pinch of ground coriander
Salt and ground black pepper, as required
¼ tablespoon olive oil

Preheat the oven to 350 degrees Fahrenheit. In a mixing bowl, thoroughly mix up all of the Ingredients. Arrange the almonds to the baking dish lined with a piece of parchment. Roast for about 10 minutes, flipping twice during the process. Remove the almonds from the oven and cool thoroughly before serving.

Nutritional information: Calories 100 Total Carbs 2.9g Net Carbs 1.2g Protein 2.6g Fat 8.5g Sugar 0.5g Fiber 1.7g

Apple Ladybug

Prep Time: 10 minutes. | Cook Time: 0 minutes. | Servings: 4

8 thin sticks of pretzel
¼ cup raisins
2 red apples
1 tablespoon peanut butter

Using a knife, cut the apples into 2 equal pieces and remove the insides. Place all the ½ apples on a small, flat plate. Brush the backs of the apple ladybugs with peanut butter and add the raisins to the sink in place. To make the antenna, slip one end of each pretzel stick into something like a raisin and slip the second end of the liquid into it. Serve and enjoy fresh apple ladybugs.

Nutritional information: Calories 187; Total Carbs 23.2g; Net Carbs 18g; Protein 2.1g; Fat 2.3g; Sugar 1.4g; Fiber 2.3g

Salsa de Tomas

Prep time: 10 minutes. | Cook Time: 00 minutes. | Serves: 1

½ of tomato, chopped
¼ of small red onion, chopped
1 tablespoon fresh cilantro leaves, chopped
¼ of jalapeño pepper, seeded and chopped finely
¼ of small garlic clove, minced finely
½ teaspoon fresh lime juice
1 teaspoon extra-virgin olive oil
Salt and ground black pepper, as required

Combine all of the Ingredients in a mixing bowl and gently toss to combine. Serve right away.

Nutritional information: Calories 55 Total Carbs 3.4g Net Carbs 2.5g Protein 0.9g Fat 4.8g Sugar 1.7g Fiber 0.9g

Roasted Peanuts

Prep Time: 5 minutes. | Cook Time: 20 minutes | Serve: 1

3 tablespoons raw peanuts
Pinch of salt

Preheat the oven to 350 degrees Fahrenheit. Spread the peanuts on a small baking sheet and roast for 15-20 minutes. Remove the peanuts from the oven and place them in a mixing dish, add the salt and toss well. Before serving, set aside to cool fully.

Nutritional information: Calories 155 Total Carbs 4.4g Net Carbs 2.1g Protein 0.5g Fat 10.5 g Sugar 1.1g Fiber 2.3g

Fat-Free Yogurt with Egg

Prep time: 10 minutes. | Cook Time: 00 minutes. | Serves: 1

1 hard-boiled egg
¾ tablespoon fat-free plain Greek yogurt
Pinch of salt
¼ tablespoon Dijon mustard
Pinch of cayenne pepper

Peel the egg and cut it in half vertically with a sharp knife. Remove the yolk using a spoon. Pulse the egg yolk, yoghurt, and salt in a small blender until smooth. Fill a bowl halfway with the yogurt mixture. Stir in the mustard and combine well. Use a spoon to place the yoghurt mixture evenly on each egg half. With a pinch of cayenne pepper on top, serve.

Nutritional information: Calories 71 Total Carbs 1g Net Carbs 3g Protein 0.9g Fat 4.8g Sugar 0.7g Fiber 0.2g

Egg with Avocado

Prep time: 10 minutes. | Cook Time: 00 minutes. | Serves: 1

1 hard-boiled egg
¼ of small avocado, peeled, pitted and chopped
¼ teaspoon freshly squeezed lime juice
Pinch of salt
Pinch of cayenne pepper

Peel the egg and cut it in half vertically with a sharp knife. Remove the yolk using a spoon. Add half of the egg yolk, avocado, lime juice, and salt to a bowl and mash with a fork until well blended. Evenly spoon the avocado mixture into each egg half. Serve with a dash of cayenne pepper on top.

Nutritional information: Calories 122 Total Carbs 2.9g Net Carbs 3g Protein 0.9g Fat 4.8g Sugar 0.7g Fiber 0.2g

Roasted Cashews with Lemon Juice

Prep Time: 5 minutes. | Cook Time: 10 minutes | Serve: 1

2 tablespoons raw cashews
⅛ teaspoon ground cumin
Pinch of cayenne pepper
Pinch of salt

¼ teaspoon fresh lemon juice

Preheat the oven to 400 degrees Fahrenheit. Toss the cashews and spices together in a dish to evenly coat them. Spread the cashews in the roasting pan lined with a piece of foil, then Roast for 8-10 minutes. Remove the cashews from the oven and cool thoroughly before serving. Serve with the lemon juice.

Nutritional information: Calories 101 Total Carbs 5.9g Net Carbs 5.3g Protein 2.7g Fat 8.1g Sugar 0.9g Fiber 0.6g

Simple Roasted Walnuts

Prep Time: 5 minutes. | Cook Time: 12 minutes | Serve: 1

2 tablespoons walnuts pieces
½ teaspoon olive oil

Preheat the oven to 375 degrees Fahrenheit. With parchment paper, arrange a baking sheet. Toss the walnuts with the oil in a mixing dish to evenly coat them. On the baking sheet lined with a piece of parchment papper, spread the walnut. Bake for 12 minutes, stirring halfway through. Before serving, remove the pan from the oven and set it aside to cool fully.

Nutritional information: Calories 43 Total Carbs 0.5g Net Carbs 0.3g Protein 0.5g Fat 4.6g Sugar 0.1g Fiber 0.2g

Easy-to-Make Banana Chips

Prep Time: 5 minutes | Cook Time1 hour | Serve: 1

½ of small banana, peeled and cut into ¼-inch thick slices

Preheat the oven to 350 degrees Fahrenheit. Place the banana slices on the baking sheet lined with a piece of baking paper and then bake for 1 hour. When done, serve and enjoy.

Nutritional information: Calories 45 Total Carbs 11g Net Carbs 9.7g Protein 0.6g Fat 0.2 g Sugar 5g Fiber 1.3g

Roasted Cauliflower Florets

Prep Time: 10 minutes. | Cook Time: 30 minutes | Serve: 1

¼ cup cauliflower florets
½ teaspoon olive oil
Pinch of red chili powder
Salt and ground black pepper, as required

Preheat the oven to 450 degrees Fahrenheit. A small roasting pan should be greased. Combine all Ingredients in a mixing basin. Spread the cauliflower mixture on the sprayed roasting pan and roast for 25-30 minutes. Serve warm.

Nutritional information: Calories 27 Total Carbs 1.5g Net Carbs 0.8g Protein 0.5g Fat 11.3 g Sugar 0.6g Fiber 0.7g

Paprika Roasted Pecans

Prep Time: 5 minutes. | Cook Time: 12 minutes | Serve: 1

2 tablespoons pecan halves
½ teaspoon extra-virgin olive oil
⅛ teaspoon fresh rosemary, chopped
Pinch of smoked paprika
Pinch of cayenne pepper
Pinch of salt

Preheat the oven to 350 degrees F. Thoroughly mix up all of the Ingredients in a mixing basin in a small bowl. Place the pecans on the baking sheet lined with a piece of parchment paper. Cook for 10 to 12 minutes, flipping twice during the cooking time. Remove the baking sheet from the oven and set it aside to cool. Serve and enjoy.

Nutritional information: Calories 126 Total Carbs 2.5g Net Carbs 0.6g Protein 1.6g Fat 8.1g Sugar 0.6g Fiber 1.8g

Nutmeg Apple Chips

Prep Time: 5 minutes. | Cook Time: 2 hours | Serve: 1

¼ teaspoon ground cinnamon
Pinch of ground ginger
Pinch of ground cloves
Pinch of ground nutmeg
½ Fuji apple rounds, thinly sliced and cored

Preheat the oven to 200 degrees Fahrenheit. Prepare a baking sheet with parchment paper. Combine all spices in a mixing dish. Arrange the apple slices on the baking sheet lined with a piece of parchment paper and generously season with the spice mixture, then bake for 1 hour. Sprinkle the spice mixture on the other side and bake for another 1 hour. When done, serve and enjoy.

Nutritional information: Calories 44 Total Carbs 11g Net Carbs 8.1g Protein 0.1g Fat 0.2 g Sugar 5g Fiber 2.9g

Oregano Chicken Nuggets

Prep Time: 10 minutes. | Cook Time: 30 minutes | Serve: 1

2-3 ounces skinless, boneless chicken breasts, cut into 2x1-inch chunks
1 small egg
2-3 tablespoons almond flour
Pinch of dried oregano, crushed
Salt and ground black pepper, as required

Preheat the oven to 350 degrees Fahrenheit. In a shallow basin, crack the egg and whisk it vigorously. In a separate shallow bowl, whisk together the flour, oregano, onion powder, garlic powder, salt, and black pepper. After dipping the chicken nuggets in the beaten egg, uniformly coat them in the flour mixture. Lay the chicken nuggets on the sprayed baking sheet and bake for 30 minutes, or until golden brown. When done, serve and enjoy.

Nutritional information: Calories 215 Total Carbs 9g Net Carbs 13.1g Protein 16.6g Fat 13.2 g Sugar 0.8g Fiber 1.6g

Salty Kale Chips

Prep Time: 5 minutes. | Cook Time: 15 minutes | Serve: 1

2 ounces fresh kale leaves, stemmed and torn
Salt, as required
¼ tablespoon olive oil

Preheat the oven to 350 degrees Fahrenheit. Arrange the kale pieces on the baking sheet lined with a piece of parchment paper and bake for 10-15 minutes. Remove the kale chips from the oven and set aside to cool before serving.

Nutritional information: Calories 58 Total Carbs 5.7g Net Carbs 4.8g Protein 0.8g Fat 3.5 g Sugar 0g Fiber 0.9g

Simple Homemade Spinach Chips

Prep Time: 5 minutes. | Cook Time: 8 minutes | Serve: 1

1 cup fresh spinach leaves
½ teaspoon extra-virgin olive oil
Salt, as required

Preheat the oven to 325 degrees Fahrenheit. Add spinach leaves to a bowl and sprinkle with the olive oil, use your hands to rub the spinach leaves until they are coated well with the oil. Arrange the leaves in a single layer on the baking sheet lined with a piece of parchment paper and bake for 8 minutes. When done, remove the spinach chips from the oven and set aside to cool before serving.

Nutritional information: Calories 27 Total Carbs 1.1g Net Carbs 4.8g Protein 0.9g Fat 2.5 g Sugar 0.1g Fiber 0.7g

Paprika Zucchini Chips

Prep Time: 10 minutes. | Cook Time: 2 hours | Serve: 1

½ of zucchini, cut into ⅛-inch thick rounds
1 teaspoon olive oil
⅛ teaspoon smoked paprika
⅛ teaspoon ground cumin,
Pinch of salt

Preheat the oven to 235 degrees Fahrenheit. With parchment paper, line a baking sheet. Use the paper towels to squeeze the zucchini slices to remove the extra moisture. Combine all Ingredients in a mixing basin. Distribute zucchini slices on the baking sheet lined with a piece of parchment paper and bake for about 1½-2 hours, or until golden and crisp. When done, remove the zucchini chips from the oven and set aside to cool before serving.

Nutritional information: Calories 51 Total Carbs 2,2g Net Carbs 1.4g Protein 0.8g Fat 4.9 g Sugar 1.1g Fiber 0.8g

Salsa with Tomatoes and Olives

Prep time: 10 minutes. | Cook Time: 00 minutes. | Serves: 1

2 ounces cherry tomatoes, quartered
¼ of shallot, chopped finely
2-3 Kalamata olives, pitted and chopped
¼ of garlic clove, minced
½ tablespoon fresh mint leaves, chopped
½ tablespoon fresh parsley, chopped
¼ teaspoon olive oil
¼ teaspoon fresh lemon juice
Salt and ground black pepper, as required

Combine all of the Ingredients in a mixing bowl and gently toss to combine. Before serving, set aside for about 10-15 minutes.

Nutritional information: Calories 37 Total Carbs 4.2g Net Carbs 3g Protein 0.9g Fat 4.8g Sugar 1.6g Fiber 1.2g

Dehydrated Orange Slice

Prep Time: 5 minutes. | Cook Time: 10 hours | Serve: 1

½ of seedless navel orange, sliced thinly
Salt, as required

Preheat the oven at 135 degrees Fahrenheit on Dehydrate mode. Place slices of orange on the suitable sheet and then dehydrate the orange slices for a 10 hours.

Nutritional information: Calories 23 Total Carbs 5.6g Net Carbs 4.4g Protein 0.5g Fat 0.1 g Sugar 4g Fiber 1.2g

Tasty Parsnip Fries

Prep Time: 5 minutes. | Cook Time: 10 minutes | Serve: 1

2 ounces parsnip, peeled and sliced
1 teaspoon olive oil

Preheat the oven to 390 degrees Fahrenheit (180 degrees Celsius). In a mixing bowl, toss the parsnip slices and oil well. Arrange the parsnip slices to the prepared baking sheet and bake for 30 minutes, turning halfway through. Serve immediately.

Nutritional information: Calories 83 Total Carbs 10.2g Net Carbs 7.4g Protein 0.7g Fat 4.8 g Sugar 2.7g Fiber 2.8g

Almond Chicken Fingers

Prep Time: 10 minutes. | Cook Time: 18 minutes | Serve: 1

1 small egg
2-3 tablespoons almond meal
Pinch of ground turmeric
Salt and ground black pepper, as required
¼ pound skinless, boneless chicken breast, cut into strips

Preheat the oven to 375 degrees Fahrenheit. Utilizing parchment paper, line a large baking sheet. Crack the egg in a small dish. Combine almond meal and spices in a separate shallow dish. Each chicken strip should be dipped in beaten egg and then evenly coated in almond meal mixture. Lay the chicken strips in a single layer on the baking sheet lined with a piece of parchment paper and bake for 16-18 minutes. Serve warm.

Nutritional information: Calories 264 Total Carbs 3g Net Carbs 1.4g Protein 32.5g Fat 13.7 g Sugar 0.8g Fiber 1.6g

Paprika Buffalo Chicken Wings

Prep Time: 10 minutes. | Cook Time: 20 minutes | Serve: 1

⅓ pound chicken wings
1 tablespoon red hot sauce
¾ tablespoon olive oil
¼ teaspoon paprika
Pinch of cayenne pepper
Salt and ground black pepper, as required

Cut the wing tips and then each wing at the joint. In a mixing bowl, combine the spicy sauce, oil, paprika, cayenne pepper, salt, and black pepper with a wooden spoon. In a small bowl, add 2 tablespoons of the marinade. Gently coat the chicken wings with the remaining marinade in the bowl and marinate for 30-40 minutes at room temperature. Preheat your oven to 425 degrees F and then arrange the suitable cooking pan in it. Remove the wings from the bowl and toss away any leftover marinade. Lay the wings on the cooking pan. Broil for about 20 minutes, flipping halfway through. Remove the chicken wings from the oven and coat evenly with the remaining marinade. Serve immediately.

Nutritional information: Calories 380 Total Carbs 0.7g Net Carbs 0.4g Protein 43.9g Fat 18.5 g Sugar 0.3g Fiber 0.3g

Sesame Spinach Fritters

Prep Time: 10 minutes. | Cook Time: 10 minutes | Serve: 1

3-4 tablespoons chickpea flour
¼ teaspoons white sesame seeds
⅛ teaspoon garam masala powder
Pinch of ground cumin
Pinch of baking soda
Salt, as required
¼ cup water
4 fresh spinach leaves
2-4 tablespoons olive oil

Mix all of the Ingredients in a bowl, except the spinach and oil, until a smooth consistency forms. Heat the oil in a small pot over moderate heat. In two batches, evenly coat each spinach leaf in the chickpea flour mixture and set in the hot oil. Cook for about 3-5 minutes with rotating occasionally, or until golden brown on both sides. Drain the fritters on a dish lined with paper towels. Enjoy.

Nutritional information: Calories 189 Total Carbs 10.4g Net Carbs 8.3g Protein 4.1g Fat 15.2 g Sugar 1.9g Fiber 2.1g

Fried Sweet Potato Wedges

Prep Time: 10 minutes. | Cook Time: 25 minutes | Serve: 1

½ of sweet potato, peeled and cut into wedges
¼ teaspoon ground turmeric
¼ teaspoon ground cinnamon
Salt and ground black pepper, as required
½ tablespoon extra-virgin olive oil

Preheat the oven to 425 degrees Fahrenheit. Wrap a piece of foil around a baking sheet. Combine all Ingredients in a mixing basin. Spread the sweet potato wedges out evenly on the baking sheet lined with a piece of foil and bake for 25 minutes, flipping once after 15 minutes. Serve right away.

Nutritional information: Calories 148 Total Carbs 13g Net Carbs 10.6g Protein 15.6g Fat 0.1 g Sugar 3.9g Fiber 2.4g

Cayenne Broccoli Tots

Prep Time: 10 minutes. | Cook Time: 35 minutes | Serves: 3

4 ounces frozen chopped broccoli
1 small egg
⅛ teaspoon dried oregano
⅛ teaspoon cayenne pepper
Pinch of red pepper flakes, crushed
Salt, as required
Freshly ground white pepper, as required
¼ cup low-fat cheddar cheese, grated
¼ cup almond flour
Olive oil cooking spray

Preheat the oven to 400 degrees Fahrenheit. Line a baking sheet with parchment paper that has been gently oiled. Place the broccoli florets in a microwave-safe basin and microwave for about 5 minutes, stirring halfway through. Remove the water from the broccoli completely. In a mixing bowl, whisk together the eggs, oregano, cayenne pepper, red pepper flakes, salt, and white pepper. Combine the cooked broccoli, cheddar cheese, and almond flour in a mixing bowl. Make small, equal-sized patties from the Ingredients using slightly wet palms. Arrange the patties in a single layer on the prepared baking pans, about 2-inch apart. Spray each patty lightly with the cooking spray. Cook for 15 minutes on each side, or until golden brown on both sides. Warm the dish before serving.

Nutritional information: Calories 161 Total Carbs 6.8g Net Carbs 3.8g Protein 7.4g Fat 10.6 g Sugar 1.7g Fiber 3g

Garlic Chicken Wings

Prep Time: 10 minutes. | Cook Time: 1 hour | Serve: 1

⅓ pound chicken wings
¼ tablespoon fresh lemon juice
1 (¼-inch) piece fresh ginger, minced
½ of small garlic clove, minced
¼ tablespoon baking powder
Salt and ground black pepper, as required

Cut the wingtips off first, then each wing at the joint. Mix up the lemon juice, ginger, and garlic in a mixing bowl. Toss in the chicken wings to thoroughly coat them. Refrigerate for 15-20 minutes to marinate. Preheat the oven to 250 degrees Fahrenheit. Place a rack in the oven's bottom third. On a baking pan, place a sprayed rack. Remove the wings from the basin and blot them dry with paper towels. Combine the wings, baking powder, salt, and black pepper in a zip-lock bag. To coat each well, close the bag and shake it. Arrange the wings on the baking sheet. Bake for about 30 minutes, tossing out the pan drippings halfway through. When the time is up, increase the cooking temperature to 425 degrees Fahrenheit. Place the baking sheet with the wings on the top oven rack and bake for 25-30 minutes, or until golden and crisp. Serve immediately.

Nutritional information: Calories 292 Total Carbs 1.8 g Net Carbs 1.7g Protein 43.8g Fat 11.3 g Sugar 0.1g Fiber 0.1g

Pepper Zucchini Sticks

Prep Time: 10 minutes. | Cook Time: 25 minutes | Serve: 1

½ of zucchini, cut into thick slices
2 tablespoons almond flour
Salt and ground black pepper, as required
1 small egg

Preheat the oven to 425 degrees Fahrenheit. Utilising parchment paper, line a baking sheet. In a shallow bowl, crack the egg and whisk it vigorously. In another shallow bowl, whisk together the flour, salt, and black pepper until thoroughly blended. After dipping the zucchini sticks in the beaten egg, uniformly coat them in the flour mixture. Lay the zucchini sticks on the baking sheet and bake for 25 minutes, or until golden brown, flipping halfway through. When done, serve and enjoy.

Nutritional information: Calories 152 Total Carbs 4.8g Net Carbs 2.6g Protein 5.4g Fat 11.3 g Sugar 1.8g Fiber 2.2g

Parmesan Pepper Chicken Wings

Prep Time: 10 minutes. | Cook Time: 30 minutes | Serve: 1

⅓ pound chicken wings
Pinch of baking powder
Salt and ground black pepper, as required
1-2 tablespoons low-fat Parmesan cheese, grated

Preheat the oven to 250 degrees Fahrenheit. Place a rack in the lower part of the oven. On a foil-lined baking sheet, place a greased rack. Toss the wings in a basin with the baking powder, salt, and black pepper to thoroughly coat them. Arrange the wings in a single layer on the preheated rack in the baking sheet Preheat the oven to 350°F (180°C) and bake for 30 minutes. Serve immediately with a cheese garnish.

Nutritional information: Calories 348 Total Carbs 0.4g Net Carbs 0.4g Protein 29.1g Fat 17.1 g Sugar 0g Fiber 0g

Baked Sweet Potato Balls

Prep Time: 10 minutes. | Cook Time: 30 minutes | Serve: 2

¾ cup cooked sweet potato, peeled and mashed
½ tablespoon coconut oil, softened
Pinch of salt
½ of egg
2-3 tablespoons almond meal

Preheat the oven to 400 degrees Fahrenheit. Utilizing parchment paper, line a large baking sheet. Combine the mashed sweet potato, coconut oil, and salt in a mixing dish. Crack the eggs into a shallow bowl and thoroughly beat them. In another shallow bowl, add the almond meal. Form the mixture into little balls and slightly flatten each one; coat the balls with the egg mixture and the with the almond meal. Arrange the coated balls to the baking sheet lined with a piece of parchment paper and bake for about 25-30 minutes, or until totally done. Serve and enjoy.

Nutritional information: Calories 148 Total Carbs 16g Net Carbs 12.8g Protein 4.2g Fat 7.5 g Sugar 6g Fiber 3.2g

Baked Chicken Thigh Pieces

Prep Time: 10 minutes. | Cook Time: 25 minutes | Serve: 1

¼ pound boneless chicken thigh, cut into bite-sized pieces
2 ounces unsweetened coconut milk
¼ teaspoons ground turmeric
Salt and ground black pepper, as required
1 tablespoon coconut flour
2 tablespoons unsweetened desiccated coconut
1 teaspoon olive oil

Combine the chicken, coconut milk, turmeric, salt, and black pepper in a mixing bowl. Refrigerate with lid on overnight. Preheat the oven to 390 degrees Fahrenheit. Combine coconut flour and desiccated coconut in a shallow dish. Coat the chicken pieces evenly in the coconut mixture. Arrange the coated thigh pieces to the baking sheet and equally drizzle with the oil. Bake for 20 to 25 minutes. When done, serve immediately.

Nutritional information: Calories 248 Total Carbs 6.8g Net Carbs 2.9g Protein 23.6g Fat 13.5 g Sugar 0.5g Fiber 3.9g

One Pot Hot Corn

Prep time: 10 minutes . | Cook Time: 20 minutes | Serves 12

6 ears corn

Corn husks and silk should be removed. Each ear should be cut or broken in half. Fill the bottom of the electric pressure cooker with 1 cup of water. Place a wire rack or trivet on the table. Cut-side down, stand the corn upright on the rack. Close and lock the pressure cooker's lid. To close the valve, turn it to the closed position. Cook for 5 minutes on high pressure. When the cooking is finished, press Cancel and release the pressure quickly. Unlock and remove the cover once the pin has dropped. To remove the corn from the pot, use tongs. Season with salt and pepper to taste, and serve immediately away.

Nutritional information: Calories 64; Total Carbs 13.9g; Net Carbs 8 g; Protein 2.1g; Fat 17.1g; Sugar 5g; Fiber 0.9g

Garlic Onion and Tomato

Prep time: 10 minutes . | Cook Time: 20 minutes | Serves 2

2 tablespoons extra-virgin olive oil
1 chopped onion
1 red bell pepper, seeded and chopped
2 minced garlic cloves
1 (14-ounce / 397-g) can crushed tomatoes
2 cups green beans (fresh or frozen; halved if fresh)
3 cups low-sodium vegetable broth
1 tablespoon Italian seasoning
½ cup dried whole-wheat elbow macaroni
Pinch red pepper flakes (or to taste)
½ teaspoon sea salt

Warm the olive oil in a large saucepan over medium heat till it shimmers. Add onion and bell pepper in the saucepan. Cook, stirring regularly, for about 3 minutes, or until the onion and bell pepper begin to soften. Then add garlic. Cook, stirring occasionally, for 30 seconds, or until the garlic is aromatic. Bring the mixture to a boil, stirring in the tomatoes, green beans, vegetable broth, and Italian seasoning. Combine the elbow macaroni, red pepper flakes, and salt in a large mixing bowl. Cook for another 8 minutes, or until the macaroni is cooked through, stirring periodically. Remove the pan from the heat and place it in a large mixing bowl to cool for 6 minutes before serving.

Nutritional information: Calories 202; Total Carbs 29.2g; Net Carbs 19.1 g; Protein 5.2 g; Fat 7.2g; Sugar 2.9g; Fiber 7.2g

Lemony Broccoli

Prep time: 08 minutes . | Cook Time: 24 minutes | Serves 8

2 large broccoli heads, cut into florets
2 tablespoons extra-virgin olive oil
3 garlic cloves, minced

¼ teaspoon salt
¼ teaspoon ground black pepper
2 tablespoons freshly squeezed lemon juice

Preheat to 425 degrees Fahrenheit (220 degrees Celsius) and grease a large baking sheet. Combine the broccoli, olive oil, garlic, salt, and pepper in a large mixing basin. Toss until the broccoli is well covered. Place the broccoli on the baking sheet that has been prepped. Roast for about 25 minutes, or until the broccoli is browned and fork-tender, in a preheated oven, flipping halfway through. Remove the pan from the oven and place it on a dish to cool for 5 minutes. Serve with a squeeze of lemon juice on top.

Nutritional information: Calories 33; Total Carbs 3.1g; Net Carbs 0.9 g; Protein 21.2g; Fat 2.1g; Sugar 1.1g; Fiber 1.1g

Tahini Zucchini with Bell Pepper

Prep time: 10 minutes . | Cook Time: 0 minutes | Serves 4

2 zucchinis, chopped
3 garlic cloves
2 tablespoons extra-virgin olive oil
2 tablespoons tahini
Juice of 1 lemon
½ teaspoon sea salt
1 red bell pepper, seeded and cut into sticks

Combine the zucchini, garlic, olive oil, tahini, lemon juice, and salt in a blender or food processor. Blend until completely smooth. Serve with the red bell pepper sticks.

Nutritional information: Calories 120; Total Carbs 6.9g; Net Carbs 0g; Protein 2.1g; Fat 11.1g; Sugar 4g; Fiber 2.9g

Squash with Black Pepper

Prep time: 08 minutes . | Cook Time: 18 minutes | Serves 4

1 (1- to 1½-pound/454-680 g) delicate squash, halved, seeded, and cut into ½-inch-thick strips
1 tablespoon extra-virgin olive oil
½ teaspoon dried thyme
¼ teaspoon salt
¼ teaspoons freshly ground black pepper

Preheat the oven to 400 degrees Fahrenheit (205 degrees Celsius). and line a baking sheet with parchment paper. In a large mixing bowl, toss the squash strips with the olive oil, thyme, salt, and pepper until well covered. Place the squash strips in a single layer on the prepared baking sheet. Roast for 20 minutes, turning the strips halfway through, until lightly browned. Remove the dish from the oven and place it on plates to serve.

Nutritional information: Calories 78; Total Carbs 11.8g; Net Carbs 6.8g; Protein 1.1 g; Fat 4.2g; Sugar 2.9g; Fiber 2.1g

Lemony Brussels Sprouts

Prep time: 09 minutes . | Cook Time: 18 minutes | Serves 4

1 pound (454 g) Brussels sprouts
2 tablespoons avocado oil, divided
1 cup chicken bone broth
1 tablespoon minced garlic
½ teaspoon kosher salt
Freshly ground black pepper, to taste
½ medium lemons
½ tablespoon poppy seeds

Trim the Brussels sprouts by removing any loose outer leaves and cutting off the stem ends. Each one should be cut in half lengthwise (through the stem). Select the Sauté/More setting on an electric pressure cooker. Pour 1 tablespoon avocado oil into the saucepan once it is hot. Half of the Brussels sprouts, cut-side down, should be added to the saucepan and left to brown for 3 to 5 minutes without being stirred. Transfer to a bowl and return to the saucepan with the remaining tablespoon of avocado oil and Brussels sprouts. Return all of the Brussels sprouts to the pot by pressing Cancel. Combine the broth, garlic, salt, and a few grinds of pepper in a mixing bowl. To evenly distribute the seasonings, give it a good stir. Close and lock the lid of the pressure cooker. Set the valve to sealing. Sauté on high pressure for 2 minutes. Close and lock the pressure cooker's lid. Set the valve to the closed position Sauté on high pressure for 2 minutes. Zest the lemon and chop it into quarters while the Brussels sprouts are cooking. When the cooking is finished, press Cancel and release the pressure quickly. Unlock and remove the cover once the pin has dropped. Transfer the Brussels sprouts to a serving bowl with a slotted spoon. Toss with the poppy seeds, lemon zest, and a squeeze of lemon juice. Serve right away.

Nutritional information: Calories 126; Total Carbs 12.9g; Net Carbs 5 g; Protein 4.1g; Fat 8.1g; Sugar 3g; Fiber 4.9g

Savory Spinach Wraps

Prep time: 10 minutes . | Cook Time: 50 minutes | Serves 8

16 fresh spinach leaves
4 sun-dried tomatoes, rinsed, drained, and diced fine
2 medium eggplants
1 green onion, diced fine
4 tablespoons fat-free cream cheese, soft
2 tablespoons fat-free sour cream
2 tablespoons lemon juice
1 teaspoon olive oil
1 clove garlic, diced fine
¼ teaspoon oregano
⅛ teaspoon black pepper
Nonstick cooking spray
Spaghetti Sauce:
½ onion, diced
½ carrot, grated
½ stalk celery, diced
½ zucchini, grated
½ (28-ounce / 794-g) Italian-style tomatoes, in puree
½ (14½-ounce / 411-g) diced tomatoes, with juice
¼ cup water

1 clove garlic, diced fine
¼ tablespoon oregano
½ teaspoon olive oil
½ teaspoon basil
½ teaspoon thyme
½ teaspoon salt
¼ teaspoon red pepper flakes

Preheat the oven to 450 degrees Fahrenheit (235 degrees Celsius). Spray cooking spray over 2 big cookie sheets. Remove the eggplant's ends and trim them. Cut the eggplant lengthwise into ¼-inch pieces. Throw away the ones with a lot of skin; there should be approximately 16 slices left. Arrange them in a single layer on the prepared pans. Brush both sides of the eggplant with a mixture of lemon juice and oil whisked together in a small basin. Cook for 20 to 25 minutes, or until the eggplant begins to become golden brown. Allow to cool on a platter. Meanwhile, prepare the spaghetti sauce as follows: In a large saucepan, heat the oil over medium heat. Toss in the veggies and garlic. Cook for about 5 minutes, or until vegetables are soft, stirring frequently. Add the remaining Ingredients and break up the tomatoes with the back of a spoon. Bring to a simmer, then cook, partially covered, for 30 minutes over medium-low heat, stirring periodically. Combine the remaining Ingredients, except the spinach, in a mixing dish and stir well. To make the eggplant, distribute 1 teaspoon cream cheese mixture equally over the slices, leaving a 12-inch border around the edges. Start rolling from the little end with a spinach leaf on top. Place the rolls on a serving platter, seam side down. Warm spaghetti sauce is served on the side.

Nutritional information: Calories 80; Total Carbs 12.1g; Net Carbs 0.1g; Protein 3.2g; Fat 3.0g; Sugar 6.0g; Fiber 6g

Stir-Fried Tofu Broccoli with Brown Rice

Prep time: 08 minutes . | Cook Time: 08 minutes | Serves 4

3 tablespoons extra-virgin olive oil
12 ounces (340 g) firm tofu, cut into ½-inch pieces
4 cups broccoli, broken into florets
4 scallions, sliced
1 teaspoon peeled and grated fresh ginger
4 garlic cloves, minced
2 tablespoons soy sauce (use gluten-free soy sauce if necessary)
¼ cup vegetable broth
1 cup cooked brown rice

In a large skillet, heat the olive oil over medium-high heat until it begins to simmer. Stir fry in the tofu, broccoli, and scallions for 6 minutes, or until the veggies begin to soften. Then add garlic and ginger and cook, stirring constantly, for about 30 seconds. Combine the soy sauce, vegetable broth, and brown rice in a mixing bowl. Cook for a further 1 to 2 minutes, stirring constantly, until the rice is well heated. Allow 5 minutes for cooling before serving.

Nutritional information: Calories 238; Total Carbs 21.2g; Net Carbs 8.2 g; Protein 5.2 g; Fat 13.2g; Sugar 8.8g; Fiber 4.2g

Veggie Fajitas with Guacamole (Homemade)

Prep time: 08 minutes . | Cook Time: 14 minutes | Serves 4

Guacamole:
2 small avocados, pitted and peeled
1 teaspoon freshly squeezed lime juice
¼ teaspoon salt
9 halved cherry tomatoes
Fajitas:
1 red bell pepper, cut into ½-inch slices
1 green bell pepper, cut into ½-inch slices
1 small white onion, cut into ½-inch slices
1 cup black beans, drained and rinsed
¼ teaspoon garlic powder
¼ teaspoon chili powder
½ teaspoon ground cumin
4 (6-inch) yellow corn tortillas
Avocado oil cooking spray

Combine the avocados and lime juice in a mixing basin. Mash with a fork until a consistent consistency is reached. Season with salt and pepper after adding the cherry tomatoes. Set aside after thoroughly stirring. Until a large skillet is heated, heat it over medium heat. Coat the pan's bottom with cooking spray. In a large skillet, combine the bell peppers, white onion, black beans, garlic powder, chilli powder, and cumin. Cook, stirring occasionally, until the beans are cooked, about 15 minutes. Place the pan on a platter and turn off the heat. Arrange the corn tortillas on a clean work area and distribute the fajita mixture evenly among them. Serve with guacamole on top.

Nutritional information: Calories 273; Total Carbs 30.1g; Net Carbs 13.7 g; Protein 8.1g; Fat 7.1g; Sugar 5.2g; Fiber 11.2g

Lemony Wax Beans

Prep time: 5 minutes . | Cook Time: 15 minutes | Serves 4

2 pounds (907 g) wax beans
2 tablespoons extra-virgin olive oil
Sea salt to taste
Freshly ground black pepper
Juice of ½ lemon

Preheat at 400 degrees Fahrenheit (205 degrees Celsius). Line aluminum foil over a baking sheet. Toss the beans with the olive oil in a large mixing dish. Toss with salt and pepper to taste. Place the beans on the baking pan and evenly distribute them. Roast the beans for 10 to 12 minutes, or until they are caramelized and soft. Serve the beans on a serving plate with a squeeze of lemon juice.

Nutritional information: Calories 100; Total Carbs 8g; Net Carbs 0g; Protein 2g; Fat 7.0g; Sugar 4.0g; Fiber 4 g

Carrot Hummus

Prep Time: 15 minutes. | Cook Time: 10 minutes. | Servings: 2

1 chopped carrot
2 oz. cooked chickpeas
1 teaspoon lemon juice
1 teaspoon tahini
1 teaspoon fresh parsley

Cook the carrots and chickpeas in instant pot for 10 minutes on "Stew" setting. Once done place all Ingredients in the blender and blend until smooth paste. Pour in the bowl top with olive oil and serve.

Nutritional information: Calories 58; Total Carbs 2g; Net Carbs 1g; Protein 4g; Fat 2g; Sugar 0.1g; Fiber 0.8g

Eggplant Pizzas

Prep time: 15 minutes . | Cook Time: 1 hour 10 minutes | Serves 4

1 large peeled eggplant, sliced into 14-inch circles
½ cup reduced-fat Mozzarella cheese, grated
2 eggs
1¼ cups Italian bread crumbs
1 tablespoon water
¼ teaspoon black pepper
Nonstick cooking spray
Spaghetti Sauce:
1 onion, diced
1 carrot, grated
1 stalk celery, diced
1 zucchini, grated
1 (28-ounce / 794-g) Italian-style tomatoes, in puree
1 (14½-ounce / 411-g) diced tomatoes, with juice
½ cup water
2 cloves garlic, diced fine
½ tablespoon oregano
1 teaspoon olive oil
1 teaspoon basil
1 teaspoon thyme
1 teaspoon salt
¼ teaspoon red pepper flakes

Preheat the oven to 350 degrees Fahrenheit (180 degrees Celsius) (180 degrees Celsius). Spray 2 big cookie sheets with cooking spray and line with foil. Eggs, water, and pepper should be whisked together in a shallow bowl. In a separate flat dish, place the bread crumbs. After dipping the eggplant slices in the egg mixture, cover them completely with bread crumbs. Place on cookie sheets that have been prepped. Cook for 15 minutes after spraying the tops with cooking spray. Spray the eggplant with cooking spray again on the other side. Bake for a further 15 minutes. Meanwhile, prepare the spaghetti sauce as follows: In a large saucepan, heat the oil over medium heat. Toss in the veggies and garlic. Cook for about 5 minutes, or until vegetables are soft, stirring frequently. Add the remaining Ingredients and break up the tomatoes with the back of a spoon. Bring to a simmer and cook for 30 minutes, stirring often, over medium-low heat, partially covered. Remove the eggplant from the oven and spread 1 tablespoon spaghetti sauce over each slice. Bake for another 4 to 5 minutes, or until the cheese has melted and the sauce is bubbling. Serve immediately.

Nutritional information: Calories 172; Total Carbs 24.1g; Net Carbs 14.1g; Protein 9.2g; Fat 5.0g; Sugar 6.0g; Fiber 4g

Roasted Brussels Sprouts with Tomatoes

Prep time: 15 minutes . | Cook Time: 20 minutes | Serves 4

1 pound (454 g) trimmed and halved Brussels sprouts
1 tablespoon extra-virgin olive oil
Sea salt, to taste
Freshly ground black pepper, to taste
½ cup sun-dried tomatoes, chopped
2 tablespoons freshly squeezed lemon juice
1 teaspoon lemon zest

Preheat the oven to 400 degrees Fahrenheit (200 degrees Celsius) (205 degrees Celsius). A large baking sheet should be lined with aluminum foil. In a large mixing bowl, toss the Brussels sprouts with the olive oil until completely coated. Season with salt and pepper to taste. Place the seasoned Brussels sprouts in a single layer on the baking sheet that has been prepared. Roast for 20 minutes, stirring the pan halfway through, or until the Brussels sprouts are crispy and browned on the outside, in a preheated oven. Remove the dish from the oven and place it in a serving bowl. Stir in the tomatoes, lemon juice, and lemon zest to combine. Serve right away.

Nutritional information: Calories 111; Total Carbs 13.7g; Net Carbs 6.1g; Protein 5.0g; Fat 5.8g; Sugar 2.7g; Fiber 4.9g

Portobello Mushrooms with Spinach

Prep time: 04 minutes . | Cook Time: 18 minutes | Serves 4

8 large Portobello mushrooms
3 teaspoons extra-virgin olive oil, divided
4 cups fresh spinach
1 medium red bell pepper, diced
¼ cup low-fat feta cheese, crumbled

Preheat the oven to 450 degrees Fahrenheit (235 degrees Celsius). Remove the mushroom stems from your cutting board. Remove the gills with a spoon and throw them away. Use 2 teaspoons olive oil to coat the mushrooms. Place the mushrooms cap-side down on a baking sheet. Roast for 20 minutes, or until browned on top, in a preheated oven. Meanwhile, heat the remaining olive oil in a skillet over medium heat until it shimmers. Add the spinach and red bell pepper to the skillet and cook, turning occasionally, for 8 minutes, or until the veggies are soft. Remove the pan from the heat and place it in a basin. Place the mushrooms on a platter after removing them from the oven. Fill the mushrooms with the vegetables and feta cheese, using a spoon to do so. Warm the dish before serving.

Nutritional information: Calories 118; Total Carbs 12.2g; Net Carbs 13.7 g; Protein 7.2 g; Fat 6.3g; Sugar 6.1g; Fiber 4.1g

Jicama Slices with Avocado

Prep time: 5 minutes . | Cook Time: 0 minutes | Serves 4

1 avocado, cut into cubes
Juice of ½ limes
2 tablespoons finely chopped red onion
2 tablespoons chopped fresh cilantro
1 garlic clove, minced
¼ teaspoon sea salt
1 cup sliced jicama

Combine the avocado, lime juice, onion, cilantro, garlic, and salt in a small bowl. Lightly mash with a fork. Dip the jicama into the sauce.

Nutritional information: Calories 74; Total Carbs 7.9g; Net Carbs 0g; Protein 4.6g; Fat 3.3g; Sugar 3g; Fiber 4.9g

Garlic Cauliflower Bowl

Prep time: 04 minutes . | Cook Time: 18 minutes | Serves 4

1 head cauliflower, separated into bite-sized florets
¼ teaspoon garlic powder
¼ teaspoon salt
⅛ Teaspoon black pepper
Butter-flavored cooking spray

Preheat the oven to 400 degrees Fahrenheit (200 degrees Celsius) (205 degrees Celsius). In a large mixing bowl, spray the cauliflower with cooking spray, making sure to coat all sides. Mix with a pinch of salt and pepper to coat. Arrange in a single layer on a cookie sheet. Cook for 20–25 minutes, or until the cauliflower begins to color. Warm the dish before serving.

Nutritional information: Calories 55; Total Carbs 11.1g; Net Carbs 1.1g; Protein 4.2g; Fat 0g; Sugar 5.0g; Fiber 5.0g

Baked Eggs with Vegetables

Prep time: 5 minutes . | Cook Time: 25 minutes | Serves 4

2 tablespoons extra-virgin olive oil
1 red onion, chopped
1 sweet potato, cut into ½-inch pieces
1 green bell pepper, seeded and chopped
½ teaspoon sea salt
1 teaspoon chili powder
4 large eggs
½ cup shredded pepper Jack cheese
1 avocado, cut into cubes

Preheat the oven to 350 degrees Fahrenheit (180 degrees Celsius). Warm the olive oil in a large skillet over medium-high heat until it shimmers. Combine the onion, sweet potato, bell pepper, salt, and chilli powder in a large mixing bowl. Cook, stirring regularly for about 10 minutes, or until the veggies are gently browned. Turn off the heat. Make 4 wells in the vegetables with the back of a spoon, then crack an egg into each well. Over the vegetables, strew the grated cheese. Bake for about 10 minutes, or until the cheese has melted and the eggs have set. Remove the pan from the heat and top with the avocado before serving.

Nutritional information: Calories 286; Total Carbs 16.2g; Net Carbs 1.9 g; Protein 12.3 g; Fat 21.3g; Sugar 9.1g; Fiber 5.2g

Garlic Spinach Quiches

Prep time: 10 minutes . | Cook Time: 15 minutes | Serves 6

2 tablespoons olive oil, divided
1 onion, finely chopped
2 garlic cloves, minced
2 cups baby spinach
8 large eggs
¼ cup 1% skim milk
½ teaspoon sea salt
¼ teaspoons freshly ground black pepper
1 cup low-fat Swiss cheese, shredded
Special Equipment:
A 6-cup muffin tin

Preheat the oven to 375 degrees Fahrenheit (190 degrees Celsius).Using 1 tablespoon olive oil, grease a 6-cup muffin tray. Warm the olive oil in a nonstick skillet over medium-high heat. In the same skillet, add the onion and garlic and cook for 4 minutes, or until transparent. Toss in the spinach and cook for 1 minute, or until soft. Place them on a plate and leave them to cool. In a mixing dish, whisk together the eggs, milk, salt, and black pepper. Toss the cooked veggies in the egg mixture, then sprinkle with the cheese. Fill the muffin cups halfway with the mixture. Preheat the oven to 350°F and bake for 15 minutes, or until puffed and golden brown around the edges. Serve the quiches hot from the oven on six small plates.

Nutritional information: Calories 220; Total Carbs 4.2g; Net Carbs 0.7 g; Protein 14.3 g; Fat 21.3g; Sugar 2.7g; Fiber 0.8g

Baked Lemony Cauliflower

Prep time: 5 minutes . | Cook Time: 25 minutes | Serves 4

1 cauliflower head, broken into small florets
2 tablespoons extra-virgin olive oil
½ teaspoon salt, or more to taste
½ teaspoon ground chipotle chili powder
Juice of 1 lime

Preheat to 425 degrees Fahrenheit (220 degrees Celsius) and grease a large baking sheet. Remove from the equation. Toss the cauliflower florets with the olive oil in a large mixing dish. Salt and chipotle Chile powder to taste. Arrange the cauliflower florets in an equal layer on the baking sheet. Roast for 15 minutes in the preheated oven until lightly browned. Continue to roast until the cauliflower is crisp and soft, about 10 minutes. Remove from the oven and season with salt as needed. Allow it cool for 6 minutes. Then drizzle over the cauliflower with lime juice and serving.

Nutritional information: Calories 100; Total Carbs 8.1g; Net Carbs 1.7 g; Protein 3.2g; Fat 7.1g; Sugar 3.2g; Fiber 3.2g

Sautéed Garlicky Cabbage

Prep time: 10 minutes . | Cook Time: 10 minutes | Serves 8

2 tablespoons extra-virgin olive oil
1 bunch collard greens, stemmed and thinly sliced
½ small green cabbage, thinly sliced
6 garlic cloves, minced
1 tablespoon low-sodium soy sauce

Warm the olive oil in a large skillet over medium-high heat. Cook for about 2 minutes, or until the collard greens begin to wilt in the oil. Mix in the cabbage well. Reduce the heat to medium-low, cover, and simmer for 5 to 7 minutes, or until the greens are softened, stirring periodically. Stir in the garlic and soy sauce until everything is well combined. Cook for another 30 seconds, or until the mixture is aromatic. Transfer to a serving platter after removing from the heat.

Nutritional information: Calories 73; Total Carbs 5.9g; Net Carbs 3g; Protein 14.3 g; Fat 4.1g; Sugar 0g; Fiber 2.9g

Spiced Swiss Chard with Cardamom

Prep time: 08 minutes . | Cook Time: 08 minutes | Serves 4

2 tablespoons extra-virgin olive oil
1 pound (454 g) Swiss chard, coarse stems removed and leaves chopped
1 pound (454 g) kale, coarse stems removed and leaves chopped
½ teaspoon ground cardamom
1 tablespoon freshly squeezed lemon juice
Sea salt, to taste
Freshly ground black pepper, to taste

Warm the olive oil in a large skillet over medium-high heat. Stir together the Swiss chard, kale, cardamom, and lemon juice in the skillet. Cook, stirring constantly for about 10 minutes, or until the greens are wilted. Season to taste with salt and pepper and stir thoroughly. While the greens are still warm, serve them on a dish.

Nutritional information: Calories 139; Total Carbs 15.8g; Net Carbs 10.9g; Protein 5.9g; Fat 6.8g; Sugar 1.0g; Fiber 3.9g

Flavorful Bok Choy with Almonds

Prep time: 15 minutes . | Cook Time: 7 minutes | Serves 4

2 teaspoons sesame oil
2 pounds (907 g) bok choy, cleaned and quartered
2 teaspoons low-sodium soy sauce
Pinch red pepper flakes
½ cup toasted sliced almonds

In a large skillet, heat the sesame oil over medium heat until it is hot. Cook for about 5 minutes, stirring periodically, or until the bok choy is soft but still crisp in the hot oil. Stir in the soy sauce and red pepper flakes until everything is well combined. Sauté for another 2 minutes. Transfer to a serving platter and garnish with sliced almonds.

Nutritional information: Calories 118; Total Carbs 7.9g; Net Carbs 0.8g; Protein 6.2g; Fat 7.8g; Sugar 3.0g; Fiber 4.1g

Butter Yams

Prep time: 7 minutes . | Cook Time: 45 minutes | Serves 8 (½ cup each)

2 medium jewel yams cut into 2-inch dices
2 tablespoons unsalted butter
Juice of 1 large orange
1½ teaspoons ground cinnamon
¼ teaspoon ground ginger
¾ teaspoon ground nutmeg
⅛ Teaspoon ground cloves

Preheat the oven to 350 degrees Fahrenheit (180 degrees Celsius). Arrange the yam dices in a single layer on a rimmed baking sheet. Remove from the equation. In a medium saucepan over medium-low heat, combine the butter, orange juice, cinnamon, ginger, nutmeg, and garlic cloves. Cook, stirring constantly for 3 to 5 minutes, or until the sauce thickens and bubbles. Toss the yams in the sauce to thoroughly coat them. Preheat the oven to 400°F and bake for 40 minutes, or until the potatoes are soft. Allow 8 minutes for the yams to cool on the baking sheet before serving.

Nutritional information: Calories 129; Total Carbs 24.7g; Net Carbs 16.8g; Protein 2.1g; Fat 2.8g; Sugar 2.9g; Fiber 5g

Baked Asparagus with Bell Peppers

Prep time: 5 minutes . | Cook Time: 15 minutes | Serves 4

1 pound (454 g) asparagus, woody ends trimmed, cut into 2-inch segments
2 red bell peppers, seeded, 1-inch-thick slices
1 small onion, quartered
2 tablespoons Italian dressing

Preheat the oven to 400 degrees Fahrenheit (205 degrees Celsius). and line a baking sheet with parchment paper. In a large mixing basin, toss the asparagus with the peppers, onion, and dressing. Arrange the vegetables on the baking sheet and roast until tender, about 15 minutes. Using a spatula, flip the vegetables once during cooking. Serve immediately on a big dish.

Nutritional information: Calories 92; Total Carbs 10.7g; Net Carbs 1g; Protein 2.9 g; Fat 4.8g; Sugar 5.7g; Fiber 4.0g

Flavorful Peppery Mushrooms

Prep time: 09 minutes . | Cook Time: 11 minutes | Serves 4

1 tablespoon butter
2 teaspoons extra-virgin olive oil
2 pounds button mushrooms, halved
2 teaspoons minced fresh garlic
1 teaspoon chopped fresh thyme
Sea salt to taste
Freshly ground black pepper

Add olive oil and butter in a large skillet over medium-high heat. Then add mushrooms in the skillet and cook about 10 minutes or until lightly caramelized and tender. While cooking, stir from time to time. Add thyme and garlic and cook for 2 minutes or more. Add salt and pepper to season. Serve and enjoy!

Nutritional information: Calories 97; Total Carbs 8g; Net Carbs 2g; Protein 7g; Fat 6.0g; Sugar 4.0g; Fiber 2 g

Zucchini Strips

Prep time: 08 minutes . | Cook Time: 08 minutes | Serves 4

3 zucchini, slice ¼- to ⅛-inch thick
2 eggs
½ cup sunflower oil
⅓ cup sugar-free coconut flour
¼ cup reduced fat Parmesan cheese
1 tablespoon water

In a large skillet, heat the oil over medium heat. In a shallow basin, mix together the egg and water. Combine flour and Parmesan in a separate shallow basin. In a separate bowl, coat the zucchini in the egg, then in the flour mixture. Put in a thin layer in the skillet. Cook for 2 minutes per side, or until golden brown on both sides. Place on a dish lined with paper towels. Repeat. Serve immediately with your favorite dipping sauce.

Nutritional information: Calories 140; Total Carbs 6.1g; Net Carbs 1.1g; Protein 6.2g; Fat 11.0g; Sugar 3.0g; Fiber 2g

Classic Brussels Sprouts

Prep Time: 10 minutes. | Cook Time: 20 minutes. | Servings: 4

1 pound (454 g) Brussels sprouts
2 tablespoons avocado oil, divided
1 cup chicken bone broth
1 tablespoon minced garlic
½ teaspoon kosher salt
Freshly ground black pepper, to taste
½ medium lemons
½ tablespoon poppy seeds

Trim the Brussels sprouts stem and removing any loose outer leaves. Cut each in ½ lengthwise. Set the electric pressure cooker to the Sauté setting. When the pot is hot, pour in 1 tablespoon the avocado oil. Add ½ of the Brussels sprouts to the pot, cut-side down, and let them brown for 3 to 5 minutes without disturbing. Transfer to a bowl and add the remaining tablespoon avocado oil and the remaining Brussels sprouts to the pot. Add the broth, garlic, salt, and a few grinds of pepper. Stir to distribute the seasonings. Close and lock the lid of the pressure cooker. Seal the pressure cooker. Cook on high pressure for 2 minutes. While the Brussels sprouts are cooking, zest the lemon, then cut it into quarters. When the cooking is complete, quick release the pressure. Using a slotted spoon, transfer the Brussels sprouts to a serving bowl. Toss with the lemon zest, a squeeze of lemon juice, and the poppy seeds. Serve immediately.

Nutritional information: Calories 126; Total Carbs 12g; Net Carbs 10g; Protein 4g; Fat 8.1g; Sugar 3g; Fiber 4g

Gingery Eggplant

Prep time: 10 minutes . | Cook Time: 40 minutes | Serves 4

1 large eggplant, sliced into fourths
3 green onions, diced, green tips only
1 teaspoon fresh ginger, peeled and finely minced
¼ cup plus 1 teaspoon cornstarch
1½ tablespoons soy sauce
1½ tablespoons sesame oil
1 tablespoon vegetable oil
1 tablespoon fish sauce
2 teaspoons Splenda
¼ teaspoon salt

Sprinkle salt on both sides of the eggplant and place it on paper towels. Allow 1 hour for the extra moisture to evaporate. Using extra paper towels, pat dry. Whisk together soy sauce, sesame oil, fish sauce, Splenda, and 1 teaspoon cornstarch in a small basin. Coat the eggplant on both sides with the ¼ cup cornstarch, adding more if necessary. Warm the oil in a big skillet over medium-high heat. Add ½ teaspoon of ginger, and 1 green onion, and then arrange on the top with 2 slices of eggplant. Pour half of the sauce mixture over both sides of the eggplant. Cook each side for 8 to 10 minutes. Repeat. Serve with the leftover green onions as a garnish.

Nutritional information: Calories 156; Total Carbs 18.1g; Net Carbs 7.1g; Protein 2.1g; Fat 9.0g; Sugar 6.0g; Fiber 5 g

Baked Asparagus with Cashews

Prep time: 10 minutes . | Cook Time: 15 to 20 minutes | Serves 4

2 pounds (907 g) asparagus, woody ends trimmed
1 tablespoon extra-virgin olive oil
Sea salt, to taste
Freshly ground black pepper, to taste
½ cup chopped cashews
Zest and juice of 1 lime

Preheat the oven to 400 degrees Fahrenheit (200 degrees Celsius) (205 degrees Celsius). A baking pan should be lined with aluminium foil. Toss the asparagus with the olive oil in a medium bowl. To taste, season with salt and pepper. Arrange the asparagus on the baking sheet and bake for 15 to 20 minutes, or until tender and lightly browned. Transfer the asparagus to a serving bowl from the oven. Toss in the cashews, lime zest, and juice to thoroughly coat. Serve right away.

Nutritional information: Calories 173; Total Carbs 43.7g; Net Carbs 33.8g; Protein 8g; Fat 7.8g; Sugar 5.0g; Fiber 4.9g

Butternut Fritters

Prep time: 15 minutes . | Cook Time: 15 minutes | Serves 6

5 cup butternut squash, grated
2 large eggs
1 tablespoon fresh sage, diced fine
⅔ cup flour
2 tablespoons olive oil

Salt and pepper, to taste

Warm the oil in a large skillet over medium-high heat. Combine squash, eggs, sage, and salt & pepper to taste in a large mixing dish. Mix in the flour. Place ¼ cup of the batter in the skillet, spacing fritters at least 1 inch apart. Cook so that both sides are golden brown, around 2 minutes per side. Place on a paper towel-lined plate. Repeat. Serve immediately with a dipping sauce of your preference.

Nutritional information: Calories 165; Total Carbs 24.1g; Net Carbs 15.1g; Protein 4.1g; Fat 6.0g; Sugar 3.0g; Fiber 6 g

Broiled Peppery Spinach

Prep time: 5 minutes . | Cook Time: 4 minutes | Serves 4

8 cups spinach, thoroughly washed and spun dry
1 tablespoon extra-virgin olive oil
¼ teaspoon ground cumin
Sea salt to taste
Freshly ground black pepper to taste

Preheat the oven to broil. Place an oven rack in the oven's upper third. On a wide baking sheet, place a wire rack. Massage the spinach, oil, and cumin together in a large mixing bowl until all of the leaves are evenly covered. Half of the spinach should be spread out on the rack with as little overlap as possible. Season the greens to taste with salt and pepper. Broil the spinach for 2 minutes, or until the edges are crispy. Remove the spinach from the baking sheet and place it in a large serving bowl. Repeat with the rest of the spinach. Serve right away.

Nutritional information: Calories 40; Total Carbs 2g; Net Carbs 1g; Protein 2g; Fat 4.0g; Sugar 0g; Fiber 1 g

Brown Rice & Lentil Salad

Prep Time: 10 minutes. | Cook Time: 10 minutes. | Servings: 4

1 cup water
½ cup instant brown rice
2 tablespoons olive oil
2 tablespoons vinegar
1 tablespoon Dijon mustard
1 tablespoon minced onion
½ teaspoon paprika
Salt and pepper to taste
1 (15-ounce) can brown lentils, rinsed and drained
1 medium carrot, shredded
2 tablespoons fresh chopped parsley

In a large pot, combine the water and instant brown rice. When boiling, cover with a lid and simmer for 10 minutes. Remove from the heat and set aside time to prepare the salad. Place olive oil, vinegar, Dijon mustard, onion, paprika, salt, and pepper in a medium bowl. Add the rice, lentils, carrots, and parsley and mix. Adjust the seasoning to your liking, stir well and serve hot.

Nutritional information: Calories 145; Total Carbs 13g; Net Carbs 10g; Protein 6g; Fat 7g; Sugar 1g; Fiber 2g

Kale and Chard with Cardamom

Prep time: 10 minutes . | Cook Time: 10 minutes | Serves 4

2 tablespoons extra-virgin olive oil
1 pound (454 g) kale, coarse stems removed and leaves chopped
1 pound (454 g) Swiss chard, coarse stems removed and leaves chopped
1 tablespoon freshly squeezed lemon juice
½ teaspoon ground cardamom
Sea salt to taste
Freshly ground black pepper

In a large skillet, heat the olive oil over medium-high heat. In a skillet, combine the kale, chard, lemon juice, and cardamom. Toss the greens constantly with tongs until they are wilted, about 10 minutes or less. Using salt and pepper, season the greens. Serve right away.

Nutritional information: Calories 140; Total Carbs 16g; Net Carbs 11g; Protein 18.1g; Fat 7.0g; Sugar 1.0g; Fiber 4 g

Spiced Brussels Sprouts

Prep Time: 5 minutes. | Cook Time: 3 minutes. | Servings: 5

1 teaspoon extra-virgin olive oil
1 lb. halved Brussels sprouts
3 tablespoons apple cider vinegar
3 tablespoons gluten-free tamari soy sauce
3 tablespoons chopped sun-dried tomatoes

Select the "Sauté" function of Instant Pot, add oil and allow the pot to get hot. Add the Brussels sprouts and cook well. Cook the sprouts in the residual heat for 2-3 minutes. Add the tamari soy sauce and vinegar, and then stir. Cover the Instant Pot, seal the pressure valve. Select the "Manual, High Pressure" setting and cook for 3 minutes. Once the cooking is done, quick release the pressure and then stir in the chopped sun-dried tomatoes. Serve immediately.

Nutritional information: Calories 62; Total Carbs 1g; Net Carbs 0g; Protein 3g; Fat 1g; Sugar 2g; Fiber 0.2g

Spiced Carrots

Prep Time: 2 minutes. | Cook Time: 18 minutes. | Servings: 3

2 tablespoons plant-based butter
1 lb. baby carrots
1 cup water
1 teaspoon fresh thyme or oregano
1 teaspoon minced garlic
Black pepper to taste
Coarse sea salt to taste

Fill the Instant Pot inner pot with water and place it in the steamer. Place the carrots in the steamer basket. With the air vents in the "Sealing" position, close the cover and close. Select the "Steam" setting and cook for 2 minutes. Quickly release the pressure, then carefully remove the steamer basket containing the steamed carrots and drain the water. Put the butter

in the Instant Pot and melt it using the "Sauté" function. Add the garlic and sauté for 30 minutes, then add the carrots. Mix well. Add the fresh herbs and cook for 2-3 minutes. Season with salt and pepper and transfer to a bowl. Keep warm and enjoy!

Nutritional information: Calories 112; Total Carbs 7g; Net Carbs 4g; Protein 1.04g; Fat 7g; Sugar 1g; Fiber 0.4g

Garlic Sautéed Spinach

Prep Time: 5 minutes. | Cook Time: 10 minutes. | Servings: 4

1 ½ tablespoons olive oil
4 cloves minced garlic
6 cups fresh baby spinach
Salt and pepper to taste

Heat the oil in a large saucepan over medium heat. Add the garlic and cook for 1 minute. Add the spinach and season with salt and pepper. Fry for 1-2 minutes until smooth. Serve hot.

Nutritional information: Calories 60; Total Carbs 2.6g; Net Carbs 1.5g; Protein 1.5g; Fat 5.5g; Sugar 0.2g; Fiber 1.1g

Rosemary Potatoes

Prep Time: 5 minutes. | Cook Time: 25 minutes. | Servings: 2

1lb red potatoes
1 cup vegetable stock
2 tablespoons olive oil
2 tablespoons rosemary sprigs

Place potatoes in the steamer basket and add the stock into the Instant Pot. Steam the potatoes in Instant Pot for 15 minutes. Pour away the remaining stock. Set the pot to sauté and add the oil, rosemary, and potatoes. Cook until brown on top and fragrant.

Nutritional information: Calories 195; Total Carbs 1g; Net Carbs 0.5g; Protein 7g; Fat 1g; Sugar 0g; Fiber 0g

Spiced Avocado Dip

Prep Time: 5 minutes. | Cook Time: 0 minutes. | Servings: 4

1 avocado, cut into cubes
Juice of ½ limes
2 tablespoons finely chopped red onion
2 tablespoons chopped fresh cilantro
1 garlic clove, minced
¼ teaspoon sea salt
1 cup sliced jicama

In a small bowl, combine the avocado, lime juice, onion, cilantro, garlic, and salt. Mash them lightly with a fork. Serve with the jicama for dipping.

Nutritional information: Calories 74; Total Carbs 7.9g; Net Carbs 4g; Protein 1g; Fat 5g; Sugar 3g; Fiber 4.9g

Low-Sugar Bok Choy

Prep time: 15 minutes . | Cook Time: 7 minutes | Serves 4

2 teaspoons sesame oil
2 pounds (907 g) bok choy, cleaned and quartered
2 teaspoons low-sodium soy sauce
Pinch red pepper flakes
½ cup toasted sliced almonds

Heat the oil in a large skillet over medium heat. When the oil is hot, sauté the bok choy for 5 minutes, or until tender-crisp. Sauté for another 2 minutes after adding the soy sauce and red pepper flakes. Place the bok choy in a serving bowl with the sliced almonds on top.

Nutritional information: Calories 119; Total Carbs 8g; Net Carbs 1g; Protein 18.1g; Fat 8.0g; Sugar 3.0g; Fiber 4 g

Curry Roasted Cauliflower Florets

Prep Time: 5 minutes. | Cook Time: 25 minutes. | Servings: 6

8 cups cauliflower florets
2 tablespoons olive oil
1 teaspoon curry powder
½ teaspoon garlic powder
Salt and pepper

Preheat the oven to 425 ° F and place the foil on a baking sheet. Toss with the cauliflower and olive oil and spread on a baking sheet. Sprinkle with curry powder, garlic powder, salt, and pepper. Bake for 25 minutes or until tender. Serve hot and enjoy.

Nutritional information: Calories 75; Total Carbs 7.4g; Net Carbs 4g; Protein 3g; Fat 4g; Sugar 1.4g; Fiber 3.5g

Braised Summer Squash

Prep Time: 10 minutes. | Cook Time: 20 minutes. | Servings: 6

3 tablespoons olive oil
3 cloves minced garlic
¼ teaspoon crushed red pepper flakes
1-pound summer squash, sliced
1-pound zucchini, sliced
1 teaspoon dried oregano
Salt and pepper to taste

Heat oil in a large skillet over medium heat. Add the garlic and crushed red pepper in it and cook for 2 minutes. Add the summer squash and zucchini and cook for 15 minutes until just tender. Stir in the oregano and season with salt and pepper to taste. serve hot and enjoy.

Nutritional information: Calories 90; Total Carbs 6.2g; Net Carbs 1.8g; Protein 6g; Fat 7g; Sugar 3g; Fiber 1.8g

Lemon Garlic Green Beans

Prep Time: 5 minutes. | Cook Time: 10 minutes. | Servings: 6

1 ½ pounds green beans, trimmed
2 tablespoons olive oil
1 tablespoon fresh lemon juice
2 cloves minced garlic
Salt and pepper to taste

Boil the green beans in salted water. Drain when done after 3 minutes and place the in the ice cold water. Cool the beans completely then drain them well. Heat the oil in a large skillet over medium-high heat and add blanched green beans. Add the lemon juice, garlic, salt, and pepper and sauté for 3 minutes until the beans are tender-crisp then serve hot.

Nutritional information: Calories 75; Total Carbs 8.5g; Net Carbs 4.6g; Protein 2.1g; Fat 4.8g; Sugar 1.7g; Fiber 3.9g

Mashed Butternut Squash

Prep Time: 5 minutes. | Cook Time: 25 minutes. | Servings: 6

3 pounds whole butternut squash (about 2 medium)
2 tablespoons olive oil
Salt and pepper to taste

Preheat the oven to 400°F and place the parchment paper on the baking sheet. Cut the zucchini in half and remove the seeds. Cut the pumpkin into cubes, grease it with oil, and lay it out on a baking sheet. Bake for 25 minutes until tender, then place in a food processor. Mix gently, then season with salt and pepper to taste.

Nutritional information: Calories 90; Total Carbs 12g; Net Carbs 10g; Protein 1.1g; Fat 4.8g; Sugar 2.3g; Fiber 2g

Cilantro Lime Quinoa

Prep Time: 5 minutes. | Cook Time: 25 minutes. | Servings: 6

1 cup uncooked quinoa
1 tablespoon olive oil
1 medium yellow onion, diced
2 cloves minced garlic
1 (4-ounce) can diced green chiles, drained
1 ½ cups fat-free chicken broth
¾ cup fresh chopped cilantro
½ cup sliced green onion
2 tablespoons lime juice
Salt and pepper to taste

Rinse the quinoa thoroughly in cold water using a fine strainer. Heat the oil in a large saucepan over medium heat. Add the onion and sauté for 2 minutes, then add the chili and garlic and sauté Cook for 1 minute, then stir in the quinoa and chicken broth. When it comes to a boil, reduce the heat, cover, and simmer until the quinoa has absorbed the liquid, about 20-25 minutes. Remove from the heat, then add the cilantro, green onions, and lemon juice and stir. Season with salt and pepper to taste and serve hot.

Nutritional information: Calories 150; Total Carbs 22.5g; Net Carbs 19g; Protein 6g; Fat 4.1g; Sugar 1.4g; Fiber 2.7g

Eggplant Spread

Prep Time: 5 minutes. | Cook Time: 18 minutes. | Servings: 5

4 tablespoons extra-virgin olive oil
2 lbs. eggplant
4 skin-on garlic cloves
½ cup water
¼ cup pitted black olives
3 sprigs fresh thyme
Juice of 1 lemon
1 tablespoon tahini
1 teaspoon sea salt
Fresh extra-virgin olive oil

Peel the eggplant leaving some areas with skin and some with no skin. Slice eggplants into big chunks and layer at the bottom of Pot. Add olive oil to the pot, and on the "Sauté" function, fry the eggplant on one side, about 5 minutes. Add in the garlic cloves with the skin on. Flip over the eggplant and then add in the remaining uncooked eggplant chunks, salt and water. Close the lid, ensure the pressure release valve is set to "Sealing." Cook for 5 minutes on the "Manual, High Pressure" setting. Once done, quick releasing the pressure. Discard most of the brown cooking liquid. Remove the garlic cloves and peel them. Add the lemon juice, tahini, cooked and fresh garlic cloves and pitted black olives to the pot. Using a hand blender, process all the Ingredients until smooth. Pour out the spread into a serving dish and season with fresh thyme, whole black olives and some extra-virgin olive oil and serve with toasted pita bread.

Nutritional information: Calories 155; Total Carbs 16g; Net Carbs 12g; Protein 12g; Fat 11g; Sugar 2g; Fiber 1g

Golden Onion Rings

Prep time: 5 minutes . | Cook Time: 15 minutes | Serves 4

1 large onion, slice ½-inch thick
1 egg
¼ cup sunflower oil
2 tablespoons sugar-free coconut flour
2 tablespoons reduced fat Parmesan cheese
¼ teaspoon parsley flakes
⅛ teaspoon garlic powder
⅛ teaspoon cayenne pepper
Salt, to taste
Ketchup, for serving

Warm the oil in a large skillet over medium-high heat. Combine flour, Parmesan, and seasonings in a small basin. The egg should be whisked. Separate the onion slices into individual rings and set them in a large mixing dish. Add the beaten egg and toss thoroughly to coat. Allow 1 to 2 minutes for resting. Coat onion in flour mixture in small batches and add to skillet. Cook for 1 to 2 minutes per side, or until golden brown on both sides. Line a cookie sheet with paper towel. Place on the cookie sheet. Serve with ketchup on the side.

Nutritional information: Calories 185; Total Carbs 8.1g; Net Carbs 3.1g; Protein 3.2g; Fat 11.0g; Sugar 2.0g; Fiber 3 g

French Lentils

Prep Time: 5 minutes. | Cook Time: 25 minutes. | Servings: 10

2 tablespoons olive oil
1 medium onion, diced
1 medium carrot, peeled and diced
2 cloves minced garlic
5 ½ cups water
2 ¼ cups French lentils, rinsed and drained
1 teaspoon dried thyme
2 small bay leaves
Salt and pepper to taste

Heat the oil in a large saucepan over medium heat. Add the onions, carrots, and garlic and sauté for 3 minutes. Add the water, lentils, thyme, and bay leaf and season with salt. When boiling, reduce heat to low and cook until tender, about 20 minutes. Remove the excess water and adjust the taste as desired. Serve hot.

Nutritional information: Calories 185; Total Carbs 27.9g; Net Carbs 14.2g; Protein 11.4g; Fat 3.3g; Sugar 1.7g; Fiber 13.7g

Coffee-Steamed Carrots

Prep Time: 10 minutes. | Cook Time: 3 minutes. | Servings: 4

1 cup brewed coffee
1 teaspoon light brown sugar
½ teaspoon kosher salt
Freshly ground black pepper
1-pound baby carrots
Chopped fresh parsley
1 teaspoon grated lemon zest

Pour the coffee into the coffee. Add the light brown sugar, salt, and pepper and mix. Add the carrots. Close the pressure cooker. Set to close. Cook for a few minutes over high heat. When done, click Cancel and quickly release. Using a spoon, divide the carrots between bowls. Garnish with parsley and lemon zest and serve.

Nutritional information: Calories 51; Total Carbs 12g; Net Carbs 8g; Protein 3g; Fat 3g; Sugar 4g; Fiber 4g

Corn on the Cob

Prep Time: 10 minutes. | Cook Time: 5 minutes. | Servings: 12

6 ears corn

Take off husks and silk from the corn. Cut or break each ear in half. Pour 1 cup water into the bottom of the pressure cooker. Insert a wire rack in it. Place the corn on the rack, cut-side down. Seal lid of the pressure cooker. Cook on high pressure for 5 minutes. When its complete, quickly release the pressure. Pull out the corn from the pot. Season with your favorite seasoning as desired and serve immediately.

Nutritional information: Calories 62; Total Carbs 14g; Net Carbs 10g; Protein 6g; Fat 3g; Sugar 1.5g; Fiber 1g

Baked Zucchini on Whole Wheat Bread

Prep time: 5 minutes . | Cook Time: 10 minutes | Serves 6

1 large zucchini, sliced into ¼-inch circle
¼ cup reduced fat, Parmesan cheese, grated fine
3 tablespoons low-fat milk
⅓ cup whole wheat breadcrumbs
½ teaspoon garlic powder
⅛ teaspoon cayenne pepper
Nonstick cooking spray

Using paper towels, pat zucchini dry after slicing. Allow for a 60-minute rest period before using. Then pat dry once again. Preheat the oven to 425 degrees Fahrenheit (220 degrees Celsius). Place a wire rack on a cookie sheet and coat the rack with cooking spray. Combine all Ingredients in a medium mixing basin, except the milk and zucchini. Fill a small basin halfway with milk. After dipping the zucchini in the milk, coat it with the bread crumb mixture. Bake 10 to 15 minutes, or until golden and crisp, on a wire rack. Serve right away.

Nutritional information: Calories 30; Total Carbs 3.1g; Net Carbs 2.1g; Protein 2.1g; Fat 11.0g; Sugar 1.0g; Fiber 0 g

Vegetable Rice Pilaf

Prep Time: 5 minutes. | Cook Time: 25 minutes. | Servings: 6

1 tablespoon olive oil
½ medium yellow onion, diced
1 cup uncooked long-grain brown rice
2 cloves minced garlic
½ teaspoon dried basil
Salt and pepper to taste
2 cups fat-free chicken broth
1 cup frozen mixed veggies

Heat the oil in a large skillet over medium heat. Add the onions and sauté for 3 minutes until translucent. Add the rice and cook until lightly browned. Add the garlic, basil, salt, and pepper and mix. Pour in the chicken broth and bring to a boil. Lower the heat, cover, and simmer for 10 minutes. Stir in frozen vegetables, cover, and cook for another 10 minutes, until heated through. Serve hot and enjoy.

Nutritional information: Calories 90; Total Carbs 2.2g; Net Carbs 1.5g; Protein 7g; Fat 4g; Sugar 0.5g; Fiber 0.8g

Roasted Veggies

Prep Time: 5 minutes. | Cook Time: 25 minutes. | Servings: 6

1 pound cauliflower florets
½ -pound broccoli florets
1 large yellow onion, cut into chunks
1 large red pepper, cored and chopped
2 medium carrots, peeled and sliced
2 tablespoons olive oil
2 tablespoons apple cider vinegar
Salt and pepper to taste

Preheat the oven to 425°F and place the parchment paper on a large baking sheet. Spread the vegetables on a baking sheet and sprinkle them with oil and vinegar. Mix well and season with salt and pepper. Put the vegetables in a single layer and bake for 20-25 minutes, stirring every 10 minutes, until tender. Adjust spices as per liking and serve hot.

Nutritional information: Calories 100; Total Carbs 12g; Net Carbs 8.2g; Protein 3.2g; Fat 5g; Sugar 5.5g; Fiber 4.2g

Parsley Tabbouleh

Prep Time: 5 minutes. | Cook Time: 25 minutes. | Servings: 6

1 cup water
½ cup bulgur
¼ cup fresh lemon juice
2 tablespoons olive oil
2 cloves minced garlic
Salt and pepper to taste
2 cups fresh chopped parsley
2 medium tomatoes, died
1 small cucumber, diced
¼ cup fresh chopped mint

Put the water and the bulgur in a small saucepan and bring to a boil, then remove from the heat. Cover with a lid and let stand 25 minutes until the water is completely absorbed. Meanwhile, whisk together lemon juice, olive oil, garlic, salt, and pepper in a medium bowl. Toss the cooked bulger with parsley, tomato, cucumber, and mint. Season with salt and pepper and season to taste.

Nutritional information: Calories 110; Total Carbs 14g; Net Carbs 10g; Protein 3g; Fat 5g; Sugar 2.4g; Fiber 3.9g

Root Vegetables with Balsamic

Prep Time: 25 minutes. | Cook Time: 25 minutes. | Servings: 3

2 Potatoes, cut into 1 ½-inch piece
2 Carrots, cut into 1 ½-inch piece
2 Parsnips, cut into 1 ½-inch piece
1 Onion, cut into 1 ½-inch piece
Pink Himalayan salt and ground black pepper, to taste
¼ teaspoon smoked paprika
1 teaspoon garlic powder
½ teaspoon dried thyme
½ teaspoon dried marjoram
2 tablespoons olive oil
2 tablespoons balsamic vinegar

Toss all Ingredients in a large mixing bowl. Roast the veggies in the preheated Air Fryer at 400°F for 10 minutes. Shake the basket and cook for 7 more minutes. Serve with some extra fresh herbs if desired. Bon appétit!

Nutritional information: Calories 405; Total Carbs 74g; Net Carbs 55g; Protein 7g; Fat 9g; Sugar 15g; Fiber 28g

Japanese Tempura Bowl

Prep Time: 20 minutes. | Cook Time: 10 minutes. | Servings: 3

1 cup all-purpose flour
Kosher salt and ground black pepper, to taste
½ teaspoon paprika
2 Eggs
3 tablespoons soda water
1 cup panko crumbs
2 tablespoons olive oil
1 cup green beans
1 Onion, cut into rings
1 Zucchini, cut into slices
2 tablespoons gluten-free tamari soy sauce
1 tablespoon mirin
1 teaspoon dashi granule

In a shallow bowl, combine the flour, salt, pepper, and paprika. In a bowl, whisk together the eggs and soda. In other shallow bowls, combine the panko breadcrumbs and olive oil. Dip the vegetables in the flour mixture, then in the egg mixture. Finally, roll over the Panko mixture to ensure a smooth layer. Shake the basket while cooking for 10 minutes at 400 ° F in a preheated air fryer. Combine the soy sauce, mirin, and dashi granules to make the sauce. Serve hot and enjoy.

Nutritional information: Calories 446; Total Carbs 63.5g; Net Carbs 45g; Protein 14.6g; Fat 14g; Sugar 3.8g; Fiber 12g

Braised Winter Vegetable

Prep Time: 25 minutes. | Cook Time: 10 minutes. | Servings: 2

4 Potatoes, peeled and cut into 1-inch pieces
1 Celery root, peeled and cut into 1-inch pieces
1 Cup winter squash
2 tablespoons unsalted butter, melted
½ Cup chicken broth
¼ Cup tomato sauce
1 teaspoon parsley
1 teaspoon rosemary
1 teaspoon thyme

Preheat the air fryer to 370 ° F. Add all the Ingredients to a small, greased casserole dish. Stir to combine well. In a preheated air fryer, gently stir the vegetables for 10 minutes, then increase the temperature to 400 ° F. Cook for another 10 minutes. Serve hot top with lemon juice on top and enjoy.

Nutritional information: Calories 358; Total Carbs 55g; Net Carbs 45g; Protein 7g; Fat 12g; Sugar 7g; Fiber 22g

Spiced Button Mushrooms

Prep Time: 10 minutes. | Cook Time: 12 minutes. | Servings: 4

1 tablespoon butter
2 teaspoons extra-virgin olive oil
2 pounds (907 g) button mushrooms, halved
2 teaspoons minced fresh garlic
1 teaspoon chopped fresh thyme
Sea salt and freshly ground black pepper, to taste

Heat butter and olive oil in a large skillet over medium heat. Add the mushrooms and sauté for 10 minutes until the mushrooms are lightly browned and cooked through. Add the garlic and thyme and cook for another 2 minutes. Season with salt and pepper and place on a plate.

Nutritional information: Calories 96; Total Carbs 8.2g; Net Carbs 4g; Protein 6.9g; Fat 6.1g; Sugar 3.9g; Fiber 1.7g

Peppery Bok Choy with Almonds

Prep Time: 15 minutes. | Cook Time: 7 minutes. | Servings: 4

2 teaspoons sesame oil
2 pounds (907 g) bok choy, cleaned and quartered
2 teaspoons low-sodium soy sauce
Pinch red pepper flakes
½ cup toasted sliced almonds

Add sesame oil to a large saucepan and heat over medium heat until hot. Fry the bok choy in hot oil for 5 minutes. Stir-fry them until tender and still crisp. Add soy sauce and red pepper powder and stir to combine evenly. Continue frying for 2 minutes. Transfer to a plate and garnish with toasted almonds.

Nutritional information: Calories 118; Total Carbs 7.9g; Net Carbs 4g; Protein 6.2g; Fat 7.8g; Sugar 3g; Fiber 4.1g

Carrots, Brown Rice, and Scrambled Egg

Prep Time: 15minutes. | Cook Time: 20 minutes. | Servings:4

1 tablespoon extra-virgin olive oil
1 bunch collard greens, stemmed and cut into chiffonade
1 carrot, cut into 2-inch matchsticks
1 red onion, thinly sliced
½ cup low-sodium vegetable broth
2 tablespoons coconut aminos
1 garlic clove, minced
1 cup cooked brown rice
1 large egg
1 teaspoon red pepper flakes
1 teaspoon paprika
Salt, to taste

In a Dutch oven or nonstick pan, heat the olive oil over medium heat until it shimmers. Add the collard greens and cook until wilted, about 4 minutes. In a Dutch oven, combine the carrots, onion, broth, coconut aminos, and garlic; cover and cook for 6 minutes, or until the carrots are soft. Cook the brown rice in the oven for 4 minutes. Throughout the cooking process, keep stirring. Break an egg over them, then heat and scramble it for 4 minutes, or until it's set. Before serving, remove from the fire and season with red pepper flakes, paprika, and salt. You may replace the coconut aminos with low-sodium soy sauce.

Nutritional information: Calories 154; Total Carbs 22g; Net Carbs 14g; Protein 6g; Fat 6g; Sugar 2g; Fiber 6g

Low Sugar Bok Choy Bowl

Prep Time: 15 minutes. | Cook Time: 7 minutes. | Servings: 4

2 teaspoons sesame oil
2 pounds (907 g) bok choy, cleaned and quartered
2 teaspoons low-sodium soy sauce
Pinch red pepper flakes
½ cup toasted sliced almonds

Place a large saucepan over medium heat and add the oil. Once the oil is hot, fry the bok choy for about 5 minutes until tender. Add the sauce and red pepper and sauté for another 2 minutes. Place the bok choy in a bowl and garnish with flaked almonds.

Nutritional information: Calories 119; Total Carbs 8g; Net Carbs 4g; Protein 6g; Fat 8g; Sugar 3g; Fiber 4g

Zucchini Tahini with Pepper Dip

Prep Time: 10 minutes. | Cook Time: 0 minutes. | Servings: 4

2 zucchinis, chopped
3 garlic cloves
2 tablespoons extra-virgin olive oil
2 tablespoons tahini
Juice of 1 lemon
½ teaspoon sea salt
1 red bell pepper, seeded and cut into sticks

In a food processor, combine the zucchini, garlic, olive oil, tahini, lemon juice, and salt. Blend until smooth puree formed. Serve with the red bell pepper and carrots for dipping.

Nutritional information: Calories 120; Total Carbs 6.9g; Net Carbs 3g; Protein 2.1g; Fat 11g; Sugar 4g; Fiber 2g

Asian Vegetable Noodle Salad

Prep time: 30 minutes. | Cooking time: 10 minutes. | Servings: 4

2 carrots, sliced thin
2 radishes, sliced thin
1 English cucumber, sliced thin
1 mango, julienned
1 bell pepper, julienned
1 serrano pepper, sliced thin
1 bag tofu shirataki fettuccini noodles
¼ cup lime juice
¼ cup basil, chopped
¼ cup cilantro, chopped
2 tablespoon mint, chopped
2 tablespoon Rice vinegar
2 tablespoon Sweet chili sauce
2 tablespoon Roasted peanuts chopped
1 tablespoon Splenda
½ teaspoon sesame oil

In a suitable bowl, add the radish, cucumbers, carrots, vinegar, coconut sugar, and lime juice, stir to coat the vegetables well. Cover and chill 15 20 minutes. For the noodles, remove the noodles from the package and rinse under cold water. Cut into

smaller pieces. Pat dry with paper towels. To assemble the salad. Remove the vegetables from the marinade, reserving marinade, and place in a suitable mixing bowl. Add noodles, mango, bell pepper, chili, and herbs. In a suitable bowl, combine 2 tablespoons of marinade with the chili sauce and sesame oil. Pour over salad and toss to coat. Top with peanuts and serve.

Nutritional information: Calories 158; Total Carbs 30g; Net Carbs 24g; Protein 4g; Fat 4g; Sugar 19g; Fiber 6g

Acorn Squash with Parmesan

Prep Time: 10 minutes. | Cook Time: 20 minutes. | Servings: 4

1 acorn squash (about 1 pound / 454 g)
1 tablespoon extra-virgin olive oil
1 teaspoon dried sage leaves, crumbled
¼ teaspoon freshly grated nutmeg
⅛ Teaspoon kosher salt
⅛ Teaspoon freshly ground black pepper
2 tablespoons freshly grated low-fat Parmesan cheese

Cut the acorn squash in half lengthwise and remove the seeds. Cut them into 4 wedges. Snap the stem off. In a small bowl, combine the olive oil, sage, nutmeg, salt, and pepper. Wipe down the cut sides of the pumpkin with the olive oil mixture. Pour 1 cup of water into the electric oven and put on a wire on it. Place the squash in a layer, skin inside, on the tripod. Close the pressure cooker lid. Adjust the valve to close. Cook 20 minutes over high heat. When cooking is complete, click Cancel and release pressure immediately. Carefully remove the squash from the pan, sprinkle with Parmesan, and serve.

Nutritional information: Calories 208; Total Carbs 10g; Net Carbs 5g; Protein 2.1g; Fat 10g; Sugar 0g; Fiber 2g

Autumn Cranberry Slaw

Prep time: 15 minutes. | Chill time: 2 hours. | Servings: 8

10 cup cabbage, shredded
½ red onion, diced fine
¾ cup Italian parsley, chopped
¾ cup almonds, slice and toasted
¾ cup dried cranberries
⅓ cup vegetable oil
¼ cup apple cider vinegar
2 tablespoon Sugar free maple syrup
4 teaspoon Dijon mustard
½ teaspoon salt
Salt and pepper, to taste

In a suitable bowl, whisk together vinegar, oil, syrup, Dijon, and ½ teaspoon salt. Add the onion and stir to combine. Let rest 10 minutes, or cover and refrigerate until ready to use. After 10 minutes, add remaining ingredients to the dressing mixture and toss to coat. Taste and season with salt and black pepper Cover and chill 2 hours before serving.

Nutritional information: Calories 133; Total Carbs 12g; Net Carbs 8g; Protein 2g; Fat 9g; Sugar 5g; Fiber 4g

Asian Slaw

Prep time: 5 minutes. | Chill time: 2 hours. | Servings: 8

1 lb. bag coleslaw mix
5 scallions, sliced
1 cup sunflower seeds
1 cup almonds, sliced
3 oz. ramen noodles, broken into small pieces
¾ cup vegetable oil
½ cup Splenda
⅓ cup vinegar

In a suitable bowl, combine coleslaw, sunflower seeds, almonds, and scallions. Whisk together the oil, vinegar, and Splenda in a large measuring cup. Pour over salad, and stir to combine. Stir in ramen noodles, cover, and chill 2 hours.

Nutritional information: Calories 354; Total Carbs 24g; Net Carbs 21g; Protein 5g; Fat 26g; Sugar 10g; Fiber 3g

Baked Potato Salad

Prep time: 15 minutes. | Cooking time: 15 minutes. | Servings: 8

2 lb. Cauliflower, separated into small florets
6-8 slices bacon, chopped and fried crisp
6 boiled eggs, cooled, peeled, and chopped
1 cup sharp cheddar cheese, grated
½ cup green onion, sliced
1 cup mayonnaise
2 teaspoon yellow mustard
1 ½ teaspoon onion powder
Salt and fresh-black pepper, to taste

Place cauliflower in a vegetable steamer, or a pot with a steamer insert, and steam 5-6 minutes. Drain the cauliflower and set aside. In a suitable bowl, whisk together mayonnaise, mustard, 1 teaspoon onion powder, salt, and pepper. Pat cauliflower dry with paper towels and place in a suitable mixing bowl. Add eggs, salt, pepper, remaining ½ teaspoon onion powder and dressing. Mix gently to combine ingredients together. Fold in the bacon, cheese, and green onion. Serve warm.

Nutritional information: Calories 247; Total Carbs 8g; Net Carbs 5g; Protein 17g; Fat 17g; Sugar 3g; Fiber 3g

Broccoli Bacon Salad

Prep time: 10 minutes. | Cook Time: 1 hour. | Servings: 4

2 cups broccoli, separated into florets
4 slices bacon, chopped and cooked crisp
½ cup cheddar cheese, cubed
¼ cup low-fat Greek yogurt
⅛ cup red onion, diced fine
⅛ cup almonds, sliced
¼ cup mayonnaise
1 tablespoon Lemon juice
1 tablespoon Apple cider vinegar
1 tablespoon Granulated sugar substitute
¼ teaspoon salt
¼ teaspoon black pepper

In a suitable bowl, combine broccoli, onion, cheese, bacon, and almonds. In another suitable bowl, whisk remaining ingredients together till combined. Pour dressing over broccoli mixture and stir. Cover and refrigerate for 1 hour. Serve.

Nutritional information: Calories 217; Total Carbs 12g; Net Carbs 10g; Protein 11g; Fat 14g; Sugar 6g; Fiber 2g

Broccoli Mushroom Salad

Prep time: 5 minutes. | Cook Time: 5 minutes. | Servings: 4

4 sun-dried tomatoes, cut in half
3 cup torn leaf lettuce
1 broccoli florets
1 cup mushrooms, sliced
⅓ cup radishes, sliced
2 tablespoon Water
1 tablespoon Balsamic vinegar
1 teaspoon vegetable oil
¼ teaspoon chicken bouillon granules
¼ teaspoon parsley
¼ teaspoon dry mustard
⅛ teaspoon cayenne pepper

Place tomatoes in a suitable bowl and pour boiling water over, just enough to cover. Let stand 5 minutes, drain. Chop tomatoes and place in a suitable bowl. Add lettuce, broccoli, mushrooms, and radishes. In a jar with a tight-fitting lid, add remaining ingredients and shake well. Pour over salad and toss to coat. Serve and enjoy.

Nutritional information: Calories 54; Total Carbs 9g; Net Carbs 7g; Protein 3g; Fat 2g; Sugar 2g; Fiber 2g

Baked Tomatoes and Navy Beans

Prep Time: 10 minutes. | Cook Time:25 minutes. | Servings:8

1 teaspoon extra-virgin olive oil
½ sweet onion, chopped
2 teaspoons minced garlic
2 sweet potatoes, peeled and diced
1 (28-ounce / 794-g) can low-sodium diced tomatoes
¼ cup sodium-free tomato paste
2 tablespoons granulated sweetener
2 tablespoons hot sauce
1 tablespoon Dijon mustard
3 (15-ounce / 425-g) cans sodium-free navy or white beans, drained
1 tablespoon chopped fresh oregano

In a large saucepan, heat the oil over medium-high heat.Sauté the onion and garlic for 3 minutes, or until transparent. Bring to a boil with the sweet potatoes, diced tomatoes, tomato paste, sweetener, spicy sauce, and mustard. Reduce the heat to low and allow the tomato sauce to simmer for 10 minutes. Stir in the beans and continue to cook for another 10 minutes. Serve with oregano on top.

Nutritional information: calories: 256 | fat: 2.1g | protein: 15.1g | carbs: 48.1g | fiber: 11.9g | sugar: 8.1g | sodium: 150mg

Kale Blackberry Salad

Prep time: 15 minutes. | Cooking time: 25 minutes. | Servings: 6

10 oz. Kale, deboned and chopped
1 blackberries
½ butternut squash, cubed
¼ cup reduced-fat goat cheese, crumbled
Maple mustard salad dressing
1 cup raw pecans
⅓ cup raw pumpkin seeds
¼ cup dried cranberries
3-½ tablespoons Olive oil
1 ½ tablespoon Sugar free maple syrup
⅜ teaspoon salt
Pepper, to taste
Nonstick cooking spray

At 400 degrees F, preheat your oven. Spray a baking sheet with cooking spray. Spread squash on the prepared pan, add 1 ½ tablespoons oil, ⅛ teaspoon salt, and pepper to squash and stir to coat the squash evenly. Bake 20-25 minutes. Place kale in a suitable bowl. Add 2 tablespoons oil and ½ teaspoon salt and massage it into the kale with your hands for 3-4 minutes.
Spray a clean baking sheet with cooking spray. In a suitable bowl, stir together pecans, pumpkin seeds, and maple syrup until nuts are coated. Pour onto prepared pan and bake 8-10 minutes; these can be baked at the same time as the squash. To assemble the salad: place all of the ingredients in a suitable bowl. Pour dressing over and toss to coat. Serve and enjoy.

Nutritional information: Calories 436; Total Carbs 24g; Net Carbs 17g; Protein 9g; Fat 37g; Sugar 5g; Fiber 7g

Lobster Roll Salad with Bacon

Prep time: 10 minutes. | Cooking time: 35 minutes. | Servings: 6

6 slices low-fat bacon
2 whole grain ciabatta rolls, halved horizontally
3 medium tomatoes, cut into wedges
2 (8 oz.) Spiny lobster tails, or frozen (thawed)
2 cups baby spinach
2 cups romaine lettuce, torn
1 cup seeded cucumber, diced
1 cup red sweet peppers, diced
2 tablespoons shallot, diced fine
2 tablespoons chives, diced fine
2 garlic cloves, diced fine
3 tablespoons White wine vinegar
3 tablespoons Olive oil

Heat a grill to medium heat, or medium heat charcoals. Rinse lobster and pat dry. Butterfly lobster tails. Place on the grill, cover and cook 25-30 minutes, or until meat is opaque. Remove lobster and let cool. In a suitable bowl, whisk together 2 tablespoons olive oil and garlic. Brush the rolls with oil mixture. Set them on grill, cut side down, and cook until crisp, about 2 minutes. Transfer to cutting board. While lobster is cooking, chop bacon and cook in a suitable skillet until crisp. Transfer to paper towels. Reserve 1 tablespoon of bacon grease. To make

the vinaigrette: combine reserved bacon grease, vinegar, shallot, remaining 1 tablespoons oil and chives in a glass jar with an air-tight lid. Remove the lobster meat carefully from the shells and cut into 1 ½-inch pieces. Cut rolls into 1-inch cubes. In a suitable salad bowl, toss spinach, romaine, tomatoes, cucumber, peppers, lobster, and bread cubes. Toss to combine. Transfer to a platter and drizzle with vinaigrette. Sprinkle bacon over top and serve.

Nutritional information: Calories 255; Total Carbs 18g; Net Carbs 16g; Protein 20g; Fat 11g; Sugar 3g; Fiber 2g

Mustard Potato Salad

Prep time: 15 minutes. | Cooking time: 5 minutes. | Servings: 8

2 pounds cauliflower, separated into small florets
1 boiled egg, peeled and diced
½ cup celery, diced
¼ cup red onion, diced
¼ cup light mayonnaise
1 tablespoon Pickle relish
1 tablespoon Dijon mustard
¼ teaspoon celery seed
¼ teaspoon black pepper

Place cauliflower in a vegetable steamer and cook 5 minutes, or until almost tender. Drain and let cool. In a suitable bowl, whisk together mayonnaise, relish, mustard, celery seed and pepper. Once cauliflower is cooled off, pat dry and place in a suitable bowl. Add egg, celery, and onion. Pour prepared dressing over vegetables and mix, gently to combine. Cover and chill at least 2 hours before serving.

Nutritional information: Calories 71; Total Carbs 9g; Net Carbs 6g; Net Carbs 2g; Protein 3g; Fat 3g; Sugar 4g; Fiber 3g

Zucchini Pasta Salad

Prep time: 45 minutes. | Chill time: 1 hour. | Servings: 5

5 oz. zucchini, spiralized
1 avocado, peeled and sliced
⅓ cup feta cheese, crumbled
¼ cup tomatoes, diced
¼ cup black olives, diced
⅓ cup green goddess salad dressing
1 teaspoon olive oil
1 teaspoon basil
salt and Black pepper, to taste

Place zucchini on a paper towel-lined cutting board. Sprinkle with a small bit of salt and let sit for almost 30 minutes to remove excess water. Add oil to a suitable skillet and heat over med-high heat. Add zucchini and cook, frequently stirring, until soft, about 3-4 minutes. Transfer zucchini to a suitable bowl and add remaining ingredients, except for the avocado. Cover and chill for almost 1 hour. Top with avocado, serve and enjoy.

Nutritional information: Calories 200; Total Carbs 7g; Net Carbs 4g; Protein 3g; Fat 18g; Sugar 2g; Fiber 3g

Spicy Baked Asparagus with Cashews

Prep Time: 10 minutes. | Cook Time: 20 minutes. | Servings: 4

2 pounds (907 g) asparagus, woody ends trimmed
1 tablespoon extra-virgin olive oil
Sea salt and freshly ground black pepper, to taste
½ cup chopped cashews
Zest and juice of 1 lime

Preheat the oven to 400 ºF. Place the baking sheet with foil. Toss asparagus with olive oil in a medium bowl. Season with salt and pepper. Place the asparagus on a baking sheet and bake for 15 to 20 minutes, or until lightly browned and soft. Remove the asparagus in a bowl from the oven. Add the cashews, lemon zest, and juice and mix well. Serve immediately.

Nutritional information: Calories 173; Total Carbs 43g; Net Carbs 20g; Protein 8g; Fat 11g; Sugar 5g; Fiber 4g

Gingery Eggplant with Green Onions

Prep Time: 10 minutes. | Cook Time: 40 minutes. | Servings: 4

1 large eggplant, sliced into 4ths
3 green onions, diced, green tips only
1 teaspoon fresh ginger, peeled and diced fine
¼ cup plus 1 teaspoon cornstarch
1½ tablespoons gluten-free tamari soy sauce
1½ tablespoons sesame oil
1 tablespoon vegetable oil
1 tablespoon fish sauce
2 teaspoons Splenda
¼ teaspoon salt

Place the eggplant on a paper towel and sprinkle with salt on both sides. Wait an hour to remove excess moisture. Pat dry with several paper towels. In a small bowl, add soy sauce, sesame oil, fish sauce, Splenda, and 1 teaspoon of cornstarch and mix. Use ¼ cup of cornstarch on both sides of the eggplant. Heat the oil in a large skillet over medium heat. Add ½ ginger and 1 green onion and place 2 eggplants on top. Gently shake both sides of the eggplant using ½ the sauce mixture. Cook 8 to 10 minutes per side. Repeat. Serve garnished with remaining green onions.

Nutritional information: Calories 156; Total Carbs 18.1g; Net Carbs 15g; Protein 2g; Fat 9g; Sugar 6g; Fiber 5g

Peppery Butternut Fritters

Prep Time: 15 minutes. | Cook Time: 15 minutes. | Servings: 6

5 cup butternut squash, grated
2 large eggs
1 tablespoon fresh sage, diced fine
⅔ cup flour
2 tablespoons olive oil
Salt and pepper, to taste

Heat the oil in a large saucepan over medium heat. In a large bowl, combine squash, eggs, sage, salt, and pepper to taste. Stir in the flour. Put ¼ cup of mixture in the pan and fry at least 1 inch. Cook until golden brown on both sides, about 2 minutes per side. Transfer to a plate lined with a tissue. repeat. Serve immediately with your favorite dip.

Nutritional information: Calories 165; Total Carbs 24g; Net Carbs 20g; Protein 4g; Fat 6g; Sugar 3g; Fiber 3g

Cauliflower Tater Tots

Prep Time: 25 minutes. | Cook Time: 10 minutes. | Servings: 4

1 lb. cauliflower floret
2 Eggs
1 tablespoon olive oil
2 tablespoons scallions, chopped
1 Garlic clove, minced
1 Cup low-fat Colby cheese, shredded
½ Cup breadcrumbs
Sea salt and ground black pepper, to taste
¼ teaspoon dried dill weed
1 teaspoon paprika

Blanch the cauliflower in salted boiling water for 3 to 4 minutes until al dente. Drain well and grind in a food processor. Add more Ingredients. Mix well. Shape the cauliflower mixture into small skewers. Spray the Air fryer basket with cooking spray. Bake in preheated 375 º F Air fryer for 16 minutes, shaking halfway. Use your favorite sauce to serve and Bon appétit!

Nutritional information: Calories 267; Total Carbs 9.6g; Net Carbs 4g; Protein 14g; Fat 19g; Sugar 2.9g; Fiber 3g

Herbed Brown Rice with Beans

Prep Time: 15 minutes. | Cook Time:15minutes. | Servings:8

2 teaspoons extra-virgin olive oil
½ sweet onion, chopped
1 teaspoon minced jalapeño pepper
1 teaspoon minced garlic
1 (15-ounce / 425-g) can sodium-free red kidney beans, rinsed and drained
1 large tomato, chopped
1 teaspoon chopped fresh thyme
Sea salt according to taste
freshly ground black pepper, to taste
2 cups cooked brown rice

In a large skillet, heat the olive oil over medium-high heat. Sauté the onion, jalapeo, and garlic for 3 minutes, or until softened. Combine the beans, tomato, and thyme in a mixing bowl. Cook, stirring occasionally, for about 10 minutes, or until completely cooked. Season with salt and pepper to taste. Serve with a side of warm brown rice.

Nutritional information: calories: 200 | fat: 2.1g | protein: 9.1g | carbs: 37.1g | fiber: 6.1g | sugar: 2.0g | sodium: 40mg

Sweet Corn Fritters with Avocado

Prep Time: 20 minutes. | Cook Time: 10 minutes. | Servings: 3

2 Cups sweet corn kernels
1 Small-sized onion, chopped
1 Garlic clove, minced
2 Eggs, whisked
1 teaspoon baking powder
2 tablespoons fresh cilantro, chopped
Sea salt and ground black pepper, to taste
1 Avocado, peeled, pitted, and diced
2 tablespoons sweet chili sauce

In a bowl, mix together the corn, onion, garlic, egg, baking powder, cilantro, salt, and pepper. Transfer the corn mixture into 6 patties and slowly transfer to an Air fryer basket. Bake 8 minutes in an air fryer to 370 ° F. Flip and cook for another 7 minutes. Serve the fritters with avocado and chili sauce.

Nutritional information: Calories 383; Total Carbs 42g; Net Carbs 20g; Protein 12g; Fat 21g; Sugar 9.2g; Fiber 4g

Sautéed Mushrooms

Prep Time: 10 minutes. | Cook Time: 10 minutes. | Servings: 4

1 tablespoon plant-based butter
2 teaspoons extra-virgin olive oil
2 pounds button mushrooms, halved
2 teaspoons minced fresh garlic
1 teaspoon chopped fresh thyme
Sea salt to taste
Freshly ground black pepper

Put the pan on medium heat and add the butter and olive oil. Sauté mushrooms, stirring occasionally, for 10 minutes until mushrooms are lightly caramelized and tender. Add the garlic and thyme and sauté for another 2 minutes. Season the mushrooms with salt and pepper before serving.

Nutritional information: Calories 97; Total Carbs 7g; Net Carbs 4g; Protein 6g; Fat 6g; Sugar 4g; Fiber 2g

Greek-Style Vegetable Bake

Prep Time: 35 minutes. | Cook Time: 10 minutes. | Servings: 4

1 Eggplant, peeled and sliced
2 Bell peppers, seeded and sliced
1 Red onion, sliced
1 teaspoon fresh garlic, minced
4 tablespoons olive oil
1 teaspoon mustard
1 teaspoon dried oregano
1 teaspoon smoked paprika
Salt and ground black pepper, to taste
1 Tomato, sliced
6 oz. halloumi cheese, sliced lengthways

First, preheat the air fryer to 370 ° F. Spray the roasting pan with nonstick spray. Place the eggplant, peppers, onions, and garlic in the bottom of the roasting pan. Add olive oil, mustard, and spices.

Transfer to a cooking basket and cook for 14 minutes. Garnish with tomatoes and cheese. Reduce heat to 390 ° F and cook for another 5 minutes until frothy. Cool for 10 minutes before eating. Bon appétit!

Nutritional information: Calories 296; Total Carbs 22g; Net Carbs 15g; Protein 9.3g; Fat 22g; Sugar 9.9g; Fiber 2g

Spiced Tofu with Spinach

Prep Time: 15 minutes. | Cook Time: 1 hour 25 minutes. | Servings: 4

1 package extra firm tofu, pressed 15 minutes, and cut into cubes
1 package fresh baby spinach
2 limes
1 tablespoon plant-based butter
½ cup plant-based butter
2 tablespoons lite soy sauce
3 cloves garlic, chopped fine
½ teaspoon ginger
¼ teaspoon red pepper flakes

Melt the plant-based butter in a large saucepan. Add the tofu and garlic and cook, stirring occasionally, for 5 to 10 minutes or until the beans are golden brown. Add the remaining spinach and bring to a boil. Lower the heat, cover, and cook, stirring occasionally, for 30 to 35 minutes. Add the spinach and cook for another 15 minutes. Serve hot and enjoy.

Nutritional information: Calories 326; Total Carbs 15g; Net Carbs 10g; Protein 18g; Fat 24g; Sugar 5g; Fiber 5g

Eggplant and Bulgur Pilaf with Basil

Prep Time: 10 minutes. | Cook Time:60 minutes. | Servings:4

1 tablespoon extra-virgin olive oil
½ sweet onion, chopped
2 teaspoons minced garlic
1 cup chopped eggplant
1½ cups bulgur
4 cups low-sodium chicken broth
1 cup diced tomato
Sea salt , to taste
freshly ground black pepper, to taste
2 tablespoons chopped fresh basil

Warm the oil in a big pan over medium heat.Sauté the onion and garlic for 3 minutes or until softened and transparent. Add the eggplant and cook for 4 minutes to soften it. Combine the bulgur, broth, and tomatoes in a mixing bowl. Bring the water to a boil in a kettle. Reduce the heat to low, cover, and cook for about 50 minutes, or until the water has been absorbed. Add salt and pepper to taste to the pilaf. Garnish with basil leaves and serve.

Nutritional information: calories: 300 | fat: 4.0g | protein: 14.0g | carbs: 54.0g | fiber: 12.0g | sugar: 7.0g | sodium: 358mg

Basil Caprese Salad

Prep time: 5 minutes. | Cook Time: 5 minutes. | Servings: 4

3 medium tomatoes, cut into 8 slices
2 (1-oz.) Slices mozzarella cheese, cut into strips
¼ cup basil, sliced thin
2 teaspoon olive oil
⅛ teaspoon salt
Pinch black pepper

Place tomatoes and cheese on serving plates. Sprinkle with salt and pepper. Drizzle oil over and top with basil. Serve.

Nutritional information: Calories 77; Total Carbs 4g; Net Carbs 2g; Protein 5g; Fat 5g; Sugar 2g; Fiber 1g

Pickled Cucumber Salad

Prep time: 10 minutes. | Cook Time: 0 minute. | Servings: 2

½ cucumber, peeled and sliced
¼ cup red onion, sliced thin
1 tablespoon olive oil
1 tablespoon white vinegar
1 teaspoon dill

Place all the recipe ingredients in a suitable bowl and toss to combine. Serve.

Nutritional information: Calories 79; Total Carbs 4g; Net Carbs 3g; Protein 1g; Fat 7g; Sugar 2g; Fiber 1g

Tomatoes and Red Kidney Beans

Prep Time: 10 minutes. | Cook Time: 12 minutes. | Servings:8

2 tablespoons olive oil
1 medium yellow onion, chopped
1 cup crushed tomatoes
2 garlic cloves, minced
2 cups low-sodium canned red kidney beans, rinsed
1 cup roughly chopped green beans
¼ cup low-sodium vegetable broth
1 teaspoon smoked paprika
Salt, to taste

In a nonstick skillet, heat the olive oil over medium heat until it shimmers. In a large mixing bowl, combine the onion, tomatoes, and garlic. Sauté for 3 to 5 minutes, or until the onion is transparent and fragrant. In a skillet, combine the kidney beans, green beans, and broth. Season with paprika and salt, then sauté until everything is nicely combined. Cook for 5 to 7 minutes, or until the vegetables are soft, covered in the skillet. Serve right away. Tip: You can replace the veggie broth with the same amount of water.

Nutritional information: Calories 187; Total Carbs 34g; Net Carbs 20g; Protein 13g; Fat 1g; Sugar 4g; Fiber 10g

Layered Lettuce Bacon Salad

Prep time: 10 minutes. | Cook Time: 0 minute. | Servings: 10

6 slices bacon, chopped and cooked crisp
2 tomatoes, diced
2 stalks celery, sliced
1 head romaine lettuce, diced
1 red bell pepper, diced
1 cup frozen peas, thawed
1 cup sharp cheddar cheese, grated
¼ cup red onion, diced fine
1 cup ranch dressing

Layer half the lettuce, pepper, celery, tomatoes, peas, onion, cheese, bacon, and dressing on a 9x13-inch glass baking dish. Repeat the layers. Serve or cover and chill until ready to serve.

Nutritional information: Calories 130; Total Carbs 14g; Net Carbs 12g; Protein 6g; Fat 6g; Sugar 5g; Fiber 2g

Cheese Coated Muffins

Prep Time: 10 minutes. | Cook Time: 20 minutes. | Servings: 4

4 egg whites
½ teaspoon fresh parsley, diced fine
3 tablespoons reduced fat Parmesan cheese, divided
2 teaspoons water
½ teaspoon salt
Truffle oil to taste
Nonstick cooking spray

Preheat the oven to 400 ºF (205 ºC). Grease two cups of muffins with cooking spray. In a small bowl, combine the egg whites, water, and salt until blended. In each muffin cup, pour the egg white mixture almost to the bottom. Sprinkle a little Parmesan cheese on each egg white. Cook for 10 to 15 minutes or until the edges are dark brown. Let cool in the pan for 3 to 4 minutes, then transfer to a small bowl and drizzle with truffle oil. Add parsley and ½ tablespoon Parmesan and toss to coat. Serve.

Nutritional information: Calories 47; Total Carbs 0g; Net Carbs 0g; Protein 4g; Fat 3g; Sugar 0g; Fiber 0g

Honeycrisp Apple Salad

Prep time: 10 minutes. | Cook Time: 5 minutes. | Servings: 10

12 oz. Salad greens
3 honey crisp apples, sliced thin
½ lemon
½ cup reduced-fat blue cheese, crumbled
Apple cider vinaigrette
1 cup pecan halves, toasted
¾ cup dried cranberries

Put the apple slices in a large plastic bag and squeeze the half lemon over them. Close the bag and shake to coat. In a suitable bowl, layer greens, apples, pecans, cranberries, and blue cheese. Just before serving, drizzle with enough vinaigrette to dress the salad. Toss to coat all the recipe ingredients evenly.

Nutritional information: Calories 291; Total Carbs 19g; Net Carbs 15g; Protein 5g; Fat 23g; Sugar 13g; Fiber 4g

Pecan Pear Salad

Total time: 15 minutes. | Servings: 8

10 oz. mixed greens
3 pears, chopped
½ cup light blue cheese, crumbled
2 cup pecan halves
1 cup dried cranberries
½ cup olive oil
6 tablespoons champagne vinegar
2 tablespoons Dijon mustard
¼ teaspoon salt

In a suitable bowl, combine greens, pears, cranberries, and pecans. Whisk remaining ingredients, except blue cheese, together in a suitable bowl, pour over salad and toss to coat. Serve topped with blue cheese crumbles.

Nutritional information: Calories 325; Total Carbs 20g; Net Carbs 14g; Protein 5g; Fat 26g; Sugar 10g; Fiber 6g

Yummy Bean and Veggie Cups

Prep Time: 10minutes. | Cook Time:05 minutes. | Servings:4

1 cup fat-free grated Parmesan cheese, divided
1 (15-ounce / 425-g) can low-sodium white beans, drained and rinsed
1 cucumber, peeled and finely diced
½ cup finely diced red onion
¼ cup thinly sliced fresh basil
1 garlic clove, minced
½ jalapeño pepper, diced
1 tablespoon extra-virgin olive oil
1 tablespoon balsamic vinegar
¼ teaspoon salt
Freshly ground black pepper, to taste

Over medium heat, heat a medium nonstick skillet. Spatula 2 tablespoons of cheese in the centre of the pan and spread out in a thin circle. When the cheese has melted, flip it over and lightly brown the other side with a spatula. Remove the cheese "pancake" from the pan and set it in the cup of a muffin tin, gently bending it to fit into the cup. Continue with the remaining cheese until you have a total of 8 cups. Toss together the beans, cucumber, onion, basil, garlic, jalapeo, olive oil, and vinegar in a mixing bowl, seasoning with salt and pepper. Just before serving, spoon the bean mixture into each cup.

Nutritional information: calories: 260 | fat: 12.1g | protein: 14.9 | carbs: 23.9g | fiber: 8.0g | sugar: 3.9g | sodium: 552mg

Pomegranate Brussels Sprouts Salad

Prep time: 10 minutes. | Cooking time: 10 minutes, serves; 6

3 slices bacon, cooked crisp and crumbled
3 cup brussels sprouts, shredded
3 cup kale, shredded
1pomegranate seeds
½ cup almonds, toasted and chopped
¼ cup reduced; Fat parmesan cheese, grated
Citrus vinaigrette

Combine all the recipe ingredients in a suitable bowl. Drizzle vinaigrette over salad, and toss to coat well. Serve garnished with more cheese if desired.

Nutritional information: Calories 256; Total Carbs 15g; Net Carbs 10g; Protein 9g; Fat 18g; Sugar 5g; Fiber 5g

Lime Yogurt Black Bean Soup with Tomatoes

Prep Time: 8 hours 10 minutes. | Cook Time: 1 hour 33 minutes. | Servings:8

2 tablespoons avocado oil
1 medium onion, chopped
1 (10-ounce / 284-g) can diced tomatoes and green chilies
1 pound (454 g) dried black beans, soaked in water for at least 8 hours, rinsed
1 teaspoon ground cumin
3 garlic cloves, minced
6 cups vegetable broth, or water
Kosher salt, to taste
1 tablespoon freshly squeezed lime juice
¼ cup plain Greek yogurt

In a nonstick skillet, heat the avocado oil over medium heat until it shimmers. Sauté for 3 minutes, or until the onion is transparent. In a large pot, combine the onion, tomatoes, green chilies, and their juices, black beans, cumin, garlic, broth, and salt. Stir everything together thoroughly. Bring to a boil over medium-high heat, then lower to a low setting. Cook for an hour and a half, or until the beans are tender. Meanwhile, in a small bowl, combine the lime juice and Greek yoghurt. Stir everything together thoroughly. Before serving, pour the soup into a large serving bowl and drizzle with lime yoghurt.

Nutritional information: Calories 285; Total Carbs 42g; Net Carbs 31g; Protein 19g; Fat 6g; Sugar 3g; Fiber 10g

Taco Salad

Prep time: 15 minutes. | Cooking time: 10 minutes. | Servings: 4

2 whole romaine hearts, chopped
1 lb. Lean ground beef
1 whole avocado, cubed
3 oz. Grape tomatoes halved
½ cup cheddar cheese, cubed
2 tablespoon Sliced red onion
½ batch tangy Mexican salad dressing
1 teaspoon ground cumin
Salt and Black pepper, to taste

Cook ground beef in a suitable skillet over medium heat. Break the beef up into small pieces as it cooks. Add seasonings and stir to combine. Drain grease and let cool for almost 5 minutes. To assemble the salad, place all the recipe ingredients into a suitable bowl. Toss to combine well, and the stir in the dressing. Top with sour cream and serve.

Nutritional information: Calories 449; Total Carbs 9g; Net Carbs 4g; Protein 40g; Fat 22g; Sugar 3g; Fiber 5g

Creamy Broccoli Salad

Prep time: 10 minutes. | Chill time: 1 hour. | Servings: 8

1 head broccoli, separated into florets
1 head cauliflower, separated into florets
1 red onion, sliced thin
2 cup cherry tomatoes, halved
½ cup Fat-free sour cream
1 cup lite mayonnaise
1 tablespoon Splenda

In a suitable bowl, combine vegetables. In a suitable bowl, whisk together mayonnaise, sour cream, and Splenda. Pour over vegetables and toss to mix. Cover and refrigerate for 1 hour. Serve.

Nutritional information: Calories 152; Total Carbs 12g; Net Carbs 10g; Protein 2g; Fat 10g; Sugar 5g; Fiber 2g

Grilled Vegetable Noodle Salad

Prep time: 15 minutes. | Cooking time: 10 minutes. | Servings: 4

2 ears corn-on-the-cob, husked
1 red onion, cut in ½-inch thick slices
1 tomato, diced fine
⅓ cup basil, diced
⅓ cup feta cheese, crumbled
1 homemade noodles, cook and drain
4 tablespoons Herb vinaigrette
Nonstick cooking spray

Heat grill to medium heat. Spray rack with cooking spray. Place corn and onions on the grill and cook, turning when needed, until lightly charred and tender, about 10 minutes. Slice the corn kernels off the cob and place them in a suitable bowl. Chop the onion and add to the corn. Stir in noodles, tomatoes, basil, and vinaigrette, toss to mix. Sprinkle cheese over the top and serve.

Nutritional information: Calories 330; Total Carbs 19g; Net Carbs 16g; Protein 10g; Fat 9g; Sugar 5g; Fiber 3g

Beans Chili

Prep Time: 20 minutes. | Cook Time:60 minutes. | Servings:8

1 teaspoon extra-virgin olive oil
1 sweet onion, chopped
1 red bell pepper, seeded and diced
1 green bell pepper, seeded and diced
2 teaspoons minced garlic
1 (28-ounce / 794-g) can low-sodium diced tomatoes
1 (15-ounce / 425-g) can sodium-free black beans, rinsed and drained
1 (15-ounce / 425-g) can sodium-free red kidney beans, rinsed and drained
1 (15-ounce / 425-g) can sodium-free navy beans, rinsed and drained
2 tablespoons chili powder
2 teaspoons ground cumin
1 teaspoon ground coriander
¼ teaspoon red pepper flakes

In a large saucepan, heat the oil over medium-high heat. Sauté the onion, red and green bell peppers, and garlic for about 5 minutes, or until the veggies have softened. Toss in the tomatoes, black beans, red kidney beans, navy beans, chilli powder, cumin, coriander, and red pepper flakes, as well as chilli powder, cumin, coriander, and red pepper flakes. Bring the chilli to a boil, then turn it down to a low heat. Cook, stirring occasionally, for at least one hour. Serve immediately.

Nutritional information: calories: 480 | fat: 28.1g | protein: 15.1g | carbs: 45.1g | fiber: 16.9g | sugar: 4.0g | sodium: 16mg

Walnut Apple Salad

Prep time: 5 minutes. | Cooking time: 15 minutes. | Servings: 4

2 green onions, diced
2 Medjool dates, pitted and diced
1 honey crisp apple, sliced thin
2 cup celery, sliced
½ cup celery leaves, diced
¼ cup walnuts, chopped
Maple shallot vinaigrette

At 375 degrees F, preheat your oven. Spread the chopped walnuts on a cookie sheet and bake 10 minutes, stirring every few minutes, to toast. In a suitable bowl, combine all the recipe ingredients and toss to mix. Drizzle vinaigrette over and toss to coat. Serve immediately.

Nutritional information: Calories 171; Total Carbs 25g; Net Carbs 21g; Protein 3g; Fat 8g; Sugar 15g; Fiber 4g

Kale and Carrots Soup

Prep Time: 8 minutes. | Cook Time: 14 minutes. | Servings:4

4 tablespoons extra-virgin olive oil
2 onions, finely chopped
2 carrots, chopped
2 cup chopped kale (stems removed)
6 garlic cloves, minced
2 cups canned lentils, drained and rinsed
2 cups unsalted vegetable broth
4 teaspoons dried rosemary (or 1 tablespoon chopped fresh rosemary)
1 teaspoon sea salt
½ teaspoons freshly ground black pepper

Heat the olive oil in a big pot over medium-high heat until it shimmers. Add the onion and carrot and cook for 3 minutes, stirring periodically, or until the vegetables soften. Cook for another 3 minutes after adding the kale. Cook, stirring regularly, for 30 seconds after adding the garlic. Add the lentils, vegetable broth, rosemary, salt, and pepper and stir to combine. After heating to a low boil, reduce to a low heat. Cook for an additional 5 minutes., stirring periodically.

Nutritional information: Calories 160; Total Carbs 19g; Net Carbs 0g; Protein 6g; Fat 7g; Sugar 15g; Fiber 6g

Watermelon Arugula Salad

Prep time: 10 minutes. | Chill time: 1 hour serves: 6

4 cups watermelon, cut in 1-inch cubes
3 cup arugula
1 lemon, zested
½ cup reduced-fat feta cheese, crumbled
¼ cup mint, chopped
1 tablespoon lemon juice
3 tablespoon olive oil
black pepper
salt to taste

Combine oil, zest, juice, and mint in a suitable bowl. Stir together. Add watermelon and gently toss to coat. Add remaining ingredients and toss to combine. Taste and adjust seasoning as desired. Cover and chill for 1 hour. when the time is up, serve and enjoy.

Nutritional information: Calories 148; Total Carbs 10g; Net Carbs 9g; Protein 4g; Fat 11g; Sugar 7g; Fiber 1g

Strawberry Spinach Avocado Salad

Total time: 10 minutes. | Cook Time: 0 minute. | Servings: 6

6 oz. Baby spinach
2 avocados, chopped
1 cup strawberries, sliced
¼ cup feta cheese, crumbled
Creamy poppy seed dressing
¼ cup almonds, sliced

Add spinach, berries, avocado, nuts, and cheese to a suitable bowl and toss to combine. Pour ½ recipe of creamy poppy seed dressing over salad and toss to coat. Add more dressing if desired. Serve.

Nutritional information: Calories 253; Total Carbs 19g; Net Carbs 13g; Protein 4g; Fat 19g sugar 9g; Fiber 6g

Cherry Tomato Corn Salad

Prep time: 10 minutes. | Chill time: 2 hours. | Servings: 8

2 avocados, cut into ½-inch cubes
1 pint cherry tomatoes, cut in half
2 cups corn kernels, cooked
½ cup red onion, diced fine
¼ cup cilantro, chopped
1 tablespoon lime juice
½ teaspoon lime zest
2 tablespoon Olive oil
¼ teaspoon salt
¼ teaspoon black pepper

In a suitable bowl, combine corn, avocado, tomatoes, and onion. In a suitable bowl, whisk together the remaining ingredients until combined. Pour over salad and toss to coat. Cover and chill 2 hours before serving.

Nutritional information: Calories 239; Total Carbs 20g; Net Carbs 13g; Net Carbs 2g; Protein 4g; Fat 18g; Sugar 4g; Fiber 7g

Quinoa with Fresh Vegetables

Prep Time: 15 minutes. | Cook Time: 30 minutes. | Servings:12

4 cups low-sodium vegetable broth
2 cups quinoa, well rinsed and drained
2 teaspoon extra-virgin olive oil
1 sweet onion, chopped
4 teaspoons minced garlic
1 large green zucchini, halved lengthwise and cut into half disks
2 red bell pepper, chopped into small strips after being sown
2 cup fresh or frozen corn kernels
2 teaspoon chopped fresh basil
Sea salt, to taste
Freshly ground black pepper, to taste

Place the veggie broth in a medium saucepan over medium heat. Bring the stock to a boil before stirring in the quinoa. Cover and reduce to a low heat setting. Cook for 20 minutes, or until the quinoa has absorbed all of the broth. It should be removed from the heat and left aside to cool. Heat the oil in a big skillet over medium-high heat while the quinoa is cooking. Sauté the onion and garlic for 3 minutes, or until softened and transparent. Sauté the zucchini, bell pepper, and corn for about 7 minutes, or until the vegetables are tender-crisp. Turn off the heat in the skillet. Stir in the cooked quinoa and basil until everything is well combined. Season with a touch of salt and pepper before serving.

Nutritional information: calories: 159 | fat: 3.0g | protein: 7.1g | carbs: 26.1g | fiber: 2.9g | sugar: 3.0g | sodium: 300mg

Mushroom and Rice Bowl with Hazelnuts

Prep Time: 20 minutes. | Cook Time:35minutes. | Servings:8

1 tablespoon extra-virgin olive oil
1 cup chopped button mushrooms
½ sweet onion, chopped
1 celery stalk, chopped
2 teaspoons minced garlic
2 cups brown basmati rice
4 cups low-sodium chicken broth
1 teaspoon chopped fresh thyme
Sea salt , to taste
freshly ground black pepper, to taste
½ cup chopped hazelnuts

Warm the oil in a big pan over medium heat. Sauté the mushrooms, onion, celery, and garlic for about 10 minutes, or until gently browned. Cook for another minute after adding the rice. Increase the heat to high and bring the chicken broth to a boil. Lower the heat to a low setting and cover the pot. Cook for about 20 minutes, or until the liquid has been absorbed and the rice is soft. Season with salt and pepper after adding the thyme. Sprinkle the hazelnuts over top and serve.

Nutritional information: calories: 240 | fat: 6.1g | protein: 7.1g | carbs: 38.9g | fiber: 0.9g | sugar: 1.1g | sodium: 388mg

Wild Rice with Blueberries

Prep Time: 15 minutes. | Cook Time:45minutes. | Servings:4

1 tablespoon extra-virgin olive oil
½ sweet onion, chopped
2½ cups sodium-free chicken broth
1 cup wild rice, rinsed and drained
Pinch sea salt
½ cup toasted pumpkin seeds
½ cup blueberries
1 teaspoon chopped fresh basil

Add the oil to a medium saucepan over medium-high heat. 3 minutes later, the onion should be softened and transparent. Bring the broth to a boil, gradually stirring. Reduce the heat to low and stir in the rice and salt. Cook for 40 minutes, or until the rice is cooked, covered. If necessary, drain any surplus broth. Combine the pumpkin seeds, blueberries, and basil in a mixing bowl. Warm the dish before serving.

Nutritional information: calories: 259 | fat: 9.1g | protein: 10.8g | carbs: 37.1g | fiber: 3.9g | sugar: 4.1g | sodium: 543mg

Savory Linguine with Pesto

Prep Time: 10 minutes. | Cook Time:20minutes. | Servings:6

½ cup shredded kale
½ cup fresh basil
½ cup sun-dried tomatoes
¼ cup chopped almonds
2 tablespoons extra-virgin olive oil
8 ounces (227 g) dry whole-wheat linguine
½ cup grated fat-free Parmesan cheese

In a food processor or blender, pulse the kale, basil, sun-dried tomatoes, almonds, and olive oil until a thick paste forms, about 2 minutes. Place the pesto in a mixing dish and set aside. Bring a big pot filled with water to a boil over high heat. Cook the pasta until it is al dente, as directed on the package. Drain the pasta and combine it with the pesto and Parmesan cheese in a large mixing bowl. Serve right away.

Nutritional information: calories: 218 | fat: 10.1g | protein: 9.1g | carbs: 25.1g | fiber: 1.1g | sugar: 2.9g | sodium: 195mg

Curried Black-Eyed Peas

Prep Time: 15minutes. | Cook Time:40 minutes. | Servings:12

1 pound (454 g) dried black-eyed peas, rinsed, and drained
4 cups vegetable broth
1 cup coconut water
1 cup chopped onion
4 large carrots, coarsely chopped
1½ tablespoons curry powder
1 tablespoon minced garlic
1 teaspoon peeled and minced fresh ginger
1 tablespoon extra-virgin olive oil
Kosher salt (optional)
Lime wedges, for serving

Combine the black-eyed peas, broth, coconut water, onion, carrots, curry powder, garlic, and ginger in an electric pressure cooker. Over the top, drizzle the extra virgin olive oil. Close and lock the pressure cooker's lid. To close the valve, turn it to the closed position. Cook for 25 minutes on high pressure. When the cooking is finished, press Cancel and let the pressure naturally release for 10 minutes before quick-releasing any leftover pressure. Unlock and remove the cover once the pin has dropped. If desired, season with salt and squeeze fresh lime juice over each serving.

Nutritional information: calories: 113 | fat: 3.1g | protein: 10.1g | carbs: 30.9g | fiber: 6.1g | sugar: 6.0g | sodium: 672mg

Kale, Squash, and Barley Risotto with Pistachio

Prep Time: 10 minutes. | Cook Time:15minutes. | Servings:6

1 teaspoon extra-virgin olive oil
½ sweet onion, finely chopped
1 teaspoon minced garlic
2 cups cooked barley
2 cups chopped kale
2 cups cooked butternut squash, cut into ½-inch cubes
2 tablespoons chopped pistachios
1 tablespoon chopped fresh thyme
Sea salt, to taste

Warm the oil in a big pan over medium heat. Sauté the onion and garlic for 3 minutes, or until softened and transparent. Stir in the barley and kale for about 7 minutes, or until the grains are heated through and the greens are wilted. Combine the squash, pistachios, and thyme in a mixing bowl. Season with salt and cook until the dish is heated, about 4 minutes.

Nutritional information: calories: 160 | fat: 1.9g | protein: 5.1g | carbs: 32.1g | fiber: 7.0g | sugar: 2.0g | sodium: 63mg

Flavorful Wax Beans

Prep Time: 05 minutes. | Cook Time:15 minutes. | Servings:4

2 pounds (907 g) wax beans
2 tablespoons extra-virgin olive oil
Sea salt, to taste
Freshly ground black pepper, to taste
Juice of ½ lemon

Preheat the oven to 400 degrees Fahrenheit (205 degrees Celsius). A baking pan should be lined with aluminium foil. Toss the beans with the olive oil in a large mixing dish. According to taste, season with salt and pepper. Place the beans on the baking pan and evenly distribute them. Roast the beans for 10 to 12 minutes, or until they are caramelised and soft. Serve the beans on a serving plate with a squeeze of lemon juice.

Nutritional information: calories: 99 | fat: 7.1g | protein: 2.1g | carbs: 8.1g | fiber: 4.2g | sugar: 3.9g | sodium: 814mg

Navy Beans with Pico de Gallo

Prep Time: 20 minutes. | Cook Time:00 minutes. | Servings:4

2½ cups cooked navy beans
1 tomato, diced
½ red bell pepper, seeded and chopped
¼ jalapeño pepper, chopped
1 scallion, white and green parts, chopped
1 teaspoon minced garlic
1 teaspoon ground cumin
½ teaspoon ground coriander
½ cup low-sodium feta cheese

In a medium mixing bowl, combine the beans, tomato, bell pepper, jalapeo, scallion, garlic, cumin, and coriander. Serve with feta cheese on top.

Nutritional information: calories: 225 | fat: 4.1g | protein: 14.1g | carbs: 34.1g | fiber: 13.1g | sugar: 3.9g | sodium: 165mg

Avocado and Farro

Prep Time: 05minutes. | Cook Time:25 minutes. | Servings:4

3 cups water
1 cup uncooked farro
1 tablespoon extra-virgin olive oil
1 teaspoon ground cumin
½ teaspoon salt
½ teaspoon freshly ground black pepper
4 hardboiled eggs, sliced
1 avocado, sliced
⅓ cup plain low-fat Greek yogurt
4 lemon wedges

In a medium saucepan over high heat, bring the water to a boil.Pour the boiling water over the farro and whisk to fully submerge the grains. Cook for another 20 minutes after lowering the heat to medium-low. Drain and set aside the water. Over medium-low heat, heat a medium skillet. Pour in the oil when the pan is heated, then add the farro, cumin, salt, and pepper. Cook, stirring periodically, for 3 to 5 minutes. Top each portion of farro with one-quarter of the eggs, avocado, and yoghurt. Serve with a squeeze of lemon on top of each serving.

Nutritional information: calories: 333 | fat: 16.1g | protein: 15.1g | carbs: 31.9g | fiber: 7.9g | sugar: 2.0g | sodium: 360mg

Traditional Texas Caviar

Prep Time: 10 minutes. | Cook Time:00 minutes. | Servings:6

For the Salad:
1 ear fresh corn, kernels removed
1 cup cooked lima beans
1 cup cooked black-eyed peas
1 red bell pepper, chopped
2 celery stalks, chopped
½ red onion, chopped
For the Dressing:
3 tablespoons apple cider vinegar
1 teaspoon paprika
2 tablespoons extra-virgin olive oil

In a large mixing basin, combine the corn, beans, peas, bell pepper, celery, and onion. Stir everything together thoroughly. In a small bowl, combine the vinegar, paprika, and olive oil. Stir everything together thoroughly. Toss the salad in the dressing to evenly distribute it. Allow it infuse for 20 minutes before serving.

Nutritional information: Calories 170; Total Carbs 29g; Net Carbs 15g; Protein 10g; Fat 6g; Sugar 4g; Fiber 10g

Black Beans with Dandelion and Beet Greens

Prep Time: 9 minutes. | Cook Time:14 minutes. | Servings:4

1 tablespoon olive oil
½ Vidalia onion, thinly sliced
1 bunch dandelion greens, cut into ribbons
1 bunch beet greens, cut into ribbons
½ cup low-sodium vegetable broth
1 (15-ounce) can no-salt-added black beans
Salt, to taste
Freshly ground black pepper, to taste

In a nonstick skillet, heat the olive oil over low heat until it shimmers. Cook for 3 minutes, or until the onion is clear. In a skillet, combine the dandelion and beet greens with the broth. Cook, covered, for 8 minutes, or until the spinach has wilted. Cook for 4 minutes, or until the black beans are tender. Season to taste with salt and pepper. Stir everything together thoroughly. Serve right away.

Nutritional information: Calories 161; Total Carbs 26g; Net Carbs 17g; Protein 9g; Fat 4g; Sugar 1g; Fiber 10g

Chickpea Spaghetti Bolognese

Prep Time: 05 minutes. | Cook Time:25 minutes. | Servings:4

1 (3- to 4-pound / 1.4- to 1.8-kg) spaghetti squash
½ teaspoon ground cumin
1 cup no-sugar-added spaghetti sauce
1 (15-ounce) can low-sodium chickpeas, drained and rinsed
6 ounces (170 g) extra-firm tofu

Preheat the oven to 400 degrees Fahrenheit (205 degrees Celsius). Squash should be cut in half lengthwise. Scoop out the seeds and toss them away. Season both sides of the squash with cumin and set cut-side down on a baking pan. Cook for 25 minutes at 350°F. Meanwhile, simmer the spaghetti sauce and chickpeas in a medium skillet over low heat. Squeeze off any excess water by pressing the tofu between two layers of paper towels. Cook for 15 minutes after crumbling the tofu into the sauce. Remove the squash from the oven and comb thin strands of flesh through each half with a fork. Divide the "spaghetti" into four sections and drizzle one-quarter of the sauce over each.

Nutritional information: Calories 276; Total Carbs 41.9g; Net Carbs 24.8g; Protein 7g; Fat 7.1g; Sugar 7g; Fiber 10.1g

Garlic Zucchini and Chicken Soup

Prep Time: 8 minutes. | Cook Time:14 minutes. | Servings:4

2 tablespoons extra-virgin olive oil
12 ounces (336 g) chicken breast, chopped
1 onion, chopped
2 carrots, chopped
2 celery stalks, chopped
2 garlic cloves
6 cups unsalted chicken broth
1 teaspoon dried thyme
1 teaspoon sea salt
2 medium zucchinis cut into noodles (or store-bought zucchini noodles)

In a large pot, warm the olive oil over medium-high heat until it shimmers. Add the chicken and simmer for 5 minutes, or until it is opaque. Remove the chicken from the saucepan with a slotted spoon and place it on a plate. In a large pot, combine the onion, carrots, and celery. Cook, stirring periodically, for about 5 minutes, or until the vegetables are tender. Add the garlic and simmer for 30 seconds, stirring regularly. Combine the chicken stock, thyme, and salt in a large mixing bowl. Stir to a boil, then reduce to a low heat. Return the chicken to the pan with the zucchini and any liquids that have gathered on the dish. Cook for another 1 to 2 minutes, stirring periodically, until the zucchini noodles are tender.

Nutritional information: Calories 236; Total Carbs 11g; Net Carbs 1.6g; Protein 27g; Fat 10g; Sugar 17.3g; Fiber 3g

Black Bean Fritters

Prep Time: 10 minutes. | Cook Time:25 minutes. | Servings: 20

1¾ cups all-purpose flour
½ teaspoon cumin
2 teaspoons baking powder
2 teaspoons salt
½ teaspoon black pepper
4 egg whites, lightly beaten
1 cup salsa
2 (16-ounce / 454-g) cans no-salt-added black beans, rinsed, and drained
1 tablespoon canola oil, plus extra if needed

In a large mixing bowl, combine the flour, cumin, baking powder, salt, and pepper, then add the egg whites and salsa. Stir in the black beans until everything is fully combined. In a nonstick skillet, heat the canola oil over medium-high heat. To make a fritter, put 1 teaspoon of the mixture into the skillet. Make extra fritters to cover the skillet's bottom. Maintain a small gap between each pair of fritters. To avoid overpopulation, you may need to work in bunches. Cook for 3 minutes, or until both sides of the fritters are golden brown. Halfway through the cooking time, flip the fritters and flatten using a spatula. Rep with the rest of the mixture. As needed, add more oil. Serve right away.

Nutritional information: Calories 115; Total Carbs 20g; Net Carbs 13g; Protein 6g; Fat 1g; Sugar 2g; Fiber 5g

Savory Sofrito Dumplings

Prep Time: 20 minutes. | Cook Time:15 minutes. | Servings:10

4 cups water
4 cups low-sodium vegetable broth
1 cup cassava flour
1 cup gluten-free all-purpose flour
2 teaspoons baking powder
1 teaspoon salt
1 cup fat-free milk
2 tablespoons bottled chimichurri or sofrito

Bring the water and broth to a slow boil in a large pot over medium-high heat. Whisk together the cassava flour, all-purpose flour, baking powder, and salt in a large mixing basin. Whisk the milk and chimichurri together in a small bowl until smooth. Combine the wet Ingredients in a mixing bowl. Place the dry Ingredients in a large mixing bowl. A bit at a time until a firm dough is formed. Pinch off a tiny piece of dough with clean hands. Form a disc by rolling the dough into a ball and gently flattening it in the palm of your hand. Repeat till there is no more dough. Insert a fork into the dumpling to check for doneness; it should come out clean. Warm the dish before serving.

Nutritional information: Calories 133; Total Carbs 25.9g; Net Carbs 20.7g; Protein 4.1g; Fat 1.1g; Sugar 2.0g; Fiber 3.2g

Black Bean and Corn Soup

Prep Time: 10 minutes. | Cook Time:25 minutes. | Servings:7

2 tablespoons olive oil
½ onion, diced
1 pound boneless and skinless chicken breast, cut into ½-inch cubes
½ teaspoon Adobo seasoning, divided
¼ teaspoon black pepper
1 (15-ounce) can washed and drained black beans with no salt added
1 (14.5-ounce) can fire-roasted tomatoes
½ cup frozen corn
½ teaspoon cumin
1 tablespoon chili powder
5 cups low-sodium chicken broth

Heat the olive oil in a stockpot over medium-high heat until it shimmers. Sauté the onion for 3 minutes, or until it is transparent. Spread the Adobo seasoning and pepper over the chicken breasts. Cook for 6 minutes, or until gently browned, with the lid on. Halfway through the cooking period, give the pot a good shake. Combine the remaining Ingredients in a mixing bowl. Reduce to a low heat and continue to cook for another 15 minutes, or until the black beans are tender. Serve right away. To make your own Adobo seasoning, combine paprika, black pepper, onion powder, dried oregano, cumin, garlic powder, chilli powder, and salt.

Nutritional information: Calories 170; Total Carbs 15g; Net Carbs 7g; Protein 20g; Fat 3.6g; Sugar 3g; Fiber 5g

Lime Yogurt Chili Soup with Tomatoes

Prep Time: 8 hours10 minutes. | Cook Time:1 hour 33 minutes. | Servings:8

2 tablespoons avocado oil
1 medium onion, chopped
1 (10-ounce / 284-g) can diced tomatoes and green chilies
1 pound (454 g) dried black beans, soaked in water for at least 8 hours, rinsed
1 teaspoon ground cumin
3 garlic cloves, minced
6 cup vegetable broth, or water
Kosher salt, to taste
1 tablespoon freshly squeezed lime juice
¼ cup low-fat Greek yogurt

In a nonstick skillet, heat the avocado oil over medium heat until it shimmers. Cook for 3 minutes, or until the onion is clear. In a large pot, combine the onion, tomatoes, green chilies, and their juices, black beans, cumin, garlic, broth, and salt. Stir everything together thoroughly. Bring to a boil over medium-high heat, then lower to a low setting. Cook for 1 hour and 30 minutes, or until the beans are soft. Meanwhile, in a small bowl, combine the lime juice and Greek yoghurt. Stir everything together thoroughly. Before serving, pour the soup into a large serving bowl and drizzle with lime yoghurt.

Nutritional information: Calories 285; Total Carbs 42g; Net Carbs 29g; Protein 19g; Fat 6g; Sugar 3g; Fiber 10g

Black Beans and Low-Sodium Veggie Greens

Prep Time: 10 minutes. | Cook Time:15minutes. | Servings:4

1 tablespoon olive oil
½ Vidalia onion, thinly sliced
1 bunch dandelion greens cut into ribbons
1 bunch beet greens, cut into ribbons
½ cup low-sodium vegetable broth
1 (15-ounce / 425-g) can no-salt-added black beans
Salt and freshly ground black pepper, to taste

In a nonstick skillet, heat the olive oil over low heat until it shimmers. Sauté the onion for 3 minutes, or until it is transparent. In a skillet, combine the dandelion and beet greens, as well as the broth. Cook, covered, for 8 minutes, or until the spinach has wilted. Simmer for 4 minutes, or until the black beans are tender. Season to taste with salt and pepper. Stir everything together thoroughly. Serve right away.

Nutritional information: Calories 161; Total Carbs 26g; Net Carbs 15g; Protein 9g; Fat 4g; Sugar 1g; Fiber 10g

Greens and Beans

Prep Time: 9 minutes. | Cook Time:14 minutes. | Servings:4

1 tablespoon olive oil
½ Vidalia onion, thinly sliced
1 bunch dandelion greens, cut into ribbons
1 bunch beet greens, cut into ribbons

½ cup low-sodium vegetable broth
1 (15-ounce) can no-salt-added black beans
Salt, to taste
Freshly ground black pepper, to taste

In a nonstick skillet, heat the olive oil over low heat until it shimmers. Sauté the onion for 3 minutes, or until it is transparent. In a skillet, combine the dandelion and beet greens, as well as the broth. Cook, covered, for 8 minutes, or until the spinach has wilted. Simmer for 4 minutes, or until the black beans are tender. Season to taste with salt and pepper. Stir everything together thoroughly. Serve right away.
Tips: Replace the beet greens or dandelion greens with collard greens, spinach, arugula, or Swiss chard.

Nutritional information: Calories 161; Total Carbs 26g; Net Carbs 5g; Protein 9g; Fat 4g; Sugar 1g; Fiber 10g

Stuffed Kale Wrap

Prep Time: 10 minutes. | Cook Time:00 minutes. | Servings: 4

1 teaspoon Dijon mustard
1 tablespoon chopped fresh dill
½ teaspoon sea salt
¼ teaspoon paprika
4 hard-boiled large eggs, chopped
1 cup shelled fresh peas
2 tablespoons finely chopped red onion
4 large kale leaves

Combine mustard, dill, salt, and paprika in a medium mixing basin. Add the eggs, peas, and onion and stir to combine. Serve with kale leaves wrapped around it.

Nutritional information: Calories 295; Total Carbs 18g; Net Carbs 10.3g; Protein 17g; Fat 18g; Sugar 3.7g; Fiber 4g

Kidney Beans Bowl

Prep Time: 10 minutes. | Cook Time: 12minutes. | Servings:8

2 tablespoons olive oil
1 medium yellow onion, chopped
1 cup crushed tomatoes
2 garlic cloves, minced
2 cups low-sodium canned red kidney beans, rinsed
1 cup roughly chopped green beans
¼ cup low-sodium vegetable broth
1 teaspoon smoked paprika
Salt, to taste

In a nonstick skillet, warm the olive oil over medium heat until it shimmers. In a large mixing bowl, combine the onion, tomatoes, and garlic. Sauté for 3 to 5 minutes, or until the onion is transparent and fragrant. In a skillet, combine the kidney beans, green beans, and broth. Season with paprika and salt, then sauté until everything is nicely combined. Cook for 5 to 7 minutes, or until the vegetables are soft, covered in the skillet. Serve right away.

Nutritional information: Calories187; Total Carbs 34g; Net Carbs 20g; Protein 13g; Fat 1g; Sugar 4g; Fiber 10g

Carolina Green Beans

Prep Time: 08 minutes. | Cook Time: 28 minutes. | Servings:8

1 pound (454 g) green beans, trimmed, cut into bite-size pieces
3 tablespoons extra-virgin olive oil, divided
8 ounces / 227-g brown mushrooms, diced
3 garlic cloves, minced
1½ tablespoons whole-wheat flour
1 cup low-sodium vegetable broth
1 cup unsweetened plain almond milk
¼ cup almond flour
2 tablespoons dried minced onion

Preheat the oven to 400 degrees Fahrenheit (205 degrees Celsius). Bring a big saucepan of water to a rolling boil. Cook the green beans for 3 to 5 minutes, or until they are just barely soft but bright green. Drain the water and set it aside. Once the 2 tablespoons oil is heated in a medium skillet over medium-high heat, toss in the mushrooms and toss to combine. Cook for 3 to 5 minutes, or until the mushrooms are golden brown and liquid has evaporated. Stir in the garlic for approximately 30 seconds, or until it is barely aromatic. Stir in the whole-wheat flour until everything is fully combined. Add the broth and simmer for 1 minute. Reduce the heat to a low setting and stir in the almond milk. Return to a low heat and cook for 5–7 minutes, or until the sauce has thickened. Turn off the heat. Stir with the green beans and then turn on the heat. Mix the almond flour, the remaining 1 tablespoon of olive oil, and the dried onion minces in a small bowl until well combined. Then Sprinkle over the beans. Cook for 12 to 20 minutes until it is bubbling and browned.

Nutritional information: Calories 241; Total Carbs 7.1g; Net Carbs 0.1g; Protein 7g; Fat 20g; Sugar 3.4g; Fiber 4.8g

Black Eyed Beans and Rice Bowl

Prep Time: 14 minutes. | Cook Time: 45 minutes. | Servings:8

1 tablespoon canola oil
2 celery stalks, thinly sliced
1 small yellow onion, chopped
1 medium green bell pepper, chopped
1 tablespoon tomato paste
2 garlic cloves, minced
2 cups brown rice, rinsed
5 cups low-sodium vegetable broth, divided
2 bay leaves
1 teaspoon smoked paprika
1 teaspoon Creole Seasoning
1¼ cups frozen black-eyed peas

In a Dutch oven, warm the canola oil over medium heat. Then add onion, celery, tomato paste, garlic, and bell pepper in the oven. Cook, stirring frequently, for 3 to 5 minutes, or until the celery, onion, bell pepper, tomato paste, and garlic are softened. Combine the rice, 4 cups broth, bay leaves, paprika, and Creole seasoning in a large mixing bowl. Reduce the heat to low, cover, and cook for 30 minutes, or until the rice is tender. Add the remaining 1 cup of broth and the black-eyed peas. Cook for 12 minutes, or until the peas soften, stirring occasionally. Remove the bay leaves and toss them out. Enjoy with Broccoli Stalk Slaw.

Nutritional information: Calories 185; Total Carbs 35.6g; Net Carbs 26.8g; Protein 4.6g; Fat 3.3g; Sugar 5.8g; Fiber 3g

Summer Vegetables with Green Lentils

Prep Time: 15 minutes. | Cook Time:00 minutes. | Servings:4

3 tablespoons extra-virgin olive oil
2 tablespoons balsamic vinegar
2 teaspoons chopped fresh basil
1 teaspoon minced garlic
Sea salt, according to taste
freshly ground black pepper, according to taste
2 (15-ounce / 425-g) cans sodium-free green lentils, rinsed and drained
½ English cucumber, diced
2 tomatoes, diced
½ cup halved Kalamata olives
¼ cup chopped fresh chives
2 tablespoons pine nuts

In a medium mixing bowl, combine the olive oil, vinegar, basil, and garlic. Salt & pepper to taste. Combine the lentils, cucumber, tomatoes, olives, and chives in a large mixing bowl. Serve with pine nuts as a garnish.

Nutritional information: calories: 400 | fat: 15.1g | protein: 19.8g | carbs: 48.8g | fiber: 18.8g | sugar: 7.1g | sodium: 439mg

Shrimp Avocado Salad

Prep time: 20 minutes. | Cooking time: 5 minutes. | Servings: 4

½ lb. Raw shrimp, peeled and deveined
3 cups romaine lettuce, chopped
1 cup napa cabbage, chopped
1 avocado, pit removed and sliced
¼ cup red cabbage, chopped
¼ cucumber, julienned
2 tablespoon Green onions, diced fine
2 tablespoon cilantro, diced
1 teaspoon ginger, diced fine
2 tablespoon Coconut oil
1 tablespoon Sesame seeds
1 teaspoon Chinese five-spice
Fat-free ranch dressing

Toast sesame seeds in a suitable skillet over medium heat. Shake the skillet to prevent them from burning. Cook until they start to brown, about 2 minutes. Set aside. Add the coconut oil to the skillet. Pat the shrimp dry and sprinkle with the five-spice. Add to hot oil. Cook for 2 minutes per side, or until they turn pink. Set aside. Arrange lettuce and cabbage on a serving platter. Top with green onions, cucumber, and cilantro. Add shrimp and avocado. Drizzle with the desired amount of dressing and sprinkle sesame seeds over the top. Serve.

Nutritional information: Calories 306; Total Carbs 20g; Net Carbs 15g; Protein 15g; Fat 19g; Sugar 4g; Fiber 5g

Pepperoni Pita

Prep Time: 10 minutes. | Cook Time:00 minutes. | Servings:2

½ cup tomato sauce
½ teaspoon oregano
½ teaspoon garlic powder
½ cup chopped black olives
2 canned artichoke hearts, drained and chopped
2 ounces pepperoni, chopped
½ cup shredded low-fat mozzarella cheese
1 whole-wheat pita, halved

Combine the tomato sauce, oregano, and garlic powder in a medium mixing basin. Combine the olives, artichoke hearts, pepperoni, and cheese in a mixing bowl. To blend, stir everything together. Spoon the mixture into the pita halves and fold them in half.

Nutritional information: Calories 376; Total Carbs 27g; Net Carbs 3.2g; Protein 17g; Fat 23g; Sugar 17.8g; Fiber 6g

Lettuce Wraps with Chestnuts

Prep Time: 10 minutes. | Cook Time:00 minutes. | Servings:2

1 tablespoon freshly squeezed lemon juice
1 teaspoon curry powder
1 teaspoon reduced-sodium soy sauce
½ teaspoon sriracha (or to taste)
½ cup drained and sliced canned water chestnuts
2 (2.6-ounce/73.7 g) package tuna packed in water, drained
2 large butter lettuce leaves

Combine the lemon juice, curry powder, soy sauce, and sriracha in a medium mixing bowl. Combine the water chestnuts and tuna in a mixing bowl. To blend, stir everything together. Wrap the lettuce leaves around the meat and serve.

Nutritional information: Calories 271; Total Carbs 18g; Net Carbs 6.9g; Protein 19g; Fat 14g; Sugar 8.1g; Fiber 3g

Veggie Macaroni Pie

Prep Time: 15 minutes. | Cook Time: 30 minutes. | Servings:6

1 (1-pound / 454-g) package whole-wheat macaroni
2 celery stalks, thinly sliced
1 small yellow onion, chopped
2 garlic cloves, minced
Salt, to taste
¼ teaspoon freshly ground black pepper
2 tablespoons chickpea flour
2 cups grated reduced-fat sharp Cheddar cheese
1 cup fat-free milk
2 large zucchinis, finely grated and squeezed dry
2 roasted red peppers, ¼-inch pieces, chopped

Preheat the oven to 350 degrees Fahrenheit (180 degrees Celsius). Bring a pot of water to a boil, then add the macaroni and cook until al dente, about 4 minutes. Drain the macaroni and place it in a big mixing dish. 1 cup of the macaroni water should be set aside. In an oven-safe skillet, heat the macaroni water over medium heat. In a large skillet, sauté the celery, onion, garlic, salt, and black pepper for 4 minutes, or until soft. Fold in the cheese and milk after gently mixing in the chickpea flour. Whisk the liquid until it is thick and smooth. Combine the cooked macaroni, zucchini, and red peppers in a large mixing bowl. Stir everything together thoroughly. Preheat the oven to 350°F and cover the skillet with aluminum foil. Bake for 15 minutes, or until the cheese has melted, then remove the foil and bake for another 5 minutes, or until the top is lightly browned. Get the pie out of the oven and serve right away. Tip: To make this meal gluten-free, substitute the macaroni with organic quinoa pasta.

Nutritional information: Calories 378; Total Carbs 67g; Net Carbs 53g; Protein 24g; Fat 4g; Sugar 6g; Fiber 8g

Baby Spinach Salad with Walnuts

Prep Time: 8 minutes. | Cook Time: 00minutes. | Servings:2

4 cups baby spinach
½ pear, cored, peeled, and chopped
¼ cup whole walnuts, chopped
2 tablespoons apple cider vinegar
2 tablespoons extra-virgin olive oil
1 teaspoon peeled and grated fresh ginger
½ teaspoon Dijon mustard
½ teaspoon sea salt

In the bottom of two mason jars, layer the spinach. Add the pear and walnuts on top. Combine the vinegar, oil, ginger, mustard, and salt in a small bowl. Place in a closed container. Before serving, give the dressing a good shake and pour it into the mason jars. To evenly distribute the dressing, close the jars and shake them.

Nutritional information: Calories 254; Total Carbs 18g; Net Carbs 6g; Protein 4g; Fat 23g; Sugar 7g; Fiber 4g

Green Beans with Onion

Prep Time: 8 minutes. | Cook Time: 28 minutes. | Servings:8

½ cup vegetable broth (here) or store-bought low-sodium vegetable broth
2 celery stalks, thinly sliced
½ Vidalia onion, thinly sliced
1 garlic clove, minced
2 (15-ounce / 425-g) cans low-sodium butter beans
¼ teaspoon Not Old Bay Seasoning

Bring the broth to a low simmer in a medium skillet over medium heat. In the skillet, add onion, celery, and garlic and then cook for 3 to 5 minutes, or until the celery, onion, and garlic are softened. Add the beans and seasonings, cover, and simmer for another 5 to 7 minutes, or until the flavors meld. Serve alongside your favorite greens.

Nutritional information: Calories 101; Total Carbs 19.02g; Net Carbs 11.2g; Protein 0.7g; Fat 0.7g; Sugar 2.3g; Fiber 5.5g

Portobello Greens Salad

Prep time: 5 minutes. | Cooking time: 10 minutes. | Servings: 4

6 cup mixed salad greens
1 cup portobello mushrooms, sliced
1 green onion, sliced
walnut or warm bacon vinaigrette
1 tablespoon olive oil
⅛ teaspoon black pepper

Warm-up 1 tablespoon of oil in a nonstick skillet over medium-high heat. Stir in mushrooms and cook for 10 minutes until they are tender, stirring occasionally. Stir in onions and reduce heat to low. Place salad greens on serving plates, top with mushrooms and sprinkle with pepper. Drizzle lightly with your choice of vinaigrette.

Nutritional information: Calories 81; Total Carbs 9g; Net Carbs 2g; Protein 4g; Fat 4g; Sugar 0g; Fiber 0g

Tomato Radish Salad

Prep time: 10 minutes. | Cook Time: 5 minutes. | Servings: 4

1 cucumber, chopped
1-pint cherry tomatoes, cut in half
3 radishes, chopped
1 yellow bell pepper chopped
½ cup parsley, chopped
3 tablespoon Lemon juice
1 tablespoon Olive oil
Salt to taste

Place all the recipe ingredients in a suitable bowl and toss to combine. Serve immediately, or cover and chill until ready to serve.

Nutritional information: Calories 70; Total Carbs 9g; Net Carbs 7g; Protein 2g; Fat 4g; Sugar 5g; Fiber 2g

Crab Cabbage Slaw

Prep time: 10 minutes. | Chill time: 1 hour. | Servings: 4

½ lb. Cabbage, shredded
½ lb. red cabbage, shredded
2 hard-boiled eggs, chopped
Juice of ½ lemon
2 (6 oz.) Cans crabmeat, drained
½ cup lite mayonnaise
1 teaspoon celery seeds
Salt and pepper, to taste

In a suitable bowl, combine both kinds of cabbage. In a suitable bowl, combine mayonnaise, lemon juice, and celery seeds. Add to cabbage and toss to coat. Add crab and eggs and toss to mix, season with salt and pepper. Cover and refrigerate 1 hour before serving.

Nutritional information: Calories 380; Total Carbs 25g; Net Carbs 17g; Protein 18g; Fat 24g; Sugar 13g; Fiber 8g

Cauliflower Soup

Prep Time: 10 minutes. | Cook Time: 15 minutes. | Servings: 6

2½ pounds (1.1 kg) cauliflower florets
½ leek, white and pale green part, halved
4 tablespoons plant-based butter
2 teaspoons fresh parsley, diced
2 tablespoons low sodium chicken broth
2 teaspoons extra virgin olive oil
4 cloves garlic, diced fine
¼ teaspoon salt
¼ teaspoon pepper

Place the cauliflower in a steamer basket over boiling water. Cover and cook for 10 to 15 minutes or until the pork is tender. Rinse the leek with water and pat dry. Cut into thin slices. Heat the oil in a large saucepan over medium heat. Add the chives and cook for 2-3 minutes until tender. Add the garlic and cook for another 1 minute. Put everything in a food processor and pulse until almost tender. Keep warm or store in the refrigerator for later use.

Nutritional information: Calories 147; Total Carbs 14g; Net Carbs 10g; Protein 5g; Fat 9g; Sugar 6g; Fiber 6g

Spicy Brown Rice with Collard

Prep Time: 14 minutes. | Cook Time: 18 minutes. | Servings:4

1 tablespoon extra-virgin olive oil
1 bunch collard greens, stemmed and chiffonade-style
1 carrot, cut into 2-inch matchsticks
1 red onion, thinly sliced
½ cup low-sodium vegetable broth
2 tablespoons coconut amino
1 garlic clove, minced
1 cup cooked brown rice
1 large egg
1 teaspoon red pepper flakes
1 teaspoon paprika
Salt, to taste

In a Dutch oven or nonstick pan, heat the olive oil over medium heat until it shimmers. Add the collard greens and cook until wilted, about 4 minutes. In a Dutch oven, combine the carrots, onion, broth, coconut amino, and garlic; cover and cook for 6 minutes, or until the carrots are soft. Cook for 4 minutes after adding the brown rice. Throughout the cooking process, keep stirring. Break an egg over them, then heat and scramble it for 4 minutes, or until it is set. Before serving, remove from the fire and season with red pepper flakes, paprika, and salt.

Nutritional information: Calories 154; Total Carbs 22g; Net Carbs 14g; Protein 6g; Fat 6g; Sugar 2g; Fiber 6g

Roasted Carrot Leek Soup

Prep time: 4 minutes. | Cooking time: 30 minutes. | Servings: 3-4

6 carrots, cut into thirds
1 cup chopped onion
1 fennel bulb, cubed
2 garlic cloves, crushed
2 tablespoons avocado oil
1 teaspoon sea salt
1 teaspoon black pepper
2 cups almond milk

At 400 degrees F, preheat your oven. Line a baking sheet with parchment paper. Add the carrots, onion, fennel, garlic, and avocado oil, and toss to coat. Season the veggies with black pepper and salt, and toss again. Transfer the vegetables to the prepared baking sheet, and roast for almost 30 minutes. Remove from the oven and allow the vegetables to cool. In a high-speed blender, blend together the almond milk and roasted vegetables until creamy and smooth. Adjust the seasonings, if necessary, and add additional milk if you prefer a thinner consistency. Pour into 2 large or 4 suitable bowls and enjoy.

Nutritional information: Calories: 55; Total Carbs 12g; Net Carbs 2g; Protein: 1.8 g; Fat: 2g; Sugar: 1g; Fiber: 2g

Lamb Vegetable Stew

Prep time: 15 minutes. | Cooking time: 35 minutes. | Servings: 2

1 lb. diced lamb shoulder
1 lb. chopped winter vegetables
1 cup vegetable broth
1 tablespoon yeast extract
1 tablespoon star anise spice mix

Mix all the recipe ingredients in your instant pot. Cook on stew for 35 minutes. Release the pressure naturally.

Nutritional information: Calories: 320; Total Carbs: 10; Net Carbs 1.2g; Protein: 42g; Fat: 8; Sugar: 1g; Fiber: 2g

Irish Lamb Stew

Prep time: 15 minutes. | Cooking time: 35 minutes. | Servings: 2

1.5 lb. diced lamb shoulder
1lb chopped vegetables
1 cup beef broth
3 minced onions
1 tablespoon ghee

Mix all the recipe ingredients in your instant pot. Cook on stew for 35 minutes. Release the pressure naturally.

Nutritional information: Calories: 330; Total Carbs: 9g; Net Carbs 2g; Protein: 49g; Fat: 12; Sugar: 1g; Fiber: 2g

Meatball Vegetable Stew

Prep time: 15 minutes. | Cooking time: 25 minutes. | Servings: 2

1 lb. Sausage meat
2 cups chopped tomato
1 cup chopped vegetables
2 tablespoon Italian seasonings
1 tablespoon vegetable oil

Roll the sausage into meatballs. Put the instant pot on sauté and fry the meatballs in the oil until brown. Mix all the recipe ingredients in your instant pot. Cook on stew for almost 25 minutes. Release the pressure naturally.

Nutritional information: Calories: 300; Total Carbs: 4g; Net Carbs 2g; Protein: 40g; Fat: 12g; Sugar: 1g; Fiber: 2g

French Onion Gruyere Soup

Prep time: 35 minutes. | Cooking time: 35 minutes. | Servings: 2

6 onions, chopped
2 cups vegetable broth
2 tablespoon oil
2 tablespoon gruyere

Place the oil in your instant pot and cook the onions on sauté until soft and brown. Mix all the recipe ingredients in your instant pot. Cook on stew for 35 minutes. Release the pressure naturally.

Nutritional information: Calories: 110; Total Carbs: 8; Net Carbs 3g; Protein: 3g; Fat: 10; Sugar: 1g; Fiber: 2g

Coconut and Jalapeño Soup

Prep time: 5 minutes. | Cooking time: 5 minutes. | Servings: 1-2

2 tablespoons avocado oil
½ cup diced onions
3 garlic cloves, crushed
¼ teaspoon sea salt
1 (13.5-ounce) can skimmed coconut milk
1 tablespoon lime juice
½ to 1 jalapeño
2 tablespoons cilantro leaves

In a suitable skillet over medium-high warmth, heat the avocado oil. Add the garlic, onion salt, and pepper, and sauté for 3 to 5 minutes or until the onions are soft. In a blender, blend together the coconut milk, lime juice, jalapeño, and cilantro with the onion mixture until creamy. Fill 1 large dish or 2 small dishes and enjoy.

Nutritional information: Calories: 75; Total Carbs 13 g; Fat: 2 g; Net Carbs 3g; Protein: 4 g; Fat: 2g; Sugar: 1g; Fiber: 2g

Lentil Potato Stew

Prep time: 10 minutes. | Cooking time: 30 minutes. | Servings: 4

2 tablespoons avocado oil
½ cup diced onion
2 garlic cloves, crushed
1 to 1½ teaspoons sea salt
1 teaspoon black pepper
1 cup dry lentils
2 carrots, sliced
1 cup peeled and cubed potato
1 celery stalk, diced
2 oregano sprigs, chopped
2 tarragon sprigs, chopped
5 cups vegetable broth
1 (13.5-ounce) can skimmed coconut milk

In a great soup pot over average-high hotness, heat the avocado oil. Add the garlic, onion, salt, and pepper, and sauté for 3 to 5 minutes, or until the onion is soft. Add the lentils, carrots, potato, celery, oregano, tarragon, and 2½ cups of vegetable broth, and stir. Get to a boil, decrease the heat to medium-low, and cook, stirring frequently and adding additional vegetable broth a half cup at a time to make sure there is enough liquid for the lentils and potatoes to cook, for almost 20 to 25 minutes, or until the potatoes and lentils are soft. Take away from the heat, and stirring in the coconut milk. Pour into 4 soup bowls and enjoy.

Nutritional information: Calories: 85; Total Carbs 20g; Net Carbs 2g; Protein: 3g; Fat: 2g; Sugar: 1g; Fiber: 2g

Tofu Soup

Prep time: 15 minutes. | Cooking time: 15 minutes. | Servings: 2

1 lb. minced tofu
0.5 lb. chopped vegetables
2 cups vegetable broth
1 tablespoon almond flour
salt and Black pepper, to taste

Mix the tofu, flour, salt and pepper. Form the meatballs from the mixture. Place all the recipe ingredients in your instant pot. Cook on stew for almost 15 minutes. Release the pressure naturally.

Nutritional information: Calories: 240; Total Carbs: 9g; Net Carbs 1.2g; Protein: 35g; Fat: 10g; Sugar: 1g; Fiber: 2g

Bacon Vegetable Stew

Prep time: 15 minutes. | Cooking time: 25 minutes. | Servings: 2

0.5 lb. soy bacon
1 lb. chopped vegetables
1 cup vegetable broth
1 tablespoon nutritional yeast

Mix all the recipe ingredients in your instant pot. Cook on stew for almost 25 minutes. Release the pressure naturally.

Nutritional information: Calories: 200; Total Carbs: 12g; Fat: 7; Net Carbs 0.5g; Protein: 41; Sugar: 1g; Fiber: 2g

Chicken Zucchini Noodle Soup

Prep time: 15 minutes. | Cooking time: 35 minutes. | Servings: 2

1 lb. cooked chicken, chopped
1 lb. zucchini, spiralized
1 cup chicken soup
1 cup diced vegetables

Mix all the recipe ingredients except the zucchini in your instant pot. Cook on stew for 35 minutes. Release the pressure naturally. Stir in the zucchini and allow to heat thoroughly.

Nutritional information: Calories: 250; Total Carbs: 5g; Sugar: 0g; Fat: 10g; Net Carbs 2g; Protein: 40g; Sugar: 1g; Fiber: 2g

Kebab Chickpea Stew

Prep time: 15 minutes. | Cooking time: 35 minutes. | Servings: 2

1 lb. cubed, seasoned kebab meat
1 lb. cooked chickpeas
1 cup vegetable broth
1 tablespoon black pepper

Mix all the recipe ingredients in your instant pot. Cook on stew for 35 minutes. Release the pressure naturally.

Nutritional information: Calories: 290; Total Carbs: 22g; Net Carbs 2g; Protein: 34g; Fat:10g; Sugar: 1g; Fiber: 2g

Garlicky Cauliflower Soup

Prep time: 10 minutes. | Cooking time: 35 minutes. | Servings: 1-2

4 cups bite-size cauliflower florets
5 garlic cloves
1½ tablespoons avocado oil
¾ teaspoon sea salt
½ teaspoon black pepper
1 cup skimmed almond milk
1 cup vegetable broth

At 450 degrees F, preheat your oven. Line a baking sheet with parchment paper. In a suitable bowl, toss the cauliflower and garlic with the avocado oil to coat. Season the cauliflower with black pepper and salt, and toss again. Transfer to the prepared baking sheet and roast for almost 30 minutes. Cool before adding to the blender. In a high-speed blender, blend together the cooled vegetables, almond milk, and vegetable broth until creamy and smooth. Adjust the salt and pepper, if necessary, and add additional vegetable broth if you prefer a thinner consistency. Transfer to a medium saucepan, and lightly warm on medium-low heat for 3 to 5 minutes. Ladle into 1 large or 2 suitable bowls and enjoy.

Nutritional information: Calories: 48; Total Carbs 11g; Net Carbs 2g; Protein: 1.5g; Fat: 2g; Sugar: 1g; Fiber: 2g

Beefless Stew

Prep time: 10 minutes. | Cooking time: 0 minutes. | Servings: 4

1 tablespoon avocado oil
1 cup onion, diced
2 garlic cloves, crushed
1 teaspoon sea salt
1 teaspoon black pepper
3 cups vegetable broth
2 cups water
3 cups sliced carrot
1 large potato, cubed
2 celery stalks, diced
1 teaspoon dried oregano
1 dried bay leaf

In a suitable soup pot over medium heat, heat the avocado oil. Add the onion, garlic, salt, and pepper and sauté for almost 2 to 3 minutes or until the onion is soft. Add the water, carrot, vegetable broth, oregano, potato, celery, and bay leaf, and stir. Get to a boil, decrease the heat to medium-low, and cook for almost 30 to 45 minutes, or until the potatoes and carrots be soft. Adjust the seasonings, if necessary, and add additional water or vegetable broth, if a soupier consistency is preferred, in half-cup increments. Ladle into 4 soup bowls and enjoy.

Nutritional information: Calories: 59; Total Carbs 12g; Net Carbs 2g; Protein: 2g; Fat: 2g; Sugar: 1g; Fiber: 2g

Herbed Chickpea Soup

Prep time: 15 minutes. | Cooking time: 35 minutes. | Servings: 2

1 lb. cooked chickpeas
1 lb. chopped vegetables
1 cup vegetable broth
2 tablespoon mixed herbs

Mix all the recipe ingredients in your instant pot. Cook on stew for 35 minutes. Release the pressure naturally.

Nutritional information: Calories: 310; Total Carbs: 20g; Sugar: 3g; Fat: 5g; Net Carbs 2g; Protein: 27g; Sugar: 1g; Fiber: 2g

Tarragon Soup

Prep time: 10 minutes. | Cooking time: 10 minutes. | Servings: 1-2

1 tablespoon avocado oil
½ cup diced onion
3 garlic cloves, crushed
¼ plus ⅛ teaspoon sea salt
¼ plus ⅛ teaspoon black pepper
1 (13.5-ounce) can full-fat coconut milk
1 tablespoon lemon juice
½ cup raw cashews
1 celery stalk
2 tablespoons chopped tarragon

In a suitable skillet over medium-high warmth, heat the avocado oil. Add the onion, garlic, salt, and pepper, and sauté for 3 to 5 minutes or until the onion is

soft. In a high-speed blender, blend together the coconut milk, lemon juice, cashews, celery, and tarragon with the onion mixture until smooth. Adjust seasonings, if necessary. Fill 1 large or 2 small dishes and enjoy immediately, or transfer to a medium saucepan and warm on low heat for 3 to 5 minutes before serving.

Nutritional information: Calories: 60; Total Carbs 13g; Net Carbs 1g; Proteins: 0.8 g; Fat: 2g; Sugar: 1g; Fiber: 2g

Mushroom Soup

Prep time: 5 minutes. | Cooking time: 20 minutes. | Servings: 4

1 tablespoon avocado oil
1 cup shiitake mushrooms, sliced
1 cup cremini mushrooms, sliced
1 cup onion, diced
1 garlic clove, crushed
¾ teaspoon salt
½ teaspoon black pepper
1 cup vegetable broth
1 (13.5-ounce) can skimmed coconut milk
½ teaspoon dried thyme
1 tablespoon coconut aminos

In a suitable soup pot over average-high hotness, heat the avocado oil. Add the mushrooms, onion, garlic, salt, pepper, and sauté for almost 2 to 3 minutes. Add the vegetable broth, coconut milk, thyme, and coconut aminos. Reduce its heat to medium-low, and simmer for almost 15 minutes, with occasional stirring. Adjust seasonings, if necessary, ladle into 2 large or 4 suitable bowls, and enjoy.

Nutritional information: Calories: 65; Total Carbs 12g; Fat: 2g; Net Carbs 2g; Protein: 2g; Sugar: 1g; Fiber: 2g

Cold Berry Mint Soup

Prep time: 5 minutes. | Cooking time: 20 minutes. | Servings: 1-2

For the sweetener:
¼ cup sugar substitute
¼ cup water
For the soup:
1 cup mixed berries (raspberries, blackberries, blueberries)
½ cup water
1 teaspoon lemon juice
8 mint leaves

To prepare the sweetener in a suitable saucepan over medium-low, heat the sugar and water, with occasional stirring for almost 1 to 2 minutes, until the sugar is dissolved. Cool. In a blender, blend together the cooled sugar water with the berries, water, lemon juice, and mint leaves until well combined. Transfer the prepared mixture to the refrigerator and allow chilling completely, about 20 minutes. Ladle into 1 large or 2 suitable bowls and enjoy.

Nutritional information: Calories: 89; Total Carbs 12g; Fat: 6g; Net Carbs 0.5g; Protein: 2.2 g; Sugar: 1g; Fiber: 2g

Italian Vegetable Soup

Prep time: 10 minutes. | Cooking time: 30 minutes. | Servings: 5

8 cups vegetable broth
2 tablespoons olive oil
1 tablespoon Italian seasoning
1 onion, large and diced
2 bay leaves, dried
2 bell pepper, large and diced
sea salt and black pepper, to taste
4 garlic cloves, minced
28 oz. tomatoes, diced
1 cauliflower head, medium into florets
2 cups green beans, chopped

Set a Dutch oven with oil over medium heat. Once the oil becomes hot, stir in the onions and pepper; cook for almost 10 minutes or until the onion is softened and browned. Spoon in the garlic and sauté for a minute or until fragrant. Add all the remaining ingredients to it. Mix until everything comes together. Bring the mixture to a boil. Lower the heat and cook for further 20 minutes or until the vegetables have softened. Serve hot.

Nutritional information: Calories 79kl; Fat 2g; Total Carbs 8g; Net Carbs 2g; Protein 2g; Sugar: 1g; Fiber: 2g

Celery Soup

Prep time: 10 minutes. | Cooking time: 30 minutes. | Servings: 4

6 cups celery stalk, chopped
2 cups water
1 onion, chopped
½ teaspoon dill
1 cup skimmed coconut milk
¼ teaspoon sea salt

Combine all elements into the direct pot and mix fine. Cover pot with lid and select soup mode; it takes 30 minutes. Release pressure using the quick release directions, then open the lid carefully. Blend the soup utilizing a submersion blender until smooth. Stir well and serve.

Nutritional information: Calories 193; Fat 15.3 g; Total Carbs 10.9 g; Net Carbs 2g; Protein 5.2 g; Sugar 5.6 g; Fat 10g; Sugar 1g; Fiber 2g

Cucumber and Lime Soup

Prep time: 5 minutes. | Cooking time: 20 minutes. | Servings: 1-2

1 cucumber, peeled
½ zucchini, peeled
1 tablespoon lime juice
1 tablespoon cilantro leaves
1 garlic clove, crushed
¼ teaspoon sea salt

In a blender, blend together the cucumber, zucchini, lime juice, cilantro, garlic, and salt until well combined. Add more salt, if necessary. Fill 1 large or 2 small dishes and enjoy immediately, or refrigerate for almost 15 to 20 minutes to chill before serving.

Nutritional information: Calories: 48; Total Carbs 8 g; Fat: 1g; Net Carbs 2g; Protein: 5g; Fat: 2g; Sugar: 1g; Fiber: 2g

Watermelon Gazpacho

Prep time: 5 minutes. | Cooking time: 5 minutes. | Servings: 1-2

2 cups cubed watermelon
¼ cup diced onion
¼ cup packed cilantro leaves
½ to 1 jalapeño
2 tablespoons lime juice

In a suitable food processor, blend the onion, cilantro, watermelon, jalapeño, and lime juice. Pour into 1 large or 2 suitable bowls and enjoy.

Nutritional information: Calories: 35; Total Carbs 12; Net Carbs 0.5g; Protein: 1.8 g; Fat: 2g; Sugar: 1g; Fiber: 2g

Chilled Tomato Soup

Prep time: 7 minutes. | Cooking time: 20 minutes. | Servings: 1-2

2 small avocados
2 large tomatoes
1 stalk of celery
1 onion
1 clove of garlic
juice of 1 lemon
1 cup water (best: alkaline water)
a handful of lavages
parsley and sea salt to taste

Scoop the avocados and cut all veggies in small pieces. Spot all fixings in a blender and blend until smooth. Serve chilled and appreciate this nutritious and sound soluble soup formula!

Nutritional information: Calories: 68; Total Carbs 15g; Fat: 2g; Net Carbs 2g; Protein: .8g; Sugar: 1g; Fiber: 2g

Onion Broccoli Soup

Prep time: 5 minutes. | Cooking time: 10 minutes. | Servings: 6

1 pound broccoli, chopped
6 cups water
1 onion, diced
2 tablespoons olive oil
Black pepper, to taste
salt to taste

Add oil into the instant pot and set the pot on sauté mode. Add the onion in olive oil and sauté until softened. Add broccoli and water and stir well. Cover pot with top and cook on manual high pressure for 3 minutes. When finished, release pressure using the quick release directions, then open the lid. Blend the soup utilizing a submersion blender until smooth. Season soup with pepper and salt. Serve fresh.

Nutritional information: Calories 73; Total Carbs 6.7 g; Net Carbs 3g; Protein 2.3 g; Fat 10g; Sugar 1g; Fiber 2g

Carrot Millet Soup

Prep time: 7 minutes. | Cooking time: 40 minutes. | Servings: 3-4

2 cups cauliflower pieces
1 cup potatoes, cubed
2 cups vegetables stock
3 tablespoons low-fat Swiss Emmenthal cheddar, cubed
2 tablespoons chives
1 tablespoon pumpkin seeds
1 touch of nutmeg and cayenne pepper
salt

Cook cauliflower and potato in vegetable stock until delicate and blend with a blender. Season the soup with nutmeg and cayenne, and possibly somewhat salt and pepper. Add Emmenthal cheddar and chives and mix a couple of moments until the soup is smooth and prepared to serve. Enhance with pumpkin seeds.

Nutritional information: Calories: 65; Total Carbs 15g; Fat: 1g; Net Carbs 0.5g; Protein: 2g; Sugar: 1g; Fiber: 2g

Carrot Mushrooms Soup

Prep time: 10 minutes. | Cooking time: 20 minutes. | Servings: 1-2

4 carrots
4 potatoes
10 large mushrooms
½ white onion
2 tablespoon olive oil
3 cups vegetable stock
2 tablespoon parsley
Salt and white pepper, to taste

Wash and strip carrots and potatoes and dice them. Heat the vegetable stock in a pot over medium heat. Cook carrots and potatoes for around 15 minutes. Meanwhile, shape onion and braise them in a container with olive oil for around 3 minutes. Wash mushrooms, slice them to the wanted size and add to the container, cooking approx. An additional 5 minutes, blending at times. Blend carrots, vegetable stock and potatoes, and put the substance of the skillet into the pot. When nearly done, season with parsley, salt and pepper and serve hot.

Nutritional information: Calories: 75; Total Carbs 13g; Fat: 1.8g; Net Carbs 0.5g; Protein: 1 g Sugar: 1g; Fiber: 2g

Chilled Parsley-Gazpacho

Prep time: 10 minutes. | Cooking time: 2 hours. | Servings: 1

4-5 middle sized tomatoes
2 tablespoon olive oil, and cold pressed
2 large cups parsley
2 ripe avocados
2 garlic cloves, diced
2 limes, juiced
4 cups vegetable broth
1 middle sized cucumber
2 small red onions, diced

1 teaspoon dried oregano
1½ teaspoon paprika powder
salt and black pepper, to taste
½ teaspoon cayenne pepper

In a suitable pan, heat up olive oil and sauté onions and garlic until translucent. Blend avocado, tomatoes, lime juice, parsley, vegetable broth, cucumber, and onion-garlic mix until smooth. Add some water if desired, and season with cayenne pepper, paprika powder, oregano, salt and pepper. Blend again and put in the fridge for at least 1-½ hours. You can add chives or dill to the gazpacho. Enjoy!

Nutritional information: Calories: 48; Total Carbs 12 g; Fat: 0.8g; Net Carbs 2g; Protein: 1g; Sugar: 1g; Fiber: 2g

Pumpkin White Bean Soup

Prep time: 10 minutes. | Cooking time: 40 minutes. | Servings: 3-4

1 ½ pound pumpkin
½ pound yams
½ pound white beans
1 onion
2 cloves of garlic
1 tablespoon of olive oil
1 tablespoon of spices
1 tablespoon of sage
1 ½ quart water
A spot of salt and pepper

Cut the pumpkin in shapes, cut the onion and cut the garlic, the spices and the sage into fine pieces. Sauté the onion and also the garlic in olive oil for around 2 or 3 minutes. Add the pumpkin, spices and sage and fry for an additional 5 minutes. At that point, add the water and cook for around 30 minutes until vegetables are delicate. At long last add the beans and some salt and pepper. Cook for an additional 5 minutes and serve right away. Serve.

Nutritional information: Calories: 78; Total Carbs 12g; Net Carbs 2g; Protein: 1g; Fat: 12g, Sugar: 1g; Fiber: 2g

Avocado-Broccoli Soup

Prep time: 10 minutes. | Cooking time: 15 minutes. | Servings: 1-2

2-3 flowers broccoli
1 avocado
1 yellow onion
1 green or red pepper
1 celery stalk
2 cups vegetable broth
Celtic sea salt to taste

Heat vegetable stock in a pot. Add hacked onion and broccoli, and warm for a few minutes. At that point, put in a blender, add the avocado, pepper and celery and blend until the soup is smooth. Serve warm.

Nutritional information: Calories: 60g; Total Carbs 11g; Fat: 2 g; Net Carbs 2g; Protein: 2g; Sugar: 1g; Fiber: 2g

Pumpkin Coconut Soup

Prep time: 10 minutes. | Cooking time: 15 minutes. | Servings: 3-4

2 pounds pumpkin
6 cups water
1 cup unsweetened coconut milk
5 ounces potatoes
2 onions
3 ounces leek
1 bunch of parsley
1 touch of nutmeg
1 touch of cayenne pepper
1 teaspoon salt
4 tablespoons olive oil

As a matter of first significance: cut the pumpkin and the potatoes just as the hole into small pieces. At that point, heat the olive oil in a suitable pot and sauté the onions for a couple of moments. At that point, add the water and heat up the pumpkin, potatoes, and the leek until delicate. Add the coconut milk. Presently utilize a hand blender and puree for around 1 moment. The soup should turn out to be extremely velvety. Season with salt, pepper, and nutmeg; lastly, add the parsley. Serve.

Nutritional information: Calories: 88; Total Carbs 23g; Net Carbs 3g; Protein: 1.8g; Fat: 2.5 g; Sugar: 1g; Fiber: 2g

Garden Vegetable Soup

Prep time: 7 minutes. | Cooking time: 20 minutes. | Servings: 1-2

2 large carrots
1 small zucchini
1 celery stem
1 cup broccoli
3 stalks of asparagus
1 yellow onion
4 cups water
4-5 teaspoons vegetable stock
1 teaspoon basil
2 teaspoons salt to taste

Put water in pot, add the vegetable stock just as the onion and bring to bubble. In the meantime, cleave the zucchini, the broccoli and the asparagus, and shred the carrots and the celery stem in a food processor. Put veggies in the hot water and hold up until the vegetables turn soft. Allow to cool somewhat, at that point put all fixings into blender and blend until you get a thick, smooth consistency.

Nutritional information: Calories: 43; Total Carbs 7g; Fat: 1 g; Net Carbs2g; Protein: 0.2g; Sugar: 1g; Fiber: 2g

Kale Cauliflower Soup

Prep time: 10 minutes. | Cooking time: 25 minutes. | Servings: 4

2 cups baby kale
½ cup unsweetened coconut milk
4 cups water
1 large cauliflower head, chopped
3 garlic cloves, peeled

2 carrots, peeled and chopped
2 onions, chopped
3 tablespoons olive oil
Black pepper, to taste
Salt to taste

Add oil into the instant pot and set the pot on sauté mode. Add carrot, garlic, and onion to the pot and sauté for almost 5-7 minutes. Add water and cauliflower and stir well. Cover pot with lid and cook on high pressure for almost 20 minutes. When finished, release pressure using the quick release directions then open the lid. Add kale and coconut milk and stir well. Blend the soup utilizing a submersion blender until smooth. Season with pepper and salt.

Nutritional information: Calories 261; Total Carbs 23.9 g; Net Carbs 2g; Protein 6.6 g; Fat 19g; Sugar 6.2g; Fiber 2g

Swiss Cauliflower Soup

Prep time: 10 minutes. | Cooking time: 15 minutes. | Servings: 3-4

2 cups cauliflower pieces
1 cup potatoes, cubed
2 cups vegetable stock
3 tablespoons Swiss omental cheddar, cubed
2 tablespoons chives
1 tablespoon pumpkin seeds
1 touch of nutmeg and cayenne pepper

Cook cauliflower and potato in vegetable stock until delicate and blend with a blender. Season the soup with nutmeg and cayenne, and possibly somewhat salt and pepper. Add Emmenthal cheddar and chives and mix a couple of moments until the soup is smooth and prepared to serve. Enhance it with pumpkin seeds.

Nutritional information: Calories: 65; Total Carbs 13g; Fat: 2g; Net Carbs 2g; Protein: 1g; Sugar: 1g; Fiber: 2g

Milky Carrot Soup

Prep time: 10 minutes. | Cooking time: 20 minutes. | Servings: 6

8 large carrots, peeled and chopped
1 ½ cups water
14 ounces unsweetened coconut milk
3 garlic cloves, peeled
1 tablespoon red curry paste
¼ cup olive oil
1 onion, chopped
Salt to taste

Combine all the ingredients into the direct pot and mix fine. Cover pot with lid and select manual mode and set timer for almost 15 minutes. Allow releasing pressure naturally, then open the lid. Blend the soup utilizing a submersion blender until smooth. Serve fresh.

Nutritional information: Calories 267; Total Carbs 13 g; Net Carbs 3g; Protein 4 g; Fat 22 g; Sugar 1g; Fiber 2g

Moroccan Lentil Soup

Prep Time: 5 minutes. | Cook Time: 1 hour 25 minutes. | Servings: 3

2 cups chopped onions
2 teaspoon olive oil
2 cups chopped carrots
1 teaspoon of ground cumin
4 cloves of garlic, minced
1 teaspoon of ground coriander
¼ teaspoon of ground cinnamon
1 teaspoon of ground turmeric
¼ teaspoon of ground pepper
4 cups fresh chopped spinach
2 cups water
6 cups low-sodium vegetable broth
2 tablespoons lemon juice
3 cups chopped cauliflower
1 chopped tomato (28-ounce of the can)
2 tablespoons tomato paste
1 ¾ cups lentils
½ cup fresh chopped cilantro

Heat a little oil in a saucepan over medium heat, then add the onions and carrots, stirring occasionally, until tender, about 10 minutes. Mix in a little garlic and cook for ½ minute. Add the cumin, cilantro, turmeric, cinnamon, and black pepper. Stir until fragrant, about 60 seconds. Add the broth, cauliflower, water, tomatoes, lentils, and tomato paste and bring to a boil. Reduce heat and cook until lentils are tender, but not half liquid, about 45-55 minutes, half volume and stir occasionally. Stir in spinach and cook for 5 minutes until soft. Add the lemon and cilantro juice before serving.

Nutritional information: Calories 27.5; Total Carbs 10g; Net Carbs 8g; Protein 9.3g; Fat 1.5g; Sugar 1g; Fiber 3g

Slow Cooker Chicken-Tortilla Soup

Prep Time: 20 minutes. | Cook Time: 8 hour 20 minutes. | Servings: 2

1 ¼-pounds skinless chicken thighs
½ of chopped bell pepper (red)
1 small chopped onion
1 chopped clove of garlic
1 can diced tomatoes
2 cups low-sodium chicken stock
1 can tomato sauce
1 teaspoon chili powder
1 can green chilies (chopped)
1 teaspoon dried oregano
Salt as per taste
¾ teaspoon ground cumin
2 ½ tablespoons fresh cilantro, chopped
Fresh black pepper, grounded
Tortilla chips and sliced jalapenos for serving
3 ounces halved green beans
2 sliced and halved yellow squash
1 tablespoon lime juice, fresh

Place onion, bell pepper, chicken, broth, garlic, tomato sauce, chopped tomatoes, chili powder, chili, cumin, and oregano in the slow cooker. Season with pepper and salt. Cover chicken until ready to simmer for 7 to 8 hours. Or heat for 3 hours and 4 hours at high. Add the green beans and zucchini, cover, and simmer for 30 minutes. Then remove the chicken, discard the bones and shred the meat. Return to slow cooker. Combine the cilantro and lemon juice. Top with jalapeño and cilantro, and tortilla chips on the side.

Nutritional information: Calories 158; Total Carbs 18g; Net Carbs 12g; Protein 26g; Fat 8g; Sugar 2g; Fiber 4g

Pumpkin Tomato Soup

Prep time: 15 minutes. | Cooking time: 30 minutes. | Servings: 3-4

4 cups of water
14 ounces tomatoes, stripped and diced
1 sweet pumpkin
5 yellow onions
1 tablespoon olive oil
2 teaspoons salt
1 pinch of cayenne pepper
Bunch of parsley, chopped

Sauté chopped onion with some oil in a suitable pot. Cut the pumpkin down the middle; at that point, remove the stem and scoop out the seeds. At long last, scoop out the fragile living creature and put it in the pot. Add the tomatoes and the water likewise and cook for around 20 minutes. At that point, empty the soup into a food processor and blend well for a couple of moments. Sprinkle with salt, pepper and other spices. Fill bowls and top with parsley. Serve!

Nutritional information: Calories: 78; Total Carbs 20g; Net Carbs 2g; Protein: 1.5g; Fat: 0.5g; Sugar: 1g; Fiber: 2g

Squash Soup

Prep time: 10 minutes. | Cooking time: 40 minutes. | Servings: 4

3 pounds butternut squash, peeled and cubed
1 tablespoon curry powder
½ cup unsweetened coconut milk
3 cups water
2 garlic cloves, minced
1 large onion, minced
1 teaspoon olive oil
salt, as needed

Add olive oil to the instant pot and set the instant pot on sauté mode. Add onion and cook until tender, about 8 minutes. Add curry powder and garlic and sauté for a minute. Add butternut squash, water, and salt and stir well. Cover pot with lid and cook on soup mode for almost 30 minutes. When finished, allow to release pressure naturally for almost 10 minutes, then release using quick-release directions then open the lid. Blend the soup utilizing a submersion blender until smooth. Add coconut milk and stir well. Serve warm and enjoy.

Nutritional information: Calories 254; Total Carbs 46.4 g; Net Carbs 2g; Protein 4.8 g; Fat 10g; Sugar 1g; Fiber 2g

Lentil Spinach Soup

Prep time: 10 minutes. | Cooking time: 20 minutes. | Servings: 4

1 ½ cups green lentils, rinsed
4 cups baby spinach
4 cups water
1 teaspoon Italian seasoning
2 teaspoons thyme
14 ounces tomatoes, diced
3 garlic cloves, minced
2 celery stalks, chopped
1 carrot, chopped
1 onion, chopped
Black pepper, to taste
Sea salt to taste

Add all the recipe ingredients except spinach into the direct pot and mix fine. Cover pot with top and cook on manual high pressure for almost 18 minutes. When finished, release pressure using the quick release directions and then open the lid. Add spinach and stir well. Serve fresh.

Nutritional information: Calories 306; Total Carbs 53.7 g; Net Carbs 0.5g; Protein 21 g; Fat 10g; Sugar 1g; Fiber 2g

Cashews Avocado-Broccoli Soup

Prep time: 10 minutes. | Cooking time: 30 minutes. | Servings: 1-2

½ cup water
½ avocado
1 cup chopped broccoli
½ cup cashew nuts
½ cup alfalfa sprouts
1 clove of garlic
1 tablespoon cold-pressed olive oil
1 pinch of sea salt and pepper
Some parsley to garnish

Blend cashew nuts in a blender, add some water and puree for a couple of moments. Add the various fixings individually and puree each, an ideal opportunity for a couple of moments. Dispense the soup in a container and warm it up to normal room temperature. Enhance taste with salt and pepper. In the interim, dice the avocado and slash the parsley. Dispense the soup in a container or plate; add the avocado and embellishment with parsley. That's it! Enjoy this excellent healthy soup!

Nutritional information: Calories: 48; Total Carbs 18g; Net Carbs 2g; Protein: 1.4g; Fat: 3g; Sugar: 1g; Fiber: 2g

Cauliflower-Coconut Soup

Prep time: 7 minutes. | Cooking time: 20 minutes. | Servings: 3-4

1 pound cauliflower
1 ¼ cup unsweetened coconut milk
1 cup water
2 tablespoons lime juice
⅓ cup olive oil
1 cup coriander leaves, slashed
salt and cayenne pepper, to taste

1 bunch of unsweetened coconut chips

Steam cauliflower for around 10 minutes. At that point, set up the cauliflower with coconut milk and water in a food processor and procedure until extremely smooth. Add lime squeeze, salt and pepper, a large portion of the cleaved coriander and the oil and blend for an additional couple of moments. Pour in soup bowls and embellishment with coriander and coconut chips. Appreciate!

Nutritional information: Calories: 65; Total Carbs 11g; Net Carbs 2g; Protein: 1.5g; Fat: 0.3g; Sugar: 1g; Fiber: 2g

White Bean Soup

Prep time: 10 minutes. | Cooking time: 40 minutes. | Servings: 6

2 cups white beans, rinsed
¼ teaspoon Cayenne pepper
1 teaspoon dried oregano
½ teaspoon rosemary, chopped
3 cups water
3 cups unsweetened almond milk
3 garlic cloves, minced
2 celery stalks, diced
1 onion, chopped
1 tablespoon olive oil
½ teaspoon sea salt

Add oil into the instant pot and set the instant pot on sauté mode. Add celery and onion in oil and sauté until softened, about 5 minutes. Add garlic and sauté for a minute. Add beans, seasonings, water, and almond milk and stir to combine. Cover pot with lid and cook on high pressure for 35 minutes. When finished, allow releasing pressure naturally, then open the lid. Stir well and serve.

Nutritional information: Calories 276; Total Carbs 44.2 g; Net Carbs 0.5g; Protein 16.6 g; Fat 4.8 g; Sugar 2.3 g; Fiber 2g

Milky Tomato Soup

Prep time: 5 minutes. | Cooking time: 20 minutes. | Servings: 4

6 tomatoes, chopped
1 onion, diced
14 oz. coconut milk
1 teaspoon turmeric
1 teaspoon garlic, minced
¼ cup cilantro, chopped
½ teaspoon cayenne pepper
1 teaspoon ginger, minced
½ teaspoon sea salt

Add all the recipe ingredients to the direct pot and mix fine. Cover the instant pot with lid and cook on manual high pressure for almost 5 minutes. When finished, allow to release pressure naturally for almost 10 minutes, then release using the quick release directions. Blend the soup utilizing a submersion blender until smooth. Stir well and serve.

Nutritional information: Calories 81; Total Carbs 11.6 g; Net Carbs 2g; Sugar 6.1 g; Protein 2.5 g; Fat 3.5 g; Fiber 2g

Basil Zucchini Soup

Prep time: 10 minutes. | Cooking time: 20 minutes. | Servings: 4

3 medium zucchinis, peeled and chopped
¼ cup basil, chopped
1 large leek, chopped
3 cups water
1 tablespoon lemon juice
3 tablespoons olive oil
2 teaspoons sea salt

Add 2 tablespoons oil into the pot and set the pot on sauté mode. Add zucchini and sauté for almost 5 minutes. Add basil and leeks and sauté for 2-3 minutes. Add lemon juice, water, and salt. Stir well. Cover pot with lid and cook on high pressure for 8 minutes. When finished, allow releasing pressure naturally, then open the lid. Blend the soup utilizing a submersion blender until smooth. Top with remaining olive oil and serve.

Nutritional information: Calories 157; Total Carbs 8.9 g; Net Carbs 2g; Protein 5.8 g; Sugar 4 g; Fat 11.9 g; Fiber 2g

Coconut Asparagus Soup

Prep time: 10 minutes. | Cooking time: 30 minutes. | Servings: 6

2 pounds asparagus cut off woody stems
¼ teaspoon lime zest
2 tablespoons lime juice
14 ounces unsweetened coconut milk
1 teaspoon dried thyme
½ teaspoon oregano
½ teaspoon sage
1 ½ cups water
1 cauliflower head, cut into florets
1 tablespoon garlic, minced
1 leek, sliced
3 tablespoons coconut oil
1 pinch of Himalayan salt

At 400 degrees F, preheat your oven. Layer a suitable baking tray with parchment paper and set it aside. Arrange asparagus spears on a baking tray. Drizzle with 2 tablespoons of coconut oil and sprinkle with salt, thyme, oregano, and sage. Bake in the preheated oven for almost 20-25 minutes. Add remaining oil to the instant pot and set the pot on sauté mode. Put some garlic and leek to the pot and sauté for 2-3 minutes. Add cauliflower florets and water in the pot and stir well. Cover pot with lid and select steam mode, and set timer for 4 minutes. When finished, release pressure using the quick release directions. Add roasted asparagus, lime zest, lime juice, and coconut milk and stir well. Blend the soup utilizing a submersion blender until smooth. Serve fresh.

Nutritional information: Calories 265; Total Carbs 14.7 g; Net Carbs 2g; Protein 6.1 g; Fat 23g; Sugar 1g; Fiber 2g

Red Pepper & Roasted Cauliflower Soup

Prep Time: 50 minutes. | Cook Time: 25 minutes. | Servings: 6

1 big head of cauliflower
2 medium-sized red peppers (sweet), seeded and halved
4 tablespoons olive oil
2 minced garlic cloves
1 cup sweet onion, chopped
2 and a ½ teaspoons fresh rosemary, minced
¼ cup flour (all-purpose)
⅛ to ¼ teaspoon cayenne pepper
½ teaspoon paprika
4 cups low-sodium chicken stock
½ teaspoon salt
1 cup 2% milk
¼ teaspoon pepper

Preheat the broiler. Place the peppers, skin side up, on the bright paper lined with the foil. Cook for five minutes or until the fire dropped or skin moves to brown. Remove the middle of the pepper out and set aside it for 20 minutes. Your oven can be preheated at 400 degrees F and set the oven on bake mode. Spread cauliflower in a pan with two tablespoons of oil. Roast, regularly stir for 25-30 minutes. Remove seeds and skin from the pepper before cutting them. Heat the extra oil in 6 quarts soup pot on high heat. Cook, soft, pepper, and cauliflower and stir regularly. Approximately 6-8 minutes. Add rosemary, garlic, and paprika and continue cooking and mix for 1 minute. After adding flour, cook and fry for a minute. Boil the stock until thickened. Put peppers and crashes and mix well. Puree the soup until creamy with a hand blender. Add hot milk and seasoning in it and cook for a while. Add cheese if desire and serve hot.

Nutritional information: Calories 263; Total Carbs 19g; Net Carbs 15g; Protein 8g; Fat 10g; Sugar 1.1g; Fiber 2.9g

Broccoli Asparagus Soup

Prep time: 10 minutes. | Cooking time: 20 minutes. | Servings: 6

2 cups broccoli florets, chopped
15 asparagus spears, ends chopped
1 teaspoon dried oregano
1 tablespoon thyme leaves
½ cup unsweetened almond milk
3 ½ cups water
2 cups cauliflower florets, chopped
2 teaspoons garlic, chopped
1 cup onion, chopped
2 tablespoons olive oil
Black pepper, to taste
Salt to taste

Add oil in the instant pot and set the pot on sauté mode. Add onion to the olive oil and sauté until onion is softened. Add garlic and sauté for almost 30 seconds. Add all vegetables and water and stir well. Cover pot with lid and cook on manual mode for 3 minutes. When finished, allow releasing pressure naturally, then open the lid. Blend the soup utilizing a submersion blender until smooth. Stir in almond milk, herbs, pepper, and salt. Serve fresh.

Nutritional information: Calories 85; Total Carbs 8.8 g; Net Carbs 2g; Protein 3.3 g; Fat 10g; Sugar 1g; Fiber 2g

Autumn Bisque

Prep Time: 25 minutes. | Cook Time: 50 minutes. | Servings: 2

2 teaspoons fresh chives, minced
¼ cup dairy-free margarine
2 teaspoons fresh parsley, minced
2 tablespoons olive oil
½ teaspoon lemon zest, grated
2 big cubed and peeled rutabagas
3 medium-sized chopped leeks only white portion
1 big cubed and peeled celery root
1 big cubed carrot
2 cups unsweetened almond milk
7 cups vegetable stock
3 cloves of minced garlic
2 teaspoons fresh thyme, minced
1 teaspoon salt
1-½ teaspoons fresh rosemary, minced
½ teaspoon ground pepper, coarsely
2 tablespoons fresh chives, minced

Put the first 4 Ingredients in a bowl. Use a measuring spoon to shape the mix in 12 packets. Cool on a baking sheet greased with foil until frozen. Heat the oil in a 6-quart soup pot and sauté the celeriac, rutabagas, carrots, and leeks over medium heat for 8 minutes. Add the garlic and simmer for 2 minutes. Add the herbs, broth, pepper, and salt and bring to a boil. Lower the heat and cover. Cook for 30 to 35 minutes or until the vegetables are cooked through. Mix the soup using a blender. Alternatively, place it in part of the blender and allow it to cool slightly before returning it to the pot. Add milk and heat until hot. Take the herbed margarine out of the freezer 15 minutes before eating it. Garnish with margarine and chives.

Nutritional information: Calories 218; Total Carbs 20g; Net Carbs 18g; Protein 3g; Fat 6g; Sugar 0.6g; Fiber 4g

Gazpacho Soup

Prep time: 7 minutes. | Cooking time: 3 hours. | Servings: 3-4

1 lb. tomatoes, diced
1 cucumber, peeled and diced
1 red pepper, chopped
1 onion, chopped
2 cloves of garlic, minced
1 chili, chopped
sea salt to taste
4 cups of water
1 dash of cayenne pepper
4 tablespoon olive oil
juice of 1 lemon

Add all the recipe ingredients except the olive oil in a blender and blend Pour in the olive oil and mix again until oil is emulsified. Put the soup in the fridge and chill for at least 2 hours. Add some salt and Black pepper, to taste, mix, place the soup in bowls. Garnish with chopped scallions, cucumbers, tomatoes and peppers and enjoy!

Nutritional information: Calories: 39; Total Carbs 8g; Fat: 0.5 g; Net Carbs 3g; Protein: 0.2g; Sugar: 1g; Fiber: 2g

Summer Zucchini Soup

Prep time: 5 minutes. | Cooking time: 20 minutes. | Servings: 10

½ cup basil, chopped
2 bell peppers, sliced
½ cup green beans, cut into pieces
8 cups water
1 summer squash, sliced
1 zucchini, sliced
2 large tomatoes, sliced
1 eggplant, sliced
6 garlic cloves, smashed
1 onion, diced
Black pepper, to taste
salt to taste

Combine all ingredients into the direct pot and mix fine. Cover pot with lid and cook on soup mode for almost 10 minutes. Release pressure using quick-release directions, then open the lid. Blend the soup utilizing a submersion blender until smooth. Serve fresh.

Nutritional information: Calories 84; Total Carbs 12.8 g; Net Carbs 2g; Protein 6.1 g; Sugar 6.1 g; Fat 1.6 g; Fiber 2g

Vegetables Soup

Prep Time: 25 minutes. | Cook Time: 1 hour 20 minutes. | Servings: 16

8 sliced of medium carrots
1 tablespoon olive oil
2 large chopped onions
1 big chopped and seeded green pepper
4 chopped celery ribs
1 minced garlic clove
2 cups frozen green beans
2 cups chopped cabbage
2 cups frozen peas
1 can garbanzo beans
1 cup frozen corn
One bay leaf
1-½ teaspoon parsley flakes, dried
2 teaspoon chicken bouillon cubes
2 cups V8 juice
1 teaspoon salt
1 teaspoon dried thyme
1 teaspoon dried marjoram
½ teaspoon dried basil
4 cups water
¼ teaspoon pepper
1 can undrained diced tomatoes

Place the onion, carrot, bell pepper, and celery in a saucepan and cook over medium to high heat until tender and crisp. Cook for 1 minute, stirring constantly. Bring the rest of the Ingredients to a boil and continue. Reduce heat to low, cover, and cook for 1 to 1 hour 30 minutes or until vegetables are tender. Remove the bay leaves before serving.

Nutritional information: Calories 218; Total Carbs 20g; Net Carbs 18g; Protein 4g; Fat 2g; Sugar 0.14g; Fiber 3.2g

Potato Pot Soup

Prep Time: 20 minutes. | Cook Time: 40 minutes. |
Servings: 5

½ cup light sour cream
2 slices of halved non-nitrate bacon
1 tablespoon unsalted butter
½ teaspoon salt
½ cup chopped onion
¼ cup chives
2 cups less sodium-containing chicken broth
1 ½ pound russet potatoes which are diced and
peeled
¼ teaspoon pepper

Add a little butter to the multicooker and heat until
the butter is melted. Add the bacon and cook for 4 to
5 minutes, turning occasionally until golden brown.
Transfer it to a paper towel to drain off and let the
bacon and butter drip into the pan. Put the onions in
the multicooker and simmer for 2-3 minutes, stirring
until tender, then add the potatoes and broth and
cook. Close the lid and cook for 10 minutes over high
heat. Reduce the pressure and puree the soup until
soft and slightly crumbly. Add a little sour cream and
stir until smooth. Mix ¼ cup of cheese with salt and
pepper. Mix until the cheese is melted. Now serve it
and top with mashed bacon, scallion greens, and the
remaining quarter cup of cheese.

Nutritional information: Calories 156; Total Carbs
10g; Net Carbs 8g; Protein 3.2g; Fat 4.1g; Sugar
0.2g; Fiber 3g

Coconut and Chicken Soup

Prep Time: 20 minutes. | Cook Time: 30 minutes. |
Servings: 2

1 pound thinly sliced chicken breast
Salt & pepper
1 tablespoon coconut oil
1 small sized onion which is thinly sliced
2 minced garlic cloves
1-inch minced and peeled ginger piece
1 medium-sized zucchini, which is cut into ¼, diced
0.75 pounds of pumpkin
1 red-colored bell pepper
1 jalapeño pepper
14 ounces part-skim coconut milk (lite)
2 cups low-sodium chicken broth
1 lime juice

Season the chicken breasts finely with salt and pepper. Heat the coconut oil over medium heat in a large
saucepan and add the chicken breast. Sauté chicken
over high heat for 4 to 5 minutes until red on the outside. Add the onion, garlic, and ginger and sauté for
2-3 minutes. Add the zucchini and pumpkin and mix.
Add the bell peppers, jalapeño peppers, chicken
broth, coconut milk, and lemon juice, and stir. When
it comes to a boil, reduce the heat, cover, and simmer for about 20 minutes. Remove from the heat and
season with salt and pepper at the end.

Nutritional information: Calories 186; Total Carbs
12g; Net Carbs 9g; Protein 17g; Fat 13g; Sugar 1.4g;
Fiber 5g

Kabocha Squash with Cauliflower Soup

Prep Time: 10 minutes. | Cook Time: 20 minutes. |
Servings: 4

½ yellow-colored diced onion
2 tablespoons olive oil
3 cloves of minced garlic
2 and a ½ cups cauliflower florets
1 tablespoon minced ginger
¼ teaspoon pepper
2 and a ½ cups kabocha squash, cubed
¼ teaspoon cayenne
½ teaspoon ground cardamom
2 leaves of bay
½ cup almond vanilla milk, unsweetened
4 cups low-sodium vegetable broth
½ teaspoon salt

Heat olive oil in a saucepan over medium heat. Put
the garlic, onion, and ginger in a mixing bowl and
mix. Sauté for 3 minutes or until the onions are
translucent and starting to flavor. In a large mixing
bowl, place the squash, cauliflower, cayenne pepper,
cardamom, and bay leaves. Mix everything then pour
into the broth. Bring the mixture to a boil then lower
the heat to low. Cook for 10 minutes or until the fork
is easily absorbed by the zucchini. Puree the Ingredients with a spoon or under high pressure. When the
soup mixes slowly, return it to the pot over low heat.
Add the almond milk and season with pepper and
salt.

Nutritional information: Calories 248; Total Carbs
12g; Net Carbs 9g; Protein 3g; Fat 8g; Sugar 0.1g;
Fiber 2.8g

Vegan Mushroom Soup

Prep Time: 10 minutes. | Cook Time: 30 minutes. |
Servings: 4

1 teaspoon olive oil
1 large diced onion
1 clove of garlic
16 ounces mushrooms
8 sprigs of thyme (leaves set aside and removed)
2 cups vegetable broth with low sodium
14 ounces coconut milk, canned and unsweetened
1 tablespoon coconut Aminos
Pepper and salt

Cut all the garlic, onion, and mushrooms into small
pieces. In a large saucepan, add the garlic, onion, oil,
and mushrooms heated to medium heat and mix.
Cook for another 8 to 10 minutes, until the mushrooms, start to lose liquid. Mix the other Ingredients
until they are well combined. Bring the soup to a boil
or simmer, then reduce the heat to low and cook for
another 15 minutes. Fill the blender halfway with the
soup. Mix until smooth, then add to the soup. This
adds extra creaminess to the soup. Garnish with a little thyme and coconut milk and serve.

Nutritional information: Calories 176; Total Carbs
13g; Net Carbs 10g; Protein 3g; Fat 16g; Sugar 0.8g;
Fiber 4g

Chicken Chili with Black Beans

Prep Time: 10 minutes. | Cook Time: 25 minutes. | Servings: 2

1 and ¾ pounds of cubed chicken breasts, skinless boneless
2 medium-sized chopped red peppers
1 big chopped onion
3 tablespoons olive oil
1 can green chilies, chopped
4 minced garlic cloves
2 tablespoons chili powder
2 teaspoons ground cumin
1 teaspoon ground coriander
2 cans of drained and rinsed black beans
1 can Italian tomatoes, stewed
1 cup low-sodium chicken broth
½-1 cup water

Cook red peppers, onions, and chicken in a greased Dutch oven, until the chicken is longer pink, about 5 minutes. Add the garlic, red pepper, cumin, red pepper powder and cilantro and boil for another 1 minute. Bring to a boil with tomatoes, beans, ½ cup water, and broth. Reduce heat to low and cook for 15 minutes, stirring frequently, adding water as needed. Serve hot and enjoy.

Nutritional information: Calories 163; Total Carbs 21g; Net Carbs 18g; Protein 22g; Fat 6g; Sugar 0g; Fiber 4g

Cabbage Roll Mexican Soup

Prep Time: 5 minutes. | Cook Time: 25 minutes. | Servings: 6

1-pound lean beef
½ teaspoon salt
¾ teaspoon garlic powder
¼ teaspoon pepper
1 tablespoon olive oil
1 medium chopped onion
6 cups chopped cabbage
3 cans of green chilies, chopped
2 cups water
1 can less sodium-containing beef broth
2 tablespoons fresh cilantro, minced

Place the beef with the Ingredients in a large saucepan and cook over medium-high heat until no pink, about 5-7 minutes, then crumble. Remove the pan from the heat. In the same skillet, heat oil over medium to high heat and sauté cabbage and onions until tender and crisp, about 4 to 6 minutes. Boil with beef, water, chili, and broth. Lower the heat, cover, and let stand 10 minutes to blend the flavors. Add the cilantro and mix well. If desired, use sour cream and Pico de Gallo.

Nutritional information: Calories 282; Total Carbs 10g; Net Carbs 8g; Protein 9g; Fat 1g; Sugar 0.4g; Fiber 4g

White Bean and Chicken Soup

Prep Time: 5 minutes. | Cook Time: 20 minutes. | Servings: 2

2 leeks, light green and white parts only, which are cut into quarter-inch rounds
2 teaspoons olive oil
1 roasted 2-pound chicken, discarded skin, removed meat from the bones, shredded
1 tablespoon fresh sage, chopped
2 cups water
2 cans of less sodium in chicken broth
1 can 15-ounce rinsed cannellini bean

Heat the oil in a Dutch oven over medium-high heat. Add a leek, then cook and stir until tender, about 3 minutes. Add sage and cook until fragrant, about ½ minute. Add the broth and a little water, increase the temperature to high, cover and bring to a boil. Add the chicken and beans and simmer, uncovered, stirring occasionally, until heated through, about 3 minutes. Serve hot.

Nutritional information: Calories 146; Total Carbs 14.8g; Net Carbs 10g; Protein 35.1g; Fat 5.8g; Sugar 1.2g; Fiber 2.9g

Beef and Mushroom Soup

Prep Time: 30 minutes. | Cook Time: 55 minutes. | Servings: 4

12 ounces trimmed sirloin beef steak
1 tablespoon canola oil
4 cups sliced mushrooms
¼ cup chopped shallot
2 minced cloves of garlic
4 cups less sodium in beef broth
¼ teaspoon black pepper
1 cup chopped carrot
½ teaspoon salt
1 can undrained diced tomatoes with no salt
½ teaspoon of dried and crushed leaf thyme
½ cup chopped celery
1 bay leaf
2 cups fresh chopped kale

Cut the beef into ¾-inch cubes and cook the beef over medium to high heat with oil in a 44 to 55-quart oven. Remove the beef and set it aside. Put the shallot, mushrooms, and garlic in a saucepan and boil for 4 to 5 minutes, stirring occasionally. Return the beef to the pan and add the broth, carrots, tomatoes, bay leaves, celery, salt, thyme, and pepper. Stir to separate the brown from the bottom of the pot. Then bring to the boil and reduce the heat. Cover and simmer for 20-25 minutes. Stir in the kale. Boil lightly for 5 -10 minutes. Remove the bay leaves before putting them in a bowl.

Nutritional information: Calories 210; Total Carbs 10.5g; Net Carbs 8g; Protein 14.9g; Fat 5.1g; Sugar 0.7g; Fiber 3g

Beans and Greens Turkey Soup

Prep Time: 15 minutes. | Cook Time: 2 hours. | Servings: 2

9 cups water
1 remaining turkey skeleton
2 ribs of celery, cut into half-inch pieces
1 can drained and rinsed northern beans,
1 medium-sized onion
1 package frozen spinach, chopped
¼ teaspoon pepper
2 teaspoons granules of chicken bouillon
3 tablespoons chopped onion
1 teaspoon salt

In a saucepan, combine the celery, turkey, water, and onion. Boil slowly. Lower the heat, cover, and cook for 2 hours. Remove the turkey and let it cool. Remove the vegetables and strain the liquid with a cotton-lined colander. Remove excess fat. Remove the bones, remove the meat, and cut it into small pieces. Discard the bones. Return the meat and broth to the pan. Beans, chopped onion, spinach, broth, pepper, and salt are added to the pan. Boil soup. Lower the heat, cover, and simmer for 10 minutes. Serve hot and enjoy.

Nutritional information: Calories 321; Total Carbs 10g; Net Carbs 9g; Protein 10g; Fat 2g; Sugar 1g; Fiber 3g

English Pub Pea Soup

Prep Time: 15 minutes. | Cook Time: 5 hours. | Servings: 2

2 chopped celery ribs
1 and a ½ cups green peas, dried and split
1 big chopped carrot
4 cups water
1 sweet chopped onion
1 bottle of light beer
½ cup 2% milk
1 tablespoon English mustard, prepared
¼ cup fresh parsley, minced
1 ham bone, meaty
¼ teaspoon pepper
½ teaspoon salt
¼ teaspoon ground nutmeg

Place ham in a 4-quart slow cooker. In it, you need to add peas, carrots, celery, and onions. In a salad bowl, put the beer, water, and mustard. Pour it over the vegetables. Cook for 5 hours and 6 hours. Cover over high heat or until the peas are cooked. Remove the ham bones from the soup. Cut the fat and let it cool slightly before removing the meat from the bones. Remove the bones and fat. Put the meat in a slow cooker and cut it into small pieces. Place the

rest of the Ingredients in a mixing bowl. Add chopped parsley on top.

Nutritional information: Calories 211; Total Carbs 25g; Net Carbs 20g; Protein 9g; Fat 1g; Sugar 0g; Fiber 6g

White Turkey Chili

Prep Time: 15 minutes. | Cook Time: 70 minutes. | Servings: 6

½ cup chopped onion
2 tablespoons canola oil
3 minced garlic cloves
1 lb. of skinless, boneless breast of turkey
2 and a ½ teaspoons ground cumin
½ pound ground turkey
1 teaspoon of water
1 can chickpeas or garbanzo beans
3 cups chicken broth
1 teaspoon minced jalapeno pepper
¼ teaspoon dried savory
½ teaspoon of dried marjoram
2 teaspoons cornstarch

Heat the oil in a large saucepan over medium heat. Add the onion and simmer until tender, about 5 minutes. Boil another 1 minute after adding the garlic, add the cumin and boil another 5 minutes. Divide the turkey chunks until no pink. Add the broth, jalapenos, beans, marjoram, pepper, and salt to taste. Boil soup. Lower the heat to low, cover, and cook for 45 minutes, stirring occasionally. Cook for another 15 minutes before serving. The cornstarch should be dissolved in water and then mixed with the chilies. Cook for 2 minutes, stirring occasionally. Serve with cheese and chopped red onions, if desired.

Nutritional information: Calories 274; Total Carbs 15g; Net Carbs 13g; Protein 29g; Fat 12g; Sugar 0g; Fiber 6g

Creamy Tomato Soup

Prep Time: 0 minutes. | Cook Time: 5 minutes. | Servings: 1

1 tablespoon cream cheese, with less fat
¼ cup less sodium-containing chicken broth
¾ cup tomato puree, canned with no salt

In a large heat-resistant bowl, put the broth, tomatoes, and cream cheese. Microwave for 2 minutes over high heat, stirring occasionally until cooked through and creamy.

Nutritional information: Calories 111; Total Carbs 18.3g; Net Carbs 11g; Protein 5.1g; Fat 2.7g; Sugar 0.2g; Fiber 5g

Crispy Apple Slices

Prep Time: 20 minutes. | Cook Time: 30 minutes. | Servings: 8

5 cups Granny Smith apples, peeled and sliced
3 tablespoons plant-based butter
What you'll need from the store cupboard
½ cup rolled oats
¼ cup + 2 tablespoon Splenda
3 tablespoon flour
1 teaspoon lemon juice
¾ teaspoon apple pie spice, divided

Preheat the oven to 375°F. Combine apples, 2 tablespoons Splenda, lemon juice, and ½ teaspoon apple pie spice in a bowl until apples are well coated. Place apples in a greased square baking pan. Combine oats, flour, ¼ Splenda, and remaining apple pie spice in a bowl. add butter and mix until mixture resembles coarse crumbs. Sprinkle the crumbs evenly over apples. Bake the apple crisp for 30 to 35 minutes, or until apples are tender and topping is golden brown. Serve warm.

Nutritional information: Calories 153; Total Carbs 27g; Net Carbs 23g; Protein 1g; Fat 5g; Sugar 18g; Fiber 4g

Apricot Soufflé

Prep Time: 5 minutes. | Cook Time: 30 minutes. | Servings: 6

4 egg whites
3 egg yolks, beaten
3 tablespoon plant-based butter
What you'll need from store cupboard
¾ cup sugar-free apricot fruit spread
⅓ cup dried apricots, diced fine
¼ cup warm water
2 tablespoon flour
¼ teaspoon cream of tartar
⅛ teaspoon salt

Preheat the oven to 325 °F for 10 minutes. In a sauce pan, melt plant-based butter over medium heat. Stir in flour and cook until bubbly. In a small bowl, stir together the fruit spread and water and add it to the saucepan with the apricots. Cook, stirring, 3 minutes or until mixture thickens. Whisk in egg yolks. Let cool to room temperature, stirring occasionally. Beat egg whites, salt, and cream of tartar in a medium bowl on high speed until stiff peaks form. Gently fold into cooled apricot mixture. Spoon the apricot batter into a 1-½ quart soufflé dish. Bake the soufflé for 30 minutes, or until puffed and golden brown. Serve immediately.

Nutritional information: Calories 116; Total Carbs 7g; Net Carbs 4g; Protein 4g; Fat 8g; Sugar 1g; Fiber 0g

Baked Maple Custard

Prep Time: 5 minutes. | Cook Time: 1 hour 15 minutes. | Servings: 6

2 ½ cup half-and-½
½ cup egg substitute
What you'll need from store cupboard
3 cup boiling water
¼ cup Splenda
2 tablespoon sugar free maple syrup
2 teaspoon vanilla
Dash nutmeg
Nonstick cooking spray

Heat oven to 325°F. Lightly spray 6 custard cups or ramekins with cooking spray. In a large bowl, combine half -n-half, egg yolks, Splenda, vanilla, and nutmeg. Pour evenly into prepared custard cups. Place the cups in a 13x9-inch baking dish. Pour boiling water around the cup, being careful not to splash it. Bake the cups for 1 hour and 15 minutes. Remove the cups from the pan and let them cool completely. Cover and let cool overnight. Drizzle with maple syrup before serving.

Nutritional information: Calories 190; Total Carbs 15g; Net Carbs 10g; Protein 5g; Fat 12g; Sugar 8g; Fiber 0g

Peach Custard Tart

Prep Time: 5 minutes. | Cook Time: 40 minutes. | Servings: 8

12 oz. frozen unsweetened peach slices, thaw and drain
2 eggs, separated
1 cup skim milk
4 tablespoon cold plant-based butter, cut into pieces
What you'll need from store cupboard:
1 cup flour
3 tablespoon Splenda
2-3 tablespoon cold water
1 teaspoon low-sugar vanilla
¼ teaspoon + ⅛ teaspoon salt, divided
¼ teaspoon nutmeg

Preheat the oven to 400 degrees F. In a large bowl, combine the flour and ¼ teaspoon of salt. With a pastry blender, chop the plant-based butter until the mixture resembles coarse crumbs. Stir in cold water, one tablespoon at a time, until moist. Roll out the dough into an 11-inch circle on a lightly floured surface. Place bottom of 9 "pie dish with removable bottom. Turn bottom edges over and pierce sides and bottom with a fork. Beat an egg white with a fork in a small bowl. Gently rub the crust with an egg. Place the pan on a baking sheet and bake for 10 minutes. cool. In a large bowl, combine the egg whites, Splenda, vanilla, nutmeg, and ⅛ tsp. salt until blended. Pour the milk into the measuring cup and microwave for 1 minute. Do not boil. Cover the egg mixture until the milk is combined. Place the peaches at the bottom of the crust and pour the egg mixture over them. Bake for 25-30 minutes or until light. Cool to room temperature. Cover and cool at least 2 hours before serving.

Nutritional information: Calories 180; Total Carbs 22g; Net Carbs 21g; Protein 5g; Fat 7g; Sugar 9g; Fiber 1g

Chocolate Cherry Cake Roll

Prep Time: 10 minutes. | Cook Time: 15 minutes. | Servings: 10

10 maraschino cherries, drained and patted dry
4 eggs, room temperature
1 cup sugar-free Cool Whip, thawed
⅔ cup maraschino cherries, chop, drain and pat dry
½ cup reduced-fat cream cheese, soft
What you'll need from the store cupboard
⅓ cup flour
½ cup Splenda for baking
¼ cup unsweetened cocoa powder
1 tablespoon sugar-free hot fudge ice cream topping
¼ teaspoon baking soda
¼ teaspoon salt
Unsweetened cocoa powder
Nonstick cooking spray

Preheat the oven to 375 degrees F. Spray a large sheet baking pan and spray with the cooking spray. In a small bowl, combine the flour, ¼ cup cocoa powder, baking soda, and salt. Beat the eggs in a large bowl at high speed for 5 minutes, slowly add the sweetener and continue beating until the mixture is thick and lemon-colored. Stir in the dry Ingredients. Spread evenly over the prepared pan. Bake for 15 minutes. Place a clean paper towel on the cutting board and sprinkle with cocoa powder. Place the cake on a towel and carefully remove the parchment. Start at the short end and wrap the towel around it. Cool on a wire rack for 1 hour. Preparing the filling: In a small bowl, beat the cream cheese until tender. Add ½ cup of the whipped topping and mix gently and slowly until combined. Stir in another ½ cup of whipped topping. Fold the chopped cherries. Unwrap the cake and remove the towel. Spread the filling to within 1-inch of the edges. Roll the cake again and cut off the ends. Cover and refrigerate for at least 2 hours or overnight. Reheat fudge toppings, drizzle over cake, garnish with whole cherries and serve in slices.

Nutritional information: Calories 163; Total Carbs 25g; Net Carbs 18g; Protein 5g; Fat 3g; Sugar 12g; Fiber 0g

Blackberry Crostata

Prep Time: 10 minutes. | Cook Time: 25 minutes. | Servings: 6

1 9-inch pie crust, unbaked
2 cup fresh blackberries
Juice and zest of 1 lemon
2 tablespoon butter, soft
What you'll need from store cupboard:
3 tablespoon Splenda, divided
2 tablespoon cornstarch

Heat oven to 425°F. Line a large baking sheet with parchment paper and unroll pie crust in pan. In a medium bowl, combine blackberries, 2 tablespoons of Splenda, lemon juice, zest, and cornstarch. Spoon onto the crust but leave a 2-inch edge. Fold and crimp the edges. Top the berries with 1 tablespoon of butter. Brush remaining butter around edges of crust and sprinkle crust and fruit with the remaining Splenda. Bake for 20 to 22 minutes or until golden brown. Chop and cool before eating.

Nutritional information: Calories 206; Total Carbs 24g; Net Carbs 21g; Protein 2g; Fat 11g; Sugar 9g; Fiber 3g

Autumn Skillet Cake

Prep Time: 10 minutes. | Cook Time: 30 minutes. | Servings: 10

3 eggs, room temperature
1 cup fresh cranberries
4 oz. reduced-fat cream cheese, soft
3 tablespoon fat free sour cream
2 tablespoon planted-based butter, melted
What you'll need from store cupboard:
2 cup almond flour, sifted
¾ cup Splenda
¾ cup pumpkin puree
1 ½ tablespoon baking powder
2 teaspoon cinnamon
1 teaspoon pumpkin spice
1 teaspoon ginger
¼ teaspoon nutmeg
¼ teaspoon salt
Nonstick cooking spray

Preheat the oven to 350 °F. Grease a 9-inch cast iron skillet or cake pan with cooking spray. In a bowl, beat Splenda, butter and cream cheese until thoroughly combined. Add eggs, one at a time, beating after each. Add pumpkin and spices in the butter mix and combine. Add the dry Ingredients and mix well. Stir in the sour cream. Pour into prepared pan. Sprinkle cranberries over the batter and with the back of a spoon, push them half-way into the batter. Bake 30 minutes or the cake passes the toothpick test. Cool completely before serving.

Nutritional information: Calories 280; Total Carbs 23g; Net Carbs 20g; Protein 7g; Fat 17g; Sugar 16g; Fiber 3g

Chocolate Orange Bread Pudding

Prep Time: 10 minutes. | Cook Time: 35 minutes. | Servings: 8

4 cups French baguette cubes
1 ½ cups skim milk
3 eggs, lightly beaten
1-2 teaspoon orange zest, grated
What you'll need from store cupboard
¼ cup Splenda
¼ cup sugar-free chocolate ice cream topping
3 tablespoon unsweetened cocoa powder
1 teaspoon low-sugar vanilla
¾ teaspoon cinnamon

Heat oven to 350°F. In a medium bowl, combine the Splenda and cocoa. Whisk milk, egg, zest, vanilla, and cinnamon until well combined. Place square bread on an 8-inch square baking sheet. Pour the milk mixture evenly over the top. Bake for 35 minutes or until a medium knife is clean. Let cool for 5-10 minutes. Place the cake on a plate and sprinkle lightly with an ice cream topping. Serve and enjoy.

Nutritional information: Calories 139; Total Carbs 23g; Net Carbs 22g; Protein 6g; Fat 2g; Sugar 9g; Fiber 1g

Café Mocha Torte

Prep Time: 15 minutes. | Cook Time: 25 minutes. | Servings: 14

8 eggs
1 cup plant-based butter, cut into cubes
What you'll need from store cupboard:
1 lb. bittersweet chocolate, chopped
¼ cup brewed coffee, room temperature
Nonstick cooking spray

Preheat the oven to 325 degrees F. Spray cooking spray on the 8-inch springform pan. Line bottom side with parchment paper and spray again. Wrap the outside with a double layer of foil and place them in a 9 x 13-inch baking sheet. Add water in a small pot and bring to boil. Beat eggs in a large bowl on medium speed until doubled in size, about 5 minutes. Place chocolate, plant-based butter, and coffee in a microwave-safe bowl stirring every 30 seconds, until chocolate melts and the mixture is soft. Fold ⅓ of the eggs in the chocolate until almost combined. Add the remaining egg, ⅓ at a time and fold until combined. Pour into the prepared pan. Pour boiling water around the pan until it reaches halfway up the side. Bake for 22-25 minutes or until the cake is slightly puffed and the edges are just starting to harden. Remove from the double boiler and let cool completely. Cover with plastic wrap and let cool for 6 hours or overnight. About 30 minutes before cooking, brush the edges and remove both sides of the pan. Cut and serve.

Nutritional information: Calories 260; Total Carbs 12g; Net Carbs 11g; Protein 5g; Fat 21g; Sugar 11g; Fiber 1g

Unbaked Blueberry Cheesecake

Prep Time: 5 minutes. | Cook Time: 0 minutes+3 hours. | Servings: 8

16 oz. fat free cream cheese, softened
1 cup sugar-free frozen whipped topping, thawed
¾ cup blueberries
1 tablespoon plant-based butter, melted
What you'll need from store cupboard
8 zwieback toasts
1 cup boiling water
⅓ cup Splenda
1 envelope unflavored gelatin
1 teaspoon sugar-free vanilla

Place the toast and plant-based butter in the food processor. Pulse until mixture resembles coarse crumbs. Press the mixture to the bottom of the 9 inches spring foam. Place gelatin in a medium bowl and add boiling water. Stir until gelatin is completely dissolved. In a large bowl, whisk the cream cheese, Splenda, and vanilla on medium speed until combined. Beat the whipping toppings. Add the gelatin in a stream while stirring at a low speed. Increase speed to medium and hold for 4 minutes or until smooth and creamy. Gently fold in the berries and spread over the crust. Cover and refrigerate for 3 hours or until frozen.

Nutritional information: Calories 316; Total Carbs 20g; Net Carbs 18g; Protein 6g; Fat 23g; Sugar 10g; Fiber 0g

Cinnamon Bread Pudding

Prep Time: 10 minutes. | Cook Time: 45 minutes. | Servings: 6

4 cups day-old French or Italian bread, cut into ¾-inch cubes
2 cups skim milk
2 egg whites
1 egg
4 tablespoon plant-based butter, sliced
What you'll need from the store cupboard
5 teaspoon Splenda
1 ½ teaspoon cinnamon
¼ teaspoon salt
⅛ teaspoon ground cloves

Preheat the oven to 350 degrees F. In a suitable saucepan, bring the milk and plant-based butter to a boil. Remove from the heat and stir until the plant-based butter is completely dissolved. Let cool for 10 minutes. Beat eggs and whites in a large bowl until foamy. Add Splenda, spices, and salt. Whisk until smooth, then add the cold milk and bread. Transfer the mixture to a 1½-quart baking sheet. Place on a rack in the roasting pan and add 1-inch of hot water to the roasting pan. Bake for 40 to 45 minutes until the pudding hardens and the knife in the middle is clean.

Nutritional information: Calories 362; Total Carbs 25g; Net Carbs 23g; Protein 14g; Fat 10g; Sugar 10g; Fiber 2g

German Chocolate Cake Bars

Prep Time: 10 minutes. | Cook Time: 5 minutes. | Servings: 20

2 cup unsweetened coconut flakes
1 cup coconut milk, divided
¾ cup chopped pecans
¾ cup dark baking chocolate, chopped
What you'll need from the store cupboard
1 ½ cup almond flour cracker crumbs (chapter 4)
½ cup + 2 tablespoon powdered sugar substitute
½ cup coconut oil
Nonstick cooking spray

Spray an 8 x 8-inch baking sheet with cooking spray. In a large bowl, combine the coconut, ½ cup sugar substitute, cracker crumbs, and pecans and mix. Add ½ cup of milk and oil to a suitable saucepan and cook over medium heat until oil and mixture are heated through. Pour in the coconut mixture and stir to combine. Spread evenly on a baking dish and let cool for 1-2 hours. In a clean saucepan, put the chocolate and milk over medium-low heat. Continue cooking, stirring, until the chocolate melts and the mixture is tender. Add 2 tablespoons of the sugar substitute and stir to combine. Pour the chocolate over the coconut layer and let cool for 1 hour or until firm. Cut into squares to serve.

Nutritional information: Calories 245; Total Carbs 12g; Net Carbs 9g; Protein 3g; Fat 19g; Sugar 7g; Fiber 3g

Apple Pear & Pecan Cups

Prep Time: 10 minutes. | Cook Time: 25 minutes. | Servings: 24

1 Granny Smith apple, sliced, leave peel on
1 Red Delicious apple, sliced, leave peel on
1 ripe pear, sliced, leave peel on
3 eggs
½ cup plain fat-free yogurt
1 tablespoon lemon juice
1 tablespoon plant-based butter
What you'll need from store cupboard:
1 package spice cake mix
1 ¼ cup water, divided
½ cup pecan pieces
1 tablespoon Splenda
1 teaspoon cinnamon
½ teaspoon vanilla
¼ teaspoon nutmeg
Nonstick cooking spray

Preheat the oven to 350°F for 10 minutes. Grease jelly-roll pan with nonstick cooking spray. In a large bowl, beat cake mix with 1 cup water, eggs and yogurt until smooth. Pour the cake batter into prepared pan and bake for 20 minutes until fully cooked. Cool completely. Toss pecans over med-high heat in a skillet until lightly browned. In a skillet, add the remaining ¼ cup water, sliced fruit, juice and spices and boil to medium heat for 3 minutes until fruits are tender crisp. Remove the fruits from heat and stir in Splenda, plant-based butter, vanilla, and toasted pecans. Spoon evenly over cake. Slice and serve.

Nutritional information: Calories 130; Total Carbs 20g; Net Carbs 18g; Protein 2g; Fat 5g; Sugar 10g; Fiber 1g

Unsweetened Chocolate Coffee Cupcakes

Prep Time: 10 minutes. | Cook Time: 20 minutes. | Servings: 24

2 eggs
½ cup fat free sour cream
½ cup plant-based butter, melted
What you'll need from store cupboard:
2 cup Splenda
1 cup almond flour, sifted
1 cup strong coffee, room temperature
4 oz. unsweetened chocolate
½ cup coconut flour
3 teaspoon of baking powder
½ teaspoon-salt

Preheat the oven to 350 degrees F. Line 12-cup muffin cups with cupcake liners. Melt the chocolate. Add the Splenda, almond and coconut powder, baking powder, and sea salt. In a small bowl, combine the coffee, sour cream, and butter. Add the butter mixture to the dry Ingredients and keep beating on low speed until well combined. Add and beat the eggs one at a time. Stir in chocolate until well combined. Pour batter into prepared cups and bake for 20-25 minutes. Let cool completely before serving.

Nutritional information: Calories 173; Total Carbs 20g; Net Carbs 19g; Protein 2g; Fat 9g; Sugar 16g; Fiber 1g

Caramel Pecan Pie

Prep Time: 5 minutes. | Cook Time: 35 minutes. | Servings: 8

1 cup pecans, chopped
¾ cup almond milk, unsweetened
⅓ cup plant-based butter, melted
1 tablespoon plant-based butter, cold
What you'll need from the store cupboard
2 cup almond flour
½ cup + 2 tablespoons Splenda for baking
1 teaspoon vanilla
1 teaspoon Arrowroot powder
¾ teaspoon sea salt
½ teaspoon vanilla
½ teaspoon maple syrup, sugar-free
Nonstick cooking spray

Preheat the oven to 350 degrees F. Spray 9-inch pie pan with cooking spray. In a medium bowl, combine the flour, melted plant-based butter, 2 tablespoons of Splenda, and vanilla. Mix until the Ingredients are well combined. Press down on the bottom and sides of the prepared pan. Bake for 12-15 minutes or until the edges are golden. Take out and set aside for later use. In a small saucepan, combine the milk, remaining Splenda, arrowroot, salt, ½ teaspoon of vanilla, and syrup. Cook over medium heat until it begins to boil, stirring constantly. Continue cooking, about 2-3 minutes. Remove from heat and let cool. Mix with the ½ pecans. Pour the filling in the crust and garnish with the remaining pecans. Bake for about 15 minutes or until filling begins to bubble. Let cool completely before eating.

Nutritional information: Calories 375; Total Carbs 20g; Net Carbs 15g; Protein 7g; Fat 30g; Sugar 14g; Fiber 5g

Mini Bread Puddings

Prep Time: 5 minutes. | Cook Time: 35 minutes. | Servings: 12

6 slices cinnamon bread, cut into cubes
1 ¼ cup skim milk
½ cup egg substitute
1 tablespoon plant-based butter, melted
What you'll need from store cupboard
⅓ cup Splenda
1 teaspoon vanilla
⅛ teaspoon salt
⅛ teaspoon nutmeg

Preheat the oven to 350 ° F. line in 12 medium muffin cups. In a large bowl, combine milk, egg yolks, Splenda, vanilla, salt, and nutmeg until blended. Add the cubed bread and stir until moist. Take 15 minutes of rest. Pour evenly into the prepared baking dish. Sprinkle plant-based butter evenly on top. Bake for 30 to 35 minutes or until puffed and golden. Remove from the oven and let cool completely.

Nutritional information: Calories 105; Total Carbs 15g; Net Carbs 15g; Protein 4g; Fat 2g; Sugar 9g; Fiber 1g

Mini Lime Pudding

Prep Time: 5 minutes. | Cook Time: 10 minutes. | Servings: 8

4 sheets phyllo dough
¾ cup skim milk
¾ cup fat-free whipped topping, thawed
½ cup egg substitute
½ cup fat free sour cream
6 tablespoons fresh lime juice
What you'll need from store cupboard
2 tablespoon cornstarch
½ cup Splenda
Butter-flavored cooking spray

In a medium saucepan, combine the milk, juice, and cornstarch. Cook over medium heat for 2-3 minutes or until thickened, stirring constantly. Remove from heat. Add the egg substitute and whisk for 30 seconds. Combine sour cream and Splenda. Cover and stay until completely chilled. Preheat the oven to 350 degrees F. Spray 8 cups of muffins with cooking spray. Place 1 sheet of phyllo on cutting board and spray gently with cooking spray. Repeat this for other sheets so that they are stacked on top. Divide the filo dough into 8 equal parts and gently place them in a muffin pan, pressing firmly on the bottom and sides. Bake for 8 to 10 minutes or until golden brown. Remove from the pan and let cool. Pour lemon mixture evenly into 8 cups and garnish with whipped toppings. Garnish with fresh lemon slices, if desired.

Nutritional information: Calories 82; Total Carbs 13g; Net Carbs 12g; Protein 3g; Fat 1g; Sugar 10g; Fiber 1g

Sweet Potato Crème Brule

Prep Time: 10 minutes. | Cook Time: 1 hour 5 minutes. | Servings: 12

7 egg yolks
1 ¼ cup sweet potato, bake, peel & mash
2 cup half-n-half
1 tablespoon fresh lemon juice
What you'll need from store cupboard:
¾ cup Splenda
¼ cup + ⅓ cup Splenda brown sugar
3 teaspoon vanilla
Butter flavored cooking spray

Preheat the oven to 325 °F. Grease a 10-inch metal quiche dish with cooking spray. Combine sweet potato, ¼ cup Splenda brown sugar, and lemon juice in a mixing bowl and pour it in prepared baking dish. In a suitable saucepan, whisk together half-n-half, Splenda, egg yolks, and vanilla over medium-low heat for 15 minutes until well incorporated. Cook and stirring frequently, until hot, do not boil. Pour the sauce over sweet potato mixture. Place dish in a shallow baking pan and put in the oven. Pour enough boiling water to cover ½ way up the sides of the quiche dish. Bake the quiche for 1 hour until full set and golden brown from top. Cool on rack. Cover and refrigerate 8 hours or overnight. Heat the oven to broil setting. Sprinkle quiche with ⅓ cup Splenda brown sugar and place it on a baking sheet. Broil it for 3-5 minutes or until sugar has melted. Cool 5 minutes before serving.

Nutritional information: Calories 193; Total Carbs 24g; Net Carbs 20g; Protein 3g; Fat 7g; Sugar 21g; Fiber 0g

Toffee Apple Pies

Prep Time: 20 minutes. | Cook Time: 25 minutes. | Servings: 12

2 9-inch pie crusts, soft
2 cup Gala apples, diced fine
1 egg, beaten
1 tablespoon plant-based butter, cut in 12 cubes
1 ½ teaspoon fresh lemon juice
What you'll need from store cupboard:
2 tablespoon toffee bits
1 tablespoon Splenda
½ teaspoon cinnamon
Nonstick cooking spray

Preheat the oven to 375 °F. Grease a cookie sheet with cooking spray. Stie apples, toffee, Splenda, lemon juice, and cinnamon in a mixing bowl. Roll pie crusts separately and cut into a 3-inch crust with cookie cutter. Place 12 crusts on greased pan. Brush the dough with ½ egg. Spoon a tablespoon of apple mixture on each crust, leaving ½- inch edge. Top with pat of butter. Place second dough round on top and seal edges closed with a fork. Brush with remaining egg. Bake the mini tarts for 25 minutes, or until golden brown. Serve warm.

Nutritional information: Calories 154; Total Carbs 17g; Net Carbs 16g; Protein 1g; Fat 9g; Sugar 6g; Fiber 1g

Chocolate Raspberry Soufflés

Prep Time: 10 minutes. | Cook Time: 10 minutes. | Servings: 6

1 cup fresh raspberries
4 egg whites
What you'll need from store cupboard:
½ oz. dark chocolate, chopped
6 teaspoon Splenda
1 teaspoon plant-based butter, soft

Preheat the oven to 400 °F for 10 minutes. Grease the 6 small ramekins with plant-based butter. Add raspberry in a blender and puree well. Stain the puree and add 1 tablespoon Splenda in it and set aside. In a mixing bowl, beat egg whites until thickened and start adding the remaining Splenda, gradually, until the mixture forms stiff glossy peaks. Gently fold ⅓ of the egg whites into the raspberry puree. Fold the raspberry puree mixture into the remaining egg whites and fold gently until evenly mixed. Spoon the raspberry egg mixture into the ramekins filling them ½ full. Divide the chopped chocolate between the ramekins and then fill to the top with soufflé mixture. Place ramekins on a baking sheet and bake for 9 minutes until golden brown and puffed up. Serve immediately.

Nutritional information: Calories 60; Total Carbs 8g; Net Carbs 7g; Protein 3g; Fat 1g; Sugar 16g; Fiber 1g

Raspberry Almond Clafoutis

Prep Time: 10 minutes. | Cook Time: 1 hour. | Servings: 8

1 pint raspberries, rinse and pat dry
3 eggs
¾ cup almond milk, unsweetened
¼ cup half-n-half
4 tablespoons plant-based butter
What you'll need from store cupboard:
½ cup almond flour
⅓ cup Splenda
¼ cup almonds, sliced
1 tablespoon coconut flour
1 ½ teaspoon vanilla
½ teaspoon baking powder
¼ teaspoon allspice
¼ teaspoon almond extract
Nonstick cooking spray

Preheat the oven to 350 °F. Grease 9-inch pie dish with cooking spray and place on a baking sheet. Spread the berries, in a single layer, in the pie dish. Add the flours, baking powder, and allspice in a mixing bowl and stir well. In a small saucepan, add the plant-based butter and melt it over low heat. Whisk Splenda in melted plant-based butter until smooth. In a bowl, pour the plant-based butter and whisk in eggs, one at a time. Add extracts and dry Ingredients in it. Stir in the almond milk and half-n-half and mix well. Pour the batter in pie dish and spread the raspberries and almonds on top. Bake it for 50-60 minutes, or center is set and top is lightly browned. Cool to room temperature before serving.

Nutritional information: Calories 273; Total Carbs 19g; Net Carbs 13g; Protein 7g; Fat 19g; Sugar 11g; Fiber 6g

Pumpkin Ice Cream with Candied Pecans

Prep Time: 15 minutes. | Cook Time: 0 minutes+ 1 hour chilling time. | Servings: 8

2 eggs
2 cup almond milk, unsweetened, divided
1 cup half-n-half
What you'll need from store cupboard:
1 cup pumpkin
1 envelope unflavored gelatin
¾ cup Splenda
¾ cup Candied Pecans
2 teaspoon pumpkin pie spice

Pour a glass of almond milk into a small bowl. Sprinkle gelatin over it. Leave it for about 5 minutes. Whisk together the Splenda and eggs in a large saucepan. Add the pumpkin and pumpkin spices. Add the gelatin in it and whisk. When the mixture begins to boil, remove it from the heat. Let cool at room temperature for 5 minutes, then refrigerate for 45 minutes uncovered, stirring occasionally. Do not refrigerate for long periods. Otherwise, the mixture will harden. Take the pumpkin out of the refrigerator and whisk half -n- half and add the cup with the almond milk. Pour into ICE FREEZER and freeze according to the manufacturer's instructions. Once the ice cream has reached the desired consistency, transfer it to a container with a lid that is suitable for the freezer.

Add the candied pecans, cover, and place in the freezer to make the ice cream firmer.

Nutritional information: Calories 254; Total Carbs 26g; Net Carbs 24g; Protein 5g; Fat 13g; Sugar 22g; Fiber 2g

Peanut Butter Pie

Prep Time: 10minutes. | Cook Time: 0 minutes+ 4 hours chilling time. | Servings: 8

1 ½ cup skim milk
1 ½ cup frozen fat-free whipped topping, thawed and divided
1 small pkg. sugar-free instant vanilla pudding mix
1 (1 ½ oz.) pkg. sugar-free peanut butter cups, chopped
What you'll need from the store cupboard
1 (9-inch) reduced-fat graham cracker pie crust
⅓ cup reduced-fat peanut butter
½ teaspoon sugar-free vanilla

In a large bowl, combine milk and pudding until thickened. Add the peanuts, vanilla, and 1 cup of whipped cream and whisk. Stir in peanut butter cups. Pour over in pie crust and spread whipped cream more on top. Cover and chill at least 4 hours before eating.

Nutritional information: Calories 191; Total Carbs 27g; Net Carbs 20g; Protein 4g; Fat 6g; Sugar 6g; Fiber 0g

Moist Butter Cake

Prep Time: 15 minutes. | Cook Time: 30 minutes. | Servings: 14

3 eggs
¾ cup plant-based butter, divided
½ cup fat free sour cream
What you'll need from store cupboard:
2 cup almond flour, packed
1 cup Splenda, divided
1 teaspoon baking powder
2 tablespoon water
1 tablespoon+ 1 teaspoon low-sugar vanilla, divided
Butter flavored cooking spray

Preheat the oven to 350 degrees F. Sprinkle cooking oil to bake on a Bundt cake pan. In a large bowl, combine the flour, sour cream, ½ cup of plant-based butter, 3 eggs, ⅔ cup of Splenda, baking powder, and 1 teaspoon of vanilla and whisk until well combined. Pour into prepared pan and bake for 30 to 35 minutes. Melt ¼ cup of plant-based butter in a small saucepan over medium heat. Add ⅓ cup of Splenda, a tablespoon of vanilla, and water and stir. Keep stirring until Splenda is completely dissolved. Use a skewer to poke holes across the cake. Pour the syrup mixture evenly over the cake so that all the holes are filled. Turn the pan for a few minutes until the syrup is absorbed into the cake. Leave to cool for 1 hour. Turn onto the plate, cut, and serve.

Nutritional information: Calories 259; Total Carbs 18g; Net Carbs 16g; Protein 4g; Fat 17g; Sugar 15g; Fiber 2g

Broiled Stone Fruit

Prep Time: 5 minutes. | Cook Time: 5 minutes. | Servings: 2

1 peach
1 nectarine
2 tablespoon sugar-free whipped topping
What you'll need from store cupboard:
1 tablespoon Splenda
Nonstick cooking spray

Heat the oven for baking. Place foil on a thin baking sheet and spray with the cooking spray. Cut the peach and nectarine in half and remove the seeds. Place one side off the prepared plate. Broil for 3 minutes. Turn fruit over and sprinkle with Splenda. Cook for another 2-3 minutes. Transfer 1 fruit each to a bowl and top with 1 tablespoon of the whipped topping. Serve and enjoy.

Nutritional information: Calories 101; Total Carbs 22g; Net Carbs 20g; Protein 1g; Fat 1g; Sugar 19g; Fiber 2g

Coffee Tiramisu

Prep Time: 15 minutes. | Cook Time: 0 minutes + 4 hours chilling time. | Servings: 15

2 (8 oz.) pkgs. reduced-fat cream cheese, soft
2 cup fat-free sour cream
2 (3 oz.) pkgs ladyfingers, split
¼ cup skim milk
2 tablespoon coffee liqueur
What you'll need from store cupboard:
⅔ cup Splenda
½ cup strong brewed coffee
2 tablespoons unsweetened cocoa powder, sifted
½ teaspoon vanilla

Combine sour cream, cream cheese, sugar substitute, milk, and vanilla in a large mixing bowl. Beat on high until smooth in texture. Stir coffee and liqueur in a small bowl. Place lady fingers, cut side up, in a 2-quart baking dish. Brush the lady fingers with ½ the coffee mixture. Spread ½ the blended cheese mixture over top. Repeat layers. Sprinkle cocoa powder over top. Cover the cake with foil and chill 4 hours or overnight. Cut into squares to serve.

Nutritional information: Calories 208; Total Carbs 24g; Net Carbs 15g; Protein 6g; Fat 8g; Sugar 14g; Fiber 0g

Raspberry Lemon Cheesecake

Prep Time: 5 minutes. | Cook Time: 40 minutes. | Servings: 12

2 cups raspberries
1 cup fat-free sour cream
¾ cup fat-free cream cheese, softened
½ cup egg substitute
2 tablespoons lemon juice
2 teaspoon lemon zest, divided
What you'll need from store cupboard:
½ cup + 3 tablespoons Splenda
1 teaspoon vanilla
Nonstick cooking spray

Preheat the oven to 350°F. Grease 8-inch square baking pan with cooking spray. Beat the cream cheese, ½ cup Splenda, and vanilla on high speed until smooth in a large mixing bowl. Add juice, 1 teaspoon zest, and egg substitute in the cream mix and beat until thoroughly combined. Pour the batter into prepared pan. Bake the batter for 40 minutes or until firm to the touch. Remove the cake from oven and cool completely. Add the sour cream and 1 tablespoon Splenda in a small bowl and stir well until smooth. Spoon the cream evenly over cooled cheesecake. Cover the cake and refrigerate overnight. Before serving, toss the berries and 2 tablespoons Splenda in small bowl and place aside for 30 minutes. Stir in the remaining zest and spoon the berry mixture over the top of the cheesecake. Cut into 12 bars and serve.

Nutritional information: Calories 114; Total Carbs 18g; Net Carbs 17g; Protein 3g; Fat 5g; Sugar 14g; Fiber 1g

Raspberry Peach Cobbler

Prep Time: 15 minutes. | Cook Time: 40 minutes. | Servings: 8

1 ¼ lbs. peaches, peeled and sliced
2 cups fresh raspberries
½ cup low-fat buttermilk
2 tablespoon cold plant-based butter, cut into pieces
1 teaspoon lemon zest
What you'll need from store cupboard
¾ cup + 2 tablespoon flour, divided
4 tablespoon+ 2 teaspoon Splenda, divided
½ teaspoon baking powder
½ teaspoon baking soda
⅛ teaspoon salt
Nonstick cooking spray

Preheat the oven to 425 °F. Grease an 11×7-inch baking dish with cooking spray. In a large bowl, stir 2 tablespoons of Splenda and 2 tablespoons of flour. Add the fruit and zest in the flour mix and toss to coat. Pour the flour coated fruits into prepared baking dish. Bake the fruits for 15 minutes until fruit is bubbling around the edges. Combine remaining flour, 2 tablespoons of Splenda, baking powder, baking soda, and salt in a mixing bowl. Cut in plant-based butter until it resembles coarse crumbs. Stir the buttermilk in the flour mix just until moistened. Remove the fruit from the oven. Pour the buttermilk mixture top on the bubbling fruits. Sprinkle the remaining 2 teaspoons of Splenda over the top and bake for 18-20 minutes or top is lightly browned. Serve warm.

Nutritional information: Calories 130; Total Carbs 22g; Net Carbs 19g; Protein 2g; Fat 3g; Sugar 10g; Fiber 3g

Tropical Fruit Tart

Prep Time: 10 minutes. | Cook Time: 10 minutes. |
Servings: 8

1 mango, peeled, pitted, and sliced thin
1 banana, sliced thin
2 egg whites
What you'll need from store cupboard
15 ¼ oz. can pineapple chunks in juice, undrained
3 ½ oz. can unsweetened flaked coconut
1 cup cornflakes, crushed
3 teaspoons Splenda
2 teaspoon cornstarch
1 teaspoon coconut extract
Nonstick cooking spray

Preheat the oven to 425 °F. Grease a 9-inch spring-form pan with cooking spray. Combine cornflakes, co-conut, and egg whites in a suitable bowl and toss until blended. Press the mix firmly over the bottom and ½-inch up the sides of the prepared baking pan to make crust. Bake the crust for 8 minutes or until edges start to brown. Cool completely. Add pineapple juice into a small saucepan along with cornstarch and stir until smooth. Stir and cook the slurry for a minutes over high heat. Remove from heat and cool completely. Once cooled, stir in Splenda and coconut extract. Combine pineapple, mango, and banana in a bowl, add over baked crust and drizzle with pineapple juice mixture. Cover and chill at least 2 hours before serving.

Nutritional information: Calories120; Total Carbs 19g; Net Carbs 17g; Protein 2g; Fat 4g; Sugar 13g; Fiber 2g

4 Weeks Meal Plan

Week 1

Day 1:
Breakfast: Scrambled Tofu with Spinach
Lunch: Pickled Cucumber Salad
Snack: Salty Kale Chips
Dinner: Asparagus & Beef Rolls
Dessert: Raspberry Peach Cobbler

Day 2:
Breakfast: Paleo Hash
Lunch: Taco Salad
Snack: Almond Chicken Fingers
Dinner: Fish Cakes
Dessert: Raspberry Almond Clafoutis

Day 3:
Breakfast: French Toast with Blueberries
Lunch: Walnut Apple Salad
Snack: Baked Sweet Potato Balls
Dinner: Honey-Soy Broiled Salmon
Dessert: Pumpkin Ice Cream with Candied Pecans

Day 4:
Breakfast: Pumpkin Topped Waffles
Lunch: Savory Linguine with Pesto
Snack: Baked Chicken Thigh Pieces
Dinner: Kabocha Squash with Cauliflower Soup
Dessert: Cinnamon Bread Pudding

Day 5:
Breakfast: Breakfast Salad with Egg
Lunch: Navy Beans with Pico de Gallo
Snack: Dehydrated Orange Slice
Dinner: Meatball Vegetable Stew
Dessert: Moist Butter Cake

Day 6:
Breakfast: Breakfast Quesadilla
Lunch: Tomatoes and Red Kidney Beans
Snack: Simple Roasted Walnuts
Dinner: Glazed & Grilled Salmon
Dessert: Chocolate Cherry Cake Roll

Day 7:
Breakfast: Waffle with Nut Butter Spread
Lunch: Low Sugar Bok Choy Bowl
Snack: Gazpacho with Strawberries
Dinner: Beef and Mushroom Cauliflower Wraps
Dessert: Apple Pear & Pecan Cups

Week 2

Day 1:
Breakfast: Pineapple Smoothie
Lunch: Autumn Cranberry Slaw
Snack: Mini Meatball with Apricot Dip
Dinner: Saigon Shrimp
Dessert: Blackberry Crostata

Day 2:
Breakfast: Pear Oatmeal
Lunch: Tomato Radish Salad
Snack: Roasted Cinnamon Almonds
Dinner: Sesame Tuna Steak
Dessert: Autumn Skillet Cake

Day 3:
Breakfast: Bean Breakfast Tacos
Lunch: Pecan Pear Salad
Snack: Garlic Chicken Wings
Dinner: Salmon with Maple and Orange Glaze
Dessert: Baked Maple Custard

Day 4:
Breakfast: Hite Sandwich
Lunch: Yummy Bean and Veggie Cups
Snack: Sesame Spinach Fritters
Dinner: Catfish in the Cajun style
Dessert: Crispy Apple Slices

Day 5:
Breakfast: Niçoise Salad Tuna
Lunch: Quinoa with Fresh Vegetables
Snack: Parmesan Pepper Chicken Wings
Dinner: Shrimp Zucchini Kabobs
Dessert: Chocolate Cherry Cake Roll

Day 6:
Breakfast: Balanced Turkey Meatballs
Lunch: Black Bean Fritters
Snack: Cayenne Broccoli Tots
Dinner: Onion Broccoli Soup
Dessert: Cinnamon Bread Pudding

Day 7:
Breakfast: Tex-mex Migas
Lunch: Kale and Carrots Soup
Snack: Dehydrated Orange Slice
Dinner: Seafood Stew
Dessert: Raspberry Almond Clafoutis

Day 1:
Breakfast: Savory Egg Muffins
Lunch: Lettuce Wraps with Chestnuts
Snack: Nutmeg Apple Chips
Dinner: Cold Berry Mint Soup
Dessert: Caramel Pecan Pie

Day 2:
Breakfast: Cheese Coated Egg Muffins
Lunch: Green Beans with Onion
Snack: Easy-to-Make Banana Chips
Dinner: Lamb Vegetable Stew
Dessert: Baked Maple Custard

Day 3:
Breakfast: Oatmeal with Sausage
Lunch: Avocado and Farro
Snack: Roasted Cashews with Lemon Juice
Dinner: Mustard Pork Chops
Dessert: Blackberry Crostata

Day 4:
Breakfast: Breakfast Salad with Egg
Lunch: Savory Sofrito Dumplings
Snack: Salsa de Strawberry
Dinner: Shrimp Bell Peppers Soup
Dessert: Pumpkin Ice Cream with Candied Pecans

Day 5:
Breakfast: Trail Mix Hot Cereal
Lunch: Savory Linguine with Pesto
Snack: Ham and Turkey Wraps
Dinner: Lentil Potato Stew
Dessert: Raspberry Lemon Cheesecake

Day 6:
Breakfast: Omelet with Greens
Lunch: Zucchini Pasta Salad
Snack: Gazpacho with Strawberries
Dinner: Halibut Packets
Dessert: Toffee Apple Pies

Day 7:
Breakfast: Pumpkin Pancakes
Lunch: Navy Beans with Pico de Gallo
Snack: Grilled Sesame Tofu
Dinner: Chicken Chili with Black Beans
Dessert: Peanut Butter Pie

Day 1:
Breakfast: Gruyère and Bacon Scrambled Eggs
Lunch: Tomatoes and Red Kidney Beans
Snack: Popcorn
Dinner: Alfredo Sausage and Vegetables
Dessert: Cinnamon Bread Pudding

Day 2:
Breakfast: Scrambled Tofu with Spinach
Lunch: Carrots, Brown Rice, and Scrambled Egg
Snack: Fruit Leather
Dinner: Scallops Egg Salad
Dessert: Mini Bread Puddings

Day 3:
Breakfast: Salad with Avocado and Chicken Dice
Lunch: Spicy Brown Rice with Collard
Snack: Fat-Free Yogurt with Egg
Dinner: Kebab Chickpea Stew
Dessert: Autumn Skillet Cake

Day 4:
Breakfast: Egg Banana Pancakes
Lunch: Carolina Green Beans
Snack: Paprika Chickpeas
Dinner: Saucy Tomato Cod
Dessert: Café Mocha Torte

Day 5:
Breakfast: Cottage Cheese with Walnuts
Lunch: Lime Yogurt Chili Soup with Tomatoes
Snack: Easy-to-Make Banana Chips
Dinner: Easy Crab Cakes
Dessert: German Chocolate Cake Bars

Day 6:
Breakfast: French Toast with Blueberries
Lunch: Navy Beans with Pico de Gallo
Snack: Simple Homemade Spinach Chips
Dinner: Steak Sandwich
Dessert: Moist Butter Cake

Day 7:
Breakfast: Avocado Pesto Zucchini Noodles
Lunch: Eggplant and Bulgur Pilaf with Basil
Snack: Fried Sweet Potato Wedges
Dinner: Broccoli Asparagus Soup
Dessert: Chocolate Raspberry Soufflés

Keeping monitoring of your blood sugar levels is an important part of type 2 diabetes management. Living a healthy lifestyle allows many people to do so. Some folks may also require medication.

A healthy lifestyle requires sticking to a well-balanced diet and doing enough exercise on a regular basis. You must learn to balance what you eat and drink with physical activity and diabetic medicine, if necessary.

Diabetes is treated with oral medicines, insulin, and a variety of injectable drugs. To control their diabetes, some patients will need to take more than one type of medication over time.

You'll need to monitor your blood sugar levels on a frequent basis. Your doctor will advise you on how often you should do it.

It's also critical to keep your blood pressure and cholesterol readings within the ranges set by your doctor. Make sure you have your screening tests done on a regular basis.

If you are overweight, you can help prevent or delay type 2 diabetes by decreasing weight, eating fewer calories, and increasing your physical activity. If you have a condition that puts you at risk for type 2 diabetes, treating it may help you avoid developing the disease.

Blood glucose, blood pressure, and cholesterol control, as well as quitting smoking if you smoke, are all significant aspects of managing type 2 diabetes. Planning healthy meals, restricting calories if you're overweight, and being physically active are all important aspects of diabetes management. Taking any prescribed medications is also a no-no. Create a diabetic treatment plan that works for you with the help of your health care team.

Appendix 1 Measurement Conversion Chart

WEIGHT EQUIVALENTS

US STANDARD	METRIC (APPROXINATE)
1 ounce	28 g
2 ounces	57 g
5 ounces	142 g
10 ounces	284 g
15 ounces	425 g
16 ounces (1 pound)	455 g
1.5 pounds	680 g
2 pounds	907 g

VOLUME EQUIVALENTS (DRY)

US STANDARD	METRIC (APPROXIMATE)
⅛ teaspoon	0.5 mL
¼ teaspoon	1 mL
½ teaspoon	2 mL
¾ teaspoon	4 mL
1 teaspoon	5 mL
1 teaspoon	15 mL
¼ cup	59 mL
½ cup	118 mL
¾ cup	177 mL
1 cup	235 mL
2 cups	475 mL
3 cups	700 mL
4 cups	1 L

TEMPERATURES EQUIVALENTS

FAHRENHEIT(F)	CELSIUS© (APPROXIMATE
225 °F	107 °C
250 °F	120 °C
275 °F	135 °C
300 °F	150 °C
325 °F	160 °C
350 °F	180 °C
375 °F	190 °C
400 °F	205 °C
425 °F	220 °C
450 °F	235 °C
475 °F	245 °C
500 °F	260 °C

VOLUME EQUIVALENTS (LIQUID)

US STANDARD	US STANDARD (OUNCES)	METRIC
2 tablespoons	1 fl.oz	30 mL
¼ cup	2 fl.oz	60 mL
½ cup	4 fl.oz	120 mL
1 cup	8 fl.oz	240 mL
1½ cup	12 fl.oz	355 mL
2 cups or 1 pint	16 fl.oz	475 mL
4 cups or 1 quart	32 fl.oz	1 L
1 gallon	128 fl.oz	4 L

CPSIA information can be obtained
at www.ICGtesting.com
Printed in the USA
LVHW060714110322
713216LV00005B/128